HILL GUIDES™ SERIES

NORTHWEST WINE COUNTRY

Wine's *New* Frontier

Third Edition

Kathleen Thompson Hill
&
Gerald Hill

S0-CFO-841

GUILFORD, CONNECTICUT

Cover design and text design by Lana Mullen
Cover painting, entitled *Vineyards at Lake Okanagan, B.C., Canada,* by Judy Theo, M.F.A. Studio address: 134 Church Street, Sonoma, CA 95476; (707) 996–5111. Medium: monotype.
Maps by Lisa Reneson © The Globe Pequot Press
Illustrations by Mauro Magellan
Photos by Kathleen & Gerald Hill
Historical photos courtesy of the Kelowna Museum Archives, Kelowna, B.C.

ISSN 1549-6082
ISBN 0-7627-2991-0

Manufactured in the United States of America
Third Edition/First Printing

CONTENTS

PREFACE

We have left a little blood, sweat, and tears on Northwest soil in the process of driving thousands of miles in order to tell you how to get to the best wineries and eateries of Oregon, Washington, British Columbia, and Idaho. In exchange for our efforts, we always take away with us an unusual gustatory, cultural, emotional, and physical experience.

We are wine and food fans who believe that you do not have to be a wine snob to enjoy wines. We strongly believe in a vital connection between food, wine, and local culture. To really understand a community, you must get to know how people grow their food, cook it, and enjoy it, as well as what they drink with it and in what settings.

The Pacific Northwest is one of the world's most beautiful regions. What greater splendor could there be than the Columbia River Gorge, the view from a hilltop winery over the lush Willamette Valley, or the charm of Ashland with its almost perpetual Shakespeare Festival? And there is the experience of a lifetime in driving through the magnificent canyons and forests, over streams and rivers, down British Columbia's perfectly engineered highway, the Coquihalla, from Merritt to Hope on the way back from the Okanagan Valley to Vancouver. This is a route we urge you to take.

So bring along your picnic basket and corkscrew, and get ready to tour, taste, and enjoy.

Cheers!

—Kathleen Thompson Hill
—Gerald Hill

ACKNOWLEDGMENTS

For all the time, information, and stories they share with us, we thank the winemakers and restaurateurs of the Northwest Wine Country, and give special thanks to the chefs who gave us recipes to share with our readers.

We also give special thanks to Dave Gamble, publisher and editor of *B.C. Wine Trails,* for his help, tips, and introductions; and to Dr. Wilf Krutzmann of The Wine Barrel in Victoria for inside information and for introducing us to Dave Gamble. Our dear friend Mary Evelyn Arnold helped us immensely this time, as always!

INTRODUCTION

*P*eople ask us "What is the Northwest Wine Country?" In a sense, we made it up. We blended British Columbia with Oregon, Washington, and Idaho in the Cascadian spirit of natural rather than political boundaries. Nature does not know governmental borders, and we believe that humans ought to ignore them a little more. We would like to encourage people to live more regionally and less provincially.

ABOUT THIS BOOK

In *Northwest Wine Country* we introduce you to the people who grow wine grapes, make wine, and prepare food for the public and tell you where and when you can join them. We also show you the restaurants, diners, and delis where locals hang out to find you the most genuine local and regional cuisine. For those who wish to bring home the best in Northwest cuisine, we have included original recipes kindly given to us by some of the region's best chefs, winery owners and managers, and winemakers. We also tell you where to find the best farmers' markets and festivals along the way.

We will take you from south to north, first through Oregon, then Washington, British Columbia, and Idaho, but you can arrive from any direction to hook up with a tour route.

We offer you sensible, logical itineraries, taking into consideration how many wineries you can get to and enjoy in a relaxed day of travel. We generally base our wine trips in the larger cities, because often that is where you can find the widest choice of overnight accommodations. We also give you a range of places to eat (excluding fast-food joints) or buy picnic supplies, and other suggested stops. Our primary criterion is value.

Kathleen is a particular connoisseur of rest rooms and can tell you their conditions along most roads in most western states. Oregon and Washington provide clean and scenic facilities at their rest stops, often with local service clubs offering homemade cookies or hot dogs, cool drinks, and coffee, while lower mainland British Columbia's are singularly awful. When traveling in British Columbia's interior, plan your stops and use washrooms whenever you come upon good ones, whether you need them or not.

Very few of the Northwest wineries offer dining, so we will happily point out those that do.

Many Northwest wineries resemble small European family enterprises in which a couple or family runs and does everything either adjoining their home or very close by. Often the husband/winemaker is in his second career now doing what he's always really wanted, and the wife/manager loves getting her hands dirty and wearing jeans every day, packs the boxes, runs the tasting room, keeps the books, and does the public relations. Occasionally the roles are reversed. Many of the men were engineers, chemists, or doctors, while many of the women were accountants, bookstore managers, and advertising executives. Most of their offspring put in their time doing grunt work (also known as "helping out") and then go off to universities.

We cover them all, from corporate giants like the sister wineries Chateau Ste. Michelle and Columbia Crest, with their large cement buildings and glorious grounds, to little family-run Gersighel Wineberg on a rocky loop of the highway with the small home's garage converted into a tasting room. We concentrate on the wineries that are open to the public, although we mention those that are not open or require appointments.

At Northwest wineries' tasting rooms you can get real bargains that you will never see in liquor stores. Tasting rooms often offer excess vintages at $5.00 or $6.00 per bottle. Yes!

Many of the smaller wineries sell exclusively from their tasting rooms or to restaurants, so visiting the winery is often your only chance to track down a favorite you may have enjoyed in a restaurant. Some sell out their entire production every year, so it is well worth the adventure of finding them and getting to know the personalities, their philosophies, and what they put of themselves into their wines. You will find yourself on some dusty, rocky roads along the way, but it will be worth it.

Oh yes! There's a popular saying among winery workers that "It takes a lot of beer to make great wine." So we feel obligated to point out our favorite microbreweries along your route just in case.

HOW TO BE A VISITOR AND NOT A TOURIST IN THE NORTHWEST WINE COUNTRY

Winemakers in the Northwest and British Columbia welcome tourists and visitors to their wineries and communities and know the value of outsiders discovering the fruits of their labors. They earnestly try to communicate with the outside world in a struggle to get their wines recognition approaching that of the more media-successful Sonoma and Napa Valleys of California's wine country. So they welcome out-of-staters with open arms.

Many Californians have moved to Oregon and Washington in search of a quieter, slower-paced life. Winemakers have moved north as well to find less expensive land and a less corporate winemaking community.

If you wish to blend in and not be pegged as a tourist, wear sensible, earthy colors and just take life a little slower and easier.

British Columbians are eager to have their work, craft, and product discovered by Canadians, Americans, and visitors from every country—generally confident, for good reason, that you will simply visit, spend some money, and leave.

Americans might consider modifying their voices and putting on their extra polite and considerate clothes, because British Columbians are remarkably nice to visitors and tourists. We would all do well to emulate their "nice" qualities: pleasant, kind, thoughtful, considerate, modest, well-mannered, reserved, tasteful, refined, and scrupulous.

HOW TO GET HERE AND GET AROUND

If you want to visit the Northwest Wine Country from outside the region, fly or take Amtrak to a major city such as Eugene or Portland, Oregon; Spokane, Walla Walla, or Seattle, Washington; or Vancouver, Victoria, or Penticton, British Columbia. From there you can rent a car. Or drive your own vehicle into Oregon, Washington, or British Columbia and follow our itineraries. You can also get to the Okanagan by driving in from Washington on Highway 97 east of the Okanogan (yes, it's spelled differently in Washington and British Columbia) National Forest.

Many major airlines fly to Portland, Seattle, Spokane, and Vancouver, and Canadian Airlines/Air Canada or its connectors fly to Victoria on Vancouver Island and Penticton in the Okanagan. All major car rental agencies operate at these airports and take almost all credit cards.

To get to some Seattle area wineries you take Washington ferries to Whidbey Island, and you can easily take British Columbia (BC) ferries from Vancouver to Victoria and Nanaimo.

To get to Idaho wineries from Oregon, take I–84 eastward along the Columbia River from Portland to Pendleton, and then southeast through LaGrande to Caldwell and Boise, Idaho. From Washington, you can drive from Kennewick south on Highway 395 or south from Walla Walla on Highway 11 to Pendleton, and then head southeast on I–84 to LaGrande, Caldwell, and Boise, Idaho. To reach northern Idaho wineries, just follow Highway 90 east about 40 miles from Spokane, Washington.

From inside the region, get your car or bike to I–5 in Oregon, Washington, or British Columbia, and follow our directions. You can also get to eastern Washington wineries by following the Columbia River Gorge eastward, and you can reach British Columbia's Okanagan Valley by following Highway 97 north from eastern Washington to Osoyoos.

You will definitely need a car or other two- or four-wheeled vehicle to move between wineries, as there is no public transportation in the quasi-rural wine country.

We tell you in each of the British Columbia and Washington chapters how to get to island wineries. So bon voyage!

> *The prices, rates, and hours listed in this guidebook were confirmed at press time. We recommend, however, that you call establishments to obtain current information before traveling.*

CHAPTER 1

OREGON

Oregon provides an ideal environment in which to travel to its wineries: heavenly landscape, several wineries close together, urban conveniences close by, and excellent wines.

Most of the Oregon wineries are either right next to or close to highways, never very far by California standards, but then what is? In Oregon it seems that the larger the highway number, the smaller the road. The smaller the road, the more beautiful the scenery.

Many of the smaller (and often more interesting) wineries are open only on weekends, and some are open to the public only by appointment or not at all. Be sure to plan your route accordingly.

There are two publications you might enjoy. Pick them up at wineries: *Oregon Wine,* a free tabloid-size newspaper with wine business insider monthly news, and *NW Palate,* a sophisticated magazine featuring the best up-to-date news on Northwest restaurants and wines.

Throughout Oregon the wine regions are named for local rivers whose surrounding fertile valleys provide soil, climate, and security for some winegrowers and, occasionally, fear of floods for others.

The Willamette Valley, Oregon's most productive wine grape growing region, runs for 100 miles from Eugene to the Columbia River north of Portland and is 60 miles wide in some places. The Willamette Valley and Highway I–5 follow the Willamette River about 50 miles inland from the Pacific Ocean, resulting in Oregon's coolest wine appellation.

Depending upon local hillside formations, many vineyards enjoy some marine air and average 40 inches of rainfall annually. Many vineyards occupy benchland hillsides along the western margin of the valley. Distinct subregions include the Red Hills of Dundee southwest of Portland, the Eola Hills northwest of Salem, the South Salem Hills, and the rolling hills near Veneta west of Eugene.

The Umpqua Valley appellation, all of which is within Douglas County, covers land just one-fourth the size of the Willamette Valley and extends from the Cascade Mountains toward the west through and around Roseburg to the

Pacific Ocean. It's a combo of lots of small hillsides around the Umpqua River and other ripply convergences unified by historic and current drainage areas known as the "hundred valleys of the Umpqua."

The Umpqua Valley is drier, hotter, and colder than the Willamette Valley. The soils are also more varied, resulting in happy growing for Cabernet Sauvignon, Sauvignon Blanc, Chardonnay, Pinot Noir, and Riesling.

The Rogue Valley appellation runs along the Rogue River in southern Oregon, has a slightly higher growing elevation than the other wine-growing regions, and includes two distinct subappellations, the Illinois Valley and the Rogue River. The Illinois Valley in the west has loads of Pacific Ocean marine air and produces great Pinot Noir and Pinot Gris. More inland, and therefore hotter, drier, and mostly protected from marine air, is the Rogue River subappellation, which runs from Ashland south to Grants Pass along I–5, producing many Bordeaux varieties. Vineyardists grow Chardonnay throughout the Rogue Valley Region. The new Applegate Valley appellation was carved out of the Rogue Valley appellation and has a warm climate that yields excellent Cabernet Sauvignon, Cabernet Franc, and Merlot.

The Columbia Valley appellation runs along the Columbia River east of Portland on both the Washington and Oregon sides of the state border. The hot, arid eastern Oregon climate collides with the cooler marine air of western Oregon and creates major climatic variations and microclimates. Here growers enjoy success with a wide range of grapes.

The Walla Walla appellation, shared with southeastern Washington, is east of the Columbia Valley region and follows the Walla Walla River in Washington and the Blue Mountains and Touchet Slope in Oregon. Both of these formations protect the valleys from cold Arctic air and moist Pacific air. The region only gets 10–25 inches of rain and enjoys a long growing season of up to 220 days, resulting in interesting Cabernet Sauvignon, Merlot, Chardonnay, Sémillon, and Cabernet Franc.

Oregon winemakers have imposed strict labeling rules upon their industry. Wines must contain 95 percent minimum of the state vintage, 100 percent of the grapes must be from within the state, and varietal wines must be at least 90 percent from the stated variety, compared to the national standard of 75 percent.

ROGUE REGION

The primary cities whose names you might recognize in the Rogue region are Ashland (home of the outstanding Oregon Shakespeare Festival), Medford,

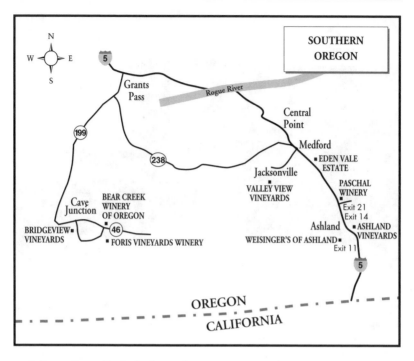

and Grants Pass, all of which are along Interstate Highway 5 (I–5). The Rogue Valley appellation is at a higher elevation than the rest of Oregon's wine-growing regions. Chardonnay is grown throughout the larger appellation.

As you cross the border from California into Oregon, you are immediately greeted by a HELMETS REQUIRED sign, which is an absolute law in the Northwest for anyone riding a motorcycle or bicycle. From here it is only 16 miles to Ashland.

The highway exits in Oregon are numbered according to their approximate distance, in miles, from the California border. Exit 4 has camping sites, and exit 6 has food of sorts. Soon you reach Siskiyou Mountains Summit (4,130 feet) and begin a downgrade trucks should care about. To the west at exit 6 you can see Mt. Ashland, a locally popular ski area, and the Rogue River National Forest. The Pacific Crest National Scenic Trail crosses I–5 at exit 6 also. You are now in the Rogue Valley appellation.

Take exit 11 to WEISINGER'S OF ASHLAND WINERY. In about 1 mile turn left (west) into Weisinger's of Ashland's gravel driveway, and you'll come to a charming Swiss chalet–like winery of white stucco and dark wood beams, reflecting Weisinger origins in Switzerland, southern Germany, and northern Austria. If

WEISINGER'S OF ASHLAND WINERY

you are traveling south, take exit 14 and turn left at Tolman Creek Road, then left again on Siskiyou Boulevard.

In the 1970s Frank Wisnovsky of Valley View Vineyards gave and sold Gewürztraminer vines to his friend John Weisinger, and Weisinger's of Ashland opened ten years later.

Weisinger's air-conditioning is most refreshing on hot summer days, their shaded deck overlooks the valley, and the gift shop's gourmet foods surpass those in most tasting rooms. Look for pesto and sun-dried tomato cheese torta, Cypress Grove chèvre, Turkey Store pastrami, Cuisine Perel products, biscuits and crackers, local cookbooks, and colorful flags and wind socks.

Weisinger's holds a warehouse case sale in the spring and fall, usually in April and November, winemaker's dinners, home winemaking classes, and an annual Grape Stomp and Harvest Festival in early September. Its Wine Club members get to attend an exclusive dinner at the winery every June and receive a 10 percent discount on rates at the Vineyard Cottage, originally an apple storage shed. Rates at the romantic cottage (with hot tub and yummiest of goodies and wine) are normally $135 from November through March, and $175 from April through October (double occupancy, $35 per extra person). No smoking, children, or pets.

Fine points: Featured wines: French-style blends such as Chardonnay, Sémillon, Gewürztraminer, Mescolare, Merlot, Petite Pompadour, and Cabernet Sauvignon. Fifty percent estate grown; aged in American and French oak. $16–$40. Owners: John and Eric Weisinger. Winemakers: John and Eric Weisinger. Cases: 3,000. Acres: 6.5.

🍃 *Weisinger's of Ashland Winery,* *3150 Siskiyou Boulevard (Highway 99),* *Ashland 97520; phone (541) 488–5989; fax (541) 488–5989; e-mail* *wine@weisingers.com; Web site www.weisingers.com. Open 11:00 A.M.–5:00 P.M.* *daily, May 1–October 1; 11:00 A.M.–5:00 P.M. Wednesday–Sunday, October 2–April* *30. Visa and MasterCard. Wheelchair accessible.*

As you leave Weisinger's, head back down their driveway and turn left on Siskiyou or Highway 99 toward Ashland. You can either continue into Ashland or go to ASHLAND VINEYARDS. In about 0.3 mile turn right on Crowson, go over the railroad tracks and under I–5, and after about 0.5 mile turn left on Route 66 toward Ashland past Country Corner. In about 0.7 mile take a soft right onto East Main Street at the "Y" and watch carefully for the Ashland Vineyards Winery sign on the right just before an overpass. Turn right (east) onto their hard-packed dirt road, still following signs for about 1 mile. Pass the end of the airport runway until you find yourselves in front of a small, green cement-block ranch house. You can also take exit 14 and turn left (east) onto the hard-packed dirt road.

Pilot Bill Knowles planted the original vines in 1988, got bored with the wine biz, and sold his property in 1994 to Phil and Kathy Kodak, who migrated to

ASHLAND VINEYARDS' COZY TASTING ROOM

Oregon via Ohio and California, where Phil had worked as a chemist with the Santa Cruz Vintners' Association. The Kodaks planted thousands of Merlot and Cabernet plants in 1995 and doubled Knowles's production.

Ashland Vineyards boasts the "largest privately owned vineyard property in southern Oregon" (120 acres, although not all is planted yet). It is the only Oregon winery with five wines rated #1 by *Wine Spectator* in its May 15, 1997, issue, and it produced the only Gold Medal–winning Merlot (1994) at the 1997 Newport Tri-State Commercial Wine Competition. Ashland has now earned *Wine Spectator*'s praise for the "World's Best Merlot."

Kathy Kodak presides over the homey tasting room, where you can taste their new upscale Shakespeare Love series of wines, created to celebrate Ashland's world-renowned Shakespeare Festival. Bring a picnic!

Every year the Kodaks give a percentage of all case sales to a scholarship for local students to attend college. Check with the winery for special case sale events.

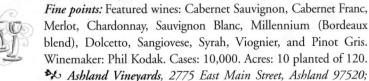

Fine points: Featured wines: Cabernet Sauvignon, Cabernet Franc, Merlot, Chardonnay, Sauvignon Blanc, Millennium (Bordeaux blend), Dolcetto, Sangiovese, Syrah, Viognier, and Pinot Gris. Winemaker: Phil Kodak. Cases: 10,000. Acres: 10 planted of 120.

❧ *Ashland Vineyards, 2775 East Main Street, Ashland 97520; phone (541) 488–0088 or (866) 4WINENET; fax (541) 488–5857; e-mail wines@winenet.com; Web site www.winenet.com or www.shakespearewine.com. Open 11:00 A.M.–5:00 P.M. Tuesday–Sunday, March–December; by appointment only January–February; closed Mondays and holidays. Tasting fee: 50 cents per taste, free with case purchase. Visa and MasterCard. Not wheelchair accessible.*

PASCHAL WINERY lives in a Tuscan villa with a panoramic mountain, vineyard, and orchard views. From the large deck you can picnic and inhale the Siskiyou Mountains and Harry & David's orchards. Roy Paschal, who is still involved in television and radio broadcasting, built his dream in 1998 and hired one of the best, Joe Dobbes, to make his wine. Take exit 21 off I–5 for 1.5 miles.

Fine points: Featured wines: Cabernet Franc, Cabernet Sauvignon, Malbec, Merlot, Pinot Noir, Rhone blends, Syrah, Chardonnay, Pinot Blanc, Pinot Gris, and Viognier. Owner: Roy Paschal. Winemaker: Joe Dobbes. Cases: 5,000. Acres: 7.5 planted of 15.

❧ *Paschal Winery, 1122 Suncrest Road, Talent 97540; phone (541) 535–7957; Web site www.paschalwinery.com. Open 11:00 A.M.–5:00 P.M. daily, not on Monday in winter. Visa and MasterCard. Wheelchair accessible.*

As you leave the Paschal Winery, go south to Ashland. You might want to explore the PACIFIC NORTHWEST MUSEUM OF NATURAL HISTORY. The museum includes fabulous exhibits of our ecological systems, a hands-on Discovery Center, and the Aspen Grove Gift Shop of natural gifts.

❧ *Pacific Northwest Museum of Natural History, 1500 East Main Street, Ashland; phone (541) 488–1084; Web site www.projecta.com/nwmuseum. Open daily 10:00 A.M.–5:00 P.M., summer; 10:00 A.M.–4:00 P.M., winter. Admission $6.00 for adults, discounts available for seniors and children.*

Nestled in the foothills of the Siskiyou Mountains and surrounded by green trees, Ashland is small, historic, well preserved, cosmopolitan, and "removed" all at once. Its cultural activities range from the world-famous Oregon Shakespeare Festival, which runs a modest eight months from late February through early November, to performances by the Oregon Cabaret Theater, Rogue Music Theater, Ashland Community Theater, the Rogue Valley Symphony, and the Rogue Valley Chorale.

This college town is only 14 miles from the California border on the south, the halfway point between San Francisco and Portland, making it a possible one-day drive from the Bay Area and a natural stopping place. It is also the natural center for a tour of the Rogue Valley wine country.

Ashland has a wealth of restaurants to try in a large price range since the town feeds thousands of Shakespeare fans most of the year. You can sample delicate Japanese food or robust Italian food, diner specials or fine French cuisine.

Among our favorites is BROTHERS' RESTAURANT, often voted by the locals as having the Best Breakfast, Best Lunch, Best Social Scene, and a few other bests. On the menu are huge servings of two eggs with hash browns or tomatoes at $3.95, surprise combos of omelettes from $5.95 to $7.95, cheese blintzes, huevos con chorizo, potato pancakes, fried matzo, granola, and bagels with lox. Sumptuous sandwiches range from carnivore Reubens and burgers to veggies Santa Fe and a broiled salmon fillet sandwich. Brothers' offers a great selection of local wines, "seasonal microbrews," and espresso drinks.

❧ *Brothers' Restaurant, 95 North Main Street, Ashland; phone (541) 482–9671. American Express, MasterCard, and Visa. All nonsmoking. Wheelchair accessible.*

For great coffees try the cart on the sidewalk in the Plaza or the STARBUCKS a block south on Main Street. City Hall folks gather here in the mornings for their java injections and out-of-the-building "work." THE BEANERY, slightly off the beaten path at 1602 Ashland Street (541–488–0700), is a popular local hangout for coffee with free live music on weekends. Open 6:00 A.M.–11:00 P.M. All nonsmoking. Wheelchair accessible.

OREGON CRAB CAKES
from Chef David Taub, Chateaulin Restaurant

½ cup fresh bread crumbs

1 large egg, beaten

½ tsp fresh chives, minced

½ tsp fresh parsley, minced

1 Tbs Dijon mustard

4 Tbs mayonnaise

2 scallions, minced

½ tsp salt

pinch of cayenne pepper

1 lb Dungeness crabmeat

1½ Tbs unsalted butter

1½ Tbs canola oil

In a large bowl mix together the bread crumbs, egg, herbs, mustard, mayonnaise, scallions, and seasonings. Add the crabmeat and mix gently. (If the crab mixture seems too dry or won't hold together, add one more Tbs of mayonnaise.) Form this mixture into six patties. Meanwhile, heat the butter and oil in a large skillet over moderate heat. When the oil is just starting to smoke, add the crab cakes and cook until golden on both sides (about four to five minutes per side).

Serve immediately with lemon wedges, parsley, and a small bowl of cocktail sauce or mustard mayonnaise. Bon appétit!

Neighbors come in every day to **ASHLAND BAKERY CAFE**, 38 East Main Street (541–482–2117), for baked goods, great vegetarian lunches, terrific sandwiches, bento, burritos, omelettes, and tender fajitas.

Storefront **CHATEAULIN**, 50 East Main Street (541–482–2264), is Ashland's best-known and most award-winning Franco/Oregon restaurant. Michael Donovan and Chef David Taub have created a comfort zone with dark wood, heavy curtains hung by thick wooden rings separating rooms, and a warm bar in the back of the dining room. Entrees from $12.50 to $30.00 including soup or salad, and a great local wine list. Full bar. All nonsmoking. American Express, MasterCard, Visa, and local checks. Wheelchair accessible.

Locals crowd **OMAR'S** for huge steaks, salads you adorn yourself, and reasonable prices. 1380 Siskiyou Boulevard (541–482–1281).

MONET offers light French cuisine in a fun, contemporary atmosphere. 36 South Second Street (541–482–1339).

One of Ashland's new culinary stars is AMUSE, featuring more contemporary French-Northwest cuisine. 15 North First Street (541–488–9000).

The newest, greatest addition to the Ashland area culinary scene is NEW SAMMY'S COWBOY BISTRO, the creation of Chez Panisse alumni Charlene and Vernon Rollins. Both closed their famous New Boonville Hotel in the middle of the night and "disappeared," surfacing near Ashland fifteen years ago. Do not miss! 2210 South Pacific Highway, Talent; (541) 535–2779.

For excellent melt-in-your-mouth steaks, chicken, seafood, and pastas, try BEASY'S ON THE CREEK, 51 Water Street (541–488–5009). Terrific small steaks with salad, vegetables, and potatoes start at $13.

ILLINOIS VALLEY AND APPLEGATE VALLEY

The wineries of the western portion of southern Oregon are a bit more difficult to get to because they are not right off I–5. Take exit 30 at Medford and head west on Highway 238 to historic Jacksonville, which is fun to visit anyway.

VALLEY VIEW VINEYARDS, technically part of the new Applegate Valley appellation, operates a tasting room in Anna Maria's gift shop, 125 West California Street in Jacksonville, as well as at their new tasting pavilion at the winery. Get to the winery by turning left on Upper Applegate Road in the town of Ruch. Valley View is on the right up a dirt road.

Swiss photographer Peter Britt arrived in the nineteenth-century boomtown

MICROBREWERY ALERT!

To get to Caldera Brewing Company, *540 Clover Lane, Ashland (541–482–HOPS), take exit 14 from I–5.* Caldera *can mean boiling kettle or cauldron, a large crater formed by the collapse of a volcanic cone like Crater Lake, or a class 5 rapid on the Upper Klamath River. Featured beers: Vanilla Wheat, Pale Ale, Amber Ale, Dry Hop Red, Porter, Oatmeal Stout, Spring Bock, Belgian Style Wit, Maple Strong Ale, Imperial Chocolate Stout, and Hibernator Dopplebock.*

and southern Oregon commercial hub of Jacksonville in 1852 and soon planted starter vines he brought from California, thus founding the wine industry
of southern Oregon. By the 1880s he was producing 3,000 gallons yearly and
grew grapes such as Tokaya, Emperors, and Black Ferrereas. At the turn of the
twentieth century the dreaded *phylloxera* from California devastated the vineyard, and in 1920 Prohibition wiped out wine production. The late Frank
Wisnovsky bought this ideal location in 1971 and originally planted twenty-
six acres of Cabernet Sauvignon, Merlot, and Chardonnay. Eighty percent of
its production is in reds.

 Fine points: Featured wines: Valley View and Anna Maria Char-
donnay, Pinot Gris, Cabernet Sauvignon, Merlot, Viognier, and
Syrah. Owners: The Wisnovsky family. Winemaker: John Guerrero.
Cases: 10–12,000. Acres: 28.

*Valley View Vineyards, 1000 Upper Applegate Road, Jacksonville 97530;
phone (541) 899–8468 or (800) 781–WINE; Web site www.valleyview
winery.com. Tasting room: Anna Maria's Wine Tasting Room, 125 West California
Street, Jacksonville; (541) 899–1001. Open 11:00 A.M.–5:00 P.M. at winery; at
Anna Maria's, noon–6:00 P.M. Wednesday–Sunday, January–April; 11:00 A.M.–6:00
P.M. daily, April–December. Wheelchair accessible.*

One of the best-known restaurants in Oregon is the JACKSONVILLE INN,
175 East California Street. This 1863 building and inn are actually elegant.
Chef Diane Menzie brings back the quasi-continental foods the early settlers
enjoyed and offers them a la carte or on a seven-course prix fixe menu, or even
more reasonably in the lounge. Entrees range from reliable veal piccata (always
a good test) and petrale sole to fashionable polenta with seasonal variations.
Owner Jerry Evans has one of the finest wine lists in Oregon, including 600
local and imported wines.

Stay upstairs in one of the eight beautifully redecorated rooms with
comforting solid brick walls, four-poster beds, private bathrooms, and air-
conditioning—not historically accurate but extremely important here in the
summer. Throw all this in with a few old Wild West fantasies and wow!
Great breakfast included.

*Jacksonville Inn, 175 East California Street, Jacksonville 97530; phone (503)
899–1900. Lunch Tuesday–Saturday, breakfast and dinner daily, brunch Sunday.
Full bar. All nonsmoking. American Express, Diners Club, MasterCard, and Visa.
Checks accepted. Not wheelchair accessible.*

Also worth a try is MᴄCᴜʟʟʏ Hᴏᴜsᴇ Iɴɴ, an 1861 mansion with four bedrooms, each with bath and antique furniture. Continental breakfast is served.
🍂 *McCully House Inn, 240 East California Street, Jacksonville 97530; phone (503) 899–1942. MasterCard, Visa, and American Express. Not wheelchair accessible.*

The Bᴇʟʟᴀ Uɴɪᴏɴ Rᴇsᴛᴀᴜʀᴀɴᴛ has pizza, great dinners, and picnic stuff. Host Jerry Hayes loves to collect and talk wine, offering thirty-five labels from his wine cellar.
🍂 *Bella Union, 170 West California Street, Jacksonville 97530; phone (503) 899–1710. Visa and MasterCard. Wheelchair accessible.*

Either follow Applegate Road along the beautiful Applegate River westward and then head south on Highway 199 toward Cave Junction and Bridgeview and Foris wineries (a good hour), or return to Medford and go north on I–5. You are now in the new Applegate appellation region.

To get to Bʀɪᴅɢᴇᴠɪᴇᴡ Vɪɴᴇʏᴀʀᴅs, go south on Highway 199 to Cave Junction and turn left (east) on Highway 46 for a couple of miles. Highway 46 is the Oregon Caves Highway, which basically dead-ends at Oregon Caves National Monument (definitely worth the extra miles). Turn right on Holland Loop Road to the winery. You are now in the Illinois Valley.

Bridgeview is one of the most spectacular winery settings in Oregon with lakes, waterfalls, decks, picnic tables, and more than one hundred acres of vineyards. Buy your picnic supplies in Cave Junction or try one of the town's twenty eateries. Bridgeview also offers a picturesque and romantic bed-and-breakfast, Kerbyville Inn in Kerby just north of Cave Junction on Highway 199.

 Fine points: *Wine Enthusiast* rates Bridgeview's 1995 Pinot Noir Reserve an 85. Featured wines: Pinot Noir, Merlot, Chardonnay, Pinot Gris, Gewürztraminer, and Blue Moon Riesling. Owners: Robert and Lelo Kerivan. Winemaker: René Eichmann. Cases: 80,000. Acres: 185.
🍂 *Bridgeview Vineyards, 4210 Holland Loop Road, Cave Junction 97523; phone (541) 592–4688; fax (541) 592–2127; e-mail bvw@bridgevieweine.com; Web site www.bridgeviewwine.com. Open 11:00 A.M.–5:00 P.M. daily. Visa, MasterCard, and Discover. Wheelchair accessible.*

Moving on to Fᴏʀɪs Vɪɴᴇʏᴀʀᴅs Wɪɴᴇʀʏ, come out of Bridgeview and turn right on Holland Loop Road and then right again on Kendall Road. Foris is off to the right. Just to confuse you, Foris is in the Illinois Valley subregion of the Rogue Valley appellation.

Foris is Oregon's southernmost winery, only 6 miles from the California-Oregon border. You can also get here from Eureka and Crescent City up Highway 1, a beautiful but somewhat harrowing drive. On the Siskiyou Terrace of the Siskiyou Mountains, Foris gets the most ocean air of any Oregon winery, yielding interesting Alsatian, Burgundian, and Bordeaux-style wines.

Transplanted Californians Meri and Ted Gerber's original five acres were planted in 1973, and they began to make their own wine on-site in 1987. Ted now has eighty-five acres planted, is planting more, and purchases grapes from other local growers. Their extremely pleasant tasting room makes you feel at home and welcomed and offers baskets and other appealing novelties. Watch for spring, harvest, and Thanksgiving case sales.

Fine points: Featured wines: Pinot Gris, Pinot Blanc, Chardonnay, Gewürztraminer, Merlot, Cabernet Sauvignon, Cabernet Franc, Pinot Noir, and Early Muscat. Owner: Ted Gerber. Winemaker: Sarah Powell. Cases: 25,000. Acres: 120 and purchase from others, including partners.

❧ *Foris Vineyards Winery, 654 Kendall Road, Cave Junction 97523; phone (541) 592–3752 or (800) 843–6747; fax (541) 592–4424; e-mail foris@foriswine.com; Web site www.foriswine.com. Open 11:00 A.M.–5:00 P.M. daily. Visa and MasterCard. Wheelchair accessible.*

What was Siskiyou Vineyards, 6220 Oregon Caves Highway, has been purchased by René Eichmann, son of Bridgeview Vineyards co-owner Lelo

MICROBREWERY ALERT!

Wild River Brewing, *595 North East Street, Grants Pass (541–471–7487), is the public house of this Cave Junction brewery, with a spectacular three-story restaurant with good grub and wood-fired pizza, salads, soups, pasta, espresso, and filling breakfasts. Featured beers: Imperial Stout, Hefeweizen, Kolsch, and Extra Special Bitter, accompanied by seasonal efforts such as Oktoberfest, Cave Bear, Barleywine, Blackberry Porter, Weizen Bock, Harbor Lights Kolsch style, Nut Brown Ale, Hefe-Weizen, and Bohemian Pilzner. Lots of calories here, but what a way to go!*

Kerivan. René worked at Bridgeview since it first opened and is restarting Siskiyou as **BEAR CREEK WINERY OF OREGON**, with a regional tasting room featuring Southern Oregon wines and eventually including his own.

From the Foris driveway turn left on Kendall Road, right on Holland Loop Road, and left on Oregon Caves Highway 46. Bear Creek (Siskiyou) will be on your right.

Bear Creek's new tasting room and grounds offer spectacular picnic sites and panoramic views of the Siskiyou Mountains.

 Fine Points: Featured wines: Bear Creek Chardonnay, Sauvignon Blanc, Pinot Noir, Cabernet Sauvignon, Cabernet Franc, Le Cave Rouge (Cabernet/Merlot), Merlot, Siskiyou Pinot Noir, Gewürztraminer, Dry Gewürztraminer, and Pinot Blanc. Owner: René Eichmann. Winemaker: René Eichmann. Cases: 2,500. Acres: 40.

❧ *Bear Creek Winery of Oregon, 6220 Caves Highway, Cave Junction 97523; phone (541) 592–3977; fax (541) 592–2127; e-mail renee@cavenet.com. Open noon–5:00 P.M. April–Labor Day. Visa and MasterCard. Not wheelchair accessible.*

As you leave Bear Creek, turn right (west) on Oregon Caves Highway 46 and return to Cave Junction, continuing north to Grants Pass and on to the Umpqua Region.

UMPQUA VALLEY

Roseburg is the obvious home base for wine touring in the Umpqua region. Lying on I–5 70 miles south of Eugene and 110 miles north of Ashland, it can be reached in less than two hours from either of those stop-offs. Downtown Roseburg is centered on the east side of the highway, just north of the Umpqua River, which flows east to west. To reach downtown get off the highway at exit 124. This will take you eastward across the river on West Harvard Boulevard.

Find a place to stay early if you are going to spend the night in Roseburg. Believe it or not, the best place to stay currently is a newer, plastic-looking HOLIDAY INN EXPRESS right off exit 124. Every room seems to hang over the Umpqua River with the inn's lawn separating the two. All rooms have lovely views. A buffet breakfast with good, healthful choices comes with the price of rooms, as does an indoor swimming pool and Jacuzzi.

❧ *Holiday Inn Express, 375 West Harvard Boulevard, Roseburg 97470; phone (541) 673–7517 or (800) 898–7666; fax (541) 673–8331. Visa, MasterCard, and American Express. Wheelchair accessible.*

Top in the B&B line is HOUSE OF HUNTER. In 1990 Walt and Jean Hunter restored this 1900 Italianate house, decorating with a mixture of antiques and newer furniture. An oasis in Roseburg, it's worth the visit for Jean's scrumptious breakfasts.

🌺 *House of Hunter, 813 Southeast Kane Street, Roseburg 97470; phone (541) 672–2335 or (800) 540–7704; e-mail walth@users.wizzards.net; Web site www.server.wizzards.net/hunter/b&b.html. Visa, MasterCard, and American Express. Not wheelchair accessible.*

There also are many other nice B&Bs and chain motels in the area.

When you are ready to grab a bit to eat, CAFE ESPRESSO, at the corner of Douglas and Jackson, is good for salads, espressos, microwaved dinner entrees, and sandwiches. LOS DOS AMIGOS, 537 Southeast Jackson (541–673–1351), has the best family-style Mexican food in the area.

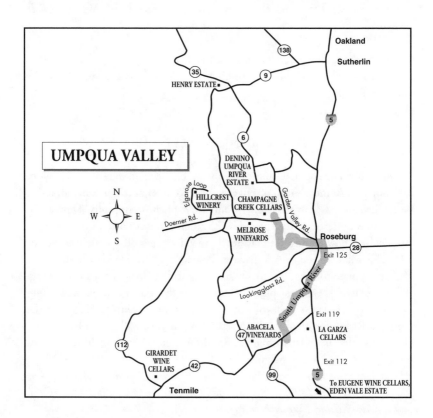

Another dining option is Tolly's in nearby Oakland. Take exit 138 off I–5, then drive about 2 short miles into town. Oakland appears like a small European village in the near distance, complete with church steeples nestled in the gentle hills. As you pass fast-food joints, yellow and white wildflowers line the road and lift your spirits instantly, no matter how hungry you are. Turn left at Fourth Street and right on Locust and you will feel as if you have turned the corner into the nine-teenth century, which you have.

Old brick buildings and a slow pace lower the blood pressure right away. TOLLY'S ANTIQUES AND SODA FOUNTAIN MERCANTILE RESTAURANT is all of that, plus candy store, elegant dining room, former bank, theater with grand piano, and tearoom. Sumptuous root beer floats spill unabashedly over the glass's edge, and a sign warns that UNATTENDED CHILDREN WILL BE SOLD TO THE ZOO. Check out the Young Bank Safe, which operated from 1892 to 1920. Tolly's steams its deli sandwiches, which has an interesting maturing effect on the ingredients. Ask about the Tollefsons' winemaker dinners, since winemakers say Tolly's is the best there is in the evening.

If you have kids along, you may want to appease them with a stop at Wildlife Safari (a right turn about 2 miles west of the left turn to La Garza Cellars and Gourmet Kitchen), an only slightly artificial 600-acre "wildlife preserve" that you can drive through to check out baby animals up close and ooh and aah at 500 wildish fenced-in cheetahs, zebras, yaks, eland, giraffes, tigers, and bears. Pet adorable creatures at the Petting Corral, have a snack at the White Rhino restaurant, or buy a souvenir at the Casbah Gift Shop. Open daily. Phone (541) 679–6761 or (800) 355–4848.

✤ *Tolly's Antiques and Soda Fountain Mercantile Restaurant, 115 Locust Street, Oakland 97462; phone (541) 459–3796. Visa, MasterCard, and American Express. Wheelchair accessible.*

To proceed on your tour of wineries in the Umpqua Region around Roseburg, we suggest you get back on I–5 heading south (yes) and take exit 119 about 5 miles south of Roseburg onto Highway 99.

A half mile from I–5, take the second left around the first hill to LA GARZA CELLARS AND GOURMET KITCHEN, 491 Winery Lane. We recommend that you call ahead to find out if they are serving lunch. Californian Jon Marker and friends founded this vineyard and winery as Jonicole in 1969. Leonard and Donna Souza-Postles purchased the property in 1992, revived the vineyards, and added to the winery and tasting room. Now a lovely patio and garden complement the tasting and dining rooms, a true oasis. Usually you can enjoy lunch Wednesday–Sunday; dinner and private parties are by reservation only.

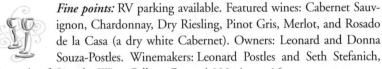

Fine points: RV parking available. Featured wines: Cabernet Sauvignon, Chardonnay, Dry Riesling, Pinot Gris, Merlot, and Rosado de la Casa (a dry white Cabernet). Owners: Leonard and Donna Souza-Postles. Winemakers: Leonard Postles and Seth Stefanich, formerly of Girardet Wine Cellars. Cases: 4,000. Acres: 16.

TRIPLE CHOCOLATE TORTE
from Donna Souza-Postles,
co-owner, La Garza Cellars and Gourmet Kitchen

For the cake:

8 eggs	*1 Tbs vanilla*
16 oz semisweet chocolate	*½ tsp salt*
2 cups soy margarine	*⅓ cup bourbon*
1 cup granulated sugar	*1½ cups toasted walnuts, chopped*
1 cup whipping cream	*fine (put aside to use after torte is glazed)*

For the glaze:

6 oz semisweet chocolate	*3 Tbs whipping cream*
2 Tbs butter	*2 Tbs corn syrup*

For the chocolate curls:

½ cup semisweet chocolate chips	*2 Tbs butter*

Cake: In a bowl beat the eggs until blended. Heat remaining cake ingredients (except walnuts), stirring slowly over low heat until smooth. Temper the eggs with some of the chocolate mixture and then slowly pour the tempered beaten eggs into the chocolate mixture and mix until well blended. Pour into a springform pan and bake at 350°F for approximately 45 minutes. Cool completely, then remove from pan.

Glaze: Melt all glaze ingredients together and blend until smooth. Glaze the entire torte. Lightly press the toasted chopped walnuts onto the sides of the torte.

Chocolate curls: Melt the semisweet chocolate chips and butter together. Chill. Grate onto top of glazed torte.

Chill the torte.

MICROBREWERY ALERT!

Umpqua Brewing Company, *328 SE Jackson Street (541–672–0452), in historic downtown Roseburg on the east side of I–5, is an oasis in a town not too concerned with gustatory arts. The barbecued hamburgers, excellent pizzas, and salads are refreshing and popular with locals. First Friday is Sushi Night. Featured beers: Umpqua Gold, Summer Wheat, Rosegarden White, Roseburg Red, Douglas Draft, Downtown Brown, plus berry beers, Stout, Weizen, and Bock. Tours during regular day hours; no food service on Mondays. No smoking.*

❧ *La Garza Cellars and Gourmet Kitchen, 491 Winery Lane, Roseburg 97470; phone (541) 679–9654; fax (541) 679–3888; e-mail lagarza@ rosenet.net; Web site www.winesnw.com/lagarzacellars.htm. Open 11:00 A.M.– 5:00 P.M. daily, June–September; noon–4:00 P.M. Wednesday–Sunday, February–May and October–mid-December. Visa and MasterCard. Wheelchair accessible.*

As you leave La Garza, turn left (west) on Highway 99/42 and travel for a total of about 10 miles. At the small town of Winston, turn right to Highway 42 toward Coos Bay, while Highway 99 turns south and east. Turn right on Broadway, then turn left on Lookingglass.

At ABACELA VINEYARDS & WINERY, Dr. H. Earl and Hilda Jones apply their scientific knowledge and approach to chemistry as dermatologist and lab technician to make fine wines available mostly at the winery. Having moved to Roseburg from Alabama in 1995, the Joneses age their wines in small oak casks, striving for deeply colored wines with intense character.

Fine points: Featured wines: Cabernet Franc, Grenache, Malbec, Merlot, Sangiovese, Syrah, Tempranillo, and Viognier. Owners and winemakers: Earl and Hilda Jones. Cases: 5,000. Acres: 35.

❧ *Abacela Vineyards & Winery, 12500 Lookingglass Road, Roseburg 97470; phone (541) 679–6642; Web site www.abacela.com. Open 11:00 A.M.–5:00 P.M. daily. Visa, MasterCard, American Express, and Discover. Wheelchair accessible.*

GIRARDET WINE CELLARS' Philippe Girardet gave up teaching astrophysics at Cal Tech in Pasadena, California, to migrate with his wife, Bonnie, to Oregon in 1972, among the very first Californians to hit the road toward Oregonian sanity. Settling here because the terrain reminded Philippe of his native Switzerland, the Girardets sold their early crops to other wineries and started their own winery in 1983 with the help of enologist Bill Nelson. Bonnie Girardet presides over the tasting room, and all five Girardet children help in this truly family endeavor.

Fine points: Featured wines: Luscious French hybrids Grand Blanc and Grand Rouge, Riesling, White Zinfandel, Pinot Gris, Maréchal Foch, Pinot Noir, and Cabernet Sauvignon. Girardet's highly unusual Baco Noir, Seyval Blanc, and Pinot Noir Barrel Select at $16 are standouts. Owners: Philippe and Bonnie Girardet. Winemaker: Marc Girardet. Cases: 25,000. Acres: 35 planted of 48.

Girardet Wine Cellars, 895 Reston Road, Roseburg 97470; phone (541) 679–7252; fax (541) 679–9502; e-mail genuine@girardetwine.com; web site www.girardetwine.com. Open 11:00 A.M.–5:00 P.M. daily. Visa and MasterCard. Not wheelchair accessible.

There are two ways to approach HillCrest Vineyards and Champagne Creek Cellars, and it is well worth the trip from either direction. You can either go back to I–5 or take the gorgeous and sometimes confusing back roads. It isn't the roads themselves that mystify; it's the signs, the directions they point, or lack of same. If you see a WINE TOUR ROUTE sign, you might know you're on the right track, although these signs give no direction.

To take the country back-road way from Girardet Wine Cellars, when you leave Girardet, turn right onto Reston Road, then right on Flournoy Road, left on Doerner Road, and then right on Elgarose Loop Road. Turn left onto Vineyard Lane and drive up the gravel driveway to HillCrest. We got lost several times, but what a way to go.

If you decide to go back to I–5, take exit 125 (Garden Valley Road) north of Roseburg for 2 miles, and go left on Melrose for 1.3 miles, right on Busenbark, and left up the driveway to Champagne Creek Cellars. To get to HillCrest Vineyards from Champagne Creek, come back down Busenbark Road, turn right on Melrose Road, right on Elgarose, left on Vineyard Lane, and into the driveway.

HILLCREST WINERY is the oldest continuously operating vinifera winery in Oregon. Founder Richard Sommer, son of a Swiss immigrant biochemist father and a nutritionist mother from Ashland, grew up in San Francisco, got the enology bug while an agriculture student at the University of California at Davis, and moved to Oregon to pursue his dream. Sommer planted his vineyard in 1961, long before anyone else currently involved in the Oregon wine business.

HillCrest is in a lovely old dark wood barnlike structure with a tasteful, subtle sign. Sommer selected this site because of the soils and western Oregon climate, which he believes best approximate German conditions for producing Rieslings.

Because of Alzheimer's, Sommer sold the winery for $1,000. The sale was undone, the winery was put in conservatorship, and Susan and Dyson DeMara bought HillCrest for a proper price.

Dyson made wine at Robert Mondavi in the Napa Valley for twenty-five years, had his own winemaking facility on Atlas Peak, and moved northward after determining this was the perfect spot to make Northern Italian varietals. The DeMaras now hope to fulfill their dream of becoming "peasant winemakers" out of the commercial Napa crush.

 Fine points: Featured wines: Riesling, Sémillon, Old Vine Zinfandel, Cabernet Sauvignon, and Pinot Noir, from $14 to $40. Owner: Della Terra, LLC. Winemaker: Dyson DeMara. Cases: 4,000. Acres: 35.

🍃 *HillCrest Winery, 240 Vineyard Lane, Roseburg 97470; phone (541) 673–3709; e-mail finewine@sorcom.com. Open 11:00 A.M.–5:00 P.M. daily. Visa and MasterCard. Not wheelchair accessible.*

As you leave HillCrest turn left (east) on Melrose Road to Champagne Creek by getting yourself back to Elgarose. Turn right on Doerner, and left on Melrose Road, then left on Buesenbard Road and up the driveway to the left to Champagne Creek Cellars.

CHAMPAGNE CREEK CELLARS was born when Janiece and well-known winemaker David Brown bought Callahan Ridge Winery in 2001, and they still use the winery's charming 1878 barn. The Browns now host a Winter Dance the fourth weekend in January and a great Rhythm on the Vine Music Festival the third Saturday in September, which features their wines and those of other wineries for which they produce wine.

 Fine points: Featured wines: Dry Gewürztraminer, Chardonnay, White and Late Harvest Rieslings, Pinot Gris, Pinot Noir, Syrah, Grenache, Cabernet Sauvignon, Merlot, and a Semillon/Cabernet Sauvignon blend. Owners: Janiece and David Brown. Winemaker: David Brown. Cases: 10,000. Acres: 15.

HENRY ESTATE WINERY

❧ *Champagne Creek Cellars, 340 Busenbark Lane, Roseburg 97470; phone (866) WINE4US or (800) 216–7690; e-mail info@champagnecreek.com; Web site www.champagnecreek.com. Open 9:00 A.M.–5:00 P.M. daily, closed Tuesday January–March. Visa, MasterCard, and American Express. Wheelchair accessible.*

To get to **HENRY ESTATE WINERY,** you again have two choices. First, you can approach it from Champagne Creek or HillCrest Winery by coming north on Melqua Road and then turning right (east) on Ft. McKay Road, which turns into Hubbard Creek Road just west of Henry. We only tell you that in case you get ever so slightly off track as we did, you can find your way back to home base, which, in this case, is Henry Estate Winery.

Or you can arrive at Henry Estate Winery by taking exit 136 off I–5 and heading west through the little town of Umpqua, across the Umpqua River— Henry Estate is on your right. You will know it by its bright-colored petunias and red geraniums set against an appealing dark green wooden tasting room.

This winery is one of our favorites, partly because the family is so pleasant. *Wine Spectator* likes it too and gave Henry's 1995 Pinot Noir an 85 rating in 1997, and *Wine Enthusiast* rated its 1994 Pinot Noir an 89.

Scott Henry Sr. gave up his career in California as an aeronautical engineer for the earth and barrel in 1972, the year he and Sylvia Henry planted their

CHICKEN BREAST HENRY ESTATE
from Scott Henry, Henry Estate Winery

4 chicken breasts, boneless and skinless	*1 Tbs fresh garlic, minced*
3 oz flour	*1 Tbs fresh ginger, minced*
8 oz mushrooms, sliced	*2 Tbs fresh basil leaves, minced*
8 oz artichoke hearts, quartered	*4 oz Henry Estate Dry Gewürztraminer*
4 oz tomatoes, diced	*olive oil, as needed*
4 oz olives, drained and sliced	*salt & pepper to taste*

Heat skillet; dredge chicken breasts in flour and sauté in 1 oz of olive oil. When lightly browned on each side, transfer to platter and place in a preheated 350°F oven for twenty minutes to finish cooking. Return skillet to stove and sauté remaining ingredients in 1 oz or so of olive oil, adding the wine last. Let cook until wine is almost cooked away, season with salt and pepper, and pour mixture over chicken breasts.

Serve with your favorite pasta and Henry Estate's Dry Umpqua Valley, Oregon Gewürztraminer.

first thirty-five acres of vinifera grapes on the ranch that had belonged to his family for nearly eighty years. Scott Henry's scientific training resulted in his development of the Henry Trellis, the support by which vineyardists around the world trellis their vines.

We were impressed when the tasting room host said he was "Scotty Henry" until we discovered that there are four or five Scottys involved in the winery and spread over four generations. Our Scotty Henry obviously had spent his time on the dirty side of the barrel and is a charming cheerleader for his family's winery, the Umpqua Region, Oregon, and life in general. The gift shop carries Oregon mustards, pasta sauces, cookbooks, T-shirts, and all the other necessary wine equipment you could need. Plan to attend the fun "Henry Goes Wine" annual anniversary event on the third Saturday in August.

Fine points: Featured wines: 90 percent estate grapes produce hearty Estate Pinot Noir (one Double Gold medal), Port-style Pinot Noir, Müller-Thurgau (Gold and Silver medals), Pinot Noir Blanc, White Riesling, and Chardonnay, ranging from $8.00 to $25.00. Owners: Scott and Sylvia Henry. Winemaker: Scott Henry IV. Cases: 15,000. Acres: 40.

❧ *Henry Estate Winery, 687 Hubbard Creek Road, Umpqua 97486; phone (541) 459–5120; fax (541) 459–5146; e-mail henryest@wizzards.net; Web site www.henryestate.com. Open 11:00 A.M.–5:00 P.M. daily. Closed Super Bowl Sunday and major holidays. Visa and MasterCard. Wheelchair accessible.*

We suggest you drive straight through to Eugene or Corvallis, spend the night, and then begin a tour of the South Willamette Region wineries, working your way northward west of Albany to Salem for the next night.

SOUTH WILLAMETTE REGION

There is no direct, sensible route to visit the wineries of this region, which includes Eugene and Salem, so we will do our best to get you there in the most pleasant itinerary possible. It's an interesting area both gustatorily and academically. The University of Oregon is in Eugene, and Oregon State University is in Corvallis. Following our route from south to north, you will end the day in the state capital of Salem.

We will take you to only the wineries that are open to the public, including Chateau Lorane, King Estate, Silvan Ridge/Hinman Vineyards, Secret House Vineyards near Veneta; and La Velle Vineyards near Monroe; Tyee Wine Cellars, Bellfountain Cellars, and Springhill Cellars near Albany; and Airlie. In the Salem area we take you to Eola Hills Wine Cellars, Chateau Bianca, Firesteed Cellars, Willamette Valley Vineyards, Honeywood right downtown, and Redhawk Vineyards.

To reach CHATEAU LORANE take exit 174 from I–5 at Cottage Grove, follow Main Street to the Cottage Grove–Lorane Road or get there from the north via the Territorial Highway. Go 12 miles from Cottage Grove to the Cottage Grove–Lorane Road's intersection with Territorial Highway. Proceed west on Siuslaw River Road for 0.2 mile, and turn right up Chateau Lorane's driveway for about 1 mile.

Linde and Sharon Kester planted their vineyard in 1984 and opened the winery in 1992, 1 mile north of the giant metropolis of Lorane. The Coast Range foothills and natural beauty here are worth the drive even if you aren't interested in wine. The surrounding forest of fir trees and the winery's twenty-four-acre lake, which are depicted on Chateau Lorane's labels, represent what Oregon and heaven should be like. Watch for the Memorial Day Festival.

 Fine points: The Kesters make the expected wines plus small lots from several rare and exotic varieties such as Huxelrebe, Viognier, Pinot Noir, Chardonnay, Riesling, Gewürztraminer, Melon de

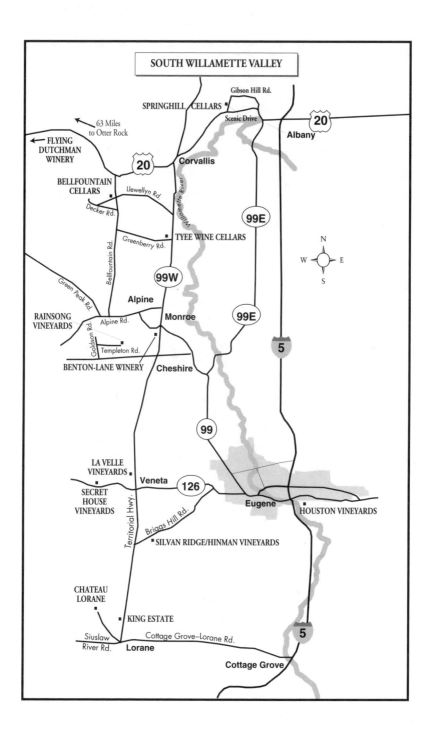

RISOTTO GAMBERONI
from Silvan Ridge Vineyards

2 large garlic cloves, sliced
2 Tbs olive oil
1 lb large shrimp, shelled, deveined, cut in half lengthwise
¾ cup simple tomato sauce
1 pkg Roland saffron, dissolved in
¼ cup boiling water
4 Tbs butter, divided
1 small onion, diced
1¾ cups Arborio rice
salt and pepper to taste
⅓ cup white wine (not Chardonnay; use Pinot Grigio or Pinot Gris)
5–6 cups chicken broth, heated in pan next to where you are cooking
¾ cup Parmesan cheese, grated

Sauté garlic in olive oil. Add shrimp; when cooked and curled add tomato sauce and stir well. Stir in saffron water mixture. Remove from heat and let cool. When cool, cover.

Melt 2 Tbs butter in a saucepan. Add onion and sauté until transparent. Add rice and stir so each kernel is covered. Add salt and pepper (lots). Add wine and stir until absorbed. Then start adding broth, one ladle at a time, until the rice is al dente. Add the shrimp mixture. Mix until all ingredients are combined and heated through. Remove from heat and add remaining 2 Tbs butter, stirring until melted. Add cheese gradually, stirring gently, and taste for seasoning. Serve immediately with Hinman Pinot Gris. Serves 8.

Bourgogne, Durif (Petite Syrah), Maréchal Foch, Baco Noir, and Pinot Meunier. This is an unusual treat and well worth the trip. Owners: Linde and Sharon Kester. Winemaker: David Hook. Cases: 5,000. Acres: 30 and buy from others.

❧ **Chateau Lorane**, *27415 Siuslaw River Road, Lorane 97451; phone (541) 942–8028; fax (541) 942–5830; e-mail info@chateaulorane.com; Web site www.chateaulorane.com. Open noon–5:00 P.M. daily, June–September; noon–5:00 P.M. weekends, October–May. Visa and MasterCard. Wheelchair accessible.*

As you leave Chateau Lorane, turn left on Territorial Highway, and then left into KING ESTATE. Although some Kings followed the Oregon Trail in covered wagons, Ed King III left his Alaskan law practice to pursue an MBA at the University of Oregon in Eugene. He never left, and he brought other families to his newfound home. Looking for hay to feed his horses, Ed answered an ad and found what is now King Estate. Planting began in 1991, and King is certified organic. Enjoy the new tasting room and garden. Watch for "open houses" with barrel tastings, music, and hors d'oeuvres.

Fine Points: Featured wines: Chardonnay, Pinot Gris, and Pinot Noir. Owners: The King family. Lead Winemakers: Bill Kremer and Ray Walsh. Cases: 90,000. Acres: 230 of 820.

❧ *King Estate, 80854 Territorial Highway, Eugene 97405; phone (541) 942–9874 or (800) 884–4441; fax (541) 942–9867; e-mail info@king estate.com; Web site www.kingestate.com. Open noon–5:00 P.M. daily, Memorial Day–Labor Day. noon–5:00 P.M. Saturday–Sunday, Labor Day–Memorial Day. Visa, MasterCard, and American Express. Wheelchair accessible.*

Next stop is SILVAN RIDGE/HINMAN VINEYARDS. From King Estate continue north on Territorial Highway. Turn right on Briggs Hill Road for about 3.5 miles, and then turn right into Silvan's driveway, one of the few paved roads to northwest wineries. What a pleasure! From Eugene, it's an 11-mile, twenty-minute gorgeous drive to Silvan by taking Eleventh Street (which is Highway

SILVAN RIDGE/HINMAN VINEYARDS

126) west, then turning left on Bailey Hill Road for about 5 miles, right on Spencer Creek Road for 2.5 miles, and left on Briggs Hill Road.

Owner Carolyn Chambers rescued this winery by purchasing it several years ago. With the help of winemaker Joe Dobbes from 1991 to 1996, she reestablished what was Hinman Vineyards at the time as one of Oregon's premier wineries. Joe's experience alongside expert winemakers in Burgundy and Germany helped him bring Hinman's Silvan Ridge reserve line accolades throughout the Northwest. They added a lovely kitchen and dining room for banquets and parties.

Today Silvan's tasting room's ecologically appropriate West Coast design invites you to try the wines, gift shop, and picnic area. You can also enjoy the Labor Day Jazz on the Vine concert at the natural amphitheater stage in front with the vineyards as the stage's backdrop. Check Silvan's Web site for quarterly dinners.

 Fine points: Featured wines at Silvan Ridge/Hinman: Pinot Noir, Chardonnay, Cabernet Sauvignon, Pinot Gris, and Riesling; $8.00–$13.00. Featured wines among Silvan Ridge reserves: Pinot Noir, Chardonnay, Pinot Gris, Gewürztraminer, Merlot, and Early Muscat Semi-Sparkling. Owner: Carolyn Chambers. Winemaker: Bryan Wilson. Cases: 30,000. Acres: 6 and buy from every appellation in Oregon.

❧ *Silvan Ridge/Hinman Vineyards, 27012 Briggs Hill Road, Eugene 97405; phone (541) 345–1945; fax (541) 345–6174; e-mail info@silvanridge.com; Web site www.silvanridge.com. Open noon–5:00 P.M. daily. Visa, MasterCard, and American Express. Wheelchair accessible.*

Next is SECRET HOUSE VINEYARDS, known as much for its music festivals and art gallery as for its wines. From Silvan Ridge Vineyards go back to Territorial Highway, turn right (north), and eventually turn left on Highway 126 toward Florence; turn right to Secret House 2.4 miles from the Territorial Highway–126 intersection. From Eugene take Highway 126 west toward the coast and from Florence go 2.4 miles past Territorial Highway (about 15 miles total).

Ron and Patty Chappel's previous passion and career was importing fine art from the Far East, so you are in for a double treat in their unique blend of fine arts and wine with their art gallery and bird sanctuary. Secret House stages an annual Wine and Blues Festival the second weekend in August and concerts throughout the summer.

 Fine points: Featured wines: Pinot Noir, Chardonnay, Late Harvest Riesling, Pinot Gris, premium *méthode champenoise* sparkling wines, White Pinot Noir, and Cabernet Sauvignon. Owners: Ron and Patty Chappel. Winemaker: Gary Carpenter, consulting.

Microbrewery Alert!

The Willamette Valley seems to attract almost as many aspiring brewers as vintners, many also transplanted Californians. The result is suds heaven for the consumer.

Oregon Trail Brewery, 341 SW Second Street, Corvallis (541–758–3527), is one of Oregon's oldest breweries.

Oregon Fields Brewing Company, Restaurant and Pub, 1290 Oak Street, Eugene (541–341–6599), in a historic building, features Northwest cuisine including crab cakes and salmon fish and chips.

Steelhead Brewing Company, 199 East Fifth Avenue, Eugene (541–686–2739), is in the heart of Eugene's Market District. They serve home-made spent-grain breads and pizza crust in an English pub atmosphere. Their own root beer soda also hits the spot.

Wild Duck Brewery and Restaurant, 169 West Sixth Street, Eugene (541–485–3825), is Eugene's newest and largest brewpub. It features a copper-clad brew kettle in the bar decorated with wild neon and curios and metal sculpture. Try the fresh ahi, salmon, swordfish, crab, and prime rib. The separate concert hall makes this place a local hangout, especially popular with U of O students. For non-Oregonians: The Oregon mascot is the duck.

Cases: 10,000. Acres: 26.

❧ *Secret House Vineyards, 88324 Vineyard Lane, Veneta 97487; phone (541) 935–3774; Web site www.secrethousewinery.com. Open 11:00 A.M.–5:00 P.M. daily. Visa and MasterCard. Wheelchair accessible tasting room, with a gravel driveway/entry.*

As you leave Secret House, turn left (east) on Highway 126 and return to the Territorial Highway intersection. Turn left on Territorial and left on Warthen Road. Turn right on Sheffler Road and right at LA VELLE VINEYARDS.

A retreat in lush, rolling hills, La Velle offers surprisingly attractive terraced gardens and lawns. The tasting room, remodeled to give it an Old World look, has a mezzanine art gallery featuring local and regional artists, as well as a few great wines. You can also visit La Velle's tasting room in downtown Eugene's historic Fifth Street Market.

Fine points: Featured wines: Pinot Gris, Riesling, Pinot Noir, and sparkling wine. Owner: Doug La Velle. Winemaker: Gary Carpenter. Cases: 4,500. Acres: 16.

La Velle Vineyards, 89697 Sheffler Road, Elmira 97437; phone (541) 935–9406 or (800) 645–8463; fax (541) 935–7202; e-mail lvvineyard@ aol.com; Web site www.lavelle-vineyards.com. Open noon–5:00 P.M. daily, May 31–Labor Day; noon–5:00 P.M. Saturday–Sunday or by appointment, November– May. Downtown tasting room, 296 East Fifth Avenue (Fifth Street Public Market), Eugene 97401; phone (541) 338–9875. Open 11:00 A.M.–6:00 P.M. Sunday– Thursday, 11:00 A.M.–10:00 P.M. Friday–Saturday. Visa and MasterCard. Wheelchair accessible.

Pinot Noir fans will be in heaven at BENTON-LANE WINERY, which makes only silken, friendly, moderately priced Pinot Noir from its own estate vineyard in both Benton and Lane Counties between Eugene and Corvallis. Formerly known as Sunnymount, just a mile north of the Diamond Wood Golf Course, Benton-Lane has an enjoyable picnic area and attractive retail shop. Steve Girard and Carl Doumani sold their superb Girard Winery on Napa's Silverado Trail and enjoy making some of the finest Pinot Noir anywhere.

Fine points: Featured wines: Pinot Noir. Owners: Steve Girard and Carl Doumani. Winemaker: Damian North. Cases: 20,000. Acres: 130.

Benton Lane Winery, 23924 Territorial Highway, Monroe 97456; phone (541) 847–5792; fax (541) 847–5791; e-mail sales@benton-lane.com; Web site www.benton-lane.com. Open 11:00 A.M.–4:00 P.M. daily, June 1–October 1; 11:00 A.M.–4:00 P.M. Monday–Friday, October–May. Visa and MasterCard. Wheelchair accessible. RVs welcome.

From Benton-Lane Winery join Highway 99W and continue north about 10 miles. Just past the Greenberry Store (hint: it's bright green), turn west on Greenberry Road for 2.3 miles and turn right to Tyee Cellars. From Corvallis take 99W south and turn right (west) on Greenberry Road.

TYEE WINE CELLARS is the most culturally sensitive winery we encountered. Before you get to the tasting room, you pass a sign announcing BUCHANAN FAMILY CENTURY FARM. Co-owner Dave Buchanan's grandfather first established the farm in 1885 and raised racehorses, sheep, and cows, which for years organically prefertilized the soil for grapes. The winery was established exactly a century later.

TYEE WINE CELLARS

Dave and wife Margy Buchanan came back to save the family farm and reflected upon whose property this really was first. Kalapooya natives lived here and worshiped Mary's Peak, which you can see through the tasting room (formerly milk tank) window. Notice the pestles dug up when the Buchanans excavated for planting their vines. You can even follow an interpretive trail on Tyee property.

Local Cherokee artist James Jordan's native designs are available in the tasting room, and he designs labels for Tyee, which means "chief," "biggest," or "best" in several Northwest First Peoples languages.

Dave started making his own wine and eventually talked U.C.–Davis graduate Barney Watson into joining Tyee and turning it professional, which he has accomplished with great success. You can picnic at Tyee before or after hiking the Beaver Pond Loop through 450 acres of meadows, views, and woodlands. Two hundred twenty acres are restored as a wetland preserve. Check Tyee's Web site for dates of the annual Pinot Gladstone comedy and music and Midsummer Night's Scream in August. Don't miss Watersheds, Wetlands, and Wineries in June, featuring author lectures, live music, an art show, and gardening demonstration. Tyee's A Summer Night to Remember, the last weekend in July, includes dinner and American Indian flute music.

Fine points: Tastes are free, and you can buy wine by the glass or bottle. Featured wines: Pinot Noir, Pinot Gris, Pinot Blanc, Chardonnay, and Gewürztraminer. Owners: Dave and Margy Buchanan, Barney Watson, and Nola Mosier. Winemaker: Barney Watson. Cases: 2,500. Acres: 10 and buy from three Coast Range vineyards.

❧ *Tyee Wine Cellars, 26335 Greenberry Road, Corvallis 97333; phone and fax (541) 753–8754; Web site www.tyeewine.com. Open noon–5:00 P.M. weekends, April–June and September–December; noon–5:00 P.M. Friday–Monday, July–August; closed January–March except by appointment. Visa and MasterCard. Wheelchair accessible.*

To get to BELLFOUNTAIN CELLARS from Tyee Cellars, return to Highway 99W and turn left (north). Turn left on Llewellyn Road into the rolling hills, pass Fern Road, and follow signs to Bellfountain Cellars on right.

Bellfountain Cellars enjoys a unique microclimate cut out of the forest, resulting in a romantic site with hot days and cool evenings. It's a pleasure just to sit on the winery's decks, overlooking the hills and valley, view local artists' work, and sip Bellfountain's fine wines. Some may find this winery too far off the beaten track, but others will find the peaceful setting and wines worth the trip.

Easterners Rob and Jeanne Mommsen left their mining business in West Virginia and headed west to live their dream. First planting ten acres of vineyards, they opened their winery/home in 1989. You'll enjoy their enthusiasm.

Fine points: Featured wines: Cabernet Sauvignon, Pinot Noir, Chardonnay, Pinot Gris, Sauvignon Blanc, dry Gewürztraminer, and dry Riesling. Owners and winemakers: Rob and Jeanne Mommsen. Cases: 3,000. Acres: 100.

❧ *Bellfountain Cellars, 25041 Llewellyn Road, Corvallis 97333; phone (541) 929–3162. Open noon–6:00 P.M. Friday–Sunday. Visa and MasterCard. Wheelchair accessible. Children welcome.*

SPRINGHILL CELLARS is alone away from other wineries but close to Albany. You may want to make the trip just for the Pinot Noirs. From Bellfountain Cellars, take 99W north to Corvallis and turn right (east) on Highway 20 toward Albany, left on Scenic Drive for 2.1 miles, and left again on Scenic, where its straight part becomes Pine View. Springhill is to the left.

Gary Budd developed the wines for Mike and Karen McLain; when Budd left the winery McLain took over the winemaking reins. Springhill's 1988 Pinot Noir won the Governor's Award at the Oregon State Fair. Thanksgiving weekend at Springhill brings a German-style Harvest Festival with live music Saturday evening.

❧

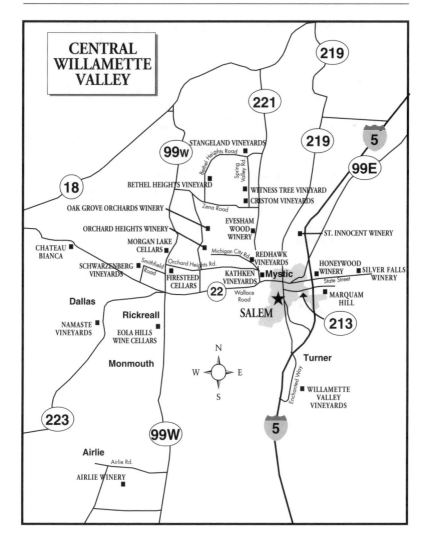

CENTRAL
WILLAMETTE
VALLEY

STANGELAND VINEYARDS
99w
Bethel Heights Road
Spring Valley Rd.
219
5
221
219
99E
18
BETHEL HEIGHTS VINEYARD
WITNESS TREE VINEYARD
CRISTOM VINEYARDS
OAK GROVE ORCHARDS WINERY
Zena Road
EVESHAM
WOOD
WINERY
ORCHARD HEIGHTS WINERY
ST. INNOCENT WINERY
MORGAN LAKE
CELLARS
Michigan City Rd.
REDHAWK
VINEYARDS
CHATEAU
BIANCA
HONEYWOOD
WINERY
SILVER FALLS
WINERY
SCHWARZENBERG
VINEYARDS
Smithfield
Road
Orchard Heights Rd.
FIRESTEED
CELLARS
KATHKEN
VINEYARDS
Mystic
State Street
22
Wallace
Road
MARQUAM
HILL
Dallas
SALEM
NAMASTE
VINEYARDS
Rickreall
213
EOLA HILLS
WINE CELLARS
Monmouth
N
W   E
S
Turner
223
99W
WILLAMETTE
VALLEY
VINEYARDS
Enchanted Way
5
Airlie
Airlie Rd.
AIRLIE WINERY

Fine points: Featured wines: Pinot Noir and Pinot Gris. Owners: Mike and Karen McLain and Merv Anthony. Winemaker: Mike McLain. Cases: 2,000. Acres: 10.

❧ *Springhill Cellars, 2920 NW Scenic Drive, Albany 97321; phone (541) 928–1009; e-mail springhill@proaxis.com; Web site www.springhill cellars.com. Open 1:00–5:00 P.M. weekends, Memorial Day weekend to Thanksgiving, or by appointment. No credit cards. Wheelchair accessible.*

The most direct route to AIRLIE WINERY is to head north from Corvallis on Highway 99W, turn left (west) at Airlie Road, left on Maxfield Creek Road in Airlie, and left again on Dunn Forest Road, about 7 miles south of Monmouth.

After a career with the telephone company, Mary Olson purchased Airlie in 1997 from founders Larry and Alice Preedy, who gave the winery, nestled here in tall Douglas firs, its laid-back nothing-flummoxes-me attitude to winemaking. The Preedys planted their thirty-five–acre Dunn Forest Vineyard in 1983 and their cavelike in-the-hill winery in 1986. Mary Olsen promptly hired Suzy Gagné from Schwarzenberg Vineyards as the winemaker.

 Fine points: Don't miss Airlie's Memorial Day Weekend Blue Grass Festival that usually attracts the Sawtooth Mountain Boys as well as local and roaming musicians to the pond-side bandstand and picnic area. Featured wines: award-winning Müller-Thurgau and Chardonnay, Pinot Noir, Maréchal Foch, Pinot Gris, Riesling, and Gewürztraminer. Owner: Mary Olson. Winemaker: Suzy Gagné. Cases: 9,000. Acres: 44.

Airlie Winery, 15305 Dunn Forest Road, Monmouth 97361; phone (503) 838–6013; fax (503) 838–6279; e-mail airlie@airliewinery.com; Web site www.air liewinery.com. Open noon–5:00 P.M. Saturday–Sunday, March to December, then by appointment. Visa and MasterCard. Wheelchair accessible.

More than forty wineries dot the landscape between Salem and Portland, so unless you want to visit them all, you may want to select those within the area where you plan to stop. We will follow a natural progression northward.

If you travel north on Highway 99W from Airlie Winery, pass slowly through Monmouth unless you want to stop at MAIN STREET PIZZA for yummy garlicky pizza or at J's RESTAURANT, 220 North Pacific Highway (Highway 99W), Monmouth (503–838–1730), for better-than-average comfort sandwiches, hamburgers, and salads. We did and enjoyed every greasy bite.

You might drop in on the JENSEN ARCTIC MUSEUM, 590 West Church Street (503–838–8468), to view a small museum of natural and cultural history of the Arctic, all based on the founder's collection and sixty others. Open 10:00 A.M.–4:00 P.M. Wednesday–Saturday.

Just past the Polk County Fairgrounds on the right, you will find Eola Hills Wine Cellars on the left in an industrial-style metal building. Or you can get to Eola by heading west on Highway 22 from Salem, turn left (south) at the signal on Highway 99W through the small burg of Rickreall (don't blink because you might miss it), go past Rickreall Road, and find Eola Hills on your right (about 10 miles total).

EOLA HILLS WINE CELLARS offers a fun and different experience. Named for the surrounding Eola Hills region, Eola Hills Wine Cellars is actually on the flatland. It's owned by Bill, Jim, and Tom Huggins and a group of fifty other investors, and it's managed by founder/co-owner Tom Huggins, who has created a fun sports-connected atmosphere in this former lumber company warehouse and cherry-processing plant. Eola Hills released its first wines in 1987. The winery's 1995 White Riesling ($5.00) was rated as one of *Wine Enthusiast's* "Best Buys" for 1997.

Scott and Lajuana "L. J." Gunderson, who host at the tasting room, met and married in the winery and have created two salesrooms with shirts, hats, wine paraphernalia, gourmet foods, and candles. Footprints on the floor announce upcoming wine trips to football games, including the "Civil War" between the University of Oregon and Oregon State.

Cyclists: Watch for special-event labels commemorating the Hood to Coast Relay and Cycle Oregon Wine Country tour of six wineries on Sundays in August. For $50, a bus follows, picks up your purchases, and then cyclists come back to Eola for a barbeque.

Make reservations for Eola Hills' famous gourmet Sunday brunches throughout the year, except during harvest. Monthly winemaker dinners are eagerly anticipated by local food and wine lovers. Sunday brunch: $19.95. Reservations required. Includes souvenir wineglass and glass of Blanc de Noir champagne.

Fine points: Featured wines: Cabernet Sauvignon, Pinot Noir, Merlot, Zinfandel, Chardonnay, Pinot Gris, Syrah, Sangiovese, Gewürztraminer, Riesling, Blanc de Noir, Port, and dessert wines Vin d'Ete, Vin d'Epice, and Vin d'Or; $7.00–$25.00. Owners: Bill, Jim, and Tom Huggins and fifty other investors. Winemaker: Steve Anderson. Cases: 50,000. Acres: 120 and buy from Oregon vineyards.

✿ *Eola Hills Wine Cellars, 501 South Pacific Highway (Highway 99W), Rickreall 97371; phone (503) 623–2405; fax (503) 623–0350; e-mail eolahill@ eolahillswinery.com; Web site www.eolahillswinery.com. Open 11:00 A.M.–5:00 P.M. daily. Visa and MasterCard. Wheelchair accessible.*

CHATEAU BIANCA is well located if you are heading for Oregon beaches. From Eola Hills, turn left (north) on Highway 99W, back through Rickreall, and then left (west) at the signal onto Highway 22 toward the coast. Ten miles later you will find Chateau Bianca on the right.

❧

Named for the owners' daughter, Chateau Bianca is a popular stop right beside the road for wine tastings, specialty foods, espresso, picnics, and even a turnaround and overnight parking for RVs and trailers. Tastes cost $1.00, which is refundable with a purchase. Check out the new bed-and-breakfast, complete with eight-person hot tub, koi pond, gazebo, evening wine tastings with the winemaker, and gourmet European breakfasts ($115–$135). Great views!

Fine points: Featured wines: Gewürztraminer, Chardonnay, Riesling, Pinot Noir, Pinot Blanc, Pinot Gris, Maréchal Foch, Meritage, Ports, dry ice wines, and some sparkling wines. Owners: The Wetzel family. Winemaker: Andreas Wetzel. Cases: 10,000. Acres: 46 planted of 100.

Chateau Bianca, 17485 Highway 22, Dallas 97338; phone (503) 623–6181 or (877) 823–6181; e-mail chateaubianca@quest.net; Web site www.chateaubianca.com. Open 11:00 A.M.–6:00 P.M. daily, February–December. Visa and MasterCard. Wheelchair accessible.

Don't miss FIRESTEED CELLARS, the under-known largest wine producer in Oregon. At the intersection of Highway 22 and 99W, turn north for about 2 miles and turn right (east) up Firesteed's driveway. If the American flags are flying at the driveway's entrance, the tasting room is open.

Commercial airline pilot and vintner Wayne Flynn first planted vines in 1982 and opened the large winery in 1990. Howard Rossbach bought the property from Flynn (Flynn Vineyards) in 2002.

The "tasting room" is right in the warehouse, so you get the feel and smell of what's going on.

Fine points: Featured wines: Sparkling Brut *méthode champenoise,* vintage Blanc de Blanc, Brut, tank-fermented Pinot Noir, Pinot Gris, and Chardonnay. Owner: Howard Rossbach. Winemaker: Bryan Croft. Cases: 60,000 under own label. Acres: 123.

Firesteed Cellars, 2200 West Pacific Highway (99W), Rickreall 97371; phone (503) 623–8683; fax (503) 623–0908; e-mail scroft@firesteed.com; Web site www.firesteed.com. Open 11:00 A.M.–5:00 P.M. daily. Visa and MasterCard. Wheelchair accessible.

Now return to I–5 and head south to WILLAMETTE VALLEY VINEYARDS, one of the most splendiferous in Oregon. Take exit 248 (Sunnyside/Turner) off I–5, which puts you on Delaney Road, then turn right (south) immediately onto Enchanted Way, and go 0.5 mile south and past Enchanted Forest amusements to 8800. Turn into the beflagged arch and gate and wind up to the top of Ilahee Hill,

VIEW FROM THE DECK AT WILLAMETTE VALLEY VINEYARDS

where you'll see the winery buildings and tasting room, named the M. Dean Cox Hospitality Center for Willamette's original winemaker, Dean Cox.

This unusual public common stock winery offers discounts for shareholders, of which there are 4,000, who pooled their financial and passion resources to establish their ideal winery. The Mediterranean-cum-Northwest architectural design features antique doors, modern sculpture, exquisite picnic selections, and a commanding view of the Willamette Valley.

Enjoy Bandon's Oregon whole-milk cheeses, Chef Wade's English plum sauce, Campagna's olive oils, delicious crisp bagel chips, and pastas. Kids can sip nonalcoholic grape juice.

Willamette Valley sells more wine under its own label than any other Oregon winery. *Wine Enthusiast* gives its 1995 Founders Reserve Pinot Noir an 89.

Special events: Jazz in the Afternoon copresented by Chemeketa Community College and Willamette Valley Vineyards, monthly year-round; Memorial Day Weekend Celebration; annual Riverboat Dinner Cruise in August; Bluegrass BBQ mid-August; Crab and Chowder Fest in January.

 Fine points: Featured wines: Pinot Noir, Chardonnay, Riesling, Gewürztraminer, and Pinot Gris. Owners: 4,000 enthusiastic shareholders. Winemaker: Forrest Klaffke. Cases: 100,000. Acres: 50 and buy from other locals.

❧ *Willamette Valley Vineyards, 8800 Enchanted Way SE, Turner 97392; phone (503) 588–9463 or (800) 344–9463; fax (503) 588–8894; e-mail*

information@wvv.com; Web site www.wvv.com. Open 11:00 A.M.–6:00 P.M. daily. Visa, MasterCard, American Express, and Discover. Wheelchair accessible.

Drive back to Salem for four more wineries and a night's rest. If your time is limited, you can get a good picture of regional winemaking diversity from these four wineries.

Right in downtown Salem is HONEYWOOD WINERY, approachable from I–5 by taking Highway 22 west. Take a soft left on Hines Street, cross the railroad tracks, and find the winery on the right between Thirteenth and Fourteenth Streets. Once a freezer plant and the home of Columbia Distilleries, producers of fruit brandies and liqueurs, the building houses the winery, a large tasting room, and monthly meetings of both the local Democratic and Republican parties.

Established on December 8, 1933, the day after the repeal of Prohibition, Honeywood is the oldest producing winery in Oregon. Founding owners Ron Honeyman and John Wood made fruit wines, still the winery's mainstay.

Current owner Paul Gallick was a banker who came out to Salem to evaluate the winery for a potential corporate purchaser, who eventually decided against the deal. Paul thought it was so good that he bought Honeywood himself. He continues to use Willamette Valley harvests of loganberries, rhubarb, blackberries, raspberries, and plums in the ever-growing fruit wine busi-

> MICROBREWERY ALERT!
> **Thompson Brewery & Public House,** *3575 Liberty Road South, Salem (503–363–7286), is in a marvelous converted old house where you can taste brews at the little bar, nosh on pub grub in the parlor, or hang out on the veranda at picnic tables. A McMenamin outpost serving their regulars: Ruby Ale, Crystal Ale, Hammerhead, and Edgefield wines.*

ness, bottling for other wineries' and retailers' fruit wine labels. Varietals have also gained respect.

 Fine points: Featured wines: Cabernet Sauvignon, Pinot Noir, Riesling, Gewürztraminer, Pinot Gris, Pinot Noir Blanc, Maréchal Foch, Müller-Thurgau, Chardonnay, and Muscat, as well as fruit and specialty wines. Owner: Paul Gallick. Winemaker: Marlene Gallick. Cases: 15,000. Acres: None, buy from Salem and Eola Hills regions.

Honeywood Winery, 1350 Hines Street SE, Salem 97308; phone (503) 362–4111 or (800) 726–4101; fax (503) 362–4112; e-mail info@honeywood

GERALD HILL ENTERS HONEYWOOD WINERY

winery.com; Web site www.honeywoodwinery.com. Open 9:00 A.M.–5:00 P.M. weekdays, 10:00 A.M.–5:00 P.M. Saturday, 1:00 P.M.–5:00 P.M. Sunday. Visa, MasterCard, American Express, Discover, and Diners. Wheelchair accessible.

KATHKEN VINEYARDS is the combo name from owners Kathy and Ken Slusser, the latter a former contractor and developer from Half Moon Bay and La Honda in California. They bought the place in 1995 and sold grapes to Sokol-Blosser, which speaks highly of their quality.

Fine points: Featured wines: Pinot Noir, Pinot Gris, and Late Harvest Ice Wine. Owners and winemakers: Kathy and Ken Slusser. Cases: 4,500. Acres: 50.

Kathken Vineyards, 5739 Orchard Heights Road NW, Salem 97304; phone (503) 316–3911; fax (503) 399–5476; e-mail kathkenvyd@ aol.com; Web site www.kathkenvineyards.com. Open noon–5:00 P.M. Saturday– Sunday, May–Thanksgiving. Visa and MasterCard.

The irreverence of REDHAWK VINEYARDS' owner Tom Robinson is worth the short ride to the northwest side of Salem to sample his humor, his Rat Race Red, Average White, Chateau Mootom, and Grateful Red. We enjoyed a minor feast of his salmon and liver pâté hors d'oeuvres.

To get to Redhawk Vineyards, go west on Highway 22 from downtown Salem, cross the Willamette River, turn right on Highway 221 (Wallace Road) about 3.3 miles north from west Salem, and turn left (west) on Michigan City Road. Partway up the road a seductive wooden girl bathing in a wine barrel directs you to turn right onto the gravel road to Redhawk.

New Zealander Robinson gave up teaching and his hot tub business to not blend into the wine business. Tom boasts that England's *Decanter Magazine* gave him *two* "worst label" awards.

Beyond the tasting room is a shaded lawn with tables and chairs on which you are welcomed to rest your wine-weary bodies, and beyond that, the Robinson family home.

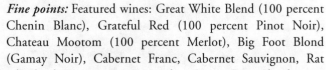

Fine points: Featured wines: Great White Blend (100 percent Chenin Blanc), Grateful Red (100 percent Pinot Noir), Chateau Mootom (100 percent Merlot), Big Foot Blond (Gamay Noir), Cabernet Franc, Cabernet Sauvignon, Rat Race Red, Punk Floyd, Donner Party Macabre, Pinot Gris, Chardonnay, Syrah, and Merlot. Owner: Tom Robinson. Winemaker: Jill Oien. Cases: 5,000. Acres: 15.

❧ *Redhawk Vineyards, 2995 Michigan City NW, Salem 97304; phone (503) 362–1596; fax (503) 589–9189. Open noon–5:00 P.M. daily, May–November, and by appointment during the winter. Tasting twelve wines (keep the glass) and hors d'oeuvres costs a whopping $4.00. Visa and MasterCard. Wheelchair accessible.*

The North Willamette Region

The Oregon Wine Advisory Board and Oregon Winegrowers' Association brochure places Salem area wineries in both the South Willamette Region and the North Willamette Region. There are about forty wineries between Salem and Portland. Hardly any of them is right on a highway, and some require several miles of bumping along rocky dirt roads. We will direct you only to the ones that are open for tasting with regular hours.

To follow the Willamette River northward, and thereby find many of the wineries between Salem and McMinnville, take Highway 221 north to visit Bethel Heights, Cristom, Witness Tree, Stangeland, and Hauer of the Dauen.

After visiting those, we will take you over to Highway 99W and Amity, from which you can take 99W north and visit Amity Vineyards, Kristin Hill, the Oregon Wine Tasting Room, and Yamhill Valley, and perhaps spend a night in McMinnville, home of the annual Pinot Noir Festival.

If you are in Portland and have a day or two to find your favorite Oregon wineries, you can make one-, two-, or three-day tours, depending on how long you like to visit and taste in each winery. We suggest you leave Portland heading south on I–5, take exit 294 to Highway 99W and Tigard, and continue on 99W to Rex Hill near Newberg, Duck Pond, Dundee Springs/Perry Bower, Argyle, Torii Mor, Lange, Erath, Sokol Blosser around Dundee, Chateau Benoit, and maybe into McMinnville for a late lunch or dinner. Then you can head north on Highway 47 to Willakenzie, Elk Cove, Kramer, Montinore, David Hill, Shafer, and Tualatin on Highway 8 and back on Highway 8 straight into Portland or south on Highway 219 to Oak Knoll and then east on Highway 210 to Ponzi and Cooper Mountain.

If you only have time to follow Highway 99W from McMinnville straight into Portland or vice versa, which is a great winery tour in itself, we will give you explicit directions to do that. In that case, you can visit Chateau Benoit, Sokol Blosser, Argyle, Erath, Lange, Duck Pond, Torii Mor, Rex Hill, and possibly Ponzi and Cooper Mountain.

If you have additional time, like another day, we will guide you up Highway 47 to Willakenzie, Elk Cove, Kramer, Montinore, Sake One/ Momokawa, David Hill, Shafer, Tualatin, and Oak Knoll, from which Portland is a short drive.

SALEM TO MCMINNVILLE

Of course the first winery you come to is Redhawk (see page 37). From there proceed north through grass seed fields on Highway 221 (Wallace Road). Bethel Heights is our next stop, about 7 miles off Highway 221.

Turn left (west) on Zena Road in Lincoln (a school, gas station, and restaurant), 2.6 miles north of Michigan City Road if your're coming from Redhawk. Drive about 4 miles west and turn right (north) on Bethel Heights Road NW. Go 0.5 mile northward and turn into Bethel Heights Vineyard's fairly steep gravel driveway.

BETHEL HEIGHTS VINEYARD enjoys an unusual microclimate in the Eola Hills, where the families of brothers Terry and Ted Casteel produce fine Pinot Noirs and Chardonnays. The original fourteen acres were planted by the previous owners, and the Casteels established their own winery in 1984 with great success.

The tasting room and picnic area offer scintillating views of Spring Valley and Mt. Jefferson, as well as the fifty-one–acre vineyard. The Casteels' love of France, coupled with the Bethel Heights climate, led them to produce

Burgundy-style wines. Bethel Heights has added three exciting new vineyard-designated Pinot Noirs.

Fine points: Featured wines: Pinot Noir, Chardonnay, Pinot Blanc, and Pinot Gris. Owners: Ted and Terry Casteel, Marilyn Webb, and Barbara and Patricia Dudley. Winemaker: Terry Casteel. Cases: 10,000. Acres: 72.

❧ *Bethel Heights Vineyard,* 6060 Bethel Heights Road NW, Salem 97304; phone (503) 581–2262; fax (503) 581–0943; e-mail info@bethelheights.com; Web site www.bethelheights.com. Open 11:00 A.M.–5:00 P.M. Tuesday–Sunday, June–August; 11:00 A.M.–5:00 P.M. weekends, March–May and September–December. Visa, MasterCard, and American Express. Wheelchair accessible.

Go back toward Lincoln, but turn left (north) on Spring Valley Road to Cristom, Witness Tree, and Stangeland wineries before you reach Highway 221. It always amazes us that the grass beside the roads here is green, even in August.

As you arrive at CRISTOM VINEYARDS, you immediately realize that these people have been other places: The building looks almost California Spanish, and the roses and flowers have a distinctly French charm.

The whole winery was built around the 150-year-old front door, which Paul and Eileen Gerrie brought all the way from a Bordeaux château. Don't try to open it, because it's locked to preserve it. Walk to your left and use the glass door with the doormat in front of it. The pleasant tasting room itself is two-storied with beamed ceilings, mustard-colored plaster walls, and Spanish tile floors. There also is a gift shop here.

Paul Gerrie gave up oil exploration to produce Burgundy-style wines; winemaker Steve Doerner gave up Calera Winery; and vineyard manager Mark Feltz gave up Chalk Hill Winery in Sonoma County to help revive the former Pellier-Mirassou Winery, which crafted wines here from 1985 to 1991. Their success is attested to by *Wine Spectator*'s 1997 rating of an 88 for their 1995 Pinot Noir Reserve and an 85 for a nonreserve Pinot Noir. While one of Cristom's Chardonnays is rated higher (91) than any from other Oregon wineries, it is actually from a Washington vineyard in the Columbia River Gorge.

Fine points: Featured wines: Pinot Noir, Pinot Gris, Chardonnay, Syrah, and Viognier. Owners: Paul and Eileen Gerrie. Winemaker: Steve Doerner. Cases: 8,000. Acres: 50 planted of 130.

❧ *Cristom Vineyards,* 6905 Spring Valley Road NW, Salem 97304; phone (503) 375–3068; fax (503) 391–7057; e-mail tasting@cristom wines.com; Web site www.cristomwines.com. Open 11:00 A.M.–5:00 P.M.

CRISTOM VINEYARDS

Tuesday–Sunday, May–October; 11:00 A.M.–5:00 P.M. Friday–Sunday by appointment only December–February. Visa and MasterCard. Wheelchair accessible.

Come back down Cristom's driveway, turn left on Spring Valley Road, and left again up the driveway to WITNESS TREE VINEYARD. Witness Tree is the only winery in Oregon that produces kosher wines.

The name "Witness Tree" is not a religious statement; it comes from an oak tree high on the hill above the winery that was used as the official surveyor's landmark for this Eola Hills part of the Willamette Valley beginning in 1854. The winery is also witness to the ability of imaginative professionals from other disciplines to make good wine.

As we were taking photos of the tree, co-owner and pharmaceutical consultant Dennis Devine, a mild-mannered intellectual-looking fellow, came roaring up on his "grape mobile," a sparkling metallic purple dune buggy. Carolyn Devine serves as managing partner. *Wine Enthusiast* gave their 1995 Pinot Noir an 88.

 Fine points: Featured wines: estate bottled Pinot Noir, Pinot Blanc, Viognier, Dolcetto, and Chardonnay Sweet Signe (Chardonnay dessert wine). Owners: Dennis and Carolyn Devine. Winemaker: Bryce Bagnall. Cases: 6,000. Acres: 100.

WITNESS TREE VINEYARD

❧ Witness Tree Vineyard, 7111 Spring Valley Road NW, Salem 97304; phone (503) 585–7874 or (888) GR8T–PNO; fax (503) 362–9765; e-mail info@ witnesstreevineyard.com; Web site www.witnesstreevineyard.com. Open 11:00 A.M.–5:00 P.M. Tuesday–Sunday, June–August; 11:00 A.M.–5:00 P.M. weekends only, March–May and September–December; closed January–February. Visa, MasterCard, American Express, and Discover. Wheelchair accessible.

As you leave Witness Tree, turn left on Spring Valley Road to Stangeland Vineyards, which is only open on weekends. When Spring Valley intersects Hopewell Road, cross to STANGELAND VINEYARDS. This is a small winery with an expansive view, great conversation, and truly crafted wines. Its slogan is "There are no strangers at Stangeland." Stangeland is the "only Eola Hills winery to win international awards for Pinot Noir."

Fine points: Featured wines: Pinot Noir, Pinot Gris, Chardonnay, Chardonnay Decadence dessert wine, and Gewürztraminer. Owners: Larry and Kinsey Miller. Winemaker: Larry Miller. Cases: 1,800. Acres: 5 and buy from four others who grow to their specifications.

❧ Stangeland Vineyards, 8500 Hopewell Road NW, Salem 97304; phone (503)

581–0355; fax (503) 540–3412; e-mail stanglnd@open.org; Web site www.stange landwinery.com. Open noon–5:00 P.M. weekends June–November; first weekend of each month, December–May. Visa and MasterCard. Wheelchair accessible, but a little rough.

To get to Hauer of the Dauen from Stangeland Vineyards, turn right on Hopewell Road to the stop sign. Go straight ahead. Hopewell Road becomes Webfoot Road. Go straight on Webfoot 3 miles. You have arrived at HAUER OF THE DAUEN, the pride and joy of the Dauenhauer family, Oregon natives who planted their vineyard in 1980. Hauer of the Dauen, a twist on the family's name, means "hour of the dawn." Opened to the public in 1999, this home of estate-grown premium wines is a haven on your way up Highway 221, with the tasting bar right in the small winery room.

Fine points: Featured wines: Chardonnay, Gamay Noir, Lemberger, Pinot Noir Rosé, Dry Gewürztraminer, Pinot Noir, Late Harvest Chardonnay, Riesling, and Pinot Gris. Owners: The Dauenhauer family. Winemakers: Carl Dauenhauer and Ted Seestedt. Cases: 7,000. Acres: 110.

✣ *Hauer of the Dauen, 16425 SE Webfoot Road, Dayton 97114-8644; phone (503) 868–7359; fax (503) 868–7216. Open noon–5:00 P.M. Saturday–Sunday. Visa and MasterCard. Wheelchair accessible.*

Or take Hopewell north and turn left (west) on the Amity-Hopewell Road, which eventually jogs left and then right and becomes Nursery Lane and takes you into the town of Amity. After a few minutes exploring Amity, turn north on Highway 99W toward McMinnville. Very soon turn right (east) on Rice Lane and then left again to AMITY VINEYARDS. You are now in Yamhill County, the most prominent of Oregon's wine-producing counties.

The loose gravel and rock road is steep as it guides you to this low-tech winery. An old wooden door between cases of wine leads you into the warehouse and the tasting bar, decorated in dark wood. Amity Vineyards is an interesting and environmentally aware winery whose Eco-Wine is Oregon's first sulfite-free wine made from organic grapes. Amity uses mostly recycled bottles and label paper and avoids "almost all agricultural chemicals in its vineyard operations."

With the goal of producing Burgundian-style Pinot Noirs, Winemaker Myron Redford moved to Oregon in 1974 from Seattle, where he began as a cellar worker for Associated Vintners winery in Seattle in 1970. With his mother, Ione, and great friend Janis Checchia, he expanded the winery in 1984. All of

GARLIC PINOT NOIR MEATBALL SAUCE
from Kinsey and Larry Miller, Stangeland Vineyards

[Note: The Millers serve Larry's hors d'oeuvres at Stangeland every day. A couple of years ago, he substituted a salmon pâté for his famous meatballs and sauce, and even new guests said, "Have you stopped serving the meatballs we've heard about?" So now, again, you can stop by for a taste of wine and Larry's meatballs. In the meantime, try making the sauce at home, and use with homemade or frozen meatballs, even Ikea's.—KT Hill]

Be sure to make sauce so that it, plus the meatballs, fits into your crockpot. This recipe makes 1½ quarts of sauce.

1 package dried onion soup mix

1 qt water

1 cup fresh minced garlic

1 tsp ground black pepper

1 can cream of mushroom soup (no extra water)

½ pint fresh sour cream

8 oz Stangeland Pinot Noir

meatballs

Combine package of dried onion soup with 1 quart water and bring to a boil. While simmering, add the minced garlic and ground black pepper. Add mushroom soup and simmer everything so far for thirty minutes.

Add sour cream and bring back to a boil, whisking until smooth. Add Pinot Noir and stir. Add enough meatballs so that sauce covers all of them, move to crockpot on high until hot, and serve or let guests serve themselves.

Amity's wines are dedicated to the memory of Myron Redford's brother Hugh and his mother.

Amity produced the first Gamay Noir, used in true Beaujolais wines, from grapes grown from cuttings provided by the French government. The winery also makes an interesting Alsatian-style Gewürztraminer. *Wine Enthusiast* gave its 1993 Reserve Pinot Noir a 90.

Fine points: Featured wines: Eco-Wine (sulfite-free) Pinot Noir, Dry and Late Harvest Gewürztraminer and Riesling, Gamay Noir, Pinot Blanc, and Oregon Blush. Owners: Myron Redford and Janis Checchia. Winemaker: Myron Redford. Cases: 12,000. Acres: 15 and buy from others.

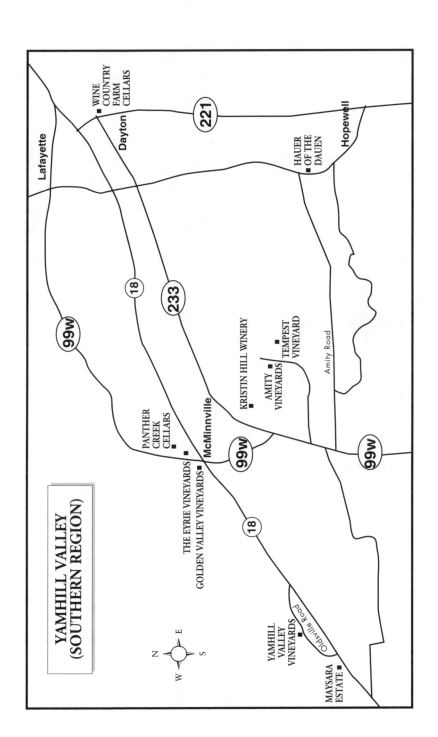

Amity Vineyards, *18150 Amity Vineyards Road SE, Amity 97101-9603; phone (503) 835–2362; fax (503) 835–6451; e-mail amity@amityvineyards.com; Web site www.amityvineyards.com. Open noon–5:00 P.M. daily, February–December 23; closed December 24–January 31.*

Go back to 99W and turn right (north) to get to KRISTIN HILL WINERY. The rural country is so gorgeous that you might forget to spot the Kristin Hill signs. Watch carefully for a slight right turn to Highway 233 (Amity-Dayton Highway) and an almost immediate right turn into the Kristin Hill driveway.

The winery is named for the one Aberg family daughter who is not involved in the winery. Kristin serves in the U.S. Army in Germany, following in the footsteps of both her parents, Linda and Eric Aberg. With the help of family and friends, the Abergs planted their first vineyard in 1985. After making wine at home for years, the Abergs began making small lots for sale in 1990 and opened their tasting room in 1993.

Visitors are greeted by the old family dog, Pinot Gris. Niece Kate Aberg Cathersal oversees the tasting room and has a deep knowledge of Kristin Hill wines. We joined a roomful of regulars who come by to stock up on their favorites and share in the generous offerings of crackers and cheeses offered by the family.

You might join Kate's grandfather in the winery/garage making sparkling wine or have your picnic on their deck overlooking the lawn and trees.

Fine points: Featured wines: *Méthode champenoise* sparkling wine, Alsatian-style Gewürztraminer, Chardonnay, Pinot Noir, Pinot Gris, Riesling, Müller-Thurgau, and Jennifer Falls Sparkling Wine. Cases: 2,000. Acres: 28.

Kristin Hill Winery, *3330 SE Amity-Dayton Highway, Amity 97101; phone (503) 835–0850; fax (503) 835–4012. Open noon–5:00 P.M. daily, March–December; weekends by appointment or chance January–February. Visa, MasterCard, and American Express. Wheelchair accessible, but a little rough.*

PORTLAND AND VICINITY

Portland is one of the West Coast's most exciting cities, having revived itself with interesting architecture and cultural events, wonderful with-it restaurants without attitude, advanced environmental appreciation, and an excellent public transportation system. And there isn't nearly as much of that famous rain as you expect.

Portland is an ideal home base for touring the northern Willamette Valley wine region, as far as McMinnville to the southwest or heading east up the

Columbia Gorge as far as Hood River. After a night in Portland or its suburb Beaverton, you may want to stay in Newberg or McMinnville or move on as far south as Salem.

For wine exploring, staying close to Highway I–5 or 99W in downtown Portland provides easy exit from the city. Cross the Willamette River from I–5 on Morrison Bridge or Marquam Bridge to reach westside downtown, including SW Sixth Avenue and SW Front Avenue (99W). Note: SW Sixth Avenue is one-way north, and SW Fifth Avenue is one-way south. NE Second Avenue is on the east side of the river. Reaching the east side off I–5, driving either north or south, exit to NE Weidler Street. If going to NE Second Avenue, then turn south from Weidler to NE Second Avenue (it is 3 blocks long).

First we'll tell you our favorite places to dine. Portland has lots of independent and creative restaurants. We happen to like GENOA, named a favorite of *Gourmet* magazine readers and *Northwest Best Places*. Arrive hungry and with the whole evening set aside to enjoy yourself, your companion, the ambience, the service, and, of course, the interpretive Italian food. Savor every one of Chef Cathy Whims's four or seven courses of classic feasts. Early (5:30 and 6:00 P.M.) and late (10:00 and 10:30 P.M.) seatings accommodate theatergoers and anyone else wanting to dine on a shorter-course dinner at those times. Beer and wine.

❧ *Genoa, 2832 SE Belmont Street at NE Twenty-ninth, Portland; phone (503) 238–1464. Open for dinner Monday–Saturday. American Express, Diners Club, MasterCard, and Visa. Wheelchair accessible.*

We also suggest you try Caprial Pance's CAPRIAL'S BISTRO AND WINE at 7015 SE Milwaukie Avenue (503–236–6457), but make reservations well ahead. Another of our drop-in favorites is PAZZO RISTORANTE in the Hotel Vintage Plaza at 627 SW Washington Street at Broadway. The bar has great light meals and excellent martinis, to say nothing of people-watching opportunities.

If you want seafood, try JAKE'S FAMOUS CRAWFISH, 401 SW Twelfth Avenue (503–226–1419), for a loud, local experience, or DAN AND LOUIS OYSTER BAR, 208 SW Ankeny (503–227–5906), for oysters from Dan and Louis Farm. The oyster stew is sublime!

HIP CHICKS DO WINE, truly the hip new fun winery in Oregon, is located in a warehouse in urban Portland. Wine Goddess Laurie Lewis and Wine Maven Renee Neely live by the premise that wine is supposed to be fun, which is why and how their home winemaking habit grew. After taking winemaking classes at Chemekta Community College, Renee worked part time at Duck Pond Cellars, and both keep their day jobs in home care and coffee sales. Check it out, just for the heck of it or for some good wines aged in barrels bought used. Watch for the purple warehouse doors.

❧

Fine points: Featured wines: Vine Nombri (Belly Button wine) and Shardoneaux ("not your mama's Chardonnay"). Owners and winemakers: Laurie Lewis and Renee Neely. Cases: 2,000. Acres: None.

❧ *Hip Chicks Do Wine, 4510 SE Twenty-third Avenue, Portland 97202; phone (503) 753–6374; e-mail winegoddess@hipchicksdowine.com; Web site www.hipchicksdowine.com. Open 1:00–6:00 P.M. Thursday–Sunday or by appointment. Visa, MasterCard, and American Express. Wheelchair accessible.*

There are also several possible wine itineraries out of Portland. East of Portland, you can travel along the Oregon side of the Columbia River Gorge and visit Edgefield Winery and historic complex in Troutdale and Hood River Vineyards and Flerchinger Vineyards in Hood River, as well as two Washington wineries across the Columbia River from Hood River.

Southwest of Portland you will find an abundance of large and family wineries to explore, some of which you can visit comfortably in a day or an afternoon, and all of which you can cover in two or three days. These include Cooper Mountain, Ponzi, Oak Knoll, Rex Hill, Torii Mor, Duck Pond, Dundee Springs, Argyle, Lange, Erath, Sokol Blosser, and Chateau Benoit. If your time is limited to a half-day or short full day, try a tour of Ponzi, Rex Hill, Torii Mor, and Duck Pond in Dundee, and then swing back to 210/219 to Oak Knoll and back to Portland on Highway 10 or 8. We will cover the southwest itineraries first.

To get from downtown Portland to Highway 99W is not difficult, but it requires attentive driving. From downtown take any street leading onto I–5 heading south. Be sure to stay to the left so that you don't get into two-lane exits you don't want to take. About 5 miles south of Portland take exit 294 toward Tigard and Highway 99W, which is also the exit for McMinnville and Lincoln City.

After you pass through the strip malls of Tigard and Tualatin, you finally glide into green forests—what Oregon is supposed to look like. Three miles later you enter Yamhill County, Oregon's richest wine county, which includes nearly 25 percent of Oregon's vineyards. Just as you descend into the valley, suddenly REX HILL VINEYARDS appears on your right, and you have to make a quick move into the right lane to turn right.

Situated in the Dundee Hills, Rex Hill is about 22 miles from Portland on Highway 99W and more outwardly sophisticated than many you will encounter. We were struck immediately by the bright petunias, terraced lawns, and attractive sculpture in Rex Hill's garden approaching the winery and parking lot, and by the basketball hoop for the staff.

Microbrewery Alert!

There are several breweries in Portland, including the following. All change their brew specialties seasonally.

Bridgeport Brewing Company, *1313 NW Marshall Street at 14th Street NW, Portland 97209; phone (503) 241–7179. Oregon's oldest brewery, with a fabulous view of the Willamette River, was created and opened by the Ponzi winery family in 1984 and now produces 25,000 barrels of beer annually. Visit the century-old brick and timber warehouse in Portland's historic "Pearl District" for locally popular pizza made fresh daily from unfermented beer wort, sandwiches, and classic salads. Featured beers: Blue Heron Amber Ale named for Portland's official bird, India Pale Ale, Porter, Black Strap Stout, and others in the Irish and English traditions. Nonsmoking pub. Also owns:* Hawthorne Street Ale House, *3632 SE Hawthorne (503–233–6540).*

Portland Brewing Company, Brewhouse, Tap Room, and Grill, *2730 NW 31st Avenue (503–228–5269), has kettles from the Sixenbrau Brewery in Nordlingen, Bavaria, Germany. Featured beers: Oregon Honey Beer, American Beer Festival gold medal–winning MacTarnahan's Scottish Style Amber Ale, international gold medal–winning Zig Zag Lager (does that tell us something?), Bavarian-style Weizen, Henry Saxer's Public Lager, Nor'Wester Hefeweizen, and Saxer Lemon Lager. Try the Taproom and Grill for fish and chips, Oregon Honey Beer steamed clams, pork loin, and spit-roasted BBQ.*

Full Sail Brewing Company, *307 SW Montgomery (503–222–5343 or 220–1865), is the urban outlet of Full Sail's brewery in Hood River, with a small state-of-the-art facility here at the Riverplace Marina on the Willamette River just south of downtown. Dine right next door at McCormich and Schmick's renowned Harborside Restaurant and Pilsner Room.*

McMenamin's Kennedy School, *5736 NE 33rd Avenue (503–249–3983), offers a truly different experience. Here you can wander an old grammar school drinking beer and smoking cigars. Spend the night in their B&B and even have a cocktail. Also try McMenamin's* St. John's Pub *in an old pavilion built to memorialize Lewis and Clark, 8203 North Ivanhoe Street (503–283–8520), or their* Ringler's Pub, *1332 West Burnside Street (503–225–0543).*

You can't miss Alameda Brewhouse, *4765 NE Fremont (503–460–9025), if you happen to be in the northeast Portland district of Beaumont, because it has a huge copper hop on the front of the building and hopyard decor. Try portersmoked oysters, salmon gyros, and smoked-chicken ravioli. There is a children's menu. Featured beers: Klickitat Pale Ale, Mozarts Golden, Alameda Wheaten, Beaumont Berry Wheat, Salzburger Fest Bier, Winter Warlock, Spring Rose Doppelbock, and Indian Summer Ale.*

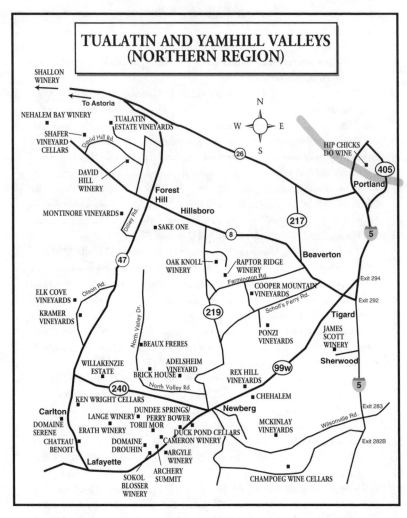

TUALATIN AND YAMHILL VALLEYS (NORTHERN REGION)

SHALLON WINERY

To Astoria

NEHALEM BAY WINERY

TUALATIN ESTATE VINEYARDS

SHAFER VINEYARD CELLARS

David Hill Rd.

DAVID HILL WINERY

Forest Hill

MONTINORE VINEYARDS

Dilley Rd.

Hillsboro

SAKE ONE

26

N
W   E
S

HIP CHICKS DO WINE

405

Portland

217

5

Beaverton

47

OAK KNOLL WINERY

RAPTOR RIDGE WINERY

Farmington Rd.

COOPER MOUNTAIN VINEYARDS

Scholl's Ferry Rd.

Exit 294

Exit 292

Tigard

ELK COVE VINEYARDS

Olson Rd.

KRAMER VINEYARDS

North Valley Dr.

219

PONZI VINEYARDS

JAMES SCOTT WINERY

Sherwood

BEAUX FRERES

WILLAKENZIE ESTATE

ADELSHEIM VINEYARD

BRICK HOUSE

240

North Valley Rd.

KEN WRIGHT CELLARS

REX HILL VINEYARDS

99w

CHEHALEM

Carlton

DOMAINE SERENE

LANGE WINERY PERRY BOWER

TORII MOR

ERATH WINERY

DUNDEE SPRINGS/

DUCK POND CELLARS

Newberg

MCKINLAY VINEYARDS

Wilsonville Rd.

Exit 283

5

CHATEAU BENOIT

DOMAINE DROUHIN

CAMERON WINERY

ARGYLE WINERY

Exit 282B

Lafayette

SOKOL BLOSSER WINERY

ARCHERY SUMMIT

CHAMPOEG WINE CELLARS

The elegantly carved wooden door leads you to the Fletcher Farr Ayotte–designed 1989 renovation and addition to what had been a historic fruit farm and nut-processing plant.

An aura of peace and calm exudes from the winery's design and its antiques. Even the rest rooms here are elegantly designed to the finest detail with brass handicapped fixtures. The owners of Rex Hill visited a clothing store in Washington, D.C., fell in love with the antiques there, and left their card in hopes that they could have a crack at buying the furniture if the store ever closed. Eventually it did, and they did.

OUTDOOR SCULPTURE AT REX HILL VINEYARDS

Be sure to check out Rex Hill's fabulous new Oregon Wine Brotherhood Museum, featuring Norman Gate's collection of masters' robes and regalia from twenty-five countries. The Oregon Brotherhood is chartered by the *Federation Internationale des Confreries Bachiques*. Rex Hill leases Maresh Red Barn and vineyards, using the barn as a second tasting room on summer weekends, and produces Maresh Red Barn Label wines at Rex Hill. Rex Hill wines are often rated among Oregon's best. Rex Hill's brands include King's Ridge and Rex Hill.

 Fine points: Featured wines: Pinot Noir, Pinot Gris, Chardonnay, Sauvignon Blanc, and White Riesling. Owners: Husband and wife Paul Hart and Jan Jacobsen. Winemaker: Aron Hess. Cases: 35,000. Acres: 225.

☙ *Rex Hill Vineyards, 30835 North Highway 99W, Newberg 97132; phone (503) 538–0666; fax (503) 538–1409; e-mail info@rexhill.com; Web site www.rexhill.com. Open 11:00 A.M.–5:00 P.M. daily. Visa, MasterCard, American Express, and Discover. Wheelchair accessible.*

When you come down Rex Hill's driveway, be extremely careful and look to the left before you turn right onto Highway 99W. If you only have a couple of hours, turn right (north) on Highway 210 just before (east of) Newberg and head north to Ponzi Vineyards, Cooper Mountain, and Oak Knoll and then back to Portland.

Otherwise, continue west on 99W. Before you get to Newberg, check out the colors and plants at WAGNER'S HANGING GARDENS. The Newberg Chamber of Commerce is extremely helpful and well signed in a lovely old Victorian house.

Follow the signs to stay on 99W as it turns and jogs through Newberg. Between Newberg and Dundee, be sure to visit DUCK POND CELLARS, on the right side of Highway 99W at 23145 Highway 99W. This is a beautiful white winery with Butchart Gardens–like grounds and is truly family owned and family run, all of which lends to a genuine warm feeling in the tasting room.

Founders Doug and Jo Ann Fries own and manage all of the vineyards, son Greg is winemaker, and daughter and son-in-law Lisa and Scott Jenkins handle sales and marketing. The family planted its first vineyard in 1993 and now has vineyards here in the Willamette Valley and in Washington. Hence, Duck Pond wines bear either Willamette Valley or Columbia Valley appellations.

Duck Pond is one of the few wineries that actually sell picnic foods in their tasting rooms. Here you can purchase sausages, hummus, feta cheese, jams, cheeses, imported olives, and sodas. You can also find wind chimes, artwork, and a broad selection of wine stuff.

Wine Enthusiast rated Duck Pond's 1995 Pinot Noir as one of the "100 Best Buys" for 1997, and *Wine Spectator* called the 1995 Pinot Noir "easy drinking," while praising its 1995 Cabernet Sauvignon, 1996 Chardonnay, and 1995 Merlot, all made with Washington grapes.

 Fine points: Featured wines: Estate-grown Willamette Valley Pinot Noir, Cabernet Sauvignon, Syrah, Sangiovese, Riesling, Gewürztraminer, Columbia Valley Merlot and Chardonnay, Port, and Sémillon Ice Wine. Owners: Doug and Jo Ann Fries, Greg Fries, Matt Fries, and Lisa Fries Jenkins. Winemaker: Greg Fries. Cases: 100,000. Acres: 280 planted in Oregon, 480 planted in Washington.
🦆 *Duck Pond Cellars, 23145 Highway 99W, P.O. Box 429, Dundee 97115; phone (503) 538–3199 or (800) 437–3213; fax (503) 538–3190; e-mail duckpond@duckpondcellars. com; Web site www.duckpondcellars.com. Open 10:00 A.M.–5:00 P.M. May–October; 11:00 A.M.–5:00 P.M. November–April. Visa, MasterCard, and American Express. Wheelchair accessible.*

Between Duck Pond Cellars and the little metropolis of Argyle is newish DUNDEE SPRINGS/PERRY BOWER VINEYARD's "La Petite Tasting Room," a lovely restored 1934 home just off Highway 99W.

Picnic in the manicured gardens and visit the demonstration vineyard. You can even park in the shade under trees right next to the tasting room. Previous owner Mary Lynne Perry selected this spot to create her "House of Three Pinots" because it reminded her of her favorite vineyards in France. She sold to the Black family in July 2003.

Fine points: Featured wines: Estate-grown Pinot Blanc, Pinot Gris, and Pinot Noir. Owner: Black Family Vineyard, LLC. Winemaker: Laureat Montalieu. Cases: 3,000. Acres: 60.

☙ *Dundee Springs/Perry Bower Vineyard,* Highway 99W and Fox Farm Road, P.O. Box 9, Dundee 97115; phone (503) 554-8000; fax (503) 554-0632; Web site www.dundeesprings.com. Open 11:00 A.M.–5:00 P.M. Thursday–Monday. Visa, MasterCard, and Discover. Wheelchair accessible.

Dick and Nancy Ponzi have opened a lovely adobe-looking wine bar, tasting room, and The Dundee Bistro right "downtown" in Dundee, where you can meet all your wining and dining needs if your time is extremely limited. In the PONZI WINE BAR, manager Tim Healy and interesting staff offer world-class Ponzi wines as well of those of the many small Oregon wineries that don't have tasting rooms. Enjoy microbrews on draft, Italian coffee, and the elegant and inexpensive light menu of cheeses, crostini, wild green salad, or other appetizers.

Adjoining Ponzi Wine Bar is THE DUNDEE BISTRO, a terrific and cheerful restaurant where Chef Michael Schreck presides over an artisan bakery, exhibition kitchen, and tandoori oven. Enjoy fireside dining, outside seating in good weather, an exceptional Oregon wine list, and a Northwest market with foods and gifts.

☙ *Ponzi Wine Bar* and *The Dundee Bistro,* corner of Highway 99 and Seventh Street, Dundee. Ponzi Wine Bar: (503) 554–1500, fax (503) 554–8800, e-mail ponziwinabar@earthlink.net, Web site www.ponziwines.com; Dundee Bistro: (503) 554–1650.

The only place to get real deli sandwiches and salads for picnics in the Dundee area is ALFIE'S and CHARDONNAY WINE CELLARS, a pink compound on the south (left) side of Highway 99W that includes a restaurant and deli–wine tasting room for local wines.

ARGYLE WINERY (THE DUNDEE WINE COMPANY), 691 Highway 99W, is right on the two-lane highway. It focuses on making "ultra premium sparkling wines in the tradition of Champagne" and succeeds!

Originally a partnership between well-known Australian vintner Brian Croser and famous Northwest vintner Cal Knudsen, Argyle Winery occupies a former hazelnut processing plant, with the tasting room next door in a meticulously restored Victorian farmhouse, a Dundee City landmark. We fantasized about entertaining in the elegant and simple dining room.

ARGYLE WINERY

Most of Argyle's sparkling grapes come from Knudsen Vineyards, some of the oldest vineyards in the Dundee Hills. Lion Nathan of Australia purchased Argyle in 2001.

  Fine points: Featured wines: Sparkling wines include Brut, Blanc de Blancs, and Rosé. Still wines include Chardonnay and Pinot Noir. Owner: Lion Nathan of Australia. Winemaker: Rollin Soles. Cases: 45,000. Acres: 235.

❧ *Argyle Winery (The Dundee Wine Company), 691 Highway 99W, Dundee 97115; phone (503) 538–8520; fax (503) 538–2055; e-mail buywine@ argylewinery.com; Web site www.argylewinery.com. Open 11:00 A.M.–5:00 P.M. daily. Visa and MasterCard. Wheelchair accessible.*

Now on to Torii Mor, Lange, and Erath. We send you in this order simply to avoid too many left turns across country roads with occasional bad visibility.

Turn north on SW Ninth Street in Dundee, which winds up through the beautiful green Dundee Hills. SW Ninth Street turns left and becomes Worden Hill Road. Turn right on Fairview Road, which itself makes a left and then a right bend. All of these wineries are up gravel roads, so roll up your windows and turn on the air-conditioning.

After you pass signs announcing Cameron Winery (which is only open by appointment) about a mile from Highway 99W, you will see the blue sign for

TORII MOR. As you climb the driveway to Torii Mor, notice the warm, deep red soil and maple and oak tree tunnels. The tasting room is in the little house on the left, surrounded by peaceful Japanese-style gardens. In Japanese Torii means gate. Mor means "earth" in some Celtic dialects, so together the two words mean Gate of Earth or Earth Gate.

At Torii Mor, owner and neurosurgeon Donald Olson and winemaker Ryan Harmes craft small quantities of Pinot Noir and Pinot Gris worth making the trip. The small chaletlike tasting room feels and looks as if it doubles as a guest room for the main house. A large futon, historic radio, and big television across from the tasting bar make you want to move right in and stay awhile. Dr. Olson welcomes guests on weekends, which he enjoys perhaps more than operating in Salem, a quick half-hour commute by the back roads. "Anyone who takes the freeway is out of their mind!"

Torii Mor has a new winery in downtown McMinnville at 905 East Tenth Street.

Fine points: Featured wines: Pinot Noir, with special reserve and single vineyard Pinots, Pinot Gris, and Pinot Blanc. Owner: Donald Olson. Consultant winemaker: Ryan Harmes. Cases: 4,000. Acres: 31.5 planted, 15 not planted, and buys from other Dundee Hills growers.

✤ *Torii Mor, tasting room, 18325 NE Fairview Drive, Dundee 97115; phone (513) 434–1439 or (800) 839–5004; fax (503) 434–5733; e-mail info@toriimor winery.com; Web site www.toriimor.com. Tasting Room open noon–5:00 P.M. Friday–Sunday, February–April; noon–5:00 P.M. Friday–Sunday, March–November. Winery open by appointment only at 905 East Tenth, McMinnville. Visa, MasterCard, American Express, and Discover. Wheelchair accessible.*

Turn right on Fairview Road and right on Buena Vista Road to LANGE WINERY. Be sure to inhale the clear air and smell the wildflowers and California poppies. Gigantic, expansive vineyards roll voluptuously over and between the Red Hills on both sides of the road. Lange Winery is unrelated to Lang Winery in British Columbia's Okanagan Valley.

Lange's own motto is "Dry Wine—Dry Humour." The Langes moved here from Santa Barbara, California, and were encouraged and even mentored by the Eraths, whose vineyards and winery are nearby.

Lange's tasting room is in what was a rumpus room on the lower level of Don and Wendy Lange's home. Wood-paneled walls, hilarious hosts, and excellent wines make this a must-stop. Kids and the Lange's dogs, Squire and Daphne, play together on the lawn. Just inside to the left of the door is a table with friends' kids' Little League and softball team photos and trophies.

Lange friends ("wine slaves") run the tasting room "for zero cash and great benefits" and readily point out their version of the alcohol consumption warning: "Drinking . . . before pregnancy can cause pregnancy." Wendy Lange is determined to build a new tasting room so she can get the rest of her home back.

Fine points: Featured wines: Pinot Noir, Pinot Gris, Chardonnay, and Pinot Blanc. Owners: Wendy and Don Lange. Winemaker: Don Lange. Cases: 5,000. Acres: 15 and buy from other locals.

Lange Winery, 18380 NE Buena Vista, Dundee 97115; phone (503) 538–6476; fax (503) 538–1938; e-mail tastingroom@langewinery.com; Web site www.langewinery.com. Open 11:00 A.M.–5:00 P.M. in summer; Wednesday–Monday 11:00 A.M.–5:00 P.M. in winter. No buses please. Visa and MasterCard. Wheelchair accessible.

Go back down Buena Vista Road and retrace your tracks down Fairview Road. Turn right on Worden Hill Road to Crabtree Park and ERATH WINERY (Knudsen-Erath). The road is a bit rough—hold on.

Originally Erath was called Knudsen-Erath for lumberman Cal Knudsen who invested money to develop the winery operation with Dick Erath. Then Erath bought out Knudsen (who went on to Argyle) in 1988 and now produces wine from his own vineyards. In 1995 he revived the Erath Vineyards label, absent the Knudsen connection.

Erath's tasting room is a cozy, big ranch house that displays a 400-year-old Italian wine press, a Burgundian tapestry replica, an excellent food and travel book selection, gifts, and a side room full of cheeses, sausages, crackers, and unusual gourmet chips and salsas. In front you will find a picnic terrace shaded by a wisteria cover and lush hanging fuchsias, and great views of the Willamette Valley with vineyards on one side and Oregon forest on the other.

Dick Erath, considered to be a wine guru to many local experts and newcomers, made his first Oregon Pinot Noir more than twenty-five years ago and currently produces some of the best Pinot Noirs anywhere.

Fine points: Featured wines: Pinot Noir, Pinot Gris, and Pinot Blanc. Owner: Dick Erath. Winemaker: Gary Horner. Cases: 38,000. Acres: 115.

Erath Winery, 9009 NE Worden Hill Road, Dundee 97115; phone (800) 539–WINE or (503) 538–3318; fax (503) 538–1074; e-mail info@erath.com; Web site www.erath.com. Open 11:00 A.M.–5:00 P.M. daily, tours by appointment. Visa and MasterCard. Wheelchair accessible.

Retrace your tracks down Worden Hill and Ninth Street to Dundee and turn right on Highway 99W. Turn right to continue our tour to Sokol Blosser.

VIEW FROM SOKOL BLOSSER PARKING LOT

It's easier to take in the beautiful view as you come back down the hill with the valley to the right and an unusual knobby hill to the south. On 99W Alfie's and the Chardonnay Wine Cellar on the south side are good places for picnic supplies and tasting local wines.

SOKOL BLOSSER is about 3 miles west of Dundee off Highway 99W. Follow the blue sign and turn right (north) on Sokol Blosser Lane for 0.9 mile (despite what the sign and industry brochures say) and *voila!* The road uphill to Sokol Blosser is a rough gravel one, but then many Northwest wineries' roads are. Just off the parking lot is Sokol Blosser's excellent "Walk-through Vineyard" educational program.

The tasting room's semicircular design makes all visitors feel as if they're having a private tasting, with tasteful wooden box displays of wine along the walls. Loads of picnic tables help you hang out and prolong your stay in what almost looks like a mini-village. The winery's Pinot Noirs usually receive high ratings from most critics.

Fine points: Featured wines: Willamette Pinot Noir, Winemaker's Reserve Pinot Noir, Riesling, Evolution (nine whites blend), Pinot Gris, and Müller-Thurgau. Owners: Bill and Susan Sokol Blosser. Winemaker: Russ Rosner. Cases: 45,000. Acres: 76 planted of 80.

Sokol Blosser, 5000 Sokol Blosser Lane, P.O. Box 399, Dundee 97115; phone (800) 582–6668 or (503) 864–2282; e-mail sbinfo@sokolblosser.com; Web site *www.sokolblosser.com. Open 11:00 A.M.–5:00 P.M. daily. Tasting fee $3.00. Visa, MasterCard, American Express, and Discover. Wheelchair accessible.*

To satisfy your dining desires in the Dundee area, we suggest the following, both on Highway 99W.

RED HILL PROVINCIAL DINING is highly recommended by *Wine Spectator, Wine Enthusiast, Northwest Best Places,* and *Pacific Northwest Magazine.* Warm and friendly Alice Halstead presides over her dining oasis in an older home's former living room, serving cosmopolitan cuisine such as pork medallions, light rosemary breads, elegant pastas (often with capers, our favorite), generous salads, and rich desserts in a very country setting, all prepared by chefs Nancy and Richard Gehrts. Outstanding local and imported wine list; beer served as well.

❧ *Red Hill Provincial Dining, 276 Highway 99W on north side of Dundee; phone (503) 538–8224. Open for lunch Wednesday–Friday, dinner Wednesday–Sunday. MasterCard and Visa. Not wheelchair accessible.*

TINA'S is a roadside restaurant whose location belies the goodies you might find inside. People who don't know about this place fly right by the colorful little "house" on the road's edge. Having cooked in many of Portland's best restaurants, Tina and David Bergen opened their own place here in 1991 in the heart of Pinot Noir country to cook food that maximizes enjoyment of both local food and wines. They now offer one of the finest wine lists around.

From the highway you walk through the front door into countryside France. You'll find specials ranging from exotic, elegant risottos and perfectly sautéed oysters to braised artichokes, rabbit, pork tenderloins, herb-roasted Oregon leg of lamb ($20.00), and wonderfully refreshing soup such as roasted squash. Do not miss the buttermilk onion rings ($5.50) or the grilled pork loin sandwich ($7.50) at lunch or the seared yellowfin tuna ($24.00) at dinner. Italian-inspired desserts are $5.00. Full bar.

❧ *Tina's, 760 Highway 99W, Dundee; phone (503) 538–8880. Open for lunch Tuesday–Friday, dinner nightly. American Express, MasterCard, and Visa. Wheelchair accessible.*

Next head for Chateau Benoit, one of Oregon's largest and most splendiferous wineries. Stay on Highway 99W into Lafayette, which you will recognize by the Lafayette School House Antique Mall and Yamhill County Museum on the right.

Turn right on Mineral Springs Road 0.7 mile from Lafayette, following the blue sign to CHATEAU BENOIT. The road is fairly flat, curvy, and actually paved complete with double line! After 1.8 miles up Mineral Springs, turn right onto Chateau Benoit's long gravel road, which goes straight up its knoll. The winery's pink château presides over the huge, perfect vineyard. As you follow the path to Chateau Benoit, a labeled herb garden greets you with aromas that stimulate the salivary glands and probably keep the bees busy away from us humans.

The tasting room at Chateau Benoit is long, lean, elegant, and sophisticatedly commercial. Its four sets of French doors face west and look out on the 100-foot-long patio, making the most of a view that extends 20 miles toward the Oregon coast. Open beamed ceilings, hardwood floors, fresh flowers, and antiques, in addition to the excellent wines, draw large crowds.

Obviously local Oregonians come here on weekends and bring guests. You can buy the finest in picnic supplies here, including Marcel and Henri pâtés and chèvre cheeses. Chateau Benoit suggests you "Bring a picnic and drink in the view." Fred and Mary Benoit retired and sold Chateau Benoit to Columbia Empire Farms, a large Oregon farming company.

Check out the new Anne Amie label of even finer wines, including single-vineyard Pinot Noirs, Pinot Gris, and dessert wines, all named for the Benoits' daughters, Anne and Amie.

CHATEAU BENOIT

Fine points: Featured wines: Barrel-fermented Chardonnay, gravity-processed Pinot Noir, Pinot Gris, and dry Riesling. Owner: Columbia Empire Farms. Winemaker: Scott Huffman, formerly assistant winemaker to Fred Benoit. Cases: 18,000. Acres: 85.

❧ *Chateau Benoit, 6580 NE Mineral Springs Road, Carlton 97111; phone (503) 864–2991; fax (503) 864–2203; e-mail steve@chateaubenoit.com; Web site www. chateaubenoit.com. Open 10:00 A.M.–5:00 P.M. daily. Factory store: Lincoln City, phone (541) 996–3981. Visa, MasterCard, and American Express. Wheelchair accessible.*

Ken Wright is doing just fine with his fabulous KEN WRIGHT CELLARS, open only by appointment and on Thanksgiving, north up Highway 47 in Carlton, 236 North Kutch Street, P.O. Box 190, Carlton 97111; phone (503) 852–7070 or (800) 571–6825; fax (503) 852–7111; e-mail info@kwcellars.com; Web site kenwrightcellars.com. Six—that's right, six—of his low-volume, carefully crafted 1995 Pinot Noirs were rated high 80s by *Wine Spectator* and *Wine Enthusiast.*

One option is to continue on Highway 99W to McMinnville and a great lunch at the Golden Valley Brewery or dinner at Nick's and a night in McMinnville. Or you can head southwest to Yamhill Valley Vineyards and the Oregon Wine Tasting Room, or turn north on Highway 47 toward Yamhill, Gaston, and Forest Grove. We will help you do any and all.

McMinnville is a delightful small town whose downtown has not been wrecked by a mall and deserted by locals. It's a functioning, ever-so-slightly urbane quasi-rural commerce and farm center. Even the Newberg Chamber of Commerce recommends the GOLDEN VALLEY BREWERY & PUB/GOLDEN VALLEY WINERY and restaurant as the best place around for wine tasters to have lunch.

Take Highway 99W or Lafayette Avenue into town, turn left (east) on Fourth Street and into the Golden Valley parking lot. You know you're there when you see the Real Deal Flea Market and Thrift Center on the left (its signs are better) and the Full Gospel Church on the opposite corner.

Owner Peter Kircher worked as sous-chef at San Francisco's St. Francis Hotel until a 5.5 earthquake rattled his pots and nerves for the last time and he decided to get out of town. For a few years he and his wife, Celia, ran a commercial fishing boat out of Kodiak Island, Alaska. Finished with that life experiment, the Kirchers found their ideal piece of land in the Dundee Hills and planted their lives and vineyard.

In 1993 the Kirchers opened the Golden Valley Brewery in an old warehouse, which is now lined with museum-quality historic photos. As you enter

PETER'S MONDO BIG SMOKIN' PORK CHOP, BABY!
from Peter Kircher, Golden Valley Brewery

Center cut pork chops with bone frenched

For the marinade:

12 oz apple cider or apple juice	*1 tsp thyme*
12 oz dry English hard cider	*1 tsp salt*
1 large apple with skin, grated	*1 Tbs fresh cracked pepper*
2 shallots, chopped	*2 oz cider vinegar*
1 large clove elephant garlic	*½ cup olive oil*
1 tsp rosemary	

For grilling:

2–3 oz apple wood or other smoking wood, soaked in water for two hours	*1 Walla Walla onion, sliced*
	6 Tbs butter
4–6 apple rings	

Combine all marinade ingredients and puree in food processor. Place pork chops in marinade for twenty-four hours.

Remove chops from marinade and pat dry. Start grill with coals on one side and apple or other smoking wood (soaked in water for two hours) on the other. Slowly smoke chops over apple wood for about twenty minutes, then grill over hot coals to brown on both sides. Grill apple rings on both sides. Caramelize onion in butter. Top each chop with grilled apple ring and onions. Serve with roasted shallot and garlic mashed potatoes and winter or summer squash, depending on the season. Serves 6.

the pub and beer/wine tasting room, enjoy the Mission-style decor with stained-glass transoms, oak booths, and even a new menu utilizing a new Tennessee smoker. Try the brew house baby back ribs ($13.95–$17.95), prime rib on Friday and Saturday nights, and jumbo ocean prawns ($17.95). Lots of great sandwiches and pastas. You can enjoy the only true Caesar salad we found in Oregon, tart with just the right amount of garlic and anchovies (add-ons extra). Here you can taste Dundee Hills beers and wines. The place is full of locals as well as wine tour vanloads.

 Fine points: Featured beers: Try the tasting menu of Red Thistle Ale (Celtic red), Erratic Rock English Bitter, Old Powerhouse Porter, St. John's Stout, and Grand Island Golden.

❧ Golden Valley Brewery & Pub/Golden Valley Winery, 980 East Fourth Street, McMinnville 97128; phone (503) 472–BREW; Web site www.golden valleybrewery.com. Visa, American Express, and Discover. Wheelchair accessible.

NICK'S ITALIAN CAFE, 521 East Third Street, McMinnville (503–434–4471), is where winemakers and winery owners gather for dinner, while you might see them at Golden Valley for lunch. Nick's is still a traditional Italian restaurant, thank heavens, based on Nick Peirano's mother's and grandmother's cooking. It reminds us of a traditional Italian restaurant in San Francisco—only better. You get a prix fixe five-course dinner ($35) always including divine garlic-laden minestrone, a light and basic green salad whose dressing you will never accurately reproduce, antipasti that vary by season, perfect pasta, and a brief choice of entrees, usually a full plate of food, none of which is stacked in a pile. Nick's menu changes daily.

Nick's is a couple of blocks west of the Golden Valley Brewery in an old storefront coffee shop across from the theater between Evans and Ford Streets.

Don't miss the "Bookshop on Third Street." Linfield College is in McMinnville, which contributes to the town's cosmopolitan ambience.

The good news is that THE EYRIE VINEYARDS, which put Oregon's Pinot Noir and McMinnville on the world wine map, is easily reached downtown at 935 East Tenth Street. The bad news is that David Lett, the white-bearded owner-winemaker who pioneered wines in the area, and his wife, Diana, only open the winery to the public on Memorial Day and Thanksgiving weekend, when the wine and music flow. Otherwise you may try to phone ahead for a special visit.

The Letts first planted in 1966 and in 1970 bottled their inaugural wine. In 1979 their little winery upset the grape cart by placing a close third with its 1975 Pinot Noir in a Paris tasting competition, beating several distinguished French wineries.

The French demanded a rematch, contending their best wines had not been entered and the jury was amateurish. So in January 1980 David Lett returned for a special blind tasting against a selected group of the best French. This time Eyrie finished second by 0.2 point to the 1959 Drouhin Chambolle-Musigny. *Wine Spectator* gave its 1995 Pinot Noir an 88.

Lett has since stimulated interest in Pinot Gris by grafting it to a sturdy White Riesling rootstock. He also produces Chardonnay and Muscat Ottonel.

Fine points: Featured wines: Pinot Blanc, Pinot Gris, Chardonnay, Pinot Noir, and Pinot Meunier. Owners: David and Diana Lett. Winemaker: David Lett. Cases: 8,000. Acres: 50.

MINESTRONE SOUP
from Nick Peirano, Nick's Italian Cafe

For the stock:

4 carrots, diced	16 oz canned tomatoes, diced
4 celery stalks, diced	½ cup tomato paste
2 green peppers, diced	¼ cup beef stock base
2 yellow onions, diced	1 Tbs black pepper
1 cup parsley leaves, finely chopped	1 Tbs rosemary, crushed
6 garlic cloves, minced	1 Tbs dried oregano, crushed
1 lb chunk of salt pork	4 Tbs dried basil, crushed
3 quarts water	

For the soup:

1 lb carrots, sliced	salt to taste
1 lb green peas, chopped,	pesto for garnish
fresh or frozen	Parmesan and Romano cheeses for garnish
12 oz green beans, fresh or frozen	

Cook diced carrots, celery stalks, green peppers, yellow onions, parsley leaves, garlic cloves, and salt pork in 3 quarts of water in a large covered pot over low to medium heat for six hours. Remove pork from stock, chop finely in food processor, then return to pot by pushing salt pork through a metal strainer. Skim several times until all fat is removed.

Add canned tomatoes, tomato paste, beef stock base, pepper, rosemary, oregano, and basil. Cook at least two additional hours, covered, over low heat until the initial vegetables are almost disintegrated. Add the carrots, green beans, and peas to the stock and cook until tender. Add salt to taste.

Garnish each bowl of soup with 2 Tbs pesto and 1 Tbs Parmesan/Romano mixture. Serves 8 to 10.

❧ *The Eyrie Vineyards, 935 East Tenth Street, McMinnville 97128 (mailing address: P.O. Box 697, Dundee 97115); phone (503) 472–6315; fax (503) 472–5124; e-mail tev@onlinemac.com. Open Memorial Day and Thanksgiving weekend only. Visa, MasterCard, and American Express. Wheelchair accessible.*

Open only by appointment or on Memorial Day and Thanksgiving is PANTHER CREEK CELLARS, a few blocks away at 455 North Irvine (between Fourth and Fifth Streets), McMinnville 97128; phone (503) 472–8080; fax (503) 472–5667; e-mail panther@viclink.com. Ron and Linda Kaplan bought Panther Creek from founder Ken Wright in 1994, resulting in four 1995 Pinot Noirs highly rated by *Wine Spectator*.

Now we'll detail some wine trips south of McMinnville. To get to Yamhill Valley Vineyards and the Oregon Wine Tasting Room, take Highway 99W south toward Amity and turn right on Highway 18 toward the ocean beaches. Then turn right at Oldsville Road and *voila!*

Slightly out of the way but intensely beautiful, YAMHILL VALLEY VINEYARDS is worth the trip. Founded by two Portland immunologists, Yamhill Valley is well designed for the Oregon Coast Range foothills and the latest in wine technologies. Motherly oak trees shade both buildings and people. Its hearty wines and beautiful settings should mean a bright future for this interesting enterprise, as should *Wine Enthusiast*'s praise for its 1995 Pinot Noir. Meditate at Yamhill's koi fishpond.

Fine points: Featured wines: Pinot Noir, White Riesling, Pinot Gris, and Pinot Blanc. Founding partners: Denis Burger, Elaine McCall, and David and Terry Hinrichs. Winemaker: Stephen Cary. Cases: 13,000. Acres: 150.

✦✧ *Yamhill Valley Vineyards, 16250 SW Oldsville Road, McMinnville 97128-8546; phone (800) 825–4845 or (503) 843–3100; fax (503) 843–2450; e-mail info@yamhill.com; Web site www.yamhill.com. Open 11:00 A.M.–5:00 P.M. daily, Memorial Day–Thanksgiving; 11:00 A.M.–5:00 P.M. weekends, mid-March–June 1; closed December–mid-March. Visa, MasterCard, and American Express. Wheelchair accessible.*

By following Highway 47 you will find Willakenzie, Elk Cove, Kramer, and Montinore Wineries and Sake One/Momokawa Sake Kura. Or you can get to these wineries by taking Highway 240 from Newberg or Torii Mor and Lange wineries west to Yamhill and heading north on Highway 47.

You can reach WILLAKENZIE ESTATE from two directions. Coming north from Highway 47, turn east on Highway 240 in the center of Yamhill, then after 2 miles turn left on Laughlin Road. Or drive west on Highway 240 (from Torii Mor, Lange, or Erath wineries) to Laughlin Road on the right. Take the well-paved flat drive for 1½ miles, through the gate with the stone sign, and then proceed ¼ mile uphill.

Forty acres of vineyards appear before you get to the deep forest ahead.

Enjoy the tasting room's cafe seating for fifty or the picnic area with gorgeous, expansive views of the vineyards below and mountains above.

Willakenzie hit the road running, with the vineyard planted in 1992, the first crush in 1995, and a gravity feed irrigation system finished the same year. In 1996 Willakenzie opened for tasting. Willakenzie has created a state-of-the-art winery—possibly the most modern in Oregon—housed in a huge gray wooden building designed by architect Ernie Munch (who also did nearby Domaine Drouhin and Archery Summit) to be compatible with an existing dairy barn.

High-tech pioneer Bernard Lacroute (originally from Burgundy via California's Silicon Valley) and his wife, Ronni, who bought 420 acres in 1990 from the descendents of the original homesteaders, planted eighty acres of vineyards and grabbed Winemaker-Manager Laurent Montalieu (a Bordeaux native) from Bridgeview Vineyards in Cave Junction after a stint in Napa Valley.

Talk about low-tech high-tech: Willakenzie is entirely gravity fed. The production is on three levels, with the grapes dropping naturally to be crushed and then the juice pouring into the underground barrel room below, all aimed at a "gentle handling of the fruit."

From their very first crush, three 1995 Pinot Noirs were rated in the high 80s by *Wine Spectator*, as were the 1996 Pinot Gris and Pinot Blanc.

Oh, yes, the name. Willakenzie is the soil native to the region, considered excellent for grape growing, first identified at the confluence of the Willamette and McKenzie Rivers.

Fine points: Featured wines: Pinot Noir, Gamay Noir, Pinot Meunier, Pinot Gris, and Pinot Blanc. Owners: Bernard and Ronni Lacroute. Winemaker: Thibaud Mandet. Cases: 15,000. Acres: 102. *Willakenzie Estate, 19143 NE Laughlin Road, Yamhill 97148; phone (503) 662–3280 or (888) 953–9463; fax (503) 662–4829; e-mail winery@willakenzie.com; Web site www.willakenzie.com. Open noon–5:00 P.M. daily, Memorial Day–Labor Day; noon–5:00 P.M. Friday–Sunday, Labor Day–Memorial Day; by appointment the rest of the time. Visa, MasterCard, and American Express. Wheelchair accessible.*

Although open only by appointment, two other wineries in Yamhill County warrant special mention: ARCHERY SUMMIT, 18599 Archery Summit Road, Dayton (503–537–4728), opened in 1993, and its Pinot Noir Arcus Estate 1995 was rated the best Pinot Noir in Oregon (tied with newcomer Siduri) with a 91 (250 cases at $60 a bottle). Archery Summit also offers tours year-round by appointment at 10:00 A.M. and 1:00 and 3:30 P.M. Thursday–Sunday.

Contact tours&tasting@archerysummit.com. **DOMAINE DROUHIN OREGON**, P.O. Box 700, Dundee (503–864–2700), is owned by French wine mogul Joseph Drouhin, who bought 180 acres in 1980s after David Lett's triumphant showing with Oregon's Eyrie Winery Pinot in France. The winery uses a modern gravity feed process. Both Archery and Drouhin back up to Sokol Blosser.

To complete the Willamette Valley sweep for its Pinot Noirs, other small wineries rate high marks from *Wine Spectator* and other prominent tasters; among them are Beaux Freres, Springhill, Brick House, Chehalem, and St. Innocent. Most seem to follow Chehalem's slogan: "Hard to find, hard to forget."

To get to Elk Cove Vineyards and Kramer Vineyards, turn left (west) onto Olson Road just south of the teensy farm center and one-sided town of Gaston, where the principal business is the "Pretty Good Grocery." For the first mile Olson Road is curvy and sometimes narrow and flat, and then it turns into a steady, twisting climb for another 3 miles before you get to Elk Cove. The surrounding hills and flora make this a gorgeous, peaceful-if-slightly-bumpy drive to **ELK COVE VINEYARDS**.

From Elk Cove's wine tasting room you can enjoy the spectacular, breathtaking view of Oregon's Tualatin Valley and Elk Cove's beautifully terraced vineyards. Love that paved driveway!

Joe, Pat, and Adam Campbell have created a magnificent facility, including the Roosevelt Room (named for the nearby Roosevelt elk) for banquets and special events.

The Campbells bring an interesting combination of backgrounds to their wine business. Pat is a fourth-generation Oregonian and is descended from Swiss immigrants whose family grew grapes, apples, and pears near Helvetia, Oregon. Joe grew up in the Hood River Valley, graduated from Harvard in history of science, and studied medicine at Stanford. After much European travel, the Campbells first made wine from grapes that grew along the streambeds of the Oglala Sioux Indian Reservation where Joe practiced medicine. This is where he first also practiced his motto, taken from the Hippocratic oath, *Primum Non Nocere*—"First Do No Harm."

The Campbells' son Adam graduated in science from Lewis & Clark College and brings new systems, advancements, creativity, and passion to his parents' winery.

 Fine points: Featured wines: Exceptional single-vineyard Pinot Noir, Pinot Gris, Late Harvest Riesling, and "Ultima" dessert wines. Owners: Joe, Adam, and Patricia Campbell. Winemaker: Adam Campbell. Cases: 24,000. Acres: 120.

Elk Cove Vineyards, 27751 NW Olson Road, Gaston 97119; phone (503)

KRAMER VINEYARDS

985–7760; fax (503) 985–3525; e-mail info@elkcove.com; Web site www.elk cove.com. Open 10:00 A.M.–5:00 P.M. daily. Visa, MasterCard, and American Express. Wheelchair accessible.

Come back out the Elk Cove drive, turn left back onto Olson Road, and in 1.4 miles turn left to KRAMER VINEYARDS. A couple miles north of Gaston and 10 miles south of Forest Grove, Kramer looks and feels like an old house, and the vivid hanging geraniums tell you something different awaits you inside. It is actually a winery that seems busy even when no one is there.

Usually several tasters fill the cozy tasting room and gift shop, enjoying winemaker and CEO Trudy Kramer's wines and her entertaining personality, tongue-in-cheek humor, and refreshing lack of ego-based seriousness. When we were last there, a band was playing in the shade of the small open-ended ware-house while picnickers enjoyed Kramer wines and music at comfortable cafe tables and chairs. The Kramers have toys, swings, and unusual activities for kids, too. Designated drivers receive a free nonalcoholic beverage. At the July Fourth Barrel Tasting you can taste and purchase futures, and you can taste Reserve Pinots the first weekend in November.

Having won a gold medal at the Oregon State Fair for her homemade raspberry wine, Trudy Kramer decided to make grape wines as a business. Husband Keith still keeps his day job as a pharmacist to support their winemaking habit.

Fine points: Featured wines: Pinot Gris, Dijon, Pinot Noir, Merlot, Carmine, Syrah, Chardonnay, Riesling, and Müller-Thurgau. Owners: Trudy and Keith Kramer. Winemaker and CEO: Trudy Kramer. Cases: 3,500. Acres: 15.

Kramer Vineyards, 26830 NW Olson Road, Gaston 97119; phone (503) 662–4545 or (800) 61–WINES; fax (503) 662–4033; e-mail kramer@heva.net. com; Web site www.kramerwine.com. Open noon–5:00 P.M. Friday–Sunday, March–May and October–December; noon–5:00 P.M. daily, June–September. Visa and MasterCard. Wheelchair accessible.

Take Olson Road back to Highway 47 and downtown Gaston and continue north to MONTINORE VINEYARDS, a winery complex combining historic and modern buildings. One of Oregon's largest wineries, Montinore proclaims itself "Oregon's Premier Wine Estate" and has even registered that statement. Montinore is 8.5 miles north of Kramer and 2 miles south of Forest Grove.

You can also get to Montinore by taking Highway 8, the Tualatin Valley Highway, which becomes Baseline Road in Hillsboro and Forest Grove. Turn left (south) onto Highway 47, right on Stringtown Road, and then left on Dilley Road. You are now in Washington County.

A historic Victorian home serves as offices, while across the lawn a Mediterranean-style building houses the vast and appealing tasting room and winery, where you can buy wine and food books, wine paraphernalia such as black-stemmed wine glasses, and local Tillamook cheeses.

An extremely friendly staff graciously handles knowledgeable or dumb questions, following the example of genial and well-informed tasting room manager Sandy Bunker.

The winery's name comes from the farm's original one, Mont-in-Ore, given to the property by John Forbis, who came to Oregon from a position as legal counsel to Anaconda Copper Company in Montana and planted walnuts and filberts here. He combined his two favorite places and came up with Montinore.

Leo and Jane Graham purchased the 361 acres in 1965. With the guidance of Jeffrey Lamy, they began planting varietals in 1983 and have nearly doubled vinifera acreage since then. The Grahams believe that wine is a food and that "your palate is the only critic that truly matters." *Wine Spectator* gave their 1995 Pinot Noir Winemaker's Reserve an 85; *Wine Enthusiast* gave it an 87.

MONTINORE VINEYARDS HISTORIC HOME/OFFICE

Fine points: Featured wines: Pinot Gris, Müller-Thurgau, White Riesling, Gewürztraminer, Chardonnay, and Pinot Noir. Owners: Leo and Jane Graham. Winemaker: Jacques Tardy. Cases: 50,000. Acres: 265.

Montinore Vineyards, 3663 Southwest Dilley Road, P.O. Box 560, Forest Grove 97116; phone (503) 359–5012; fax (503) 357–4313; e-mail info@monti nore.com; Web site www.montinore.com. Open 11:00 A.M.–5:00 P.M. daily. Visa and MasterCard. Wheelchair accessible.

You're in for a different taste experience 1.5 miles up Highway 47 at the SAKE ONE/MOMOKAWA SAKE KURA, the only American-owned sake kura (brewery). From Montinore go north on Highway 47 toward Forest Grove and follow the Tualatin Valley Highway (47) as it shortcuts over to Highway 8 around the edge of Forest Grove just east of Hillsboro. Momokawa is at the corner of Highway 47 and Elm Street.

Momokawa was a highly respected and famous Japanese rice wine "brewer" that brought its methods, craft, knowledge, Japanese garden, and culture to Oregon's wine country. In the SakeOne/Momokawa tasting room you will find it a treat to learn just how rice wine has been brewed traditionally for centuries and experience the calm of traditional Japanese interior design. Here you can taste both Oregon-made and imported Momokawa sakes. Try the new releases of sake infused with Oregon-grown Asian pear, black raspberry, and roasted hazelnut flavors. *Sugoi!* (Cheers!)

Fine points: Featured wines: Momokawa semi-dry Diamond, Ruby, dry Silver, and partially filtered pearl; SakeOne fruit infused sakes, including Momokawa and Moonstone premium sakes. Owners: Frost International Group and partners. Toji: Abednego Barnes. Cases: 21,000. Acres: 25.

᭜ *Sake One/Momokawa Kura, 820 Elm Street, Forest Grove 97116; phone (503) 357–7056; fax (503) 357–1014; e-mail info@momokawa.com; Web site www.sakeone.com. Open noon–5:00 P.M. daily. Tours by appointment. Visa, MasterCard, and American Express. Wheelchair accessible.*

From here you may want to start back to Portland or continue to three more wineries in the Tualatin Valley. To the west (farther away from Portland) you visit David Hill and Shafer Wineries, both of which are interesting wine and environmental experiences but require winding climbs a few miles up rocky roads.

You have a choice of two routes back to Portland: If you have to get back right away, take Highway 8 to Beaverton and then follow the signs to Portland or, even faster, take Highway 26 right into downtown Portland (our favorite).

First we'll tell you how to get to David Hill and Shafer wineries.

From Forest Grove take Highway 8 (Pacific Avenue in Forest Grove and Tualatin Valley Highway west of town) by staying in the right lane past Pacific University and through the cute town toward Tillamook. Highway 8 eventually becomes Gales Creek Road. Suddenly you are in the middle of cornfields and open land in a gorgeous valley.

Five miles west of Forest Grove turn right up David Hill Road, a gravel road that becomes steep and rough. About 3.5 miles up this car-tester, just beyond the point where you think you missed it or are on the road to oblivion, off to the right you will see a gorgeous view of a yellow house and dramatic rolling vineyards and a sign to David Hill Winery. You have to pull over to the left to make the hairpin right turn down the driveway.

If you're coming from Portland, take Highway 8 through Forest Grove, make a soft right up Thatcher/Kansas City Road, and eventually turn left onto David Hill Road to the David Hill sign and driveway. David Hill Road is not for motorhomes or buses, nor is DAVID HILL WINERY.

David Hill Winery, whose buildings formerly housed Laurel Ridge Winery, is one of the most beautiful, albeit hard to get to, winery sites anywhere. Lumberman Milan and Jean Stoyanov bought the property, the oldest licensed

VIEW OF DAVID HILL WINERY AND THE TUALATIN VALLEY

winery site in Oregon, in 1992 and took over the winery in 2000. In addition to the lovely Victorian on the property, the Soyanovs have now remodeled the winery and still offer the most breathtaking views of the Tualatin Valley. Laurel Ridge is now located in tiny Carlton, Oregon.

If you are allergic to bees, walk on the lawn around the plants along the path to avoid them.

The beautifully restored nineteenth-century farmhouse housed the Charles Coury Winery and the Reuter's Hill Winery in the 1970s, the latter of which sold its stock for $1.00 a bottle as a Thanksgiving Day, 1980 farewell gesture.

 Fine points: Featured wines: Pinot Noir, Chardonnay, Gewürztraminer, Pinot Gris, Riesling, Sauvignon Blanc, Muscat, Tawny Port, Muscat Port, Estate Muscat. Owners: Milan and Jean Stoyanov. Winemaker: Pascal Valadier. Cases: 6,000. Acres: 40.

❧ *David Hill Winery, 46350 NW David Hill Road, Forest Grove 97116; phone (503) 992–8545; Web site www.davidhillwinery.com. Open noon–5:00 P.M. Tuesday–Sunday. Visa and MasterCard. Partly wheelchair accessible.*

SHAFER VINEYARD CELLARS is farther north through the gracious farmlands along Gales Creek Road and up another gravel road into a tree tunnel to another gorgeous site and view.

Shafer is small and charming. You almost always get to talk with the owner/ winemaker, which is a real plus, and enjoy his hand-crafted wines along with Miki Shafer's handmade Christmas crafts and art. Bring a picnic to the gazebo.

Fine points: Featured wines: *Méthode champenoise* sparkling wines, Pinot Noir, Chardonnay, Fumé Blanc, White Riesling, Müller-Thurgau, Gewürztraminer, and special dessert wines. Owners: Harvey and Miki Shafer. Winemaker: Harvey Shafer. Cases: 10,000. Acres: 40.

Shafer Vineyard Cellars, 6200 NW Gales Creek Road, Forest Grove 97116; phone and fax (503) 357-6604; e-mail shafer@msn.com; Web site www.shafervine yardcellars.com. Open 11:00 A.M.–5:00 P.M. daily, March–December; weekends only in January. Closed February. Visa and MasterCard. Wheelchair accessible.

Established in 1973, TUALATIN'S ESTATE VINEYARDS' motto is "Old Vines—New Vision." Besides the fine wines, you must inhale the panoramic view of the Coast Range from the winery's picnic area in the vineyard, just thirty minutes from downtown Portland. You can either double back on Gales Creek Road (Highway 8) from Shafer Vineyard Cellars, or take Highway 6 from Highway 26 heading west, and then left on Gales Creek. From Gales Creek (Highway 8), turn right onto Thatcher Road, left on Clapshaw Hill Road, and then ease right on Seavey Road to Tualatin. Lovely picnic area.

Fine points: Featured wines: Chardonnay, Pinot Blanc, Pinot Noir, and semi-sparkling Muscat. Owner: Willamette Valley Vineyards. Winemaker: Joe Dobbs. Acres: 145.

Tualatin Estate Vineyards, 10850 NW Seavey Road, Forest Grove 97116; phone (503) 357-5005; fax (503) 357-1702; Web site www.wvv.com. Open noon–5:00 P.M. Saturday–Sunday, March 1–December 31; closed January–February. Visa, MasterCard, American Express, and Discover. Wheelchair accessible.

To come back down to Earth—both spiritually and physically—get back onto Gales Creek Road (Highway 8) and head east toward Forest Grove, Hillsboro, and Beaverton.

The don't-miss wine tasting alternative is to first take Highway 219 south from Hillsboro to Oak Knoll Winery and make a loop back to Portland, stopping at Ponzi and Cooper Mountain.

If you are in Portland and want to take a quick or slow afternoon wine tour, just make the Ponzi, Cooper Mountain (weekends), and Oak Knoll loop. Here's how: Take I–5 and then I–405 for 9 miles south to the Highway 217 turnoff toward Tigard. Turn south on Highway 217 and then southwest on Highway 210 (Scholls Ferry Road) for 4.5 miles toward Newberg.

Turn left on Vandermost Road and left again into the Ponzis' Winery Lane to PONZI VINEYARDS, with elegant Mediterranean architecture and a quiet atmosphere. Dick and Nancy Ponzi moved their family from northern California to the Willamette Valley in the late 1960s and made their first four barrels of Pinot Noir in 1974. Dick Ponzi, who taught engineering at Portland Community College, has been hailed as an artist, innovator, perfectionist, and de facto leader of the quality wine movement in Oregon. He has been lauded by *Wine Spectator* as one of the "People Who Made a Difference" and by Robert M. Parker in the *Wine Advocate*, the *New York Times*, and *USA Today*. Dick's engineering background led him to invent and fabricate machinery and winemaking techniques now used throughout the industry. *Wine Spectator* rates Ponzi's 1995 Pinot Noir Reserve at 89 and its nonreserve Pinot Noir at 86.

The Ponzis' children, Michel, Anna-Maria, and Luisa, have taken over management of the winery. Luisa collaborates as winemaker with her father, bringing her degree in oenology and viticulture from the C.F.P.P.A. in Beaune, France, and firsthand Burgundian techniques to the creative mix.

The Ponzis redecorated their former home with Italianate decor and objets d'art and now offer it as an event space.

Tours are available by appointment.

 Fine points: Featured wines: Possibly the best Pinot Noir, Pinot Gris, Chardonnay, Vino Gelato dessert wine, and Arneis. Owners: Dick and Nancy Ponzi. Winemakers: Dick and Luisa Ponzi. Cases: 10,000–14,000. Acres: 100 and buy from other local vineyards, all at 100–500-foot elevations with south and southeast exposures.

❧ *Ponzi Vineyards, 14665 SW Winery Lane, Beaverton 97007; phone (503) 628–1227; fax (503) 628–0354; e-mail info@ponziwines.com; Web site www.ponziwines.com. Open 11:00 A.M.–5:00 P.M. daily; closed in January. Visa, MasterCard, and American Express. Wheelchair accessible.*

To get from Ponzi to COOPER MOUNTAIN VINEYARDS, come back out Vandermost Road to Scholls Ferry Road and turn left. At a fork in the road, take the right side, which is Tile Flat Road. Turn right soon onto Grabhorn Road, which jogs to the left then right. Just past the right corner, turn into Cooper Mountain Vineyards. This is all exquisite Oregon farm country.

In 1987 Bob and Corrine Gross established their dream winery on this 1865 homestead perched on an extinct volcano overlooking the Tualatin River Valley. Currently Cooper Mountain bottles small quantities of premium estate

HARVEST PARTY HALIBUT
from Ponzi family friends, Jules and Joan Drabkin,
Beaverton, Oregon, and Alaska

[Note: *Every year Ponzi holds a harvest party where friends can get dirty, pick grapes, and have fun. Ponzi friends Jules and Joan Drabkin desert Oregon for Alaska's Inland Passage every summer and make it their project to catch enough halibut to supply the Ponzi party, to which the Drabkins deliver a huge cooler of marinating halibut. This is the recipe for the fabulous marinade.—KT Hill.*]

⅓ *lb halibut per person*
1 cup olive oil
1 cup melted butter
lemon zest ("lots")
fresh thyme, parsley, tarragon, oregano to taste
dried blended herbs de Provence
Pinot Gris juice (which you probably don't have, so use a light grape juice)
3 Tbs butter, melted for grilling
[Note: *"Don't use acid—wine, vinegar, lemon juice. It's incompatible with halibut."*]

Prepare the marinade and be adventurous with your doses of herbs. Marinate halibut for several hours, twenty-four hours maximum. Keep cold.

For the grilling: Oil your grill before cooking to prevent sticking. The cooking time varies by size of fillets—approximately four to five minutes each side, keeping fish moist by brushing or dribbling with oil or butter. "To test doneness, press the flesh with your finger. Raw flesh is soft and springy, just right is barely firm, and overdone is hard and firm."

wines and sells the rest of their grapes to other vintners.

The tasting room nestles under huge oak trees with a patio with round glass tables and green and white umbrellas. Wine barrels function as an informal tasting bar, signaling the ambience of the whole winery. Enjoy Cooper Mountain's lovely new two-story Tuscan tasting room with the barrel cellar underground downstairs.

Located in a beautifully refreshing woodsy setting, Cooper Mountain stands today as a near shrine to co-owner Corrine Gross, who died of breast cancer in 1995. (Part of the profits from some Cooper Mountain wines go to Race for the

COOPER MOUNTAIN VINEYARDS

Cure.) Corrine rode horses here as a child, and the area and winery are named for Oregon pioneer Perry Cooper. All of Cooper Mountain's wines come from 100 percent certified organic grapes grown biodynamically on its property.

Wine Spectator and *Wine Enthusiast* both gave Cooper Mountain an 88 for its 1995 Pinot Noir Reserve and an 87 for its 1995 Nonreserve Pinot Noir.

Fine points: Featured wines: Pinot Noir, Pinot Gris, Pinot Blanc, and Chardonnay. Owner: Dr. Robert Gross. Winemaker: Rich Cushman. Cases: 10,000. Acres: 150.

Cooper Mountain Vineyards, 9480 SW Grabhorn Road, Beaverton 97007; phone (503) 649–0027; fax (503) 649–0702; e-mail sales@coopermountainwine.com; Web site www.coopermountainwine.com. Open noon–5:00 P.M. daily, February–December. Visa and MasterCard. Wheelchair accessible.

Next you must go to **OAK KNOLL WINERY** for the cultural and viticultural experience. To get here from Cooper Mountain go north on Grabhorn Road, left on Farmington Road (Highway 10), and wander through sublime flat and rolling green hills. Turn right on Rood Bridge Road, then left on Burkhalter Road. Or you can take Tile Flat road off Grabhorn and turn left on Farmington (Highway 10).

Coming from Portland, just take Highway 10 (Farmington Road) from Beaverton and turn right on Rood Bridge Road and left on Burkhalter Road.

When we turned into Oak Knoll Winery for the first time, something made us smile instantly. It didn't look like a winery, because it wasn't. It looked like a dairy, because it was. The milking parlor is now the winery, and the dairy office is now a cozy and cheerful tasting room.

Marj Vuylsteke presides over the tasting room while her sister supervises the local food samples. Both entertain with great, honest stories of their personal and winery pasts. Portland folks drop in, growers come by at their first chance to sample the fruits of their labor (or the juice from their fruits), and visitors love the whole scene. The huge shade trees offer great picnic protection on the very green lawns.

Marj and her family used to bake with the local wild berries until they were purple. Marj had the bright idea of making some berry wine but didn't know how and mentioned her inspiration to her then-husband Ron. He told her to find a recipe and he would make her some; she did, and he did. They got one gallon of berry wine for their efforts, and their family and neighbors raved and wanted more. So they made more. After a while, Marj thought, "Gosh, we should be able to do this with grapes. They're fruit!"

A short thirty years later, Oak Knoll Winery now produces the eighth largest volume in Oregon. You can taste both fruit and varietal "food friendly" wines and purchase them as well as a wide collection of Oregon food products in the air-conditioned tasting room.

Oak Knoll is a true family operation: Ron and Marj are no longer married but work very well together; and sons Steve, John, and Tom work at Oak Knoll. *Wine Enthusiast* gives Oak Knoll's 1994 Pinot Noir Reserve a 91.

 Fine points: Featured wines: Chardonnay, Pinot Noir, White Riesling, Pinot Gris, Niagara, and Frambrosia (raspberry dessert wine—try it!). Owners: Marj Vuylsteke and Ron Vuylsteke. Winemaker: Ron Vuylsteke. Cases: 40,000. Acres: None.

🍇 *Oak Knoll Winery, 29700 SW Burkhalter Road, Hillsboro 97123; phone (503) 648-8198 or (800) 625-5665; fax (503) 648-3377; e-mail oakknoll@ ipinc.net; Web site www.oakknollwinery.com. Open 11:00 A.M.–4:00 P.M. Monday–Friday, October–April; 11:00 A.M.–6:00 P.M. Monday–Friday, May–September; 11:00 A.M.–5:00 P.M. Saturday–Sunday, all year. Visa, Master-Card, American Express, and Discover. Wheelchair accessible.*

The quickest way back to Portland is to retrace your tracks and take Farmington Road into Beaverton and follow the signs.

HOOD RIVER AND THE COLUMBIA RIVER GORGE

Within an hour's drive from Portland you can sample excellent wines at three small wineries typical of the region. Edgefield is in Multnomah County, and Flerchinger and Hood River are in Hood River County.

Take I–205 north from Portland and turn east on Highway 84 toward Troutdale and Hood River. Since the 1920s the Columbia Gorge Highway has provided visitors with breathtaking views of spectacular geological formations, and the scenic highway bypass can take you to Multnomah Falls, voluptuous deep green canyons, and Bonneville Dam.

Take exit 16A, also known as the Wood Village exit. Take 242nd Street south and then turn left on SW Halsey Street to EDGEFIELD WINERY. The McMenamin family, best known for their popular breweries and brewpubs, bought the old 1911 Multnomah County Poor Farm in 1990 and turned it into a non-Disney pleasure complex.

Once a farm, dairy, cannery, and meat-packing plant, and later a nursing home, the compound now includes a lovely 105-room bed-and-breakfast-style inn in the old main lodge; the Black Rabbit Restaurant and Bar, recommended by most vintners as the best restaurant in the area; Edgefield Winery with a candle-lit tasting cellar; a brewery; the Power Station Pub and Theater; beautiful gardens; an amphitheater; lots of Northwest artwork; and tons of fun.

The Black Rabbit Restaurant and Bar serves the finest in local and regional cuisine, and the bed-and-breakfast is the place to stay in this vicinity. You may consider it seriously if you've had a long day of wine or beer tasting.

Edgefield offers monthly gardening seminars on herbs and vegetables, with lunch at the Black Rabbit Restaurant included.

 Fine points: Featured wines: Riesling, Pinot Gris, Chardonnay, Pinot Noir, Cabernet, Merlot, Zinfandel, Syrah, Port, and sparkling wines. Owners: The McMenamin family. Winemaker: Clark McCool. Cases: 25,000. Acres: 5 and buy from others in Oregon.

Edgefield Winery, 2126 SW Halsey Street, Troutdale 97060; phone (503) 665–2992; fax (503) 661–1968; e-mail winery@mcmenamins.com; Web site www.mcmenamins.com. Open noon–8:00 P.M. Sunday–Thursday and noon– 10:00 P.M. Friday–Saturday in winter; noon–10:00 P.M. daily in summer through crush. Visa, MasterCard, American Express, and Discover. Wheelchair accessible.

Another dining option is TAD'S CHICKEN 'N' DUMPLINGS, 943 SE Crown Point, Troutdale (503–666–5337), for truly down-home country comfort food.

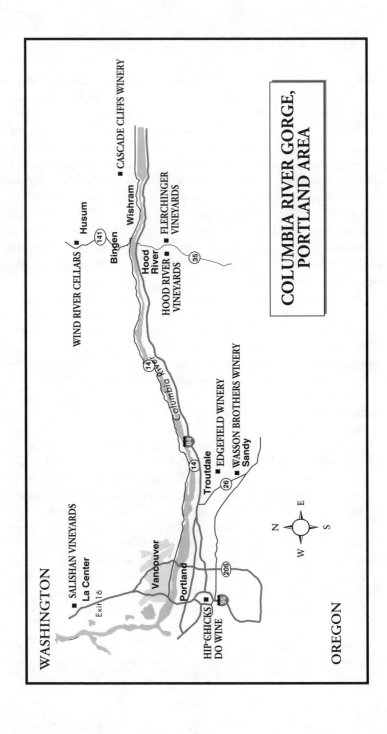

COLUMBIA RIVER GORGE,
PORTLAND AREA

WASHINGTON

OREGON

- SALISHAN VINEYARDS
La Center
Exit 16

Vancouver

Portland

HIP CHICKS
DO WINE

205

95

WIND RIVER CELLARS

- Husum
141

Bingen

Wishram

Hood
River

Columbia River

14

84

Troutdale

14

26

EDGEFIELD WINERY

WASSON BROTHERS WINERY
Sandy

CASCADE CLIFFS WINERY

FLERCHINGER
VINEYARDS

35

HOOD RIVER
VINEYARDS

N
W   E
S

Locals pack this place and have for generations. Sunday dinner is especially popular for chicken, local salmon and halibut, steaks and prime rib, and sublime
homemade pies and ice cream. Full bar.

Get back onto Highway 84 and point yourselves eastward toward Hood
River, a charming town that is currently enjoying its current tag as a world-class
windsurfing center, second only to Maui. The sport has brought interesting
people from all over the world and has spawned appropriate shops and cafes.

Hood River is also the center of Hood River County's "Fruit Loop," a self-
guided and well-posted tour you can take all or part of from close in town to
more rural farming communities to the south. The Hood River Valley is
Oregon's largest fruit-growing district, producing 30 percent of the nation's winter pears (Anjou, Bosc, and Comice) and Newtown Pippin apples.

Nathaniel Coe planted the area's first fruit trees in 1854 when he arrived to
establish Oregon's first post offices and mail routes. In the horrible 1919 freeze,
many apple trees died and were replaced by pear trees.

The Hood River Valley's exceptional fruit productivity comes from fertile
volcanic soil produced by now dormant Mt. Hood combined with cool nights
and warm growing days. At more than twenty fruit stands, staffed by owners
and growers, you can enjoy many varieties of apples, pears, apricots, cherries,
peaches, nectarines, marionberries and lots of other berries, organic juices, jams,
jellies, syrups, dried fruits, nuts, pumpkins, winter squash, loads of flowers and
honey, and farm animals.

Both Flerchinger Vineyards and Hood River Vineyards are west of Hood
River city. Take exit 62 south off Highway 84 and immediately turn right on
Country Club Drive to Post Canyon Drive, which winds a little uphill through
trees and then straightens out at the top of the hill. Frankton Road will also get
you to Post Canyon Drive. From Country Club turn left onto Post Canyon and

MICROBREWERY ALERT!

Edgefield's Brewery *is one of the premier microbreweries in Oregon, owned
by the McMenamin family. In the extremely convivial and pleasant atmosphere
of the brewery or the* Power Station *Pub and Theater (503–669–8610), also at
Edgefield, you can sample brews including Black Rabbit Porter, Rogueingreuven,
Purple Haze, and Sweet Vienna pale ale.*

from Frankton turn right to FLERCHINGER VINEYARDS. Once inside the tasting room, don't miss the family crest over the door and the new 38-foot mural depicting a Bavarian-style vineyard in the barrel room.

The Flerchingers are some of the most enthusiastic winemakers and merchants around. The Flerchingers recently won medals for all three red wines they entered in the Newport (Oregon) Wine and Seafood Festival. Their Riesling was just rated Most Outstanding Riesling by *Northwest Wine Press.* If you are interested in holding your wedding in an Oregon Bavarian atmosphere, this is the place!

Manager Gavin McAlpine has added the best gift shop around, featuring handblown, hand-painted Romanian crystal; gourmet snacks and picnic foods; twenty different corkscrews; bottle stoppers; wine literature; and great hats and shirts. Watch for Flerchinger's annual barrel tasting, appropriately on the Saturday after April 15, and lots of other special events!

 Fine points: Featured wines: Merlot, Cabernet Sauvignon, Pinot Noir, Chardonnay, White Riesling, Blush Riesling, Halbtrocken Wein, Pinot Gris, Cabernet/Merlot Blend, and Syrah. Owners: Don and Joe Flerchinger. Winemaker and cellar master: Joe Flerchinger. Cases: 4,000. Acres: 6 and buy from others.

Flerchinger Vineyards, 4200 Post Canyon Drive, Hood River 97031; phone (541) 386–2882 or (800) 516–8710; fax (541) 386–5363; e-mail flerchingervine yards@gorge.net; Web site www.flerchinger.com. Open 11:00 A.M.–5:00 P.M. daily. Visa and MasterCard. Wheelchair accessible.

MICROBREWERY ALERT!

Full Sail Ale *comes from Full Sail's brewery in Hood River, at 506 Columbia (541–386–2247 or 541–386–2281). Take exit 63 going south a few blocks, turn right on Cascade Street, right again on Fifth Street, and left on Columbia. Visit the tasting room and pub for hourly brewery tours, specialty brews on tap, and a light meal menu. Kids are welcome with parents. Featured beers: Full Sail Amber and Brown Ales, Golden Ale, Wassail, Oktoberfest, Main Sail Stout, Pilsner, and many more.*

FLERCHINGER VINEYARDS

To get to HOOD RIVER VINEYARDS, just turn right out of Flerchinger's drive-way onto Post Canyon Road, cross Country Club Road, continue 0.8 mile, and turn right on Westwood Drive. Wander up the gravel road and hill past the owners' home to Hood River Vineyards.

Bernie Lerch has made wine since he was young and has put his Ph.D. in biochemistry to excellent use in this second professional life, having first served as a professor at the University of California at Santa Cruz. Anne Lerch grew up in Santa Cruz, graduated from U.C. Santa Cruz, and made a gradual career pro-gression toward manager at renowned Kepler's Books in Menlo Park.

Bernie and Anne decided to give it all up, move to Oregon, and pursue a dream: farming. Bernie's penchant for winemaking and his professional back-ground led to the obvious. In 1993 they bought the vineyards and winery from local businessman and grower Cliff Blanchette and continued and improved upon his fine work and reputation.

The setting is unique: vineyards covering rolling hills, tall fir trees sur-rounding the little wood-covered winery, and views of the Columbia River Gorge and the Hood River Valley. Heaven! The informal, cozy tasting room is separated by only a thin wall from the working area of the winery. Everyone involved is friendly, relaxed, and informative.

Bernie ("Don't call me doctor") has become active in the Oregon Wine Growers Association and leads the effort to establish a Hood River appellation, including the wineries across the Columbia in Washington.

Fine points: Featured wines: Estate-grown Pinot Noir, Merlot, Grenache, Syrah, Chardonnay, Gewürztraminer, Cabernet Sauvignon, Cabernet Franc, Zinfandel, Nebbiolo, and a few dessert wines. Owners: L. Bernard and Anne Lerch. Winemaker: L. Bernard Lerch. Cases: 7,000. Acres: 33.

Hood River Vineyards, 4693 Westwood Drive, Hood River 97031; phone (541) 386–3772; fax (541) 386–5880; e-mail hoodriverwines@gorge.net. Open 11:00 A.M.–5:00 P.M. daily March–December or by appointment or when they are there; closed January–February. Visa, MasterCard, American Express, Discover, and Diners Club. Wheelchair accessible.

If you cross the Columbia River into Washington, you can try a Washington winery that would be included in the proposed Hood River appellation.

To get there is a bit of a project. Take the Hood River Bridge (50 cents toll) north into Washington, and turn right (east) on Highway 14. From Highway 14 turn left (north) on Highway 141 and wander through spectacular forests and across the White Salmon River to Husum. Turn left on Spring Creek Road, following the signs to WIND RIVER CELLARS. Once you are up there it feels as if you are truly in some other alpine country.

Kris and Joel Goodwillie took over Charles Hooper Family Winery in 1996, changing the name to Wind River Cellars, after Joel did a stint at Gallo.

White-water rafting fans can even book a trip through Wind River Cellars or River Drifters (800–972–0430), ending here at the winery with a fabulous lunch on the winery deck overlooking Mt. Hood. Mystery fans enjoy first Saturday Murder Mystery Dinner Theatre, June–September. Wind River also celebrates its new releases on Presidents' Day weekend in February.

Fine points: Featured wines: Chardonnay, Gewürztraminer, Riesling, Cabernet Sauvignon, Merlot, Pinot Noir, Syrah, Lemberger, Port, and Finale ice wines. Owners: Kris and Joel Goodwillie. Winemaker: Joel Goodwillie. Cases: 2,500. Acres: 12 planted of 17.

Wind River Cellars, 196 Spring Creek Road, P.O. Box 215, Husum, WA 98623; phone (509) 493–2324; e-mail kris@windrivercellars.com; Web site www.windrivercellars.com. Open 10:00 A.M.–6:00 P.M. daily. Visa and MasterCard. Wheelchair accessible.

From Hood River you can continue east to Washington's Tri-Cities and Walla Walla Valley appellations on Highway 14 on the Washington side, or cross the Columbia River at The Dalles, Biggs, or Umatilla. At Milton-Freewater you can turn north to Walla Walla.

Coming into Oregon from southern Washington in the Yakima Valley, Walla Walla, and/or the Paterson area, the best route is to cross the Columbia River from Highway 14 at Highway 142 into Biggs, a little town that clings to the hills above the Gorge. Highway 30 on the Oregon side is wider and straighter, with splendid views looking across at the Washington bluffs above the river. If it is late in the day, Biggs is a possible stopover, but The Dalles, 14 miles to the west, and Hood River, 22 miles farther along the Columbia, offer more in local amenities.

OREGON WINERIES TO WATCH

Oregon wineries are sprouting like wildflowers. Here we list new and smaller wineries to watch that are worth a trip to explore, many of which are off the beaten wine path. Wine collectors will enjoy discovering these new finds and investing in some really good wines.

CARLTON WINEMAKERS STUDIO, Oregon's first cooperative winery opened in fall 2002, Andrew Rich Vintner, Bryce Vineyard, Domaine Meriwether, Dominic, Hamacher Wines, Penner-Ash Wine Cellars, and Soter Vineyard; 801 North Scott Street, Carlton 97111; phone (503) 852–6100; Web site www.winemakersstudio.com. Cuneo Winery is next door.

CHAMPOEG WINE CELLARS, 5 miles west of Highway 5, next to Champoeg State Park; 10375 Champoeg Road NE, Aurora 97002; phone (503) 678–2144.

DENINO UMPQUA RIVER ESTATE, spectacularly sited on bank of south Umpqua River, also owns Denino's Ristorante Italiano in Roseburg; 451 Hess Lane, Roseburg 97470; phone (541) 673–1975; e-mail vinovino@internetcds.com.

EDEN VALE ESTATE, an active newcomer in the Rogue Valley; 2310 Voorhies Road, Medford 97501; phone (541) 512–2955; Web site www.edenvalewines.com.

EUGENE WINE CELLARS, award-winning "urban winery" in downtown Eugene; 255 Madison Street, Eugene 97402; phone (541) 342–2600; Web site eugenewinecellars.com.

MARQUAM HILL VINEYARDS, an ideal picnic spot on the way to Oregon Garden; 35803 South Highway 213, Molalla 97038; phone (503) 829–6677; e-mail jandmd@iglide.net.

MAYSARA ESTATE WINERY, a new (2001) entry in Yamhill Valley, already getting high ratings; 15765 Muddy Valley Road, McMinnville 97128; phone (503) 843–1234; Web site www.maysara.com.

MELROSE VINEYARDS, located on an historic site on the South Umpqua River 5 miles west of I–5, opened in fall of 2002; 885 Melqua Road, Roseburg 97470; phone (541) 672–6080.

NAMASTE VINEYARDS, hilltop tasting room just opened in natural environment to match philosophy of "peace, balance and harmony"; 5600 Van Well Road, Dallas 97338; phone (503) 623–4150; Web site www.namastevineyards.com.

ORCHARD HEIGHTS WINERY, just west of Salem and open daily in a region of successful wine production; 6057 Orchard Heights Road NW, Salem 97304; phone (503) 391–7308; e-mail oheightswinery@aol.com.

BRANDIED PEARS
from Ashley Campanella, Eden Vale Estate Winery

[Note: "Pears need about a month to absorb the brandy. Make before Thanksgiving for Christmas gifts."]

¼ cup fresh lemon juice (about 2 lemons)
5½ lbs Eden Valley Orchards Seckel pears
4 quarts water
1½ cups sugar
2 cinnamon sticks
3 cups brandy

Fill a large bowl half full of cold water and add lemon juice. Peel pears as carefully and smoothly as possible, leaving stems attached. Place pears in water as you peel them.

Combine sugar, cinnamon sticks, and 3 quarts water in a large stockpot. Drain pears and add to pot contents. Bring mixture to a boil, reduce heat, and simmer for ten to thirty minutes, depending on size and ripeness of pears.

Remove pears from liquid with slotted spoon and divide evenly among 3 quart jars.

Raise heat under pot to high and cook liquid until reduced to 2 cups, about fifty minutes. Remove from heat. Strain liquid into a bowl through a sieve lined with cheesecloth. Divide the liquid evenly among the jars and add about 1 cup brandy, or enough to cover pears, to each jar. Allow jars to cool and screw on lids. Refrigerate for several weeks before eating to allow flavors to develop. Makes about 3 quarts.

OREGON TASTING ROOMS

The following tasting rooms offer wines of several wineries, which is great for visitors with limited time. Here you will often find wines of specialty, family, and boutique wineries that don't have tasting rooms of their own.

Great Wine Buys (Starr & Brown Winery)
1515 NE Broadway, Portland; (503) 287–2897
Open 10:30 A.M.–7:00 P.M. Monday–Saturday; noon–5:00 P.M. Sunday

La Velle's Tasting Room (La Velle)
Fifth Street Public Market, Eugene; (541) 338–9857
Open 11:00 A.M.–6:00 P.M. Sunday–Thursday;
11:00 A.M.–10:00 P.M. Friday–Saturday

Oregon Wine Tasting Room (Amity Vineyards)
The Lawrence Gallery, 19690 Highway 18, McMinnville; (503) 843–3787
Tasting room open 11:00 A.M.–6:00 P.M. daily;
market 9:00 A.M.–6:00 P.M. daily

Oregon Wines on Broadway
515 SW Broadway, Portland; (503) 228–4655
Open noon–8:00 P.M. Tuesday–Saturday

Ponzi Wine Bar (Ponzi Vineyards)
Corner of SW Seventh and Highway 99, Dundee; (503) 554–1500
Open 11:00 A.M.–5:00 P.M. daily; later in summer

UMPQUA REGION

Dino's Ristorante Italiano and Wine Bar (DeNino Estate)
404 SE Jackson Street, Roseburg; (541) 673–0848
Open 5:00–9:00 P.M. Tuesday–Saturday

ROGUE REGION

Anna Maria's (Valley View Winery)
125 West California Street, Jacksonville; (541) 899–1001
Open noon–6:00 P.M. Wednesday–Sunday

OREGON COAST

Chateau Benoit Wine & Food Center (Chateau Benoit)
Factory Stores, 1524 East Devils Lake Road, Lincoln City; (503) 996–3981
Open 10:00 A.M.–5:00 P.M. daily

OTHER

Marquam Hill Vineyards Tasting Shop (Marquam Hill)
Sisters Drug Store, Highway 20, Sisters; (541) 549–2240
Open 11:00 A.M.–5:00 P.M. weekends

CHAPTER 2

WASHINGTON

*W*ashington State is known to many people outside its borders *for its fabulous forests, fabulous coffee, fabulous minds, and more fabulous coffee, most of which is centered in Seattle.*

Gradually and steadily the Evergreen State is gaining a reputation for its fine wines, made in gigantic wineries owned by huge corporations and in tiny enterprises owned by individuals. Outside the state, many wine aficionados have heard only of Columbia Crest and Chateau Ste. Michelle, which are components of a corporation that produces 75 percent of Washington's wines.

We suggest you visit their spectacular facilities to experience the elegance and luxury and taste their beautiful wines. We also highly recommend that you take the time to explore and visit smaller and medium wineries too, where you just might discover local secrets to some of the finest wines in the Northwest.

Which wineries you visit in Washington depends on where you begin and how much time you have. If you are based in Seattle on a brief trip, you might visit four wineries on Bainbridge, Vashon, and Whidbey Islands if you plan far enough ahead to call and make appointments. An hour's drive northeast from Seattle, you can visit another six wineries if you go to Woodinville (avoid commute hours, though).

We took ourselves on a motor trip that you can just barely compress into three or four days or stretch to a more comfortable week from Seattle to Yakima, Wapato, Zillah, Outlook, Granger, Sunnyside, Grandview, Prosser, Benton City, West Richland, the Tri-Cities area of Richland, Kennewick, and Pasco (which all run together), to Walla Walla and back to Portland, Oregon, via the Columbia River and the Columbia River Gorge to Hood River.

There are other area tours you may want to try. If you are in Oregon visiting the Hood River area wineries, you might head east and cross the Columbia River at Biggs, where there are a couple of decent motels and restaurants, and then continue eastward on Highway 14 to Columbia Crest Winery and slip up to the Tri-Cities area or go on to Walla Walla. Plan so that you're in Walla Walla on a weekend and maximize your visit to local wineries, several of which are closed during the week.

The Yakima Valley winery tour can easily take at least two days if you want to visit all twenty wineries. There are some exceptional small ones here, and the distances up local roads are often farther than wine association maps suggest. The Tri-Cities tour can take a full day or two, and the Spokane area wineries take a full day with some hefty driving.

The Evergreen State has four recognized viticultural appellations: Puget Sound, Columbia Valley, Yakima Valley, and Walla Walla Valley. The Yakima Valley and the Walla Walla Valley appellations are also located within the larger Columbia Valley region and appellation. Got that? And furthermore, there are five subappellations.

The Puget Sound appellation applies to wine made in the Puget Sound basin's temperate climate, reaching from Olympia up through Tacoma, Seattle, and the islands of Puget Sound past Bellingham to the Canadian border.

The Columbia Valley appellation covers Washington's largest viticultural region, stretching from Washington's Okanogan wilderness east to within 50 miles of Spokane, south to Yakima, and east along the Snake River to the Idaho border, then it squeezes down through the Tri-Cities area and gushes out again along the Columbia River on both the Washington and Oregon sides. More wine grapes are grown here than in any other region of the state.

The Yakima Valley appellation became Washington's first officially approved viticultural area in 1983. It runs from the Cascades' foothills on the west to the Kiona Hills near Richland on the east. The Yakima Valley region has the state's highest percentage of vineyard plantings per square mile in the state, partly due to the natural irrigation network provided by the Yakima River and the Roza and Sunnyside canals. Interstate Highway 82 runs right through the vineyards within this appellation, allowing relatively easy travel to its wineries.

The Walla Walla Valley runs through both Washington and Oregon and is primarily served by the city of Walla Walla.

Washington vineyardists and vintners have discovered microclimates and microsuitabilities within the appellations' geographic boundaries, resulting in at least five subappellations. They are Red Mountain–Benton County; Wahluke Slope, Royal Slope, and Cold Creek; Lower Snake River; Canoe Ridge; and Southwest Washington.

Red Mountain–Benton County contributes to outstanding Cabernet Sauvignons with grapes grown on the slope of Red Mountain that runs toward the Yakima River just above Benton City near Richland. Specialty: Cabernet Sauvignon.

Wahluke Slope, Royal Slope, and Cold Creek are all part of a strikingly beautiful high plateau that runs along the north side of the Columbia

River from Vantage to Othello. Specialties: Cabernet Sauvignon, Chardonnay, and others.

Lower Snake River includes vineyards planted on both sides of the rolling broad hills on both sides of the Snake River east of the Tri-Cities of Richland, Kennewick, and Pasco. Specialties: Merlot, Sauvignon Blanc, and Sémillon.

Canoe Ridge is a slightly remote, new grape-growing area located above Crow Butte State Park on the Columbia River and facing south-southeast toward the river near the Tri-Cities area. Specialties: Merlot, Cabernet Sauvignon, and Chardonnay.

The Southwest Washington appellation runs along the Lewis River in the north part of Clark County. Specialties: Pinot Noir and Chardonnay.

SOUTHWESTERN WASHINGTON

After you enter Washington on I-5 from Portland, Oregon, take exit 16 on your right eastward toward La Center for SALISHAN VINEYARDS to meet delightful wine pioneers Joan and Lincoln Wolverton. After 1.5 miles, cross a bridge over Lewis River's east fork, arriving at La Center, a giant metropolis of 800. Turn right just past the bank, go 1 block, then turn left on Aspen Street, which becomes North Fork Road. About 1 mile beyond La Center, you see the barn-like winery on the right. (See map on p. 78.)

Joan was a reporter for the *Seattle Times,* and Lincoln had a fresh master's degree in economics in 1971, when they decided to go country and planted their vineyard. Lincoln had been an exchange student in Dijon, France, where he caught the wine bug. Joan, however, ended up running the tractor and became Washington's first female expert winemaker. Lincoln helps out when not working as an economist for the utilities industry. They learned by their mistakes, raised two sons, and should write *The Grape and I* to regale readers with their adventures.

Situated only 30 miles north of Portland, Salishan (named for the Salish northwest Indians) is Washington's only winery in the same maritime region as northern Willamette Valley and, as Joan says immodestly, produces the best Pinot Noir in Washington.

Fine points: Featured wines: Pinot Noir, a Merlot-Cabernet blend, and Chardonnay. Owners: Lincoln and Joan Wolverton. Winemaker: Joan Wolverton. Cases: up to 500. Acres: 12 with 9 currently planted.

❦ *Salishan Vineyards, 35011 North Fork Road, La Center 98629; phone (360) 263–2713. Open 1:00–5:00 P.M. Saturday and by appointment. No credit cards. Wheelchair accessible.*

GREATER PUGET SOUND AREA

It seems as if half the world wants to move to Seattle, idealized by all the great minds attracted to Microsoft, a peaceful but booming downtown, good politics, good coffee, and a pace slightly slower than San Francisco, Los Angeles, and New York. Seattle makes a good launching pad for touring Washington's, or even British Columbia's, wine country.

Seattle's traffic patterns and freeways almost make sense when you've been there a few times, but initially they seem insane, including a freeway that obliterates the views—both of Seattle from the water and of the water from downtown Seattle.

An excellent transportation feature of this city is that you can ride its Metro buses for free all day in the downtown commercial core until 7:00 P.M.

Seattle now spreads in almost every direction, with Boeing and Microsoft employees leading the way along with all the rest of us looking for the perfect community. Traffic is terrible.

Pioneer Square, which seems boundless but stretches almost from the waterfront east to Second or Third Avenue, is old, charming Seattle where miners stopped for provisions on their way north to British Columbia and the Yukon in that ever-evasive quest for gold. It is an ideal place to deposit yourself if you only have a few hours in Seattle. You can take an excellent self-guided or guided Underground Tour complete with history and a half-hour walk. Underground shops abound here. Pick up the tour at First Avenue between Cherry and James at the totem pole.

We always stop first at Elliott Bay Book Company at First and Main, one of the best independent bookstores anywhere. No matter what time it is, we make an excuse to drop into the cafe downstairs for healthy, vegetarian-or-not food and excellent coffee.

Many of Seattle's finest private art galleries are located in Pioneer Square, so just enjoy a stroll in these few blocks and catch them as they come along.

For an excellent view of Northwest history, particularly regarding gold rush migration, be sure to visit the Klondike Museum at the Klondike Gold Rush National Park Visitor Center, 117 South Main Street.

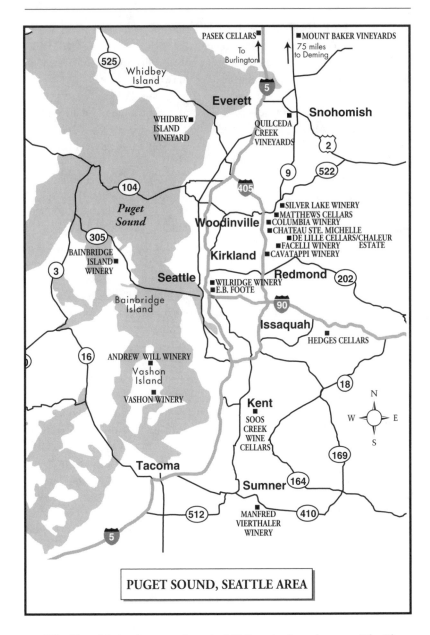

PUGET SOUND, SEATTLE AREA

Pike Place Market has spread up the hill from its focus between Pike Place, Post Alley, and First Avenue between Pike and Virginia Streets, with steps called the Pike Place Hillclimb connecting the market to the waterfront below. Here you can watch whole salmon (dead) sail by your head as shouting fishmongers order from each other and deliver extremely directly—at about eye level. Fresh local fish, produce, poultry, meats, flowers, baked delicacies, entertainers, souvenir shops, and excellent restaurants cram into two levels.

Two of our favorite restaurants in Seattle are Campagne and Cafe Campagne, the latter slightly less expensive and slightly more fun than the former. CAMPAGNE is in The Inn at the Market, 86 Pine Street (206–728–2800). Dinner entrees range from $24; a tasting menu is $60. Family dinner prices are much less during nonsummer months.

CAFE CAMPAGNE, 1600 Post Alley (206–728–2233), is Campagne's little sister and has an excellent wine bar and a changing menu. Have the lamb burger with aioli. French emphasis. Try CHEZ SHEA, 94 Pike Street (206–467–9990), a small restaurant with a great view of Puget Sound if weather permits.

On the lower level of Pike Place Market, John Farias sells beer- and wine-making supplies and makes his own wine for sale at MARKET CELLAR WINERY, a tiny shop right near Pike Place Brewery. A different fun experience!

Fine points: Featured wines: Chardonnay, Cabernet Sauvignon, Market Red, Merlot, and Gewürztraminer. Owner and winemaker: John Farias. Cases: 300. Acres: None.

Market Cellar Winery, 1432 Western Avenue, Seattle, WA 98101; phone (206) 622–1880; fax (206) 264–7886. Open 11:00 A.M.–6:00 P.M. Monday–Saturday. Visa, MasterCard, and Discover. Not wheelchair accessible.

Seattle Center, at the north end of downtown, is a world attraction. It was developed after the 1962 World's Fair was held here in the neighborhood known as the Denny Regrade. The Space Needle is Seattle's trademark at Fifth Avenue and Broad Street and offers fabulous views of Puget Sound and Seattle. It's open 8:00 A.M.–midnight, varying by weather and season. You can take Seattle's famous ninety-second Monorail ride out here from the downtown station in Westlake Center every ten to fifteen minutes. To get to Seattle Center you can take the Monorail or buses 3, 4, 6, or 16 to the Space Needle side, and buses 1, 2, 13, 15, and 18 stop on First Avenue North by the Coliseum. Lots of car parking is available, with valet parking for Space Needle restaurant customers.

Seattle's hottest new attraction is Microsoft original Paul Allen's Experience Music Project (EMP) near the Space Needle. EMP is an interactive center for pop, soul, jazz, country, hip hop, and rock and roll, with 80,000 artifacts, Turntable Restaurant, and Liquid Lounge. Phone (425) 450–1997; Web site www.emplive.com.

Don't miss the Children's Museum in the lower level of Center House, with hands-on exhibits and a child-size play neighborhood to delight us all. The Fun Forest amusement park covers the ground between the Space Needle and Center House, with rides divided between those for older and younger children, miniature golf, video arcade, refreshments, and souvenir shops. The Pacific Science Center, on the Second Avenue side of Seattle Center, holds the Planetarium, a Native American longhouse, science exhibits, a Laserium, and an IMAX movie theater. The Pacific Arts Center offers children's art classes and exhibits, and the Northwest Crafts Center exhibits and sells Northwest pottery and other crafts.

Kathleen's brother, Kirk Thompson, a longtime professor at Evergreen State University in Olympia, especially favors EL PUERCO LLORON. You can sit back and enjoy the informality, cheerful decor, great Mexican food cooked by Mexicans, and exceptional lemonade.

 *El Puerco Lloron, 1501 Western Avenue on the Hillclimb steps to Pike Place Market and the Aquarium, Seattle; phone (206) 624–0541. Open for lunch and dinner daily. Beer and wine. American Express, MasterCard, and Visa. Wheelchair accessible*

Kirk and his friends also always check in at the THAI RESTAURANT, near the Seattle Center. That is its name, its whole name. Just entering this place makes you feel soothed and safe, due partly to the almost embarrassingly wonderful

WINE SHOPS

If you can't leave Seattle but would like to buy some Washington wines to take home, try the following excellent wine shops.

Pike & Western Wine Merchants, Pike Place at Virginia Street (206–441–1307), has an excellent Northwest wine section among others, as well as tastings and winemaker dinners. Open 9:30 A.M.–6:30 P.M. Monday–Friday, 9:30 A.M.–6:00 P.M. Saturday, noon–5:00 P.M. Sunday.

McCarthy & Schiering, 2401B Queen Anne Avenue N (206–282–8500), is extremely popular with locals, who rely on owners Dan McCarthy and Jay Schiering for advice and tips. You can attend tastings here on Saturdays. Open 10:00 A.M.–5:00 P.M. Monday–Friday, 10:00 A.M.–6:00 P.M. Saturday.

and respectful service, cool Thai decor and music, and mouthwatering aromas. Watch for a few innovative twists on Thai menus you have seen before.

➤✴ *Thai Restaurant, 101 John Street at First Avenue, Seattle; phone (206) 285–9000. Open for lunch Monday–Friday, dinner daily. Full bar. American Express, MasterCard, and Visa. Wheelchair accessible.*

A special treat for food and wine lovers is the SPIRIT OF WASHINGTON DINNER TRAIN (800–876–7245), which you can ride from the Seattle suburb of Renton to Columbia Winery in Woodinville with views of Lake Washington, famous people's homes, and the Seattle skyline.

Within an hour's drive of downtown Seattle you can visit several of the best, largest, smallest, best known, and least known of Washington's wineries.

Bainbridge Island Winery (appointment only) is on Bainbridge Island, and Vashon Winery and Andrew Will Winery (both open by appointment only) are on Vashon Island. Both islands are short ferry rides from Seattle.

You can visit several fine wineries on Seattle's east side, conveniently located within commuting distance to Seattle in Woodinville, Belleview, Mill Creek, Snohomish, and Issaquah. These wineries seem even closer to Seattle than the Sonoma and Napa Valleys are to San Francisco and include the huge and elegant Chateau Ste. Michelle, Columbia Winery, Paul Thomas Winery, Silver Lake Sparkling Cellars, Red Hook Brewery, and Hedges Cellars in downtown Issaquah.

You can take the ferry from Seattle without a car and walk around downtown Winslow and to BAINBRIDGE ISLAND VINEYARDS AND WINERY. "This is strictly a family winery where four people do everything," according to co-owner JoAnn Bentryn.

Check out JoAnn's marvelous collection of antique wineglasses and wine-related antiques in the wine museum and tasting room in the handsome barn-like building. You can picnic in the fragrance garden and enjoy a self-guided educational tour of the vineyard and grape-growing process.

The Bentryns' first vines were planted in 1978 to produce German-style wines appropriate to Bainbridge Island's climate, and theirs is the only Seattle-area winery that actually grows its own grapes. Locals flock here to pick up their annual holiday Strawberry Wine. These wines are sold only locally and at the winery. Great vineyard tours at 2:00 P.M. Sunday.

Fine points: Featured wines: Estate-grown Müller-Thurgau and Dry Müller-Thurgau, Dry Madeleine Angevine, Pinot Noir and Pinot Gris, Late Harvest Botrytized Siegerrebe, and of course their "picnic wine," Ferry Boat White, and fruit wines. Owners: Gerard and JoAnn Bentryn. Winemaker: Gerard Bentryn. Cases: 3,500. Acres: 7.

MICROBREWERY ALERT!

The Seattle area is microbrewery and brewpub heaven. We will simply mention the best-known breweries that you might actually visit.

Hart Brewing Company, *91 Royal Brougham and 1201 First Avenue (206–682–8322), is an elegant taproom and show brewery. This is also the showplace of Thomas Kemper Brewery, part of Hart. The excellent food here elevates pub grub to a new orbit. Featured beers: Hefe Weizen, Wheaten Ale, Espresso Stout, Apricot Ale, and other seasonal specialties.*

Taste and watch at Pike Place Brewery, *1432 Western Avenue (206–622–3373), on the lower level of Pike's Place Market. You can also buy home brewing supplies at their shop across the street. Featured beers: Stout, Pale Ale, Porter, and East India Pale Ale.*

Hale's Ales Microbrewery, *4301 Leary Way NW (206–706–1544), is the largest producing brewery within Seattle. Check out this enormous state-of-the-art facility, to say nothing of the good beer and food. Featured beers: Wee Heavy, American Pale Ale, India Pale Ale, Amber Ale, and Honey Wheat.*

✻ *Bainbridge Island Vineyards and Winery, 682 Highway 305, Bainbridge Island 98110; phone (206) 842–9463; e-mail gbentryn@seanet.com. Open noon–5:00 P.M. Wednesday–Sunday, Saturday–Sunday only in January–February. No credit cards. Wheelchair accessible.*

Everyone needs to stop for lunch or dinner during a pleasant trip to Bainbridge Island. If you brought a picnic, enjoy it at the winery or at Waterfront Park right by where the ferry docks. You can also rent kayaks and canoes here for a leisurely paddle.

Maura and Aaron Crisp have turned a storefront next to the movie theater into a fine restaurant, RUBY'S ON BAINBRIDGE. To get here follow the signs toward the Fort Ward State Park Boat Ramp and then into Lynwood Center.

With the aroma of soups and garlic wafting through the air (ahhhh!), Maura and Aaron's cozy restaurant has a strong and grateful local following as well as plenty of business from commuters and tourists. All entrees are healthful and light combinations of local seafood, pastas, and produce.

❧ *Ruby's on Bainbridge*, 4569 Lynwood Center Road, Bainbridge Island; phone (206) 780–9303. Open for lunch and dinner Tuesday–Sunday, brunch Saturday and Sunday. Beer and wine. Visa and MasterCard; checks accepted. Wheelchair accessible.

Vashon Island is home to several companies that do business nationally from here and two small but excellent wineries. Only Vashon Winery is open to the public.

From Seattle, take I–5 south to the West Seattle Freeway and head west. This will become Fauntleroy. Follow Fauntleroy 4 miles to Fauntleroy/Vashon Ferry terminal. Take the ferry ($12.50 for car and driver) to Vashon Island. Follow Vashon Highway for 6 miles, turn right (west) on Cemetery Road, and drive 2 miles to the winery on the left.

VASHON WINERY's previous owners, Karen Peterson and Will Gerrior, produced four handmade wines: Cabernet Sauvignon from grapes grown at Portteus Vineyard near Zillah, Washington, as well as Merlot, Chardonnay, and Sémillon.

Ron Irvine, author of *The Wine Project: Washington State's Wine Making History* and former owner of Pike & Western Wine Shop in Seattle's Pike's Market, bought Vashon Winery in 2001. In addition to the above wines, Ron makes a great traditional cider.

❧ *Vashon Winery*, 10317 SW 156th Street, Vashon 98070; phone (206) 567–0055. Open by appointment noon–5:00 P.M. Saturday, Memorial Day–Labor Day, otherwise by appointment. Visa and MasterCard. Wheelchair accessible.

Whidbey Island is as culturally interesting as it is beautiful—one of those places we never want to leave but, certainly, the locals are glad we do, eventually. Heading north from the Bothell/Woodinville area on Highway 405, which merges with Highway 5, 11 miles north of Lynnwood on the left (west) is the road to Mukilteo and a twenty-minute ferry ride (auto or walk-on) to the southern tip of 45-mile-long Whidbey Island. You can also reach it by bridge on Highway 20 near the north end, or by ferry from Port Townsend on the Olympic Peninsula in the west.

Langley has especially wonderful cafes and restaurants, and more than its share of good bookstores: Boomerang Books and Moonraker Books. Downtown is two streets, basically, so don't get lost. There are two wine facilities of interest here: Whidbey Island Vineyard & Winery and Whidbeys.

To get to WHIDBEY ISLAND VINEYARD & WINERY, take the Clinton Ferry from Mukilteo and follow Highway 525 once you're on Whidbey Island. Turn north on Langley Road almost to the water and turn left to the winery.

The red barn marks Whidbey Island Vineyard & Winery. Delightful picnic space faces the vineyard and an old apple orchard. *Wine Spectator* praises Whidbey Island's 1995 Cabernet Sauvignon made from Yakima Valley grapes. This is a real family winery.

 Fine points: Featured wines: Estate-grown Island White, Chardonnay, Pinot Gris, Lemberger, Merlot, Syrah, Madeleine Angevine, Cabernet Sauvignon, Cabernet Franc, Sangiovese, Viognier, Siegerrebe, and rhubarb wine. Owners: Greg and Elizabeth Osenbach. Winemaker: Greg Osenbach. Cases: 3,500. Acres: 7.

꒱ *Whidbey Island Vineyard & Winery, 5237 South Langley Road, Langley 98260; phone (360) 221–2040; e-mail winery@whidbeyislandwinery.com; Web site www.whidbeyislandwinery.com. Open noon–5:00 P.M. Wednesday–Monday, May–October; Wednesday–Sunday, November–April. Visa and MasterCard. Wheelchair accessible.*

WHIDBEY ISLAND GREENBANK FARM was originally planted in loganberries in the 1940s, and local kids went to school in this barn in the early 1900s. The farm was recently purchased from Stimson Lane Vineyards & Estates (owners of Ste. Michelle, Columbia Crest, and a few other wineries) by island residents. You can take a self-guided tour of the loganberry farm and learn about making liqueurs, pick loganberries, taste northwest Washington wines, and buy picnic supplies to eat right outside on the lush lawns. The gift shop is better than many. Greenbank's wines are now made by Hoodsport Winery up the Olympic Peninsula.

꒱ *Whidbey Island Greenbank Farm, Wonn Road off Highway 525, Greenbank 98253; phone (360) 678–7700; fax (360) 678–3276; Web site www.greenbank farm.com. Open 10:00 A.M.–5:00 P.M. daily. Visa and MasterCard. Wheelchair accessible.*

Back on the Washington mainland, the beautiful and mostly woodsy Olympic Peninsula is one of those places we wish fewer visitors loved as we do, but then, we must share our national treasures. Three wineries here are open to the public daily; two only on weekends.

HOODSPORT WINERY is in an exquisite setting, nearly surrounded by national forests and Native American reservations. It conveniently fronts right on the highway in this area popular for waterskiing, scuba diving, shrimping, and oyster harvesting.

The Patterson family started out making fruit wines from locally grown berries and selling them to locals and a few visitors. Their well-known raspberry wine enabled them to plant varietal grapes as well.

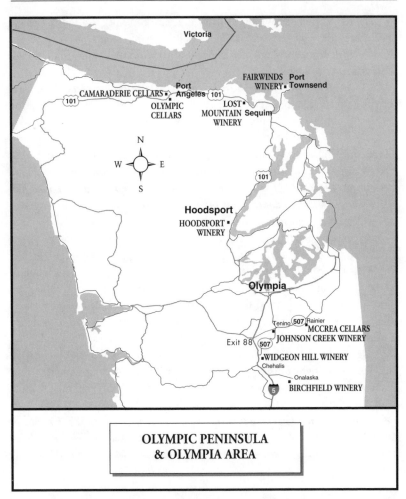

OLYMPIC PENINSULA
& OLYMPIA AREA

Peggy and Edwin Patterson host their annual grape-picking orgy in their vineyard on little Stretch Island every October, when friends and strangers come to help pick Island Belle grapes, a cross of a vinifera wine grape with a labrusca Concord eating grape, developed on this island in the early 1900s. Do not miss Hoodsport's raspberry wine chocolate truffles and their own canned smoked trout and smoked king salmon.

 Fine points: Featured wines: Raspberry, loganberry, and rhubarb wines; Island Belle Merlot; Cabernet Sauvignon; Cabernet Franc; Madeleine Angevine; Lemberger-Cabernet; Merlot; Chardonnay-Sémillon; Chardonnay; Island Belle Merlot; Syrah;

Sauvignon Blanc; Chenin Blanc; and Gewürztraminer, including some half bottles. Owner: Hoodsport Winery, Inc., Peggy Patterson, CEO. Winemaker: Edwin R. Patterson. Cases: 25,000. Acres: None, buy from Yakima Valley and Puget Sound.

*♥ *Hoodsport Winery, North 23501 Highway 101, Hoodsport 98548; phone (360) 877–9894 or (800) 580–9894; fax (360) 877–9508; e-mail wine@hoods port.com; Web site www.hoodsport.com. Open 9:00 A.M.–6:00 P.M. daily. Visa and MasterCard. Not wheelchair accessible, but staff will help.*

For a gustatory pause, try some oysters at the excellent fish-and-chips joint across the road from Hoodsport Winery in summer, or the Hoodsport Inn Restaurant in "downtown" Hoodsport north of the winery.

At Hoodsport Restaurant you will find hilarious attitude, history, fresh flowers on the tables, slot machines, a bar, a counter, local lore and gossip, and breakfast at 6:00 A.M. There is nothing on the entire menu more than $8.25.

The new freeway caused OLYMPIC CELLARS (formerly Neuharth Winery) to move from its great century-old barn a half-mile north of Sequim (say "skwim") to another charming old dairy barn up the road, halfway between Sequim and Port Angeles.

In 1999 Texas Instruments leader Kathy Charlton and friend Molly Rivard bought Olympic Cellars and were joined by winemaker Sara Gagnon. While the "girls" are very serious about traditional wines and win lots of gold medals, they have launched their sell-out "Working Girl Series," which includes Working Girl White and Go Girl Red. All profits from the Working Girl Series and T-shirts benefit the Gynocare Fund, which provides mammograms and gynecological exams and treatment for women without health insurance on the Olympic Peninsula. Let's help this cause! Don't miss the grape stomp party in September and the summer music series Friday nights.

Fine points: Featured wines: Riesling, Cabernet Sauvignon, Merlot, Dungeness White, Red, White Lemberger, Chardonnay, Red Lemberger (great values and named for nearby Dungeness River), Working Girl White, and Go Girl Red. Owners: Kathy Charlton and Molly Rivard. Winemaker: Sara Gagnon. Cases: 2,500. Acres: None, all grapes from Columbia Valley.

*♥ *Olympic Cellars, 255410 Highway 101, Port Angeles 98362; phone (360) 452–0160; e-mail wines@olympiccellars.com; Web site www.olympiccellars.com. Open 11:00 A.M.–6:00 P.M. daily. Visa, MasterCard, and Discover. Wheelchair accessible.*

To get to LOST MOUNTAIN WINERY, turn south from Highway 101 onto Taylor Cutoff Road, turn right on Lost Mountain Road to the winery (a total of 6 miles from Highway 101).

Taste wines in this serene old-growth forest of the Olympic Mountains foothills above Sequim in Lost Mountain's new tasting room, or catch the Annual Open Winery celebrating new releases during the last weekend in June and the first week of July.

Steve Conca took over from his father and makes fine Italian-style wines as his father and grandfather did.

Fine points: Featured wines: Lost Mountain Red (a blend including Muscat), Cabernet Sauvignon, Cabernet Franc, Merlot, Washington Syrah, and Pinot Gris. Owners and winemakers: Steve and Susan Conca. Cases: 1,500. Acres: None, buy from eastern Washington and California.

❧ *Lost Mountain Winery, 3174 Lost Mountain Road, Sequim 98382; phone (360) 683–5229; fax (360) 683–7572; e-mail wine@lostmountain.com; Web site www.lostmountain.com. Open daily Memorial Day–Labor Day, weekends April–May; call for seasonal hours December–March; make an appointment or take your chances. Visa and MasterCard. Entrance is wheelchair accessible, but rest room requires help from staff.*

Explore a little further into the lovely old town of Port Townsend and find FAIRWINDS WINERY, a small, hands-on, four-person winery. Approach Port Townsend on Highway 20, turn left on Jacob Miller Road to Hastings Avenue. From downtown Port Townsend, turn right off Highway 20, then right on Sheridan and left on Hastings to FairWinds Winery.

Labeling, corking, capping, and filtering are done either by hand or with devices designed and built at the winery, relying on innovation rather than automation. Two retired Coast Guard couples are having the time of their lives. "Y2K was never a problem here!" Home winemakers will enjoy.

Fine points: Featured wines: Gewürztraminer, Lemberger, Cabernet Sauvignon, and Aligote (only three acres grown in Washington). Owners and winemakers: Harvey and Zoe Ann Dudley, Michael and Judy Cavett. Cases: 1,000. Acres: None, buy from central Washington.

❧ *FairWinds Winery, 1924 Hastings Avenue West, Port Townsend 98368; phone (360) 385–6899. Open noon–5:00 P.M. Saturday–Sunday. Visa and MasterCard. Wheelchair accessible.*

CAMARADERIE CELLARS is just west of Port Angeles. Camaraderie's handcrafted wines are excellent and worth the trouble of calling ahead for rare tastes. One of the smallest wineries you will experience, it is just ¼ mile off Highway 101. A visit here is worth the trip for the fabulous Olympic Mountains views and some time in the woods.

Co-owner Vicki Corson says they believe strongly in "good food, good wine, good friends, and good music." While developing these superb wines, Don keeps his day job managing real estate for a lumber company.

Fine points: Featured wines: Premium Cabernet Sauvignon and Sauvignon Blanc, Bordeaux-style Cabernet-Merlot-Cabernet Franc blend, Merlot, Cabernet Franc, and Sauvignon Blanc-Sémillon. Owners: Don and Vicki Corson. Winemaker: Don Corson. Cases: 2,500. Acres: None, buy from eastern Washington.

➳ *Camaraderie Cellars, 334 Benson Road, Port Angeles 98363; phone (360) 452–4964; fax (360) 542–8196; e-mail corson@tenforward.com. Open 11:00 A.M.–5:00 P.M. weekends, May–October, or by appointment. Visa and MasterCard. Wheelchair accessible.*

Now we'll head for the northeast Seattle area, headquarters for the state's largest wine producers, and then on to Yakima Valley, Walla Walla, and Spokane.

Take I–405 north from Seattle, aiming for the town of Woodinville and SILVER LAKE WINERY. To get to Silver Lake, turn at exit 23 to Highway 522 going east toward Woodinville, and turn right (south) on 132nd Avenue NE.

Silver Lake started out making Spire Mountain Ciders from apples, pears, and other local fruits. Today they make their hard ciders and still wines in what had been French Creek Cellars, purchased in 1995, and they have developed a lovely tasting room, gift shop, and picnic grounds for your enjoyment. *Wine Spectator* recently rated their Chardonnay, Sémillon-Chardonnay, Merlot, Reserve Red blend, and Cabernet-Merlot blend all between 85 and 88. Their sparkling wines are produced under the Silver Lake Sparkling Cellars label.

Fine points: Featured wines: *Méthode champenoise* sparkling wines nearby at 15029 Woodville-Redwood Road, Cabernet Franc, Zinfandel, Merlot, Sauvignon Blanc, Off-Dry Riesling, Riesling Ice Wine, and Spire Mountain Hard Fruit Ciders. Owner: Washington Wine & Beverage Company. Winemakers: Mike Haddox and Cheryl Barber Jones. Cases: 40,000. Acres: None, buy from Yakima Valley and Columbia Valley.

➳ *Silver Lake Winery, 15029 Woodinvale-Redmond Road, Suite A, Woodinville 98072; phone (425) 486–1900; e-mail info@silverlakewinery.com; Web site www.silverlakewinery.com. Open noon–5:00 P.M. daily; closed Monday and Tuesday, January–March. Visa and MasterCard. Wheelchair accessible.*

MATTHEWS CELLARS is now actually open on Saturday, and what a treat! We met Matthew Loso at Blackwood Canyon Winery in eastern Washington. He's hardly ever at his own winery because he sells all of his wine in one week, except what he saves for his mailing list and some for visitors.

Matthew began making wine when he was only seventeen, worked in Seattle restaurants as a wine steward and, starting at the ripe old age of twenty-nine, now turns Yakima Valley varietals into some of the best Bordeaux-style wines around. Get on Matthew's mailing list—a must!

Fine points: Featured wines: Cabernet Sauvignon, Cabernet Franc, and Merlot. Owner and winemaker: Matthew Loso. Cases: 3,000. Acres: 8.

ᐳᏖ *Matthews Cellars, 18658 142nd Avenue NE, Woodinville 98072; phone (425) 487–9810; fax (425) 483–1652; Web site www.matthews cellars.com. Open noon–5:00 P.M. Saturday or by appointment.*

Next, get back onto Highway 522, then head south on SR 2 into Woodinville, turn right (west) on NE 175th, and then left (south) on SR 202, which is NE 145th. This will bring you to must-stops Columbia Winery, Chateau Ste. Michelle, and the Redhook Brewery.

Columbia and Chataeau Ste. Michelle are right across the road from each other, like dueling wineries. The ambience at the two wineries could not be more strikingly different. Redhook is just a smidge farther around the bend on the Columbia Winery side and is a great place for lunch while wine tasting.

COLUMBIA WINERY is Washington State's first premium winery, founded in 1962 by ten friends, seven of whom were University of Washington professors led by Dr. Lloyd Woodbume, dean of the College of Arts and Sciences. The founding ten called themselves Associated Vintners.

Wine Spectator gave high ratings to many recent vintages of Columbia's, including its 1995 Chardonnay, Sémillon, Pinot Gris, Gewürztraminer, Riesling, 1992 and 1993 Cabernet Sauvignon, 1994 Cabernet Franc, Syrah, and Merlot.

After leaving Dr. Woodbume's home garage in the 1970s, the winery effort moved several times and finally landed in its current majestic Victorian building in 1989. The interior is vast, peaceful, soothing, relaxed, casual, and elegant. One of the most interesting wine- and food-related book collections is here. Watch for the annual holiday cookbook sale.

Special note on Columbia's winemaker, Canadian David Lake: David joined Columbia in 1979 after spending ten years in the English wine trade and having already become the only Master of Wine in the United States in 1975. *Wine Spectator* called him the "Dean of Washington winemakers." David Lake is legendary, as are his wines, which can be ordered by visiting the winery's Web site.

Columbia is the destination of the Washington Dinner Train and also hosts several events annually, many of which pair wine and food, such as the Columbia Gorge Food Show, "Gorge"; Summer Fest; and Taste of Red as well as monthly classes.

Columbia's ownership recently changed its name from Corus Brands to Canandaigua Wine Company, and also owns Covey Run and Paul Thomas Winery.

 Fine points: Featured wines: Dry whites Riesling and Pinot Gris; Chardonnay; Gewürztraminer; David Lake's Signature series including Cabernet Sauvignons from the Otis, Red Willow, and Sagemoore Vineyards; and Cabernet Franc, Merlot, and Washington's first Syrah from Mike Sauer's Red Willow Vineyard. Owner: Canandaigua Wine Company. Winemaker: David Lake. Cases: 140,000. Acres: 1,600.

Columbia Winery, 14030 NE 145th, Woodinville 98072; phone (425) 488–2776; sales (425) 482–7300; fax (425) 488–3460; Web site www.columbia winery.com. Open 10:00 A.M.–7:00 P.M. daily. Visa, MasterCard, American Express, and Discover. Wheelchair accessible.

COLUMBIA WINERY

CHATEAU STE. MICHELLE and its sister winery, Columbia Crest, are the two biggest and most beautiful and luxurious wineries in the Northwest, as well as the flagships of Stimson Lane Vineyards & Estates, owned by U.S. Tobacco Co.

Strikingly breathtaking, with the feeling of a new Parisian park and estate combined, Chateau Ste. Michelle's grounds cover eighty-seven acres. The grounds were once the site of Seattle lumber baron Frederick Stimson's summer home, which was originally designed in 1912 by the noted Olmsted firm of New York. *Wine Spectator* gives it high marks for several wines, including Chardonnay (tied for best in the state), White Riesling, Sauvignon Blanc, Cabernet Sauvignon, and Merlot, and gave it a 95 for its 1995 Ice Wine Reserve. *Wine Enthusiast* rated Chateau Ste. Michelle's 1994 Chateau Reserve Merlot tenth among red wines with a score of 95 and its 1996 Johannisberg Riesling ($4.00) among its "100 Best Buys" for 1997.

Chateau Ste. Michelle is the oldest winery in Washington (1934); its Woodinville chateau was built in 1976. It offers many programs and events, including an exhilarating summer performing arts series. Culinary Director John Sarich creates special Pacific Northwest food and wine luncheons, dinners, cooking classes, and a popular summer concert series, "Summer Festival on the Green." Previous performers have included Tony Bennett, Mary Chapin Carpenter, and B. B. King. For schedules call (425) 488–3300.

In this complex you will also find an elegant wine tasting room and shop with excellent gourmet picnic supplies, wonderful cultural posters and gifts, and another large tasting bar. The main building, where tours begin every half hour, is elegant with deep red and blue rugs, Spanish-style tile, and earth-toned rustic plaster walls. Between this building and the shop, you can rest or nosh at green cafe tables.

Chateau Ste. Michelle's white wines are made here, while its red wines are made at their Canoe Ridge Vineyard (equally beautiful) in eastern Washington, 15 miles west of Paterson on the Columbia River (see page 144).

 Fine points: Featured wines: Columbia Valley Cabernet Sauvignon, Chardonnay, Chenin Blanc, Dry Riesling, Gewürztraminer, Johannisberg Riesling, Merlot, Sauvignon Blanc, Sémillon, White Riesling; Single Vineyard Wines Artist Series Meritage, Cold Creek Cabernet Sauvignon, Canoe Ridge Estate Chardonnay, Cold Creek Chardonnay, Indian Wells Chardonnay, Canoe Ridge Estate Merlot, Cold Creek Merlot, Indian Wells Merlot; Reserve Chardonnay, Merlot, Ice Wine, Late Harvest Sémillon, and Late Harvest White Riesling; Domaine Ste. Michelle's *méthode champenoise* Cuvee Brut, Extra Dry, and Blanc de Blancs; and sparkling wines. Owner: Stimson Lane Vineyards & Estates. White wine

OLD-FASHIONED SPAGHETTI SAUCE
from John Sarich, executive chef,
Chateau Ste. Michelle Winery

1 2-lb pork shoulder roast (or chuck roast)
1–2 Tbs olive oil
2 yellow onions, chopped
4 cloves garlic, finely chopped
¼ cup celery tops, chopped
1 carrot, grated
2 16-oz cans of ready cut tomatoes in juice, juice drained
1 6-oz can tomato paste
¼ cup Chateau Ste. Michelle Cabernet Sauvignon
pinch of sugar
salt and pepper to taste
pinch of allspice
2 Tbs fresh Italian parsley, chopped
1 Tbs fresh basil, chopped
1 Tbs fresh oregano, chopped

Salt and pepper pork shoulder roast. Brown roast well in olive oil in heavy saucepan. Remove roast and sauté onions, garlic, celery, and carrot until very soft. Add tomatoes. Mix tomato paste with Chateau Ste. Michelle Cabernet Sauvignon and add to sauce. Add sugar, salt, pepper, and allspice. Return roast to pan and cover. Simmer 1½ hours or until meat is literally falling apart. Remove meat and keep in warm oven. Add parsley, basil, and oregano to sauce and simmer fifteen more minutes.

Serve with spaghetti noodles accompanied with pork shoulder roast and Chateau Ste. Michelle Cabernet Sauvignon.

winemaker: Bob Bertheau; red wine winemaker: Ron Bunnell; sparkling wine winemaker: Rick Casqueiro. Culinary director: John Sarich. Cases: 975,000. Acres: 4,200 in Washington.

Chateau Ste. Michelle, 14111 NE 145th, P.O. Box 1976, Woodinville 98072; phone (425) 488–1133 or (800) 267–6793; fax (425) 415–3657; Web site www.chateau-ste-michelle.com. Open 10:30 A.M.–4:30 P.M. daily. Visa, MasterCard, and American Express. Wheelchair accessible.

MICROBREWERY ALERT!

Redhook Brewery *is where "craft brewery" Redhook actually makes its brew. Notice the almost abstract design of Redhook Brewery's angular tank buildings in contrast to Columbia Winery and Chateau Ste. Michelle Winery.*

Drive toward the back of the complex to the Forecasters Public House pub. To your left as you walk in are long fifties-style booths with rounded-edge purple tables. A subtle Jet Ski hangs from the ceiling in the middle of the room, just to set the tone. Enjoy the lush beer garden just on the other side of the plate glass windows, where cyclists pass by (or maybe stop) on the adjoining Sammamish Slough bike trail.

The food is advanced, healthy pub grub, which may include a Thai shrimp salad, jerk or honey-mustard chicken breast sandwiches, a substantial Greek plate, or rotini pasta with pesto and smoked sausage.

Daily brews are on the chalkboard over the bar/counter. Servers are young and extremely pleasant and well informed. Great weekend entertainment—the music, that is. Featured beers: Blackhook Porter, Hefe-Wiezen, IPA, Double Black Stout, ESB, and Blue Line special seasonal beers.

Redhook Brewery is at 14300 NE 145th, Woodinville; phone (425) 483–3232; Web site www.redhook.com. Call for current tour times. Open 11:00 A.M.–10:00 P.M. Monday–Saturday, 11:00 A.M.–7:00 P.M. Sunday. Visa, MasterCard, and American Express. Wheelchair accessible.

In Seattle, you can visit Redhook's location at 3400 Phinney Avenue (206-548-8000) in the old streetcar barn of the Seattle Electric Company. Sample the beers, excellent pub grub, and some imaginative specials.

REDHOOK BREWERY

If you are in the Woodinville area on a weekend afternoon, you might stop by FACELLI WINERY, located in a warehouse in an industrial park. To get there from I–405, take exit 23 east, which becomes Highway 522. From 522, take the Woodinville exit and keep right. At the second signal, turn right on NE 175th, cross the railroad tracks, and proceed to the stop sign. Turn left onto Highway 202 (Woodinville-Redmond Road NE). Go 1 mile and turn left into KS Business Park.

Veteran winemaker Louis Facelli is friendly, knowledgeable, and willing to explain. He and his family opened the small winery in 1988 after working in wines first in California and then Idaho. *Wine Spectator* praises its 1995 Chardonnay and 1994 Merlot.

 Fine points: Featured wines: Merlot, Cabernet Sauvignon, Riesling, Rosato, Sangiovese, Late Harvest Syrah, Lemberger, Fumé Blanc, Chardonnay, Cabernet Franc, and Syrah. Owners: The Facelli family. Winemaker: Lou Facelli. Cases: 4,000. Acres: None, buy from Columbia Valley and Yakima Valley.

🍇 *Facelli Winery, 16120 Woodinville-Redmond Road NE, #1, Woodinville 98072; phone (425) 488–1020; fax (425) 488–6383; e-mail facelliwinery@ msn.com; Web site www.facelliwinery.com. Open noon–4:00 P.M. Saturday and Sunday. Visa, MasterCard, American Express, and Discover. Wheelchair accessible.*

To get to HEDGES CELLARS tasting room from Seattle, take I–405 north, take the exit to I–90 going east toward Spokane, and take exit 17 off I–90. Exit 17 becomes Front Street; turn left on Gilman Boulevard at the Arco and Texaco gas stations. When we visited, the sky above was crystal clear, while pockets of fog hovered below the skyline in crevices of the surrounding forested hills.

Hedges was founded in 1987 by Tom and Anne-Marie Hedges, who opened this tasting facility in August 1997 with a cavernous, mural-covered interior. It is really just a tasting room for this fairly new winery in Benton City, using grapes planted in 1991 on Red Mountain, now a hopeful appellation in the Yakima Valley. The winery in Benton City is open to the public only by appointment, so this is your best chance at tasting excellent new wines.

The Hedges' goal is to provide affordable red wines, and they have succeeded, particulary with their Merlot–Cabernet Sauvignon blends. *Wine Spectator* has praised them in the "Best Buys" category and gave them a 92 (second in the state) for their 1993 Red Mountain Reserve Cabernet-Merlot blend, an 87 for the 1994 vintage, and an 86 for the 1996 Fumé-Chardonnay blend.

MURAL AT HEDGES CELLARS TASTING ROOMS

 Fine points: Featured wines: Red Mountain Reserve and Fumé-Chardonnay. (Note: Do not confuse this Red Mountain with a jug wine many of us drank too much of in the sixties and seventies.) Owners: Tom and Anne-Marie Hedges. Winemaker: Pete Hedges. Cases: 55,000. Acres: 70.

🍇 *Hedges Cellars, Tasting room, 195 NE Gilman Boulevard, Issaquah 98027; phone (425) 391–6056 or (800) 859–9463; fax (425) 391–3827; e-mail general@ hedgescellars.com; Web site www.hedgescellars.com. Open 11:00 A.M.–5:00 P.M. Monday–Saturday. Winery: 53511 North Sunset Road, Benton City 99320; phone (509) 588–3155. Open 11:00 A.M.–5:00 P.M. Friday–Sunday, April–December. Visa, MasterCard, and American Express. Wheelchair accessible.*

YAKIMA VALLEY

Yakima Valley is the primary wine region you should visit in Washington. Father Charles Pandosy, who eventually moved on to British Columbia, introduced irrigation to the Eyakima ("Well-Fed People") who were here first. The Yakima Indian Nation still controls about half of Yakima Valley's acreage. There are so many excellent wineries and fruit stands that you should plan at least two days, preferably four, to visit. The volcanic "Fruit Bowl of the Nation," this is

Washington's most fertile valley, spreading from the Rattlesnake Hills on the north to the Horse Heaven Hills to the south. We will guide you to all wine and food producers who welcome visitors.

Driving southwest from the Seattle area (after visiting wineries in Woodinville and environs), take I–90 to a junction with I–82 just south of Ellensburg where I–90 turns east toward Spokane in eastern Washington some 175 miles away.

Take I–82 southeast to Yakima. The total mileage from the Seattle area to Yakima is about 155 miles: 119 miles from Seattle to Ellensburg and 36 from Ellensburg to Yakima. Although several chain retail stores recently left Yakima, we find that this city, at the western head of the Yakima Valley, is a good home base for a wine tour of this end of the valley. The wineries are all southeast of Yakima.

You drive through spectacular rock formations and steep cliffs near North Bend (don't forget "Twin Peaks Pies"), and then you reach the Ireland-like green Snoqualmie Pass. You'll cross the Snoqualmie River several times and pass Lake Kachess, the gorgeous Wenatchee National Forest, access to the John Wayne Trail, and shocking clear-cutting.

About 5 miles later you can exit to the Indian John Hill Rest Area where the Upper Kitticas County Seniors Club "sells" excellent cookies, coffee, and punch to help keep drivers awake. Here the air is mountainy—clear, crisp, and refreshing, all at only 2,141 feet elevation.

When we asked the Club ladies how far it was to Yakima, one replied, "When you smell the cows, you know it's time to turn onto Highway 82 to Yakima." She was right, of course. There's a huge feed lot right near the turnoff.

You drop into the valley and rolling hills with high buttes off to the left—a real Wild West scene. Soon you're traveling through alfalfa and horse fields and true buttermilk skies. In a couple of miles you may want to stop at the Thorp Fruit & Antique Mall, where thirty dealers sell their treasures and you can buy great ciders.

Approaching Ellensburg you begin to see fields of growing corn. Remember to stop at the National Historic Museum at Ellensburg.

Take exit 110 to Highways 82 and 97 to Yakima. Crucial!

Immediately you begin to feel the richness of green or brown valleys and neatly laid out farms and apple orchards (so this is where they all come from). Down to the left don't miss the verdant valley that seems so incongruous with the desertlike hills on your right speckled with dry shrubs and gray-green sagebrush.

At 2,672 elevation you cross through the barren hills of Manastash Ridge. For miles you have been in a moonscape "military area," otherwise known as the Yakima Training Center, on a U.S. Military Reserve.

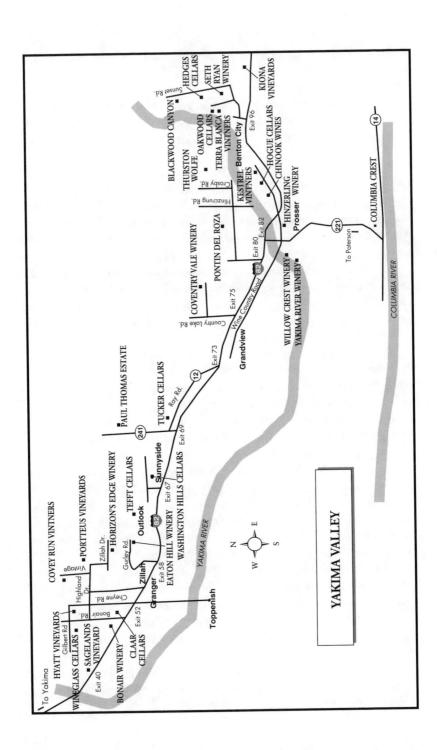

YAKIMA VALLEY

Soon you cross parched Squaw Creek, then in 5 miles you cross Umptanum Ridge, and in another 2.3 miles you begin the descent into Yakima County.

At exit 29 there's another Fruit, Antiques, and Espresso barn if you're desperate for any of the above. Exit 33B takes you to the Visitors Center, downtown, and to Yakima's Mall. East Yakima Avenue is Yakima's main street.

Yakima is relatively small and easy to walk. We stay at the Holiday Inn, which is more than adequate. This is the local favorite for community dinners and events and is practically next door to the Yakima Center, the local convention center, which also houses the Yakima Visitors Bureau, an especially helpful and informative group.

As we took our early morning walk through Yakima, it quickly became clear that the mall has, again, harmed a once-thriving downtown city center. But it actually looks as if downtown is starting to pick up speed again. Nordstrom is the downtown's anchor, with Seattle's Best Coffee nearby, along with Santiago's and Amigos.

On Front Street you can look from the outside at Yakima's Original (and only) Opera House, City Hall, and the train station. The western side of the train station still functions to process railroad passengers, while the eastern side houses shops.

On the south side of East Yakima Avenue there's an interesting small park with a one-in-every-town statue, but this one salutes the memory of Company E and Company F of Washington Volunteers and says on it that it was erected in 1802(!).

You can settle into tasting and noshing at BERT GRANT'S ALE (YAKIMA BREWING COMPANY), next to the train station and right across from the vacant old City Hall, which is for lease, in case you're interested, and next to the old train station.

Friendly locals like the outstanding inexpensive British-style pub food, from pasties to chips, soups, and Mexican specials. Featured beers: Scottish Ale, Amber Ale, India Pale Ale, HefeWeizen, Perfect Porter, Imperial Stout, and several seasonal brews.

❧ *Bert Grant's Ale (Yakima Brewing Company), 32 North Front Street near East Yakima; phone (509) 575–2922; Web site www.grants.com. Open for lunch and dinner daily. Beer and wine. MasterCard and Visa. Not wheelchair accessible.*

The CENTRAL WASHINGTON AGRICULTURAL MUSEUM is practically adjacent to Yakima. You can take South First Street south from Yakima into Union Gap, where it becomes Main Street, and continue south through Old Town and the Old Town Mill, or take exit 38 off Highway 82.

❧

Yakima Valley Museum & Children's Underground *displays special collections of American Indian art and artifacts; an exhibit on Yakima Nation life, historic tools, clothing, and furniture; and one of the largest collections of wagons, carriages, and early motorized vehicles west of the Mississippi. There is also a reconstruction of the late Yakima native Justice William O. Douglas's U.S. Supreme Court office.*

The Children's Underground invites kids of all ages to try its 2,500-square-foot hands-on learning center with interactive displays, videos, computer programs, games, and play areas. Don't miss the museum's Soda Fountain, a functioning 1930s art deco replica.

Directions: Take East Yakima Avenue heading west, turn left (south) on Sixteenth Avenue, go 4 blocks to first traffic light and turn right (west) on Tieton Drive, 4 blocks to Franklin Park and Yakima Valley Museum.

❧ *Yakima Valley Museum & Children's Underground, 2105 Tieton Drive (Franklin Park), Yakima; phone (509) 248–0747; fax (509) 453–4890; e-mail museum@wolfenet.com; Web site www.wolfe.net/museum. Admission: adults $3.00, students and seniors $1.50, children five and under free, entire family $7.00, members free. Museum open 10:00 A.M.–5:00 P.M. Monday–Friday, noon–5:00 P.M. Saturday and Sunday; Children's Underground open 1:00–5:00 P.M. Wednesday–Sunday. Mostly wheelchair accessible.*

This is a fifteen-acre developing museum in Fulbright Park, south of the original Yakima City, now called Union Gap, one of two towns in the state of Washington still operating under a territorial charter of the "Washington Territory."

Here you can see a fascinating collection of historic farm equipment, period household wares, hand tools, a Burlington-Northern boxcar full of railroad memorabilia, and nature trails lined with identified plants along Ahtanum Creek.

❧ *The Central Washington Agricultural Museum, 4508 Main Street, Union Gap 98903; phone (509) 457–8735 or 248–0432. Partially wheelchair accessible.*

toward Bonair Winery, Wineglass Cellars, Hyatt Vineyards Winery, Covey Run Winery, Portteus Vineyards, Horizon's Edge Winery, and Tefft Cellars and Eaton Hill Winery, whose addresses are technically in Outlook and Granger, respectively.

If you continue straight instead of turning on Cheyne, you end up on First Avenue, Zillah's main street and one you should visit.

To get to BONAIR WINERY, take Cheyne Road for 2 miles, turn left on Highland Drive for 1 mile, then left onto South Bonair Road, a rocky, bumpy gravel road through beautiful apple orchards. Go between the stone gateposts to the Tudor-style buildings.

Most Yakima Valley winemakers insist that you not miss Bonair, partly for its institutional humor, where they "make the best wines we can, and refuse to take ourselves seriously." Ask to meet Bung the wonder dog who watches over the Puryear family's "little hobby that got out of hand."

Both husband Gail and wife Shirley Puryear grew up in the Yakima Valley, where Gail served as school principal and Shirley was a dedicated social worker. They left the valley for California in the early sixties and fell in love with Napa Valley wines. They came back to Washington in 1969, hoping to grow grapes and make wine. They cleared the alfalfa from their new five-acre farm and hired prized winemaker Mike Januik as consultant. Shirley Puryear is a riot and usually wears her baseball cap to greet you.

The shady gazebo on the lawn and the lovely pond provide the perfect setting for a picnic while you feast your eyes on Mt. Adams off in the Yakama Indian Nation Reservation. Most of Bonair's wines and meads are available only at the winery, so make the most of your visit, and don't forget the art gallery.

Mead fans: Don't miss the unique Mead Faire the first weekend in October. Groups of twelve or more can call ahead for a special sitdown tasting.

 Fine points: Featured wines: Bonnie Bonair Red, Chardonnay, BFD Riesling, Cabernet Sauvignon, Merlot, Sunset Blush, Frankensauv, Camerlot, and four Mead wines: Sweet, Winter Solstice Mead, Sunset Blush Mead, and Chili Mead. Owners: The Puryear family, Shirley Puryear, Wine Goddess. Winemaker: (Mr.) Gail Puryear. Cases: 6,000. Acres: 35.

Bonair Winery, 500 South Bonair Road, Zillah 98953; phone (509) 829–6027; fax (509) 829–6433; e-mail winemaker@bonairwine.com; Web site www.bonairwine.com. Open 10:00 A.M.–5:00 P.M. daily; 10:00 A.M.–4:30 P.M. weekends in midwinter, or by chance during the week. Visa and MasterCard; checks accepted. Wheelchair accessible.

BONAIR WINERY

When you leave Bonair, go back north on South Bonair Road and cross Highland. Keep going about ½ mile to WINEGLASS CELLARS on your left.

At Wineglass Cellars, Linda and David Lowe produce small lots, and David's computer industry job keeps him away from the winery during the week. Nevertheless, Wineglass celebrates its tenth anniversary in 2004.

 Fine points: Featured wines: Zinfandel, Cabernet Sauvignon, Merlot, Chardonnay, Capizinno, Rich Harvest red blend, and very special Fran's White. Owners: David and Linda Lowe. Winemaker: David Lowe. Cases: 3,000. Acres: None, buy locally.

↝ *Wineglass Cellars, 260 North Bonair Road, Zillah 98953; phone (509) 829–3011; fax (509) 829–6666; e-mail wgcellars@attglobal.net; Web site www.wineglasscellars.com. Open 10:30 A.M.–5:00 P.M. Friday–Sunday, Presidents' Day through Thanksgiving; closed December–February. Visa and MasterCard. Wheelchair accessible.*

From Wineglass or Bonair, take Bonair Road north about 1.2 miles and turn right on Gilbert Road to HYATT VINEYARDS WINERY. You'll know you're here when you see the windmill on the right and pass through the iron gateposts that look like velvet.

The Hyatts began growing Concord grapes in the Yakima Valley in the early seventies to supply the local juice and jelly makers. They became intrigued with growing wine grapes, initially planting ninety-seven acres and maturing into one of the finest wineries around.

Their Chardonnay, Johannisberg Riesling, and 1996 Black Muscat Ice Wine have received scores above 85 from *Wine Spectator.* Hyatt's Old West Wine Fest in late September features lunch, a wild band, and local television newsman Dave Ettle's card tricks.

Fine points: Featured wines: Chardonnay, Fumé Blanc, Johannisberg Riesling, Black Muscat, Syrah, Merlot, Cabernet Sauvignon, Cabernet-Merlot, Late Harvest Riesling, and a special ice wine. Owners: Leland and Lynda Hyatt. Winemaker: Greg Chappell. Cases: 30,000. Acres: 147.

❧ *Hyatt Vineyards Winery, 2020 Gilbert Road, Zillah 98953; phone (509) 829–6333; fax (509) 829–6433; e-mail hyattvineyards@msn.com; Web site www.hyattvineyards.com. Open 11:00 A.M.–5:00 P.M. daily spring, summer, and fall; 11:00 A.M.–4:30 P.M. winter, weekends only in February. Closed January. Visa and MasterCard; checks accepted. Wheelchair accessible.*

To get to COVEY RUN VINTNERS, the closest and next winery, turn right on Gilbert Road when you come out of Hyatt and then turn right (south) again on Roza Drive, which to the south becomes Fifth Avenue in Zillah. Turn left (east) on Highland Drive, and then in 1½ miles turn left (north) on Vintage Road past the Let Annie Do It Trading Post, unless you want to stop. We did!

Notice the lush apple orchards and the heavily laden branches barely holding up those succulent round apples. The pavement ends on Vintage Road, but you don't. Keep going and turn left uphill into Covey Run's driveway.

Covey Run began as Quail Run Vintners in 1980 and flew off to a great start, distracted only slightly by California's Quail Ridge Winery's successful legal efforts to force Washington's Quail Run to change its name. When Associated Vintners acquired Quail Run, it changed the name to Covey Run. Associated Vintners has changed its name to Corus Brands, which recently sold Covey Run to Silver Lake Vintners, parent company of Silver Lake Winery and Silver Lake Sparkling Cellars.

The rocky drive up here, the beautiful concrete and cedar building, and the breathtaking view of what seems like the entire Yakima Valley with its shades of green and purple, Horse Heaven Hills, and Mt. Adams in the distance, all make it worthwhile. To say nothing of the wine. Inhale the sweet air and view of rolling peach and apple orchards and vineyards that seem to go on forever.

The wine vats are right in the tasting room separated from you by only a thin glass window, and the wine shop sells eco-fabric clothing made from recycled cotton. *Wine Spectator* rates its 1995 Gewürztraminer 89, 1996 Riesling 88, 1995 Chardonnay 87, and 1996 White Riesling 86.

 Fine points: Featured wines: Johannisberg Riesling, Dry Riesling, Late Harvest Riesling, Sémillon, Sémillon-Chardonnay, Chenin Blanc, Fumé Blanc, Chardonnay, Gewürztraminer, Lemberger, Merlot, Morio Muskat, and Icewine Riesling and Chenin Blanc, plus Reserves. Owner: Silver Lake Vintners. Winemaker and manager: Kerry Norton. Cases: 150,000. Acres: 180.

❧ *Covey Run Vintners, 1500 Vintage Road, Zillah 98953; phone (509) 829–6235; fax (509) 829–6895; Web site www.coveyrun.com. Open 10:00 A.M.–5:00 P.M. Monday–Saturday, noon–5:00 P.M. Sunday. Visa, MasterCard, American Express, and Discover. Wheelchair accessible.*

Now, on to PORTTEUS VINEYARDS. Get yourselves back to Highland by going down Vintage, and follow Highland east. In about 1.8 miles the pavement ends and it becomes a gravel road. When you reach the T, turn left and wind your way toward Portteus, with vineyards on your left and orchards on your right. Even though Portteus's address is on Highland Road, you have to turn left up Houghton Drive toward the Rattlesnake Mountains for about 0.8 mile.

Paul Portteus III started to make beer on his Lake Union houseboat when he was an underage nineteen, and for his twenty-first birthday he received a box of twenty-one wines from around the world. In 1982 Paul and his wife, Marilyn, planted their forty-seven-acre vineyard on what they believe is the finest wine grape growing land in Washington.

The winery is the building on the left as you arrive. (We accidentally walked right into the house on the right.) As you enter the one-room winery, you are greeted instantly by a dusty and well-used Ping-Pong table and three large vats. Paul Portteus holds court at the tasting bar to the right. Knowledgeable, generous with information, and lots of fun, Paul was the first winemaker in Washington to make Zinfandel.

 Fine points: Featured wines: Chardonnay, Rattlesnake Ridge Red, hearty Cabernet Sauvignon, Zinfandel, Merlot, Cabernet Franc, Petite Syrah, Sangiovese, and Port. Owners: The Portteus family. Winemaker: Paul Portteus III. Cases: 5,000. Acres: 47.

❧ *Portteus Vineyards, 5201 Highland Drive, Zillah 98953; phone (509) 829–6970; fax (509) 829–5626; e-mail paul@portteus.com; Web site www. portteus.com. Open noon–5:00 P.M. daily. Visa and MasterCard. Wheelchair accessible.*

In the next cluster you can visit Horizon's Edge Winery, Tefft Cellars, and Eaton Hill Winery. We will take you to these from Portteus, although you might want to take a break for lunch.

From Portteus Vineyards, come back down to the paved part of Highland Drive, turn right onto it, then left on Lucy Lane, and left again onto East Zillah Drive past Thacker Road to HORIZON'S EDGE WINERY.

After getting a degree in zoology from the University of Montana and studying viticulture and enology at U.C. Davis, Tom Campbell worked as assistant winemaker at Jekel Vineyards in California, cellarmaster at Chateau Ste. Michelle's Grandview winery, and winemaker at Tucker Cellars and Stewart Vineyards while helping Mike Moore set up Blackwood Canyon. He found his spot of heaven right here in the Yakima Valley and founded Horizon's Edge in 1985. Hemma Campbell is a pharmacist in Yakima where she met store manager and pre-med student David Padgett. Dave began to deliver wine and work in Horizon Edge's tasting room. Instead of going off to medical school, Dave bought the winery with his wife, Lisa.

Take in the view that includes Mt. Adams and Mt. Rainier on a clear day, picnic under the grape arbor next to the winery, and stroll freely through the vineyard.

Fine points: Featured wines: Dry, sweet, and Nouveau Riche Muscat Canelli; Monster Chardonnay; Champagne; Cabernet Sauvignon; Dry Riesling; Dry Gewürztraminer; Fumé Rosé; Devil's Canyon red table wine; Pinot Noir; Merlot; and Cream Sherry. Owners: Dave and Lisa Padgett. Winemaker: Dave Padgett. Cases 1,200. Acres 20.

❧ *Horizon's Edge Winery, 4530 East Zillah Drive, Zillah 98953; phone (509) 829–6401; e-mail yvwine@aol.com. Open 10:00 A.M.–5:00 P.M. daily, April–October; call ahead in winter. Visa and MasterCard. Not wheelchair accessible, but staff will bring wines downstairs.*

To get to Tefft Cellars and Eaton Hill Winery, come out of Horizon Edge's drive, turn left (west) on East Zillah Drive, left on Thacker Road, and right on Gurley Road. From Highway I–82 take exit 58 to the north side of the highway, turn right (east) on Van Belle Road, left on Beam Road, and right on Gurley Road, which becomes Independence Road. You will see the sign for Tefft Cellars and Outlook Inn, the Teffts' bed-and-breakfast.

TEFFT CELLARS is a winemaker's winery. Restaurant and winery hosts say, "Be sure you go to Tefft" or "Have you been to Tefft?"

Both Joel and Pam Tefft honed their winemaking skills by working as volunteers at nearly every winery in the area to fill in for family or staff members, thus learning on the spot from some of the best. Joel served as winemaker at both Hyatt Vineyards and Stewart Vineyards.

Tefft's Cabernet and Merlot won the Governor's Trophy three out of four years for "Best Red." *Wine Spectator* rated the Cabernet 88 and the Merlot 87, while its 1994 Cabernet Sauvignon received an 85.

The Teffts honor local waterfowl in their sensuous label designs, with the motto "Elegance, Finesse, Harmony." Either Joel or Pam or both greet you in the friendly tasting room, where you just might want to move in.

 Fine points: Featured wines: Cabernet Sauvignon, Merlot, Sangiovese, Proprietor's Red table wine (Bordeaux-style blend of Cabernet Sauvignon, Merlot, and Cabernet Franc), Pinot Grigio, Nebbiolo, Syrah, Pinot Noir Port, Rosey Outlook, and dessert-style wines including River Mist sauterne style, Black Ice Wine (Muscat Hamburg), Champagne, Cream Sherry, Cabernet Port, and Starboard port-style wine from huckleberries. Owners: Joel and Pam Tefft. Winemaker: Joel Tefft. Cases: 5,000. Acres: 12.

❧ *Tefft Cellars, 1320 Independence Road, Outlook 98938; phone (509) 837–7651; fax (509) 839–7337; Web site www.tefftcellars.com. Open 11:00 A.M.–5:00 P.M. daily. Note: The Teffts operate the three-room Outlook Inn bed-and-breakfast next door to the winery with reasonable rates of $50–$75 per night. Visa and MasterCard. Wheelchair accessible.*

Next is EATON HILL WINERY, which will bring you back closer to Zillah and Toppenish for lunch or dinner. From Tefft Cellars turn left on Independence Road, which becomes Gurley Road to the west. After you pass Beam Road, Eaton Hill will be on the left. Notice the famous Yakima Valley hop fields with the tall prop posts.

If you come from I–82, take exit 58 to the north side of the freeway, turn right on Van Belle Road, left on Beam Road, and left again on Gurley Road to Eaton Hill Winery.

Eaton Hill's tasting room is one of the more unusual and interesting anywhere. The winery and tasting room are located in a cement block building built in 1933 as a fruit and vegetable cannery, behind the house built in 1906 by Floyd Rinehold, a Yakima Valley master builder, for his bride, Emma Eaton. Cyclists and RVs welcome.

 Fine points: Featured wines: Cabernet Sauvignon, Cabernet Franc, Muscat, Sémillon, Merlot, Riesling, Gewürztraminer, Cabernet Port, and Orange Muscat. Owners: Edwin and JoAnn Stear. Winemaker: Gary Rogers. Cases: 1,500. Acres: None, buy from other locals.

❦ *Eaton Hill Winery, 530 Gurley Road, Granger 98932; phone (509) 854–2220 or (866) EATON HILL; fax (509) 854–2508. Open 10:00 A.M.–5:00 P.M. Friday–Wednesday; noon–4:00 P.M. daily in December–January. Visa, MasterCard, and American Express. Wheelchair accessible.*

EL RANCHITO RESTAURANT, TORTILLA FACTORY, BAKERY, AND GIFT SHOP in Zillah is south of town (don't give up) on First Avenue before it merges into the Yakima Valley Highway.

El Ranchito's mission is to serve the local Hispanic population, and everyone wins. You order at a counter by number in English or Spanish, and individual requirements are tolerated. Local businesspeople and workers of every background hang out here. There is nothing, nada, on the menu over $8.00, except a pound of BBQ beef at $9.50.

The gift shop sells authentic Mexican goodies. We even bought our children blue-and-white speckled cooking spoons like the ones their grandmother bought us in Mexico thirty years ago. El Ranchito makes tortillas for most of the grocery stores in the area.

❦ *El Ranchito Restaurant, Tortilla Factory, Bakery, and Gift Shop, 1319 First Avenue, Zillah 98952; phone (509) 829–5880. Open for breakfast, lunch, and dinner. Beer and wine. American Express, MasterCard, and Visa. Wheelchair accessible.*

Mid Valley Performing Arts presents at least two musicals or other plays every summer at the restored LIBERTY THEATRE in Toppenish. Try the dinner show for $50 including dinner, show, tax, and gratuity Friday and Saturday evenings and Sunday at 3:00 P.M., or a Saturday luncheon show for $45 at noon through the summer—first Friday in July through August.

❦ *Dinner Theatre at the Historic Liberty Theatre, 211 South Toppenish Avenue, Toppenish 98948; phone (509) 865–5995. Visa and MasterCard. Wheelchair accessible.*

Thirty-eight miles southeast of Yakima on Highway 82, in the heart of the valley, is Sunnyside, centered just to the east of the highway, which is paralleled on its north side by the Yakima Valley Highway (Highway 12), an old two-laner. The lower Yakima Valley is home to an abundance of farm produce, wine grapes, wine, and Christian churches. They're all easy to find and definitely have their seasons.

On your arrival, try WASHINGTON HILLS CELLARS. To get here take exit 67 off I–82 for 0.3 mile, turn left on Midvale, go under the freeway, and Midvale becomes First Street. Turn right at Lincoln Avenue, and Washington Hills Cellars is immediately on your right.

Washington Hills looks like an old dairy because it was a 1940s Carnation Dairy plant and later became Cascade Estates Winery. Harry Alhadeff and Brian Carter make excellent wines and show special talents at marketing them, resulting in one of the Northwest's largest and most successful wineries.

Washington Hills' other labels include APEX and W. B. Bridgman, named for Sunnyside's pioneer lawyer–grape grower–vintner. Instead of the oyster crackers many Washington wineries serve to cleanse your palate, Washington Hills offers bowls of chocolate chips!

Five of their 1995 wines received *Wine Spectator* ratings from 86 to 90, including the APEX Cabernet Sauvignon, Washington Hills Sémillon-Chardonnay blend, Bridgman Merlot, Washington Hills Johannisberg Riesling, and Bridgman Syrah.

Fine points: Featured wines: APEX Outlook Chardonnay, Cabernet Sauvignon, Merlot, and Gewürztraminer Ice Wine; Washington Hills blends and Chardonnay, Gewürztraminer, Dry Riesling, White Riesling, Dry Chenin Blanc, Sémillon, Cabernet Sauvignon, and Merlot; Bridgman Chardonnay, Merlot, and Cabernet Sauvignon. Owners: Harry Alhadeff and Brian Carter. Winemaker: Brian Carter. Cases: 200,000. Acres: 95.

❧ **Washington Hills Cellars**, *111 East Lincoln Avenue, Sunnyside 98944; phone (509) 839–WINE (9463) or (800) 814–7004; fax (509) 839–6155; e-mail winery@washingtonhills.com; Web site www.washingtonhills.com. Open 9:00 A.M.–5:00 P.M. daily. Visa and MasterCard. Wheelchair accessible.*

To get to TUCKER CELLARS from Washington Hills, turn right as you come out of Washington Hills' driveway on Lincoln for about 2 miles. Take a soft right onto Yakima Valley Highway (12) and follow it 2 more miles to Ray Road. Turn left to Tucker Cellars and Tucker Farms Produce Barn. Directions from I–82: Take exit 73, head northwest on Yakima Valley Highway (12), and turn right (north) on Ray Road to the winery and produce barn.

The Tucker family has been growing grapes, asparagus, spinach, and sugar beets here since 1933 and established their winery in 1981, making them pioneers in the Washington wine business. First Melvin and Vera Tucker sold grapes to William B. Bridgman, the Canadian-born leader of Washington's grape growers and vintners.

The huge doors to the produce market open wide on the left; the winery tasting room doubles as farm office. Besides the very good, modestly priced wines, you can buy jarred vegetables and popcorn made from Tucker produce. We love the asparagus and green beans. Great picnic lawn.

Fine points: Featured wines: Johannisberg Riesling, Chenin Blanc, Chardonnay, Gewürztraminer, Pinot Noir, Muscat Canelli, and a special rosé of Indian Summer White Pinot Noir and Gewürztraminer. Owner: Rose Tucker. Winemaker and manager: Randy Tucker. Cases: 12,000. Acres: 70 in wine grapes, 500 total.

❧ *Tucker Cellars and Tucker Farms Produce Barn, 70 Ray Road, Sunnyside 98944; phone (509) 837–8701; fax (509) 837–8701; e-mail wineman@tdevar. com; Web site www.businesslink.com/tucker. Open 9:00 A.M.–5:00 P.M. daily, summer; 9:00 A.M.–4:30 P.M. winter. Visa, MasterCard, and American Express. Wheelchair accessible.*

To experience a smaller winery, take exit 80 or 82 off I–82, heading north on Hinzerling Road past Johnson, Kingtull, and McCreadie Roads. New county signs direct visitors to all local wineries. PONTIN DEL ROZA will be on your left. "Roza" refers to the Roza Canal irrigation project that transformed the Yakima Valley from a dustbowl desert to the Northwest's fruit basket.

WHITE FISH WITH LEMON AND CAPER SAUCE
from Randy Tucker, Tucker Cellars

⅓ *cup chicken broth*
¼ *cup Tucker Chardonnay wine*
1½ *tsp cornstarch mixed with 1 Tbs water*
1 *tsp grated lemon peel*
1 *tsp sugar*
24-oz *whitefish steak*
2 *Tbs lemon juice*
1½ *Tbs capers*
coarsely ground pepper (optional)

In a 1 to 1½ quart pan combine broth, wine, cornstarch mixture, lemon peel, and sugar. Set aside.

Fish may be baked, broiled, or steamed. Cook fish until it is no longer translucent but is still moist looking in the center (five to ten minutes).

While fish is cooking, quickly stir chicken broth mixture over high heat until boiling. Add lemon juice and drained prepared capers and pour over cooked fish.

Sprinkle with pepper and serve. Serves 4.

Angelo Pontin planted terraced vineyards like his family's in Italy here in the 1920s. In the 1950s Angelo's son Nesto and his wife, Dolores, farmed this land north of Prosser, and in 1975 they made a pilgrimage to the original family vineyards in the hills of Italy, finding their roots in more ways than one. Their children, Scott, Colleen, and Diane, now farm and run the winery, and usually you will be able to chat with one of the Pontins in the tasting room.

Fine points: Featured wines: Chenin Blanc, White Riesling, Pinot Grigio, Sangiovese, Merlot, and Cabernet Sauvignon. Owners: The Pontin family. Winemaker: Scott Pontin. Cases: 5,000. Acres: 100 planted of 300.

➶ *Pontin del Roza, 35502 North Hinzerling Road, Prosser 99350; phone (509) 786–4449; e-mail pontindelroza@msn.com. Open 10:00 A.M.–5:00 P.M. daily. Visa and MasterCard. Wheelchair accessible.*

To get to WILLOW CREST WINERY, take exit 80 off Highway 82 (first Prosser exit) and follow signs to wineries. One of Washington's newest wineries, Willow Crest is nestled in hundreds of acres of vineyards. Enjoy the panoramic view, beautifully renovated farmhouse, and picnic area.

Fine points: Featured wines: Pinot Gris, Syrah, Mourvedre, Cabernet Franc, Sangiovese blend, Cabernet Sauvignon rosé, Black Muscat, Cabernet/Syrah blend, Syrah Port, and Sparkling Syrah. Owners: David and Mandy Minick. Winemaker: David Minick. Cases: 5,000. Acres: 185.

➶ *Willow Crest Winery, 55002 North Gap Road, Prosser 99350; phone and fax (509) 786–7999. Open 10:00 A.M.–5:00 P.M. Friday–Monday. Visa and MasterCard. Wheelchair accessible.*

Head back toward I–82 and cross it and the Yakima River on Hinzerling Road to downtown Prosser and Hinzerling Winery, Yakima River Winery, Chinook Wines, The Hogue Cellars, Thurston Wolfe, and Kestrel Vintners. All six wineries are close together and make an excellent afternoon tasting tour.

HINZERLING WINERY is Yakima Valley's oldest family-owned and -operated winery, founded in 1976 in a garage by Mike Wallace, who began growing grapes here in 1972. The tasting room is small, but the wines are special, and Wallace is a font of wine knowledge and is locally famous for his opinions.

In the late 1960s Wallace studied enology and viticulture at the University of California at Davis and worked as research assistant to Dr. Walter Clore, known in Washington as "Mr. Grape."

Mike has served as chair of the Washington Wine Institute and as a consultant to other wineries, including Preston. The entire family works in the winery and are often on hand to meet you. Be sure to try their Rainy Day Fine Tawny Port and Three Muses Ruby Port.

Fine points: Featured wines: Cabernet Sauvignon, Merlot, and Dry Gewürztraminer. Dessert wines include Angelica, Vintage port, and Muscat. Owners: The Wallace family. Winemaker: Mike Wallace. Cases: 1,500. Acres: None, buy from locals.

✢⚘ *Hinzerling Winery, 1520 Sheridan at Wine Country Road, Prosser 99350; phone (509) 786–2163 or (800) 727–6702; fax (509) 786–2163; Web site www.hinzerling.com. Open 11:00 A.M.–5:00 P.M. Monday–Saturday, 11:00 A.M.–4:00 P.M. Sunday; call for winter hours. Visa and MasterCard. Wheelchair accessible.*

If you are willing to backtrack slightly and are curious about fine dessert wines, you might want to try YAKIMA RIVER WINERY, obviously named for its location. Take exit 80 or 82 to Wine Country Road, turn southwest onto North River Road, which makes a couple of turns and lapses into Buena Vista Road, but be sure to follow the river.

A former welder and steamfitter from upstate New York, John Rauner and his wife, Louise, sipped some Yakima Valley wines and decided to head west to make their own. They started their winery in 1978, and in 1983 moved the winery from their home garage into a big red barn.

Their dessert wines have been called "delicious" and "harmonious," and *Wine Spectator* rated their port at 87. Recently the Rauners converted to making red wines only to concentrate on perfection, and the results are in— don't miss the Merlot.

Fine points: Featured wines: John's Vintage Port, Cabernet Sauvignon, Merlot, Cabernet/Merlot blend, Shiraz Port, and two types of Lemberger. Owners: John and Louise Rauner. Winemaker: John Rauner. Cases: 12,000. Acres: 2.5 experimental, buy from four local growers.

✢⚘ *Yakima River Winery, 143302 West North River Road, Prosser 99350; phone (509) 786–2805; fax (509) 786–3203; e-mail: redwine@yakimariverwinery.com; Web site www.yakimariverwinery.com. Open 9:00 A.M.–5:00 P.M. daily. Visa and MasterCard. Wheelchair accessible.*

Now we head back onto Wine Country Road to make stops at Chinook Wines, The Hogue Cellars, Thurston Wolfe, and Kestrel Vintners.

To visit the cozy, homelike tasting room at CHINOOK WINES, take exit 82 off I–82 across Yakima River into Prosser, turn left on Wine Country Road, and Chinook is on your right at Wittkopf.

Kay Simon and Clay Mackey, owners and mates, have tremendous reputations in the wine business of the Northwest and beyond.

Kay originally served as a lab technician at United Vintners in California and later joined Joel Klein, another California transplant who served as winemaker at Geyser Peak in Sonoma County, and at Chateau Ste. Michelle's Woodinville facility in 1977. In 1981 she became winemaker at River Ridge,

Chateau Ste. Michelle's Paterson winery now called Columbia Crest.

Clay came from a Napa Valley wine family and managed vineyards for Freemark Abbey and Rutherford Hill there. He joined Chateau Ste. Michelle in 1979 and managed their 2,000-acre vineyard at River Ridge.

Now partners in business and life, Kay and Clay were married in August 1984, combining a celebration of their union with the release of their first Chinook wine.

Plan a picnic on the lawn under the huge oak tree.

 Fine points: Featured wines: Chardonnay, Sauvignon Blanc, Sémillon, Cabernet Sauvignon, Merlot, and Cabernet Franc. Owners: Kay Simon and Clay Mackey. Winemaker: Kay Simon. Cases: 3,000. Acres: 2.

Chinook Wines, Wine Country Road at Loop, P.O. Box 387, Prosser 99350; phone (509) 786–2725; fax (509) 786–2777; e-mail info@chinook wines.com; Web site www.chinookwines.com. Open noon–5:00 P.M. Saturday and Sunday, May–November; closed December–April. Visa and MasterCard. Not easily wheelchair accessible, but staff will help.

To get to THE HOGUE CELLARS from Chinook Wines, return to Wine Country Road and turn left, then left again on Lee Lane. The Hogue Cellars is at Lee Lane and Lee Road.

The Hogue family has been farming and ranching 1,200 acres of hops, cattle, spearmint, potatoes, asparagus, and Concord grapes since the 1950s. For years they sold their mint to Wrigley's and their juice to Welch's. In the 1970s they planted 300 acres of premium varietals, resulting in several fine wines.

The Hogue family sold the winery to Canadian mega–wine company Vincor International in 2001.

You can sample Hogue's wines and preserved fruits and vegetables from its own farms and cannery and enjoy the gift shop.

 Fine points: Featured wines: Chardonnay, Cabernet Sauvignon, Merlot, and Cabernet-Merlot; Terroir label Sangiovese, Sauvignon Blanc, Sémillon, Syrah, Blue Franc Lemberger, and Cabernet Sauvignon; Late Harvest Riesling. Owner: Vincor International. Director of winemaking: David Forsyth. Senior winemakers: Coman Dinn for whites and Nicolas Quille for reds. Cases: 615,000. Acres: 9.

The Hogue Cellars, Lee Road at Wine Country Road, P.O. Box 31, Prosser 99350; phone (509) 786–4557 or (800) 565–9779; fax (509) 786–4580; Web site www.hoguecellars.com. Open 10:00 A.M.–5:00 P.M. daily. Closed January 1–15. Visa and MasterCard. Tasting room is wheelchair accessible.

Just 100 yards down Lee Road from Hogue is THURSTON WOLFE. Highly respected vineyard manager and winemaker Dr. Wade Wolfe and Becky Yeaman (Mrs. Wolfe) started their winery in the wonderful old City Hall in Yakima's Historical District in 1987 and moved it here in 1996. Another marriage of business and life's passion.

Fine points: Featured wines: Lemberger, Zinfandel, Syrah, Sangiovese, Pinot Gris, Viognier, and unusual dessert wines including Ports and Muscats. Owners: Wade Wolfe and Becky Yeaman. Winemaker: Wade Wolfe.

Thurston Wolfe, 3800 Lee Road, Suite C, Prosser 99350; phone (509) 786–3313; e-mail whwolfe@bentonrea.com; Web site www. winesnorthwest.com. Open 11:00 A.M.–5:00 P.M. Thursday–Sunday or by appointment, April–Thanksgiving; closed after Thanksgiving–March. Visa and MasterCard. Wheelchair accessible.

Just beyond Thurston Wolfe Winery is KESTREL VINTNERS in Prosser Wine & Food Park. Kestrel set out explicitly to create a line of "elegant, distinctive wines" via their "obsession" to craft the perfect wines. To get to Kestrel, take exit 82 off I–82 onto Wine Country Road to Lee Road.

Enjoy Kestrel's new winery and tasting room, and the terrific cheeses and Classic Breads. The Kestrel Festival in June features live kestrels.

Fine points: Featured wines: Chardonnay, Cabernet Sauvignon, Merlot, Meritage, Viognier, Sangiovese, Raptor Red, and Syrah. Owner: John Walker. Winemaker: Ray Sandidge. Cases: 8,000. Acres: 128.

Kestrel Vintners, Prosser Wine & Food Park, 2890 Lee Road, Prosser 99350; phone (509) 786–CORK (2675) or (888) 343-2675; fax (509) 786–2679; e-mail winery@kestrelwines.com; Web site www.kestrelwines.com. Open 10:00 A.M.–5:00 P.M. daily. Visa and MasterCard. Wheelchair accessible.

Slightly off the local and tourist beaten paths, DYKSTRA HOUSE RESTAURANT is well worth investigating. Take exit 73 off I–82, then Wine Country Road 1½ miles to Birch Avenue.

Linda Hartshorn welcomes you into her 1914 restored stone home in this quiet neighborhood with her warm personality and her outstanding food. Forget the diet and enjoy the locally grown foods, hand-ground locally grown whole-wheat bread, and gooey sweet desserts. Locals hang out here for meals and meetings. This is the place.

❧ Dykstra House Restaurant, 114 Birch Avenue, Grandview; phone (509) 882–2082. Shop opens at 10:00 A.M., lunch 11:00 A.M.–4:00 P.M. Tuesday–Saturday, dinner 6:00–10:00 P.M. Friday–Saturday (reservations required). Beer and wine. Visa, MasterCard, American Express, and Discover. Not wheelchair accessible.

Another dining option is THE BLUE GOOSE. Take exit 80 or 82 off I–82 to Wine Country Road, next to the Exxon (hate to mention it) Jackpot station. A surprise find with good food and reasonable prices, The Blue Goose has received accolades from the London *Daily Mirror* and *Times*, as well as many Northwest publications and television food shows.

Owners Jim Weber and Dick Denson feature local wines and microbrews to accompany their excellent salads, burgers, hearty pastas, and dinner entrees ranging from New York steak or tempura prawns at $16.95 to chicken piccata at $12.95, blackened halibut at $17.95, and French onion soup from "the original recipe from Les Halles, Paris, France," $6.95.

❧ The Blue Goose, 306 Seventh Street, Prosser; phone (509) 786–1774. Open for breakfast, lunch, and dinner 7:00 A.M.–8:00 P.M. Sunday–Thursday, 7:00 A.M.–9:00 P.M. Friday–Saturday. Full bar. Visa, MasterCard, American Express, Discover, and Diners Club. Wheelchair accessible.

You can take Highway 221 south out of Prosser 25 miles to Columbia Crest, the large winery at Paterson overlooking the Columbia River. A better plan, however, is to tour the Tri-Cities wineries first and Walla Walla to the east before going to Paterson. Patience pays.

There are five wineries in the Benton City area, of which Black-

---

EPPIE'S ESTATE RIESLING PUMPKIN CUSTARD
from Eppie Skelton, owner, Oakwood Cellars

1½ cups Oakwood Cellars Estate Riesling

1 tsp cream of tartar

1 tsp pumpkin pie spice or more to taste

5 unbeaten eggs

½ cup brown sugar

½ cup white sugar

Place all ingredients in top of a double boiler over warm water initially, not boiling water. Beat vigorously with a wire whisk. Cook custard until it thickens, whisking continually while cooking. Serve hot or cold. Takes about thirty to forty-five minutes. Cool, then chill. Serving idea: After chilling, spoon into prebaked miniature piecrust shells and top with a spoonful of whipped cream.

wood Canyon, the farthest out, is an absolute must visit. To get to these wineries, take exit 96 (Benton City exit) off I–82 and go north. Before you cross the Yakima River, turn right on Highway 224 beside the BP station and the Cactus Jack Cafe. At its fork, turn leftish with 224, and do not take Kennedy Road straight ahead. To visit Terra Blanca Vintners and Oakwood Cellars, turn left almost immediately up Demoss Road.

TERRA BLANCA VINTNERS and its spectacular tasting room opened in 1998 on Red Mountain just east of the Yakima River. Estate wines are fermented in small lots and aged in small French oak barrels in Washington's first barrel storage caves. Watch for the new additions to the facility, including caves, a demonstration kitchen, banquet room, and tasting room.

Fine points: Featured wines: Chardonnay, Bordeaux-style white wine, Merlot, Cabernet Sauvignon, Syrah, Malbec, Barbera, Viognier, and five late harvest wines. Owner and winemaker: Keith Pilgrim. Cases: 25,000. Acres: 300.

✣ *Terra Blanca Vintners, 34715 North Demoss Road, Benton City 98320; phone (509) 588–6082; fax (509) 588–2634; e-mail info@terrablanca.com; Web site www.terrablanca.com. Open 11:00 A.M.–6:00 P.M. daily, February 15–December 24, by appointment only Christmas–Valentine's Day. Visa, MasterCard, and American Express. Wheelchair accessible.*

Right next door at OAKWOOD CELLARS, Bob and Evelyn "Eppie" Skelton described their winery, founded in 1986, as a "boutique winery." The Skeltons dedicated their winemaking to French and German traditions and revisited those countries regularly to renew and update their art and craft. Bob died in 1998, and Eppie continues Oakwood's traditions as winemaker.

Picnic right there on the farm with a great view of Rattlesnake Mountain.

Fine points: Featured wines: Chardonnay, Rieslings, Lemberger Blanc, Syrah, Lemberger, Merlot, Cabernet Sauvignon, and a special Muscat Canelli. Owner: Evelyn "Eppie" Skelton. Winemaker: Evelyn "Eppie" Skelton. Cases: 3,000. Acres: 2 Riesling, buy from Prosser growers.

✣ *Oakwood Cellars, 40504 North Demoss Road, Benton City 99320; phone (509) 588–5332. Open noon–5:00 P.M. Thursday–Sunday, February 15–December 15; noon–5:00 P.M. Saturday–Sunday, December 15–February 15. Closed between Christmas and New Year's. Visa and MasterCard. Wheelchair accessible via the patio.*

To get to Blackwood Canyon, Kiona Vineyards, and Seth Ryan Winery, go back to Highway 224 and turn left (north) on Sunset Road, which leads to all

OAKWOOD CELLARS' ROADSIDE VINEYARD

three. From I–82 take exit 96 (Benton City exit) and go north, turn right just before the Yakima River beside the BP station and the Cactus Jack Cafe, and then left on Highway 224 to Sunset Road.

So you don't miss it, go all the way out to BLACKWOOD CANYON VINTNERS first (about 2 miles up Sunset to the driveway) and come back to the other two. The huge châteaulike building you see up to the right past Seth Ryan and Kiona is Hedges Cellars, which is only open to the public occasionally, but you can taste their wines at their new tasting room in Issaquah (see pages 107–8).

As you drive toward the winery, the terrain in the Red Mountains begins to resemble a mountain desert, but don't give up. When you turn at the sign pointing to Blackwood Canyon Vintners, the road gets a little rockier and a little dustier, and the vines along the road look a little more emaciated. And that is how you know you have arrived. M. Taylor Moore's vineyards are chemical free and cultivated to stress the vines to produce rich grapes.

Following an earlier career as a Range Conservationist in Idaho, Moore studied at U.C. Davis and then apprenticed at several wineries, including Almaden, Domaine Chandon, and Louis Martini.

With a $5,000 nest egg, Moore released his first Chardonnay and Cabernet in April 1985, but during the fall crush of 1985 a fire destroyed the winery and the year's crop. Moore began reconstruction in 1985.

Moore is a true genius and character to match, and totally in charge. He combines century-old French methods with his own ideas, many of which other

INSIDE BLACKWOOD CANYON VINTNERS

vintners disdain. His goal is to create world-class wines without time as a factor. Chardonnays are not released until they are ten years old. Moore believes that "the sociology of the people who make up a winery is as important as the micro-climate," and that as a winemaker you should "bend yourself to the wine, not the wine to you. I learned winemaking from cooking—it's the same thing." Enjoy many local cheeses and olive oils to nibble at the outpost.

Blackwood Canyon's wines were served at Julia Child's eightieth birthday. The Chardonnay is consistently rated in the top 100 worldwide. Be sure to try the Two Ladies Merlot (two ladies across the road grow the superb grapes). Don't miss Moore's fabulous Blackwood Canyon Chardonnay Vinegar.

Fine points: Featured wines: Chardonnay, Sémillon, Pinot Noir, Cabernet Sauvignon, Merlot, and late harvest wines. Owner and winemaker: M. Taylor Moore. Cases: 20,000. Acres: 80 in grapes, 350 total.

Blackwood Canyon Vintners, *53258 North Sunset Road, Benton City 99320; phone (509) 588–6249; e-mail Blackwdc@3-cities.com. Open 10:00 A.M.–6:00 P.M. daily. Visa, MasterCard, and Discover. Wheelchair accessible.*

The gravel driveway to **KIONA VINEYARDS WINERY** takes you 1 mile off Sunset Road, but the trip is well worth it.

In the 1970s John Williams and fellow metallurgical engineer and friend Jim Holmes began to turn their winemaking hobby into a tremendous success, making the wine in Jim's garage and aging and bottling it in John's home here in the Red Mountain foothills. They bought vineyard property from Ann Williams's father, acquired the Ciel du Cheval vineyard next door, and make and sell wine right here. "Kiona" is a Yakima Indian name for the location, specifically "brown hills."

As you drive up to the large house, you can't help but smile at the basketball hoop over the garage and children's play equipment under the trees. Bus tours are welcome with advance notice.

 Fine points: Featured wines: Special Late Harvest and Chenin Blanc Ice Wines from Riesling, Chenin Blanc, and Gewürztraminer; Chardonnay; Dry White Riesling, White Riesling, Sémillon; Cabernet Sauvignon; Merlot, Lemberger, Zinfandel, Sangiovese, and Syrah. Owners: The John Williams family. Winemaker: Scott Williams. Cases: 25,000. Acres: 65.

❧ *Kiona Vineyards Winery, 44612 North Sunset NE, Benton City 99320; phone (509) 588–6716; fax (509) 588–3219. Open noon–5:00 P.M. daily. Visa, MasterCard, American Express, and Discover. Wheelchair accessible.*

At SETH RYAN WINERY, Jo, Ron, and Kirk Brodzinski and Robert and son Khris Olsen moved their winery operation from the Brodzinskis' garage to this modern facility, finally bringing their distinctive wines to public tasting.

Founded in 1986, Seth Ryan boasts "spirited adventures, guaranteed!" if you visit their winery, with its lawns and view of the valley. (The Olsens were recently bought out.)

 Fine points: Featured wines: Riesling, Gewürztraminer, Chardonnay, Merlot, Cabernet Franc, Cabernet Sauvignon, and a blush wine called Rapture. Owners and winemakers: Jo, Ron, and Kirk Brodzinski. Cases: 20,000. Acres: 10 planted, 51 in process.

❧ *Seth Ryan Winery, Sunset Road, Route 2, Box 2168-01, Benton City 99320; phone (509) 588–6780. Open 11:00 A.M.–6:00 P.M. Thursday–Monday. Visa and MasterCard. Wheelchair accessible.*

From here you can travel farther east to the Tri-Cities Area wineries and then on to the Walla Walla appellation, in and around Walla Walla, Washington.

TRI-CITIES: RICHLAND, KENNEWICK, AND PASCO

Southeast of Benton City take I–182 where I–82 turns southeast toward Paterson at exit 102. Richland is 41 miles from Sunnyside, and its interlocking neighbor Kennewick is 8 miles farther.

The Tri-Cities form a slightly awkward triangle, with the cities' limits completely unidentifiable to the nonnative. Exit 3 on the left (south) leads to Kennewick on Columbia Drive, which merges with State Route 240 just before Center Boulevard on the right, the route to several hotels and motels. Exit 5B takes you north onto George Washington Way (State Route 240) to Richland and a motel/hotel row that parallels the Columbia River. The Columbia turns eastward in Kennewick before the Snake River empties into it on the eastern city limits of Kennewick. I–182 continues across the Columbia into Pasco and becomes I–12 headed east for Walla Walla.

While the Columbia Valley Tri-Cities Winery Association includes the Benton City area wineries (Terra Blanca, Oakwood, Blackwood Canyon, Kiona, and Seth Ryan) in its map, they are technically part of the Yakima Valley appellation, whose boundary ends west of the Tri-Cities. We found it most convenient, though, to spend the night in the Tri-Cities area and venture out from there to Benton City's wineries the next day.

Each Tri-Cities winery offers soft drinks for your lucky designated driver.

The easiest wineries to get to from I–182 are Bookwalter and Barnard Griffin, which are next door to each other. In fact, you can walk out the back patio door of Bookwalter and around the fence to Barnard Griffin.

To get to **BOOKWALTER WINERY**, take exit 3 off I–182 heading south on Kennedy Road, turn left on Columbia Drive and left again on Windmill Road. Or you can come out Columbia Drive from downtown Kennewick and turn right on Windmill Road to the winery.

Founders Jerry and Jean Bookwalter met in the first coed dorm at U.C. Davis in the late 1950s and have been together ever since. Son John Bookwalter now runs the show, but Jerry and Jean are still around. Enjoy great aprons, cookbooks, and tables with umbrellas overlooking the lawn and creek. Check out the gallery of Northwest artists' work, as well as live classical guitar music on holiday weekends. In the wine lounge and on the patio, you can also buy wine by the glass, artisanal cheese plates, and gourmet chocolates!

Bookwalter has won its share of awards for wine and its sensuous labels. *Wine Spectator* has given it a 90 and a 91 for its 1994 Cabernet Sauvignon, and 86s for its 1995 Chardonnay and 1996 Riesling.

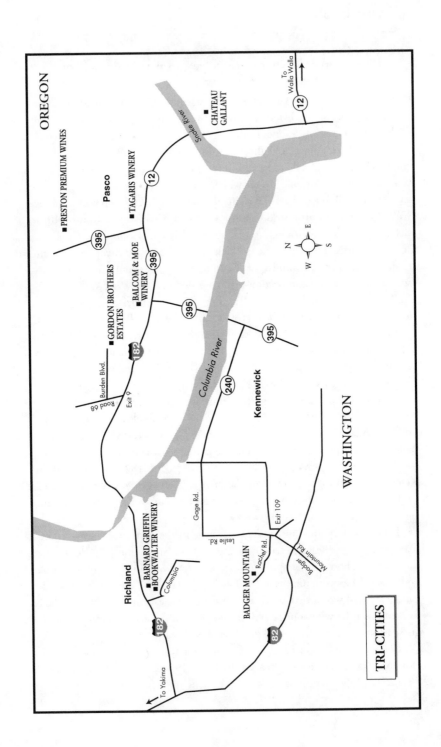

Fine points: Featured wines: Johannisberg Riesling, Chenin Blanc, Muscat Blanc, Chardonnay, Gewürztraminer, NV Red Table Wine (100 percent Cabernet), Merlot, and Cabernet Sauvignon. Owner: The Bookwalter family. Winemaker: John Bookwalter. Cases: 12,000. Acres: 7 of their own and manages 600 of others'.

❧ Bookwalter Winery, 894 Tulip Lane, Richland 99352; phone (509) 627–5000 or (877) 667–8300; fax (509) 627–5010; e-mail info@bookwalter wines.com; Web site www.bookwalterwines.com. Open 10:00 A.M.–6:00 P.M. Sunday–Tuesday, 10:00 A.M.–9:00 P.M. Wednesday–Saturday. Visa, MasterCard, American Express, and Discover. Wheelchair accessible.

BARNARD GRIFFIN is right next door to Bookwalter. Rob Griffin served as winemaker at Preston Cellars for eight years and then at Hogue Cellars, crafting award-winning and admired wines for both groups. Griffin and his wife, Deborah Barnard, formerly director of development for St. Luke's Valley Hospital in Spokane, started their own winery on the side in 1983.

Their 1997 Cabernet Sauvignon won Double Gold at the Los Angeles International Wine Festival. Don't miss the excellent selection of domestic and imported cheeses.

Fine points: Featured wines: Chardonnay, Fumé Blanc, Sémillon, Pinot Gris, White Riesling, Syrah, Zinfandel, Merlot, Cabernet Franc, Cabernet Sauvignon, and Muscat. Owners: Deborah Barnard and Rob Griffin. Winemaker: Rob Griffin. Cases: 45,000. Acres: None, buy from Columbia Valley.

❧ Barnard Griffin, 878 Tulip Lane, Richland 99352; phone (509) 627–0266; fax (509) 627–7776; e-mail linda.johnson@barnardgriffin.com; Web site www.barnardgriffin.com. Open 10:00 A.M.–6:00 P.M. daily; call for winter hours. Visa, MasterCard, and American Express. Wheelchair accessible.

Still in the neighborhood, try BADGER MOUNTAIN VINEYARD/POWERS WINERY. From Bookwalter or Barnard Griffin, turn left on Columbia Drive, then right on Leslie, and right again on South Jurupa Street. Or you can take exit 109 of I–82 and turn left on Leslie and right on South Jurupa Street. While it's a bit of a drive out of the way, the bucolic scenery and wines make it well worth it.

Badger Mountain/Powers was the first Washington State certified organic vineyard making estate wines. Rob Griffin of Barnard Griffin serves as consultant.

Wine Spectator rates Badger Mountain/Powers in the high 80s for the Powers 1995 Merlot, 1995 Chardonnay blend, and 1996 Muscat Canelli, and for the Badger Mountain 1995 Merlot.

MICROBREWERY ALERT!

Rattlesnake Mountain Brewery, *1250 Columbia Center, Richland 99352 (509–783–5747), right down Columbia Drive from Bookwalter and Barnard Griffin wineries, has the most authentically English atmosphere we have ever seen in a brand-new brewpub and some excellent hearty food.*

Fine points: Featured wines: Chardonnay, Gewürztraminer, White Riesling, Chenin Blanc, Cabernet Franc, Merlot, Cabernet Sauvignon, red Meritage blend, blush, rosé, Syrah, and Seve, a house blend. Owners: Bill Powers and Tim DeCook. Winemaker: Greg Powers. Cases: 45,000. Acres: 76.

Badger Mountain/Powers Winery, 1106 South Jurupa Street, Kennewick 99337; phone (509) 627–2148 or (800) 643–WINE; fax (509) 627–2071; e-mail bmvwine@aol.com; Web site www.badgermtnvineyard.com. Open 10:00 A.M.–5:00 P.M. daily. Visa and MasterCard. Wheelchair accessible.

TAGARIS WINERY has a retail shop in downtown Pasco where you can purchase wines made for them at Badger Mountain Winery.

Fine points: Featured wines: Chardonnay, Fumé Blanc, Chenin Blanc, Riesling, Cabernet Sauvignon, and Merlot. Owners: Mike and Kristine Taggares. Winemaker: Greg Powers. Cases: 3,000. Acres: 145.

Tagaris Winery, Retail Store, 1625 West A Street, Suite E, Pasco 99301; phone (509) 547–3590 or (877) 862–7999; e-mail tagaris@charterinternet.com; Web site www.tagariswines.com. Open 8:00 A.M.–5:00 P.M. Monday–Friday. Visa and MasterCard. Wheelchair accessible.

The next winery on our route is GORDON BROTHERS ESTATES. Take exit 9 off Highway 182 up Road 68 for ¼ mile and turn right on Burden.

Jeff and Bill Gordon and their families planted their vineyard in 1980 on a south-facing slope above the Snake River 2 miles north of the Ice Harbor Dam.

The Gordons had been growing potatoes here since 1977, switched to grapes, and then the price of Washington grapes dropped drastically. What to do? Start a winery and use your own grapes, of course. *Wine Spectator* gave them an 89 for their 1995 Chardonnay and an 85 for their 1994 Merlot.

Fine points: Featured wines: Chardonnay, Cabernet Sauvignon, Merlot, Tradition (Cabernet and Merlot blend), Sauvignon Blanc, Syrah, and Late Harvest Gewürztraminer. Owners: Jeff and Vicky Gordon. Winemaker: Dave Harvey. Cases: 23,000. Acres: 95.

Gordon Brothers Estates, 5960 Burden Road, Pasco 99301; phone (509) 547–6331; fax (509) 547–6305; e-mail info@gordonwines.com; Web site www.gordonwines.com Open 11:00 A.M.–5:00 P.M. daily. Visa, MasterCard, and American Express. Wheelchair accessible.

Next is must-stop **PRESTON PREMIUM WINES** (formerly Preston Wine Cellars), which is easy to get to from downtown. From Highway 182 take Highway 395 north toward Spokane at Pasco. In about 4 miles a billboard announces Preston in "3 miles on right." The row of tall poplar trees to the right lines Preston's driveway.

Bill Preston planted fifty acres of wine grapes in 1972. Preston is now the largest family-owned winery in Washington, with a fascinating compound of buildings and family interests, including an upstairs tasting room (steep ramp for wheelchairs), a petting zoo, gazebo, railroad caboose, a view for 20 miles, an amphitheater, and ducks and geese that wander the vast lawns.

Extremely knowledgeable Cathy Preston-Mouncer helps out in the tasting room, and, in fact, she was happily unpacking wine cases when we visited. You can buy anything you might want to go with wine: great sandwiches and light lunches, elegant cigars, sculpture, wineglasses, books, and aprons. The tasting room itself feels like a log cabin, with decks facing west, south, and

---

DAVE'S SYRAH MUSTARD GLAZE FOR GRILLED RACK OF LAMB
from Preston Premium Wines

---

4 Tbs Preston Syrah Mustard
¼ cup Preston Syrah
crushed fresh garlic, to taste
peppercorns, to taste
sea salt, to taste
crushed rosemary, to taste
rack of lamb for 2

Mix all ingredients and rub on lamb. Let marinate for thirty to sixty minutes. Grill lamb until medium-rare; timing depends on gas, charcoal, or stove grilling. Drink the rest of the Syrah with dinner. Serves 2.

ENTRANCE TO PRESTON PREMIUM WINES TASTING ROOM

north. On the decks are carved wooden chairs and tables where you sit, nibble, and taste.

Do not miss the self-guided tour downstairs to see the corkscrew collection, including historic, modern, obscene, and elegant models, and even the "world's largest." You can also view an art exhibit and fascinating old autographed photos of U.S. Air Force Blue Angels and Thunderbirds.

 Fine points: Featured wines: Chardonnay, Cabernets, Merlots, sparkling wines, and ports. Owners: The Preston family. Winemaker: Del Long. Cases: 12,000. Acres: 180 in grapes.

❧ *Preston Premium Wines, 502 East Vineyard Drive, Pasco 99301; phone (509) 545–1990; fax (509) 545–1098; e-mail info@preston wines.com; Web site www.prestonwines.com. Open 10:00 A.M.–5:30 P.M. daily. Visa, MasterCard, and debit cards. Wheelchair accessible, but may need push up a long ramp.*

You can visit COLUMBIA CREST WINERY on your way to or from Oregon via Biggs and the Columbia River Gorge, or by driving south from Pasco when you visit the Tri-Cities area wineries. From Prosser take Highway 221 south for 28 miles. From Walla Walla or Oregon, take Highway 14 along the Columbia River to the two-diner town of Paterson and turn north on Highway 221.

Columbia Crest is one of the two largest wineries owned by Stimson Lane. It was originally Chateau Ste. Michelle's River Ridge winery. As you walk into the winery's entry courtyard, you feel as if you've just entered a private courtyard in France. We expected to see little old ladies leaning out the windows on their elbows to keep track of who's coming and going.

Every detail of the winery's decor is perfectly executed, from hanging tapestries to antiques, wood detail, and production room displays. The staff is genteel, kind, considerate, and responsive to the dumbest of questions. Self-guided tours are well mapped out, easy, and informative.

 Fine points: Featured wines: Chardonnay, Sémillon-Chardonnay, Sauvignon Blanc, Merlot, Cabernet Sauvignon, as well as Barrel Select bottlings. Owner: Stimson Lane Wine and Spirits (U.S. Tobacco subsidiary). Winemaker: Doug Gore. Cases: 500,000. Acres: 2,150.

CHOCOLATE RASPBERRY CABERNET CAKE
from Cathy Preston-Mouncer, Preston Premium Wines

[Note: Cathy Preston-Mouncer's recipes are always easy, fun, and really good.]

1 chocolate cake mix

1 pkg (3 oz) raspberry flavored gelatin

¾ cup oil

4 eggs

¾ cup Preston Cabernet Sauvignon

¾ cup raspberries

Grease and flour Bundt cake pan and preheat oven to 325°F. Combine ingredients in a mixing bowl. Fill greased pan and bake for one hour. Let cake cool in pan before removing, then dust with powdered sugar.

Recommended wine: Preston Cabernet Sauvignon.

❧ *Columbia Crest, Highway 221, Paterson 99345–0231; phone (509) 875–2061; Web site www.columbia-crest.com. Open 10:00 A.M.–4:30 P.M., tours on weekends. American Express, MasterCard, and Visa. Wheelchair accessible.*

PATERSON STORE & RESTAURANT is five minutes south from Columbia Crest. Judy Crow runs this local diner in a town so small a dog is the Police Chief. The police radio plays in the background, and the local copy machine sits on top of the jukebox.

About the menu: You can't spend more than $3.95 here. Biscuits and sausage gravy cost $1.60 or $2.00, a side order of gizzards costs $2.95, and the salads are really okay.

ENTRANCE COURTYARD, COLUMBIA CREST

The "store" part of this establishment sells Alka-Seltzer and white bread, and flowered oilcloth tablecloths cover the square tables.

Paterson Store & Restaurant "caters" lunches for Columbia Crest. It's the best place around, truly.

❧ *Paterson Store & Restaurant, Highway 221 near Highway 14, Paterson; phone (509) 875–2741. Wheelchair accessible.*

If you decide to travel to or from the Tri-Cities area, Walla Walla, or Columbia Crest at Paterson by way of Highway 14 on the Washington side of the Columbia River, stop at CASCADE CLIFFS WINERY & VINEYARD, which is about 10 miles west of the Maryhill Museum and 88 miles east of Portland, Oregon. The view of the river from here is stunning.

Previous owners Kenn and Linda Adcock built the winery in 1985 between the highway and the river with high cliffs as a backdrop, thus fulfilling the dream of Seattle attorney Sam Hill, who had planted vines around the Maryhill estate in the early 1900s.

Robert Lorkowski and group purchased Cascade Cliffs in 1997 and adds a little humor to the wine mix with his upcoming Shatoe du Bob line.

Fine points: Featured wines: Nebbiolo, Merlot, Syrah, Petite Syrah, Cabernet Sauvignon, Zinfandel, Goat Head red blend, and Barbera. Owners: Robert Lorkowski and group. Winemaker: Robert Lorkowski. Cases: 4,000. Acres: 23.

ᣠᣢ *Cascade Cliffs Winery & Vineyard, 8866 Highway 14, P.O. Box 14, Wishram 98673; phone (509) 767–1100; Web site www.cascadecliffs.com. Open 10:00 A.M.–6:00 P.M. daily. Visa and MasterCard. Wheelchair accessible.*

The lonely, gigantic mansion that now houses the MARYHILL MUSEUM OF ART is worth a visit. First owner Sam Hill made his fortune by suing James J. Hill's Great Northern Railway. The railroad magnate was so impressed with Sam's work that he hired Sam as the company lawyer. Sam eventually married the boss's daughter, Mary.

A devoted Quaker and pacifist, Sam Hill purchased 7,000 windswept acres above the Columbia Gorge for a cooperative community he envisioned and named the nonexistent utopia Maryhill, believing the property to be too dry for wine grapes.

Hill began building the mansion, but Mary didn't like it. The mansion was finally completed by San Francisco heiress and art patron Alma Spreckles in 1941, ten years after Sam Hill's death. The replica of Stonehenge close to the highway east of Maryhill and next to Maryhill State Park was another of Sam Hill's projects. Enjoy the new cafe, gift shop, and fascinating sculpture garden (including Rodins).

ᣠᣢ *Maryhill Museum of Art, 35 Maryhill Museum Drive (near the intersection of Highway 14 and Highway 97), Goldendale 98620; phone (509) 773–3733. Open 9:00 A.M.–5:00 P.M. March 15–November 15. Admission is $6.00 for adults and $1.50 for children 6–12. Visa and MasterCard. Wheelchair accessible.*

WALLA WALLA VALLEY

The Walla Walla Valley produces unusually good wines because of its limestone soil, lots of heat (whew!), and a 200-day growing season. The Walla Walla Valley appellation includes vineyards in Washington and Oregon.

Walla Walla may be the pleasant surprise of your wine country tour. Whitman College is right downtown and brings a cultural vitality to an old, in-the-middle-of-nothing county seat, partially devastated by its modern mall on the outskirts.

At one time Walla Walla was the largest city in Washington, until someone started Seattle. If you arrived on the Oregon Trail from the east, Walla Walla was the first city you came to. We think it's worth rediscovering. Walla Walla is full of history, Wild West activities, college students and professors, art galleries, bookstores, and a few good restaurants.

Lewis and Clark passed through here in 1805, fur trappers founded Fort Walla Walla in 1818, and missionary Marcus Whitman set up a "medical mission" 7 miles west to treat and convert Cayuse Indians who massacred the white guys in 1847 in thanks for giving all the Native people deadly measles. Walla Walla also boasts the longest continuing (i.e., never miss a winter season) symphony west of the Mississippi.

Some Walla Walla Valley wineries are open to visitors, including L'Ecole No. 41 and Woodward Canyon Winery, which are actually in nearby "downtown" Lowden, Canoe Ridge Vineyard, Walla Walla Vintners, Glen Fiona, and Patrick M. Paul Vineyards. Not open to the public is the highly praised Leonetti.

One of our favorites is L'ECOLE NO. 41. From the Tri-Cities area take Highway 12 south along the Columbia River and Lake Wallula and then east toward Walla Walla when the highway turns that way. The "town" of Lowden (a don't-blink-or-you'll-miss-it settlement complete with grain elevator), L'Ecole No. 41, and Woodward Canyon are all about 16 miles from the turnoff.

Turn left on Lower Dry Creek Road, and then immediately left on Lowden School Road. From Oregon, come along Highway 730 and the Columbia River, turn right (east) on Highway 12, or follow Highway 11 from Pendleton up through Milton-Freewater to Walla Walla.

The winery's 1915 building was once the only school in Lowden, then dubbed "French Town" because of the French-Canadian migration here. The school closed in 1974, and in 1977 Walla Walla community leaders Baker and Jean Ferguson bought the building, beautifully restored it, added the upstairs, and began making wine here in 1983. Megan Ferguson Clubb, now president of Baker Boyer Bank, and her husband, Martin, run the winery. Crandall Kyle serves as "chief wine guy."

Upstairs, enjoy the fine woodwork, elegant dining room for winemaker's dinners, romantic deck, and an interesting book collection in etched-glass-covered bookcases. The pine floors still smell like old classrooms.

To come up with the design on L'Ecole No. 41's outstanding, colorful labels, the Clubbs held a family contest among their nieces and nephews. Young Ryan Campbell won, and his charming painting of the school decorates the wine bottles.

 Fine points: Featured wines: Chardonnay, Chenin Blanc, Sémillon, Merlot, Cabernet Sauvignon, Syrah, and late harvest Sémillon/Bordeaux. Owners: Martin and Megan Clubb. Winemaker: Mike Sharon. Cases: 27,000. Acres: 200.

com. Open 11:00 A.M.–5:00 P.M. daily in summer, 11:00 A.M.–4:00 P.M. daily in winter. Visa and MasterCard. Wheelchair accessible.

GLEN FIONA means "Valley of the Vine" in Gaelic. This winery operates out of a renovated carriage house on the historic Kibler-Finch Farmstead, which is also home of the Mill Creek Inn Bed & Breakfast. Berle "Rusty" Figgins Jr. makes Rhone-style reds from Syrah, Grenache Noir, Cinsault, and Viognier grapes. *Wine Spectator* gave high ratings to Paul's 1995 Sauvignon Blanc (125 cases), Syrah (279 cases), and Grenache Noir (167 cases).

❧ *Glen Fiona, Mill Creek Road, Walla Walla 99362; phone (509) 522–2566; fax (509) 522–1008. Open house tastings second weekends of May, September, and December, or by appointment.*

At WALLA WALLA VINTNERS, owners and winemakers Myles Anderson and Gordon Venneri make handcrafted wines including Cabernet Franc, Cabernet Sauvignon, and Merlot.

❧ *Walla Walla Vintners, Mill Creek Road, Walla Walla 99362; phone (509) 525–4724; fax (509) 525–4134. You can attend the two yearly open weekends by getting on their mailing list. Open 10:30 A.M.–4:30 P.M. March–December, 1:00–4:30 P.M. January–February.*

We always try to find the restaurants where true locals hang out and enjoy local foods, such as the PASTIME CAFE, a downtown, really local, old-time joint within walking distance of all hotels and motels. The restaurant's layout is important to understand.

As you walk in the front door you are smack-dab on top of the Formica tabletop booths of the coffee shop, where you can have breakfast and lunch, as some regulars do every day. To the right is the local hangout bar, and we mean bar. To the left of the front door, the Pastime serves "Italian dinners" in the large two-room dining area.

The back room of the dining room is the obvious local rancher comfort zone, where men in short-sleeved plaid cowboy shirts, dark blue Wrangler jeans, and cowboy boots savor their salad, pasta, and steak with their just-coiffed brides of many years.

The front room is where the hostess seats newcomers, as well as college students and their parents. The pasta sauces are well aged and well integrated, the pasta is fresh and perfectly cooked, some days there are two-for-one specials, and the beef, veal, and fried chicken are terrific. Prices are even better. The House Special is baked lasagna, which you can have with meatballs,

Italian sausage, fried chicken, french-fried prawns, soup or salad, and French bread from $7.50 to $11.95. Try the Hamburger Royal with french fries and salad or soup at $5.25, a fried-egg sandwich for $3.00, or grilled cheese at $3.10.

❧ *Pastime Cafe, 215 West Main Street, Walla Walla; phone (509) 525–0873. Open 5:30 A.M.–11:30 P.M. Full bar. Visa and MasterCard. Wheelchair accessible.*

What a surprise we found on our early morning walk around town! MERCHANT'S LTD. & FRENCH BAKERY is where we would spend our cafe time in Walla Walla, without a doubt. A true food emporium with high ceilings, old wood floors, and a mix of specialties around every corner: fine French and local wines on the west wall, the best-looking deli meats and salads in eastern Washington, espresso drinks, house-baked pastries, muffins, and breads, a soda fountain in the window, and an upstairs buffet dining room.

❧ *Merchant's Ltd. & French Bakery, 21 East Main Street, Walla Walla; phone (509) 525–0900. Open for breakfast and lunch Monday–Saturday, dinner until 8:00 P.M. Wednesday (spaghetti night). Beer and wine. Visa and MasterCard. Wheelchair accessible.*

WATERBROOK WINERY's tasting room is now right here in river city, downtown Walla Walla.

Eric and Janet Rindal converted an asparagus storage house into a winery in

---

UPSIDE-DOWN ONION CORN BREAD
from Waterbrook Winery

6 medium Walla Walla onions, thinly sliced	2 Tbs sugar
3 Tbs butter	1 tsp salt
1 cup yellow cornmeal	⅓ cup shortening
1 cup flour	1 egg
	1 cup milk

Preheat oven to 350ºF. In skillet, sauté onion rings in butter until soft, five to eight minutes. Spoon into bottom of buttered 8 x 8 x 2-inch square baking pan. Combine dry ingredients in bowl and mix well. Cut in shortening until well blended. Beat egg and milk together; mix with dry ingredients until just blended. Pour batter evenly over onions. Bake twenty-five to thirty minutes, or until done. Turn out onto serving plate; cut into squares. Serve hot.

1984 and turned it into the largest winery in Walla Walla Valley, until they were passed up in size by Walla Walla's Canoe Ridge. Enjoy their new downtown Walla Walla tasting room, pairing fine art with fine wine, right across the street from Starbucks.

Wine Spectator gave them a 92 for their Cabernet Sauvignon, a 91 for their Merlot, and high ratings for their Cabernet Franc and Sauvignon Blanc.

Fine points: Featured wines: Chardonnay, Sauvignon Blanc, Ciel du Cheval, Meritage, Viognier, Mélange Red Table Wine, Merlot, and Cabernet Sauvignon. Owners: Eric and Janet Rindal. Winemaker: Eric Rindal. Cases: 40,000. Acres: 47.

🍇 **Waterbrook Winery,** *31 East Main Street at First Street, Walla Walla 99362; phone (509) 522–1262; fax (509) 529–4770; e-mail info@waterbrook.com; Web site www.waterbrook.com. Open 10:30 A.M.–4:30 P.M. daily. Visa and MasterCard. Wheelchair accessible.*

SPOKANE

To reach Spokane take I–90 from just south of Ellensburg heading east, cross the Columbia River at Vantage, jog north and then east again through George and Moses Lake to Ritzville, where the highway heads northeast through Sprague to Spokane, a total of 174 miles.

On your way from Ellensberg to Spokane you can visit **WHITE HERON CELLARS** by turning south at exit 149 onto Washington Way. In 1990 Phyllis and Cameron Fries set up shop in a converted gasoline station after Cameron studied winemaking in Switzerland for five years and trained further with two Washington wineries.

Vines cover the red front door of fortune. Picnic on the lawn under the spreading trees and have a wine chat with the Frieses. Visitors will enjoy the new tasting room, amphitheater featuring jazz and classical music, and Petanque tournaments in June and September.

Fine points: The Frieses grow grapes in the Columbia Gorge and purchase from Yakima Valley growers for their Riesling, Pinot Noir, Syrah, Rousanne, and blended Chantepierre. Owners: Phyllis and Cameron Fries, president of the Columbia Cascades Winery Association. Winemaker: Cameron Fries. Cases: 2,000. Acres: 11.5.

🍇 **White Heron Cellars,** *10035 Stuhlmiller, Quincy 98848; phone (509) 797–9463; e-mail info@whiteheronwine.com; Web site www.whiteheronwine.com. Open 11:00 A.M.–6:00 P.M. Thursday–Monday in summer, but call ahead in winter. Visa and MasterCard; checks accepted. Wheelchair accessible.*

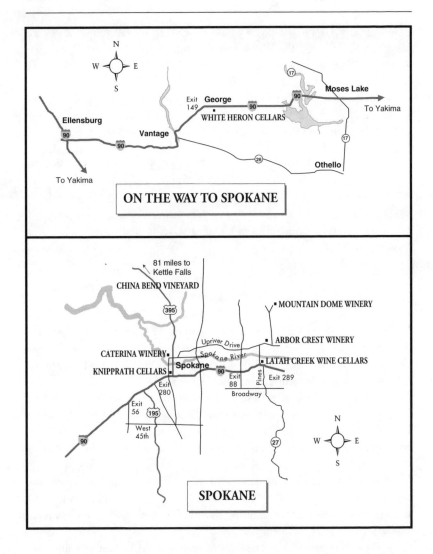

ON THE WAY TO SPOKANE

SPOKANE

There are five wineries in the Spokane area, four of which are close to Highway 90 and within Spokane's city limits. The Spokane River flows through the city, creating a parklike setting along its banks.

First we suggest KNIPPRATH CELLARS. Take exit 287 off Highway 90, go north on Argonne Road, left on Trent Avenue, right on Fancher Road, and left on East Commerce. Go just to visit the 1913 brick schoolhouse with great parking and great Ports.

Knipprath was founded in 1991 by a small group of friends led by jolly Henning Knipprath, an Air Force pilot based at nearby Fairchild Air Force Base. His talent for winemaking has been acknowledged by *Wine Spectator,* which gave high ratings to various vintages (top Washington State Pinot Noir, high on list of best bargain Merlot). Knipprath's seasoned Alpine Wine, heated in the winter, outdoes mulled wine.

Fine points: Featured wines: Dry Riesling, Riesling, Merlot, Chocolate Port, Vanilla Port, White Port, Late Harvest Syrah, Ruby Style Port, Cabernet Franc, and Alpine Spiced. Owners: Henning and Patricia Knipprath. Winemaker: Henning Knipprath. Cases: 8,000. Acres: None, buy from Yakima and Columbia Valley.

Knipprath Cellars, 5634 East Commerce Avenue, Spokane 99212; phone (509) 534–5121; fax (509) 534–5148; e-mail winemaker@knipprath-cellars.com; Web site www.knipprath-cellars.com. Open noon–5:00 P.M. Thursday–Sunday and by appointment. Visa, MasterCard, American Express, and Discover. Not wheelchair accessible.

To get to CATERINA WINERY, take exit 281 off Highway 90 and cross the Spokane River on Division Street. Turn left on North River Drive, and Caterina Winery faces you where North River runs into North Washington Street.

Once the Steven Thomas Winery, Caterina is run by winemaker and cellarmaster Monica Meglasson, a product of the University of California, Davis. Located in the historic Broadview Dairy Building, in addition to the Italian-style tasting room and gift shop, the winery is the venue for music programs (blues, jazz, folk, and flamenco) Wednesday through Saturday evenings in the summer and Friday and Saturday during winter.

Caterina, named for the Italian great-grandmother of one of the owners, is next door to the Red Lion Hotel.

Fine points: Featured wines: Sauvignon Blanc, Merlot, Cabernet Sauvignon, Pinot Gris, Cabernet della Rosa, Viognier, Late Harvest Viognier, and Late Harvest Riesling. Owner: The Caterina Trust. Winemaker: Monica Meglasson. Cases: 5,000. Acres: None, buy from Tri-Cities, Prosser, Sunnyside, and Walla Walla area.

Caterina Winery, 905 North Washington, Spokane 99201; phone (509) 328–5069; fax (509) 328–9694; e-mail monica@caterina.com. Open noon–5:00 P.M. daily. Visa, MasterCard, American Express, and Discover. Wheelchair accessible.

Don't miss LATAH CREEK WINE CELLARS. Take exit 289 off Highway 90 onto Pines Road and turn right on Indiana Avenue.

After Mike Conway's original career as a microbiologist for giant Gallo and

Franzia wineries in California, he learned to make wine at Parducci in Sonoma County. Moving north to Washington, he worked for Worden Washington Winery and then joined Mike Hogue in an exchange by which Conway would become Hogue's winemaker if Hogue would help Conway start his own winery here. Conway later bought out Hogue's share.

Latah Creek's charming California-Spanish mission-style architecture offers a huge tasting bar, and the gift shop displays an extensive collection by Yakima wildlife artist Floyd Broadbent, whose paintings decorate Latah Creek's labels, reminding us of the delicate balance we must maintain with nature.

Wine Spectator has called Latah Creek one of Washington's finest producers of Merlot.

Latah Creek holds several special events, including a July anniversary party and an Oktoberfest, and participates in area-wide tastings.

 Fine points: Featured wines: Chardonnay, Riesling, Huckleberry Riesling, Maywine, Syrah, Merlot, Cabernet Sauvignon, Sangiovese, and Muscat Canelli. Owner: Mike Conway. Winemaker: Mike Conway. Cases: 15,000. Acres: None, buy from Tri-Cities area and Sunnyside.

❧ *Latah Creek Wine Cellars, East 13030 Indiana Avenue, Spokane 99216; phone (509) 926–0164 or (800) 528–2427; fax (509) 926–0710; Web site www.latahcreek.com. Open 9:00 A.M.–5:00 P.M. daily. Visa, MasterCard, and American Express. Wheelchair accessible.*

For a different winery experience, visit ARBOR CREST WINERY. Take exit 287 off Highway 90 and go north on Argonne Road. Turn right on Upriver Drive and left on Fruithill Road.

Dave and Harold Mielke, scions of an old Spokane agribusiness family, bought a defunct Emeryville, California, winery, transported its equipment to Spokane, and purchased one of Spokane's charming and legendary 1924 historic homes, the Riblet Mansion, on a 475-foot cliff overlooking the Spokane River.

They renamed it Cliff House, restored it perfectly, and filled it with appropriate antiques. Now a national historic landmark, Cliff House also serves as Arbor Crest's wine tasting facility and visitor center. Surrounding lawns, gardens, and pools present a breathtaking oasis in eastern Washington. The winery received excellent ratings for its 1994 Cabernet Franc, 1994 Cabernet Sauvignon, 1995 Cabernet/Merlot blend, 1995 Chardonnay, 1995 Grand Cepage White, and 1996 Sauvignon Blanc. Watch for open houses on Mother's Day and Thanksgiving weekends.

MICROBREWERY ALERT!

Birkebiner Brewpub, *West 35 Main, Spokane (509–458–0854).*

Bayou Brewing Company, *1003 East Trent Avenue (509–484–4818).*

Ram Restaurant & Big Horn Brewery, *908 North Howard Street (509–326–3745), across from the Arena.*

Fort Spokane Brewery, *401 West Spokane Falls Boulevard (509–838–3809), across from Riverside Park.*

Fine points: Featured wines: Chardonnay, Blush, Sauvignon Blanc, Syrah, Cabernet Sauvignon, Cabernet Franc, and Merlot. Owners: Harold and Marcia Mielke. Winemaker: Kristina Mielke van Loben Sels. Cases: 25,000. Acres: 5 and buy from Pasco area.

✿❦ Arbor Crest Winery, *North 4705 Fruithill Road, Spokane 99207–9562; phone (509) 927–9894; fax (509) 927–0574; e-mail info@arborcrest.com; Web site www.arborcrest.com. Open noon–5:00 P.M. daily. Visa and MasterCard. Wheelchair accessible. Special note: No one under twenty-one years of age is allowed because of the dangerous cliffs.*

For an 85-mile scenic side trip, take I–395 north to Kettle Falls.

At CHINA BEND VINEYARD AND WINERY, the growers and processors of certified organic foods at Victory's Organic Garden on the banks of the Columbia River at Lake Roosevelt now make fabulous organic and sulfite-free wines for those of us who hate headaches and for other connoisseurs. If you get to China Bend, you are bound to enjoy the refreshingly uncomplicated wines, tasting room, and organic foods and gift shop. You can even enjoy lunch by reservation.

China Bend presents a Grand Release Party Memorial Day weekend, a Garlic Festival mid- to late August, and a Nouveau Festival the third weekend in November.

China Bend is the only winery we know of that offers a complete bed-and-breakfast with a "wine, dine, and recline" option on Lake Roosevelt. You can boat or fly in to a dirt landing strip on neighbors' property, and winery personnel will pick you up at your boat or plane.

Fine points: Featured wines: Maréchal Foch, Victory Red, Lake Roosevelt Red, Lemberger, Cabernet Sauvignon, Merlot, and Rosé; Royal Raspberry, Very Cherry, and Blackberry Velvet dessert wines. Owner and winemaker: Bart Alexander. Cases: 1,500. Acres: 6.

❧ *China Bend Vineyard and Winery, 3751 Vineyard Way, Kettle Falls 99141; phone (509) 732–6123 or (800) 700–6123; fax (509) 732–1401; e-mail winery@chinabend.com; Web site www.chinabend.com. Open noon–5:00 P.M. daily, April–October, by appointment November–March. Visa, MasterCard, American Express, and Discover. Wheelchair accessible.*

CHAPTER 3

BRITISH COLUMBIA

ritish Columbia wines and wineries are the most under-discovered and underpublicized in North America. As you travel throughout this region, you will enjoy a distinctly European ambience, and for good reason. Many of the vintners and growers immigrated to Canada from Europe, some having worked in vineyards and wineries in Germany, France, and Switzerland, as well as others who followed different careers in Europe. We found engineers, chemists, oilmen, and two former officials of Mercedes Benz in Germany, all pursuing two of their true loves: wine and winemaking. We also discovered that nearly one-fourth of British Columbia's winemakers are women. Many of the businesses resemble European family wineries in which the winery is the downstairs level of the house and the winemaking family lives upstairs or in a home close by.

Almost all BC wineries have their own vineyards, except for a few of the large commercial ventures that buy from growers. Estate wineries are required to grow the majority of their own grapes.

We see a couple of attitudinal differences that distinguish BC wineries from U.S. wineries, particularly those in California. Generally BC vintners help each other instead of competing against each other. Over and over again we were told by a proprietor "Don't leave without visiting . . ." or "You must stop at . . ."

In addition, many BC vintners are content to sell the wine they make and stay small, instead of aggressively striving to top their own or someone else's sales figures. The emphasis seems to be more in creating the best wines one can and sharing that product with others. Many BC wineries sell out their releases each year.

You'll find varieties here you may not have encountered before, such as Auxerrois, Ehrenfelser, Bacchus, Müller-Thurgau, Faber, Kerner, Optima, Oraniensteiner, Ortega, Seyval Blanc, Siegerrebe, Sovereign Opal, Verdelet, Schonburger, Scheurebe, Pinot Blanc, Baco Noir, Chancellor, Maréchal Foch, Chasselas, and Rotberger, many of which have their origins in France and

Germany. True ice wines are crafted here from grapes plucked frozen from the vines and crushed.

Most winemakers submit their wines to the British Columbia Wine Institute for judgment and selection for VQA (Vintners Quality Alliance) status, identified with the VQA decal on each approved bottle. A few wineries refuse to offer their wines for approval because they believe their own integrity and the consumer should be the only judge of their art and craft.

Wines from the majority of BC's small wineries are sold primarily in the winery tasting rooms and at finer restaurants. Fine wines from small, independent BC wineries are often not available at BC liquor stores, so we encourage you to visit the wineries or exclusive wine shops.

British Columbia's wine country is divided between two geographic climates, which are formed by local terrain and water bodies. Vancouver Island and the lower mainland Fraser Valley make up the coastal region, and the interior Okanagan and Similkameen Valleys form the inland wine country.

Vancouver Island is British Columbia's newest wine-growing region. Within an hour's drive of downtown Victoria you can visit fourteen wineries, including five new wineries on the Saanich Peninsula.

An ideal one-day tour from Victoria includes Venturi-Schulze Vineyards, Cherry Point Vineyards, Blue Grouse Vineyards & Winery, Vigneti Zanatta, Godfrey-Brownell Vineyards, and Alderlea Vineyards, with Chateau Wolff near Nanaimo.

Fraser Valley is east of the city of Vancouver on the lower mainland of British Columbia and is easily accessible as a one-day trip from Vancouver or from Seattle. The extremely fertile Fraser Valley is actually the largest agricultural region of the province. You can visit Domaine de Chaberton in Langley within a half-hour drive of Vancouver, depending on urban traffic. The Fraser Valley boasts twenty to thirty hectares (forty to sixty acres) of grapes.

The Okanagan Valley in central British Columbia resembles the Sonoma and Napa Valleys, with an even more startlingly beautiful landscape, including cliffs sloping dramatically into vineyards and vineyards dropping spectacularly into rivers and lakes.

The south end of the Okanagan is Canada's only desert, with less than 6 inches of rain each year, providing the perfect climate for classic red vinifera grapes. The northern end of the Okanagan is cooler and gets only 16 inches of rain, supporting French and Germanic white grape varieties. The Okanagan also yields some of the richest fruit crops in Canada, including 96 percent of Canada's peaches. Fruit stands abound along the roads as you travel between the wineries in summer and early fall.

The Okanagan is a favorite summer vacation destination of British Columbians for its beaches, where you can water-ski, sail, hike, and fish. Winter snow skiers love the close-to-town lifts and slopes.

Often the Okanagan and Similkameen Valleys get lumped together as the Okanagan/Similkameen Valley. Similkameen Valley's Crowsnest Vineyards is west of the Okanagan Valley and nestled along the beautiful, crisp Similkameen River, where eighty acres of vineyards grow on the lee side of the Coast Mountain Range. This is high desert cattle country, and the growing season is hot with long hours of sunshine and low humidity.

We will start with Vancouver Island, move on to the Fraser Valley, and then travel inland to the Okanagan Valley.

Note: All prices listed in this chapter are given in Canadian dollars.

VANCOUVER ISLAND

We usually begin our visits to Vancouver Island wineries in Victoria, simply because we love the city. By New York/London/Paris/Los Angeles standards Victoria is a small town, but it's full of urban conveniences, including excellent traditional, experimental, and ethnic restaurants. The Royal British Columbia Museum holds major exhibits and is respected worldwide, and galleries abound. Local and imported theater troupes thrill small and large audiences, particularly with Shakespeare at the Inner Harbour in August. European designers have boutiques, and you can buy Cuban cigars—if you are so inclined—in a tobacco shop right on Government Street, a cultural shock to most Americans.

Following are some of our favorite places to visit in this romantic city.

THE PARLIAMENT BUILDINGS, facing the southern bank of the Inner Harbour, beckon anyone interested in grand architecture or British Columbian politics and history. Queen Elizabeth and Princess Diana each visited here; you can see their photos upstairs. Here the aisle between the majority and loyal opposition legislators was designed to be just wide enough to prevent members from reaching their political opponents with their swords. Notice the small throne at the head of the chamber; it is reserved for the queen when she comes, because, after all, she is the Queen of Canada.

✤ *The Parliament. Belleville and Government Streets, Victoria; (250) 387–6121. Open 8:30 A.M.–5:00 P.M., except holidays. Admission is free. A wheelchair ramp is on Government Street; rest rooms, however, are not wheelchair accessible.*

WINE SHOPS

*Dr. Wilf Krutzmann's shop, **The Wine Barrel**, 644 Broughton, Victoria (250–388–0606), now offers a broad selection of BC's best wines and all the wine paraphernalia a wine aficionado could want, including wineglasses; gourmet foods such as Gigi biscotti, Cuisine Perel chocolate sauces, and wine soup; wine racks; gift wrapping papers; corkscrews; the best in wine literature; and Shoffeitt spices. We joyously celebrate Wilf's triumph over governmental bureaucracy and politics to get one of the first licenses in the province to sell wine outside a government store. Open 9:30 A.M.–5:30 P.M. Monday–Saturday, noon–5:00 P.M. Sunday, sometimes later. MasterCard, Visa, and Diners/enRoute.*

***The Wine Shoppe at Ocean Pointe Resort**, 45 Songhees Road, Victoria (phone 250–360–5804; fax 250–360–1041), stocks a most interesting selection of BC wines, from cool-climate whites to Okanagan reds, as well as sparkling wines and ice wines for your sweet tooth. Ocean Pointe Resort is visible from the Inner Harbour. To get there, cross the blue bridge and take the first exit, then follow the signs. You'll find the Wine Shoppe on the hotel's lower level next to the Boardwalk Restaurant (best Sunday brunch anywhere). The Wine Shoppe's staff helps tremendously with wine and food pairing advice. Open noon–8:00 P.M. Tuesday–Saturday, 10:00 A.M.–6:00 P.M. Sunday.*

***Cook Street, Village Wines**, 242 Cook Street, Victoria (phone 250–995–2665; fax 250–995–2224). Open 10:00 A.M.–9:00 P.M. daily.*

***Government liquor stores** with some BC wines (excluding farmgate and estate wineries) can be found at the Bay Centre shopping mall between Government and Douglas Streets at Fort Street, in the James Bay Mews at 230 Menzies Street, and 1520 Fairfield near Fort Street.*

Just across Government Street from the Parliament, you must visit the ROYAL BRITISH COLUMBIA MUSEUM, BC's outstanding museum of provincial and First Peoples history, with important permanent exhibits and world-class visiting collections. The gift shop is an outstanding place to find unusual books about the area as well as Native jewelry and art.

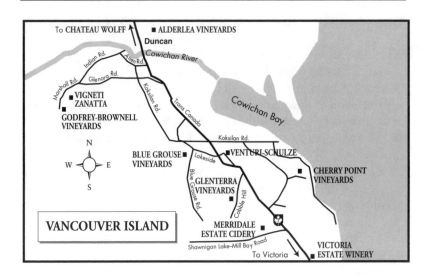

Royal British Columbia Museum, *675 Belleville Street, Victoria; phone (250) 387-3701. Open daily 9:30 A.M.–7:00 P.M., July through first full week in September; 10:00 A.M.–5:30 P.M. the rest of the year, except Christmas and New Year's Day. Admission for adults, $5.35; over 65, $3.21; 6–18, $2.14; under 6, free.*

Visit the **ART GALLERY OF GREATER VICTORIA**, 1040 Moss Street (250–384–1531), to see the best of Canadian art, including a permanent exhibit of Emily Carr's paintings. You can also buy all of her written work in the museum gift shop. Be sure to look in the garden for the only Shinto shrine in North America.

Art Gallery of Greater Victoria, *1040 Moss Street, Victoria V8V 4P1; phone (250) 384–4101. Open 10:00 A.M.–5:00 P.M. Monday–Saturday, until 9:00 P.M. on Thursday; 1:00–5:00 P.M. Sunday. Admission for adults is $5.00, seniors and students $3.00, under 12 free. Monday is "pay what you can" day.*

BEACON HILL PARK, just southeast of the Empress Hotel and Royal British Columbia Museum, is a refreshing place to stroll, watch cricket matches, listen to music on Sunday afternoons, and watch flowers grow. Children of all ages love the Children's (petting) Farm. At the southern end of the park, Dallas Road runs along the water; you can walk all the way to Ogden Point and the Ogden Point Dive Shop and Cafe.

EMILY CARR'S HOUSE, 207 Government Street (250–383–5843), offers a glimpse of old Victoria and the birthplace of Canada's most beloved painter and writer. Tour the Victorian home with well-informed docents. Open 10:00 A.M.–5:00 P.M. daily, mid-May through mid-October. Admission $2.25–$4.25. Wheelchair accessible downstairs only.

THE MARITIME MUSEUM, 28 Bastion Square (250–385–4222), is right off Government Street in a former courthouse that now houses more than 5,000 artifacts, pieces of equipment, historic boats, ship models, pictures, and maps for boating buffs. Check out the fascinating gift shop. Open 9:30 A.M.–4:30 P.M. Admission for adults, $5.00; over 65, $4.00; 6–11, $2.00; under 6, free. No credit cards.

On the Inner Harbour you may enjoy street artists and performers (comic jugglers in the evening), Undersea Gardens, and Royal London Wax Museum.

Right next to each other on Government Street are Munro's Books (considered by many the best in Canada) at 1108 and Murchie's Coffee and Tea (with sidewalk tables in good weather) at 1110, both Victoria institutions you should experience. Sam's Deli, 805 Government, has the best made-to-order sandwiches and people-watching seating in the city. Antique Row on Fort Street is antiquers' heaven. Along Government Street and its side streets from the Inner Harbour for almost a mile you can "shop till you drop."

Reasons to spread out your enjoyment over one long day or two more-relaxed ones include the many specialty growers of rhododendrons, vegetables, eggs, apples, and free-range poultry and meats, as well as craftspeople, farm markets, the Cowichan Bay Maritime Centre, and the Native Heritage Centre in Duncan. The more slowly you can go, the better.

Starting out from Victoria, take Douglas Street north past the automobile dealerships and the Mayfair Mall (you really can make it past without stopping!). Douglas Street becomes Highway 1 North, also known as the TransCanada Highway. From here it is about 32 miles (54 kilometers) to Duncan.

The entrance to Thetis Lake Park, a great place to picnic, comes up on the right. Kids love All Fun Water Slides & Recreation Park at 2207 Millstream Road (250–474–2535), just north of Langford—it might be just the right payoff for being good while you go wine tasting.

For a peaceful moment, visit Goldstream Provincial Park, a favorite refuge just a half hour from downtown Victoria, where you can experience a near rain forest and picnic under 450- to 500-year-old red cedars, reputed by some authorities to be the oldest trees in Canada. Across from Goldstream are reserves of the Malahat, Pauquachin, Tsawout, Tsartlip, and Tseycum bands.

As you approach the Malahat summit, you will see a left turn to the south end of Shawnigan Lake and Shawnigan Lake Provincial Park, where you can

CIDER ALERT!

Merridale Estate Cidery, *1230 Merridale Road, RR #1, Cobble Hill (250–743–4293), is Canada's only orchard dedicated solely to cider and wine apples. You can catch the orchard in splendiferous bloom in April or watch the fragrant pressing process in October and November. Featured ciders: Estate Cider, Merridale Scrumpy, Cyser, Merridale Pub Draft, Normandie Bubbly, Summer Berry Cider, and Summerset Select Dry, plus berries and nonalcoholic ciders. Open 10:30 A.M.–4:30 P.M. Monday–Saturday. Visa and Mastercard.*

hike, swim, or camp. Shawnigan Lake is the site of the historic "Last Spike" of the E&N Railroad, an old restored church that now houses the Auld Kirk Gallery, and the Shawnigan Historical Museum.

Soon you come upon the community of Cobble Hill, where you will find beautiful rolling hills, loads of specialty food and craftspeople, and some excellent independent wineries.

Notice the frequent blue and white signs designating an artisan's working studio, where you can often watch craftsmen at work and even purchase some signed pieces. Golfers can play at Arbutus Ridge, which you can reach by following Kilmalu Road along the coast north of Mill Bay past Arbutus Ridge through Cowichan Bay, Maple Bay, Crofton, and Chemainus.

Now we'll leave the well-beaten path and visit two of the island's finest wineries.

Call ahead to visit VENTURI-SCHULZE VINEYARDS, one of our favorites and the smallest in the Cowichan Valley. We rarely include a winery in our books that isn't open to the public, but this one is more than worth making special arrangements. Venturi-Schulze is hard to find because the family prefers not to post a sign on the road.

Giordano and Marilyn Schulze Venturi and their daughters produce some of the finest wines in North America, as well as a much-sought-after balsamic-style vinegar. (Daughter Michelle has returned to the winery, after studying and working abroad, to serve as apprentice and assistant winemaker to Giordano.) Their lovely tasting room is upstairs over the winery and adjoins the family home. The family has added a brand-new winery and planted an additional vineyard.

BALSAMIC VINEGAR MAYONNAISE
from Marilyn Schulze Venturi
of Venturi-Schulze Vineyards

2 large egg yolks
1 tsp Dijon mustard
enough vegetable oil to make a thick mayonnaise
juice of ½ lemon or to taste
2 Tbs Venturi-Schulze balsamic vinegar
salt and white pepper to taste

Put the egg yolks and the mustard in a bowl and whisk thoroughly together. Start adding the oil, drop by drop at first, then in a stream as you keep beating with the whisk. When you have a very thick sauce, the consistency of sour cream or thicker, add the lemon, the balsamic vinegar, and the salt and pepper. Beat again until smooth. Whisk in more oil if the sauce is too thin or runny. Excellent with boiled meats and poached or baked salmon.

All of Venturi-Schulze's wines are scooped up instantly by the highly rated Sooke Harbour House, the Empress Hotel, and the Wickinninish Inn on Vancouver Island, as well as Diva in Vancouver's Metropolitan Hotel and a few other lucky restaurants. Their sparkling wine was served to Queen Elizabeth at the Empress Hotel during the 1994 Commonwealth Games.

Fine points: Featured wines: Sparkling wine, Millefiori, Kerner, Schonburger, Müller-Thurgau, Madeleine Sylvaner, Siegerrebe, and an experimental Pinot Gris. Owners: Giordano Venturi and Marilyn Schulze Venturi. Winemakers: Giordano Venturi and Marilyn Schulze Venturi. Cases: 600. Acres: 10 in grapes, 15 total.

Venturi-Schulze Vineyards, 4235 TransCanada Highway, RR #1, Cobble Hill V0R 1L0; phone (250) 743-5630; fax (250) 743-5638. Open by appointment only. Credit cards are not accepted. Not wheelchair accessible.

To get to **CHERRY POINT VINEYARDS**, take the Fisher Road exit south of Duncan, head left for a minute on Telegraph, and take an immediate right on Cherry Point Road. When you reach the huge wooden wine vat/sign, you've just passed the driveway.

The fastest growing winery on Vancouver Island, Cherry Point runs on Ecotopia principles. Winemaker Todd Moore came to Cherry Point from Quail's Gate in the Okanagan Valley and serves on the VQA panel.

Notice the Swiss chalet–style architecture of the tasting room and Ulrich family home, surrounded by lawns, a large deck and elegant patio, tall cedars, and a hot tub. Co-owner Helena Ulrich and her culinary staff serve lunch or dinner to groups of ten or more at lunch or at least twenty at dinner, often including lamb fed on the porous grape skins and winter weeds from the vineyards. Soon you will be able to dine in the vineyards at the Ulrichs' new restaurant.

If no one seems to be around, ring the doorbell at the tasting room door. Adjacent to the tasting room you must have a look at the art gallery where the Arbutus Ridge Artists' Association and the Maple Bay Painters exhibit members' work.

Fine points: Cherry Point wines all cost around $10. Featured wines: Valley Mist white, Valley Sunset red, Ortega, Pinot Noir, Pinot Blanc, the first Agria (vines from Hungary) in BC Ortega, Siegerrebe, Auxerrois, and Gewürztraminer. Owners: Wayne and Helena Ulrich. Winemaker: Chris Otley. Cases: 3,500. Acres: 26.

❦ *Cherry Point Vineyards, 840 Cherry Point Road, RR #3, Cobble Hill V0R 1L0; phone (250) 743–1272; fax (250) 743–1059; Web site www.cherrypointvineyards.com. Open 10:00 A.M.–6:00 P.M. daily. MasterCard and Visa. Wheelchair accessible.*

LAMB CHOPS AU VIN
from Helena Ulrich,
Cherry Point Vineyards

---

1 Tbs vegetable oil
8 lamb chops, 1" thick
salt and pepper to taste
4 Tbs shallots, chopped
½ cup Cherry Point Pinot Noir wine
¼ cup beef broth
1 Tbs tomato paste
2 Tbs green peppercorns
¼ cup heavy cream

Heat the vegetable oil in heavy skillet until smoking. Cook lamb chops with salt and pepper to taste in skillet over high heat until done, reduce heat, pour off fat, and remove to warm plate.

Cook shallots over medium heat in skillet until wilted. Turn heat to high. Add Pinot Noir wine to skillet, reduce by three-quarters. Add beef broth to skillet, cook, stir, and scrape skillet. Add tomato paste and green peppercorns to skillet along with any meat juices from chops. Reduce by half. Stir heavy cream into sauce, and pour sauce over chops.

Take the TransCanada Highway 1 north into the Cobble Hill area, where you will find a fascinating collection of artisans and small, personal farms where you can buy superb products. (See the list of farmers' markets on page 266.)

Dolly and Cordell Sandquist open their cottage at COUNTRY TREASURES COTTAGE CRAFTS, 1133 Fisher Road, Cobble Hill (250–743–4374), for you to enjoy woodcrafts, jams, honey, beeswax candles, pottery, braided rugs, and "Christmas in the Country" the last weekend in November.

At THISTLEDOWN NURSERY, 2790 Cameron Taggert Road, Cobble Hill (250–743–2243), Peter Versteege offers hanging flower baskets, planter bowls, planter boxes, bedding plants, annuals, and perennials.

If you want to catch one more winery before lunch or dinner, don't miss BLUE GROUSE VINEYARDS & WINERY. Going north on Highway 1, turn left on Lakeside Road, and Blue Grouse's sign will be on the left. Going south on Highway 1, turn right at the light at Koksilah Road, turn left on Hillbank Road, and then right at Lakeside Road. Follow signs through the metal gate and up a gravel road to the top of the hill, where you will see an expansive vista of forest and vineyards.

Dr. Hans Kiltz, a Berlin native who comes from a family of winegrowers, has a doctorate in microbiology and is also a veterinarian specializing in tropical animals. He spent twenty years working with large animals in Africa and Asia before coming to Canada in 1988 with his Philippine-born wife, Evangeline, and their children.

Hans and Evangeline bought this secluded farm near a school their two children could attend and found it included what had been John Harper's experimental vineyard in the 1980s. Eventually, the Kiltzes imported Pinot Gris vines directly from France and now have developed their salvage project into a successful, sophisticated winery. Now the Kiltzes' delightful daughter Sandrina manages marketing and tasting.

Like Cherry Point, Blue Grouse is a farmgate winery, which means they can only produce 5,000 cases and cannot sell to provincial liquor stores. They are, however, allowed to sell at their wineries or provincial wine and beer stores.

Fine points: Featured wines: Siegerrebe, Ortega, Bacchus, Pinot Gris, Gamay Noir, Pinot Noir, and Black Muscat. Owners: Dr. Hans and Evangeline Kiltz. Winemaker: Dr. Hans Kiltz. Cases: 3,000. Acres: 10.

Blue Grouse Vineyards & Winery, 4365 Blue Grouse Road, Duncan V9L 4W4; phone (250) 743–3834; fax (250) 743–9305; e-mail skiltz@islandnet.com; Web site www.bluegrousevineyards.com. Open 11:00 A.M.–5:00 P.M. Wednesday–Sunday, April–September; 11:00 A.M.–5:00 P.M. Wednesday–Saturday, October–March. MasterCard and Visa. Wheelchair accessible.

Now we will head back to Cowichan Bay for lunch or dinner; it is forty-five minutes north of Victoria and south of Nanaimo, and its village is reminiscent of California's Sausalito and Stinson Beach as they used to be. You might try Myron's by-the-Sea or the Bayshore Fish Market.

Don't miss Cowichan Bay Maritime Centre Museum and home of the Wooden Boat Society, which acquired and renovated the pier in 1988. Many boats built here are on display, and you can watch boatbuilding and -painting and even attend workshops if you stick around a while.

Also visit the fascinating Marine Ecology Station with views of minihabitats and aquariums displaying coastal marine life. Be aware that you are experiencing the Cowichan Chemainus Ecomuseum, a museum without walls, funded by the BC Heritage Trust and the Heritage Canada Foundation.

Be sure to check out local art galleries, which include works by residents of the native Coastal Salish band. You can stroll or cycle along the estuary and Hecate Park to enjoy shorebirds and wildlife.

If you want to go a few miles farther to Duncan, we highly recommend that you visit the QUW'UTSUN CULTURAL AND CONFERENCE CENTRE. Drive across the double green bridge and turn left on Cowichan Way to this elegant and tastefully designed tribute to BC's First Peoples. Take a guided or self-guided tour, watch and meet totem pole carvers, Cowichan knitters, and Salish weavers and beaders, and try Native cuisine in the Riverwalk Cafe or Bighouse Restaurant.

๕ The Quw'utsun Cultural and Conference Centre, 200 Cowichan Way, Duncan V9L 4W4; phone (250) 746–8119; e-mail askme@quwutsun.ca; Web site www.quwutsun.ca. Open 9:00 A.M.–6:00 P.M. daily, May–September; 10:00 A.M.–5:00 P.M. daily, October–April. Admission varies by season and age, $3.25–$7.25, with a family pass at $19.00. MasterCard and Visa. Wheelchair accessible.

Farther northwest and south of Duncan, within just a few miles of Venturi-Schulze, Blue Grouse, or Cherry Point wineries, stop in at VIGNETI ZANATTA. From Highway 1, turn west at the light at Allenby Road, then turn left on Indian Road, which becomes Marshall Road when it crosses Glenora Road. The winery is on your left.

Founder Dennis Zanatta grew up in Treviso, Italy, and purchased this 120-acre dairy farm on Vancouver Island in 1958 because the area climate reminded him of home. Being a good Italian, he planted a few vines to make himself some wine, while maintaining the family marble business, Cowichan Tile & Terrazzo, in Duncan.

Tea, Please

The Fairmont Empress Hotel, *721 Government Street (250–389–2727)*, *provides Victoria's most famous tea experience. In the summer you must book reservations three days ahead. Considering ambience, decorum, and service, this is the ultimate tea in Victoria at $40 in high season.*

James Bay Tearoom & Restaurant, *322 Menzies Street (250–382–8282)*, *is just a block beyond the southwestern back corner of the Parliament Buildings. This is many locals' and visitors' favorite for value and friendliness at only $6.55, with High Tea on Sunday afternoons for $9.55.*

The Blethering Place Tea Room & Restaurant, *2250 Oak Bay (250–598–1413)*, *is a delightfully cozy and comfortable tearoom in Oak Bay Village frequented by locals, with teas served 11:00 A.M.–7:00 P.M. or any other time if you ask. Light Tea is $7.95, Full Tea is $10.95.*

Oak Bay Tea Room & Restaurant, *2241 Oak Bay (250–370–1005)*, *offers another friendly, welcoming tea experience with finger sandwiches, raisin scones, clotted cream, and the works for $22.95 for two people.*

The Oak Bay Beach Hotel, *1175 Beach Drive (250–598–4556)*, *is a must-visit and a historic hotel and room with a pleasant, informal English ambience and incomparable views of the Oak Bay Marina in the summer for $14.25.*

You can reach Point Ellice House, *2616 Pleasant Street (250–387–4697)*, *either by Harbour Ferry in front of the Empress Hotel or by road through industrial Victoria. Point Ellice is a heritage home where teas are served outside on the lawn on white wicker furniture overlooking the Gorge. You may enjoy one of the best teas in Victoria here and a tour of the museum-quality home for High Tea at $9.95 plus $2.00 for a tour; Light Tea is $5.95 plus $2.00 for a tour.*

White Heather Tea Room, *1885 Oak Bay (250–595–8020)*, *is Agnes Campbell's new Scottish tearoom with made-from-scratch soups, tea sandwiches, delicate shortbreads, scones, and miniature tarts. At once elegant and casual. Teas range from The Wee Tea ($6.95) to the Big Muckle Giant Tea ($27.95 for two people).*

Windsor House Tea Room and Restaurant, *2540 Windsor Street at Newport (250–595–3135)*, *is in a Tudor-style building facing Windsor Park, with set teas ranging from $6.95 to $25.95, Welsh rarebit, and deep-dish chicken potpies ($7.95).*

Dennis's daughter Loretta, who is the winemaker, grew into the wine business by studying plant science at the University of British Columbia and sparkling wine production in a family winery in Italy, then by getting a degree in enology at Piacenza, Italy.

The Zanattas turned the old family farmhouse into an excellent restaurant and wine shop, where guests can enjoy lunch or dinner on the deck, combining foods grown on the Zanattas' farm or close by. Go inside the house and find the tasting room to your right. Vinoteca Restaurant at Vigneti Zanatta is an absolute must-stop for lunch!

Fine points: Featured wines: Pinot Grigio, Ortega, Glenora Fantasia Brut sparkling wine, Auxerrois, and Damasco appetizer or sipping wine. Owner: Dennis Zanatta. Winemaker: Loretta Zanatta. Cases: 3,000. Acres: 30 of 120.

❧ *Vigneti Zanatta, 5039 Marshall Road, RR #3, Duncan, V9L 2X1; phone (250) 748–2338; fax (250) 746–5684; e-mail zanatta@seaside.net; Web site www. zanatta.ca. Open noon–4:30 P.M. Wednesday–Sunday and holiday Mondays, April– December; by appointment November–April. Lunches served noon–4:30 P.M. Wednesday–Sunday, Mother's Day–October. Dinners served Thursday–Saturday, July–September. Visa and MasterCard. Not wheelchair accessible.*

THE ZANATTA FAMILY HOME, NOW VIGNETI ZANATTA WINERY & VINOTECA RESTAURANT

As you leave Vigneti Zanatta, turn right on Marshall Road to heavenly gorgeous **GODFREY-BROWNELL VINEYARDS**, which the Godfreys cultivate without pesticides or herbicides. A professor at the University of Victoria, Dave Godfrey is also a distant relative of the Godfrey who received the 1886 land grant for this property, which he bought from local businessman, lawyer, and leader George Asp. The Godfreys first planted varietal grapes in 1999 and purchase grapes from the Okanagan Valley. Visit to enjoy the forest and salmon stream.

Fine points: Featured wines: Pinot Grigio (Pinot Gris), Chardonnay, Merlot, Cabernet Sauvignon, and Pinot Noir. Owners: Ellen and David Godfrey. Winemaker (consultant): Eric von Krosigk. Acres: 20 of 60.

❧ *Godfrey-Brownell Vineyards, 4911 Marshall Road, Duncan V9L 6T3; phone (250) 748–4889; e-mail info@gbvineyards.com; Web site www.gbvineyards.com. Open 11:00 A.M.–twilight daily. Visa and MasterCard.*

Go all the way through Duncan (originally called Alderlea) or stop and enjoy it on your way to **ALDERLEA VINEYARDS LTD.**, the pride of Roger and Nancy Dosman. The Dosmans say they gave up crushed cars at their Vancouver collision repair business to crush grapes here in the Cowichan Valley. Turn right onto Herd Road off TransCanada Highway, turn right on Lakes Road, then left on Stamps Road.

The Dosmans' newish, lovely tasting room across the driveway from their home, with a view of Quamichan Lake, features their very good estate-grown wines aged in American and French oak barrels. Bring a picnic, or stop at Cowichan Cheese Company Ltd. (250–715-0400), located in a renovated brick church on Norcross Road off Highway 1 between Duncan and Herd Road, for melt-in-your-mouth St. Paulin and Gouda, among other European-style cheeses.

Fine points: Featured wines: Pinot Auxerrois, Pinot Noir, Pinot Gris, Bacchus, Angelique white blend, Clarinet (Maréchal Foch), and Hearth Port. Owners: Roger and Nancy Dosman. Winemaker: Roger Dosman. Cases: 1,000. Acres: 8 of 10.

❧ *Alderlea Vineyards Ltd., 1751 Stamps Road, RR1, Duncan V9L 5W2; phone and fax (250) 746–7122. Call ahead for varying hours. Visa only. Wheelchair accessible.*

WINERY EXPLOSION ON VANCOUVER ISLAND

The sudden growth in the number of wineries on Vancouver Island is remarkable evidence of the confluence of favorable weather, the right soil, and the hard work and skill of the vineyardists and vintners.

Particularly impressive is the development of several wineries on the Saanich Peninsula north of the city of Victoria. Between 2000 and 2003, six new wineries were born here and two more were in gestation. The new facilities on the peninsula, long known as an ideal site for growing berries and vegetables, include CHALET ESTATE VINEYARD, 11195 Chalet Road, North Saanich, BC V8L 5M1, phone (250) 656–2252; NEWTON RIDGE VINEYARDS, 1595 Newton Heights Road, Saanichton, BC V8M 1T6, phone: (250) 652-8810; VICORI WINERY, 1890 Haldon Road, Saanichton, BC V8M 1T6, phone (250) 652–4820; and Victoria Estate Winery, described below.

The new vintners were drawn to winemaking from varied backgrounds— Michael Betts of Chalet was a yacht builder, and Newton Ridge owner Dutch-born Peter Sou is a retired Bechtel Corporation executive engineer (who does not even drink).

VICTORIA ESTATE WINERY is right up the road from the Victoria Butterfly Gardens and well worth the visit to stimulate the palate. Opened in 2003, this winery is the baby of British Columbia's best-known winemakers, Erik von Krosigk and Edd Moyes. Boasting an actual Viticulture Centre, a 21,000-square-foot facility on a twenty-five-acre former hay field, Victoria Estate is one of the most interestingly designed wineries in BC. Here visitors can sip wine, learn about the winemaking process, and have lunch of tapas, pizza, or deli picnic foods at the Mediterranean Deli, right on the Saanich Peninsula. Wines include a Madeleine Sylvaner, Pinot Gris, Merlot, Riesling, and Chardonnay.

Victoria Estate Winery, 1445 Benvenuto Avenue, Brentwood Bay, BC V8M IR3 (250) 652–9385; fax (250) 652–2672; e-mail info@victoriaestatewinery.com; Web site www.victoriaestatewinery.com. Open 10:00 A.M.–10:00 P.M. daily. Visa and MasterCard. Take Victoria Transit bus #75 or Gray Line Tours from the Fairmont-Empress Hotel.

Over the Malahat grade (Highway 1) north to Cobble Hill and Duncan is **Glenterra Vineyards,** which is developed, owned, and operated by John Kelly, who is distinguished by the "burr" in his brogue. Kelly has mentored

other newcomers who lacked his expertise. Glenterra is a terrific and tiny winery not on winery association maps but worth the entertaining visit. John partners with Ruth Luxton to create wines in a garagelike building across the gravel driveway turnaround from their home. Ruth is an accomplished chef and Culinary Institute of America graduate who has cooked with John Ash in Sonoma County, California, and now cooks locally at Livingston's Café in Duncan.

John Kelly relies on files left to him by original owner John Harper, who started to grow grapes here after serving and sipping in Italy during World War II. Harper originally grew forty-two grape varieties in twenty rows on one little acre at this site. Now Kelly has four-and-a-half acres planted of a total seventeen and farms with organic fertilizers and no pesticides or herbicides.

As a testament to the quality of Glenterra's limited estate-grown 500-case production, their wines are available at the best restaurants in BC, including the Wickaninnish Inn, The Aerie, Sooke Harbour House on Vancouver Island, and Bishop's in Vancouver.

Glenterra Vineyards, 3897 Cobble Hill Road, Cobble Hill, BC VR 1L; (250) 743–2330; e-mail glenterravineyards@shaw.ca. Open 11:00 A.M.–6:00 P.M. daily. Visa and MasterCard.

New in the Duncan area is ECHO VALLEY VINEYARDS, 4681 Waters Road, P.O. Box 816, Duncan, BC V9L 3Y2; phone (250) 748–1470, founded by Albert Brennink, a retired Dutch architect. Brennink and his son Edward planted their vineyard on the corner of their cattle ranch.

West of Victoria is TUGWELL CREEK FARM, opened in 2003 by professional beekeepers Robert Liptrot and Dana LeComte, who maintain more than a hundred hives. From the gathered honey, they ferment mead—the ancient drink of England's Middle Ages.

Even more adventurous is the enterprising CHASE & WARREN ESTATE VINEYARDS in the mountains in the center of the island at 6253 Drinkwater Road, Port Alberni, BC V9Y BH9; phone (250) 724–4906.

Equally impressive is the growth of wineries in the Gulf Islands in the Georgia Strait between southern Vancouver Island and the mainland. The BC Ferries thread their way among the islands from Swartz Bay north of Victoria to Tsawwassen terminal south of Vancouver city. Before 2000 no wineries existed on

these islands, except for some homemade wines pressed from the island-grown grapes. As of 2003 we have **SATURNA ISLAND VINEYARDS AND WINERY,** 8 Quarry Road, Saturna Island, BC V0N 2Y0; phone (250) 539–5139. On the well-developed, popular tourist destination and artists' colony, Salt Spring Island, three others have opened: **GARRY OAKS ESTATE WINERY,** 1880 Fulford-Ganges Road, Salt Spring Island, BC V8K 2A5, phone (250) 653–4687; **SALT SPRING ISLAND VINEYARDS,** 151 Lee Road, Salt Spring Island, BC V8K 2A5, phone (250) 653–9463; and **LONG HARBOUR VINEYARDS,** 301 Mansell Road, Salt Spring Island, BC V8K 1P9, phone (250) 537–2904. In September 2002, Salt Spring Island Vineyards beat Garry Oaks Estate by thirty minutes to get the first winery license on the island.

After taking a ferry, one can drive to the island wineries as well as enjoy the beauty and shops. It would be wise to telephone ahead to be sure the wineries are open for visitors, although the Saturna Island Winery maintains regular hours 11:30 A.M.– 4:30 P.M. Wednesday–Sunday, May–September, and closes at 2:30 P.M. in March and April.

The new owners of the island wineries are as interesting as the vintages because they all have unusual histories and different occupations. Well-known winemakers Eric von Krosigk and Ross Mirko have now joined Saturna Island Vineyards and Garry Oaks Estates, respectively. Several more vineyards are in the planting stage on the islands.

FRASER VALLEY

The Fraser Valley runs along the Fraser River and was named for Simon Fraser, the North West Fur Company explorer who crossed the Great Divide to its west side in 1808 and canoed down the river into what he dubbed New Caledonia, a poetic name for Scotland. Queen Victoria changed the name to British Columbia, and occasional discontents refer to it now as British California.

The city of Vancouver probably will be your home base to travel to Fraser Valley's four open wineries, although you can easily visit them from Victoria via a ninety-minute ferry ride and return to Victoria the same evening.

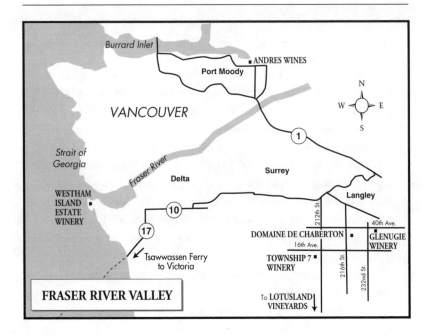

FRASER RIVER VALLEY

Vancouver is a fabulous large city that seems like a small town, partly because the sections most visitors want to see are close to each other. You can easily see why film companies come here to tape television and movie segments. Few places have beaches, densely populated residential neighborhoods, glamorous shopping, international communities, produce and artists' markets, and skiing all within an hour of each other.

Recently Vancouver has grown faster than any other metropolis in Canada, and perhaps on the West Coast of North America. Billions and billions of dollars have been invested by developers in Vancouver and nearby Richmond, resulting in a dramatic increase in high-rises replacing smaller neighborhoods and shopping centers replacing corner stores. A positive result is the increase in ethnic restaurants throughout Vancouver and Richmond.

You will find Italian neighborhoods east of Vancouver proper on Commercial Drive or out around the 2400 block of East Hastings for real Italian food from real Italian-Canadians. East Indian foods and culture focus around Punjabi Market at Main and Forty-ninth Streets, while the Greek neighborhood encircles West Broadway and MacDonald. Greek restaurants, though, seem to be everywhere in BC. A great variety of restaurants, particularly moderately priced, is located east to west on Fourth and Tenth Avenues. We especially like Las Margaritas, for great, fun Mexican food, and Chianti, for excellent pastas and veal piccata.

Vancouver's General Motors Place, called "The Garage" by British Columbians, hosts professional sports and large musical events right across the street from the Vancouver Public Library in the Library Square complex, a modern and innovatively designed center at Robson and Homer Streets. Architect Moshe Safdie's work truly takes Vancouver into the twenty-first century. Visiting the library is a cultural experience one should not miss.

Robson Street is Vancouver's version of Rodeo Drive and Melrose Avenue rolled into one. Follow it almost to English Bay, to stroll or strut along the beach. Good restaurants are everywhere, and Chinatown is on East Pender Street.

Art galleries pop up in many neighborhoods. One of the most outstanding galleries is the Vancouver Art Gallery, 750 Hornby Street (604–662–4719), where you can see works by the best Canadian and European artists. Try the Canadian Craft Museum in Cathedral Place at 639 Hornby Street (604–687–8266).

An absolute must-visit is Granville Island in the center of the city, where you can visit the Emily Carr Institute of Art and Design. The Granville Island Market has fresh vegetables, fish, poultry, breads, lunch counters, artisans and craftspeople, and the fabulous candy maker's counter where they ring a loud bell when they put out samples of fudge just out of the cauldron.

We highly recommend a visit to the University of British Columbia's Museum of Anthropology, 6393 Northwest Marine Drive (604–822–3825). Artifacts of British Columbia native cultures, Africa, and Asia are all on display much more openly than we have seen in other museums, with hundreds of drawers for you to open and explore. While out at the university, food lovers might want to visit the Physick Garden, an herb garden re-created to resemble a sixteenth-century monastic medicinal garden, and the Food Garden, to learn how we can efficiently cultivate our own.

Vancouver has exceptional parks where you can relax, exercise, rejoice in beauty, and even learn. Vancouver has twice the rain of Victoria or San Francisco, sprinkled with "sun breaks." It's generally the perfect climate to grow flowers such as snapdragons, geraniums, impatiens, and rhododendrons. Stanley Park includes a small rain forest you can walk in. Queen Elizabeth Park is loaded with winding paths that seem to close out the rest of the world. The Bloedel Conservatory is funded as a conscience move by one of the largest clear-cutting lumber companies in North America.

Close to Vancouver, as well as to Tsawwassen, where the BC ferries from Victoria land, is the established **DOMAINE DE CHABERTON**. From the ferry, follow Highway 17 then turn east on Highway 10. From Vancouver, get on the

TransCanada Highway and take the 200th Street South exit, continue south, turn left on Sixteenth Avenue, turn right on 216th Street, and watch for the Domaine de Chaberton sign. From Highway 10, turn south onto 200th Street at Fraser Highway, turn left onto Sixteenth Avenue, turn right on 216th, and Domaine de Chaberton will be on your left.

Owner/winemaker Claude Violet traces his wine roots deeper than any other BC winemaker, to his family's first vineyard planted in 1644 near Perpignan, France. Here Violet's family produced the fine red aperitif Byrrh, which his father merged with Dubonnet and Cinzano.

After Claude and his immediate family sold their interest in the resulting enterprise, he set off to pursue banking in Munich, where he met and married his German wife, Ingeborg. They moved to Switzerland, and Claude began representing Spanish wines there, eventually moving to Canada. He carefully checked out the Okanagan Valley and decided vinifera grapes might not survive occasional deep cold. He found an old raspberry farm in a warm weather pocket just beyond the bad weather belt around Vancouver. The Violets named their BC estate Domaine de Chaberton to remind them of a family farm near Montpelier, France.

The Violets have smartly added an excellent restaurant, Bacchus Bistro, to their winery, serving Mediterranean food at lunch Tuesday–Sunday and at dinner Thursday–Sunday (604–530–9694).

 Fine points: Featured wines: Estate Bacchus, Bacchus Dry, Chardonnay, Madeleine Sylvaner, Ortega, Merlot, Gamay Noir, and special Late Harvest Bottyris Affected Ortega dessert wine. Owners: Claude and Ingeborg Violet. Winemaker: Elias Phiniotis. Cases: 60,000. Acres: 33 of 55.

🍇 *Domaine de Chaberton, 1064 216th Street, Langley V2Z 1R3; phone (604) 530–1736 or (888) 332–9463; fax (604) 533–9687; e-mail info@domainede chaberton.com; Web site www.domainedechaberton.com. Open 10:00 A.M.–6:00 P.M. Monday–Saturday, 11:00 A.M.–6:00 P.M. Sunday. Tours daily at 2:00 and 4:00 P.M. Visa and MasterCard. Wheelchair accessible.*

NEW WINERIES TO WATCH IN FRASER VALLEY

Since 2000, new wineries have sprung up in Fraser Valley south and east of the city of Vancouver at an optimistic rate. While giant Andres (Peller) closed its doors to the public, Westham Island Estate Winery, Township 7 Vineyards, Glenugie Winery, A'Very Fine Winery (its actual name), and Columbia Valley Classics Winery opened theirs.

WESTHAM ISLAND ESTATE WINERY was the dream of fruit grower Andy Bissett to create a winery on Westham Island featuring fruit wines. After he died suddenly in 2002, his wife and daughter turned their home into a winery tasting room, which opened in the summer of 2003; 2170 Westham Island Road, Delta, BC V4K 3N2; phone (604) 940–9755; e-mail info@westham-island-winery.com; Web site www.westham-island-winery.com.

GLENUGIE WINERY, owned by Gary and Christina Tayler and named for a family farm in Scotland, opened in 2002; 3033 232nd Street, Langley, BC V2Z 3A8; phone (604) 539–9463; Web site www.glenugiewinery.com.

TOWNSHIP 7 VINEYARDS AND WINERY, opened by Corey and Gwen Coleman in 2000 after they spent six years working at leading Okanagan Valley wineries in winemaking and wine marketing, respectively; 21152 Sixteenth Avenue (corner 212th Street), Langley, BC V2Z 1K3; phone (604) 532–1766; Web site www.township7.com.

LOTUSLAND VINEYARDS (aka A'Very Fine Winery) is a cozy boutique winery. Owners David and Liz Avery make wine using all BC grapes; 28450 King Road (Sixteenth Avenue), Abbotsford, BC V4X 1B1; phone (604) 857–4188; e-mail info@avery finewine.ca; Web site www.averyfinewine.ca.

COLUMBIA VALLEY CLASSICS WINERY overlooks Cultus Lake, south of Chilliwak, an hour east of Vancouver via Highway 1, and concentrates on fruit wines; 1385 Frost Road, Lindell Beach, BC V2R 4X8; phone (604) 858–5233; e-mail info@cvwines.com; Web site www.cvcwines.com.

OKANAGAN VALLEY

Most of British Columbia's wineries are located in the warmer Okanagan Valley, which is at least a five-hour drive from Vancouver. We will give you directions to the Okanagan from Washington as well as from Vancouver and the BC Ferries terminal at Tsawwassen.

From Washington: You can take the easier border crossing at Osoyoos via Highway 97 instead of going through long lines and waits between Seattle and Vancouver. Winemakers caution that guns are checked and not allowed into Canada. Canadian border officials search most RVs on the basis that they figure most RV owners carry guns "for self-protection," which is not an acceptable excuse in Canada. Highway 97 goes right to and through Osoyoos at the southern end of the Okanagan Valley.

From Vancouver: Two highways of vastly different qualities take you to the Okanagan and back. We recommend that you go eastward the "long" way from Vancouver to Penticton via Highways 10 to 1 then 3 and 3A, passing through beautiful country. Then visit wineries around and south of Penticton; work your way northward through Summerland, Peachland, and Westbank; stay in Kelowna; and then return to Vancouver by driving west from Westbank on the Coquihalla Connector (Highway 97C) to Highway 5A, then to the town of Merritt, and south on the spectacular Coquihalla (Highway 5) down to Hope. It's about 250 miles (417 kilometers) from Vancouver each way. Great news for cyclists: Both highways have bike lanes. Be sure to take plenty of provisions.

If you wish to visit Domaine de Chaberton (see page 171) on this trip, turn off Highway 10 before the Langley Bypass onto 200th Street and head south. Turn left on Sixteenth Avenue and then turn right on 216th Street and the winery will be on your left.

While heading east on Highway 1, if you have the kids along, appease them (and yourselves) by taking exit 95 to Wonderland Amusement Park, 2.1 miles (3.5 kilometers) east of the Abbotsford turnoff.

Near exit 129, you can reach Bridal Falls Travel Centre and Chilliwack RV Park. Exit 135 takes you to Bridal Falls Provincial Park, Master Gardens, Dino Town, Bridal Veil Falls (hugely crowded but worth the wait), TransCanada Water Slides & Bumper Boats, the Bridal Falls Motel, and the very local China Chef Diner. And with all this, the crisp, clear Fraser River is still on your left. Stay on Highway 1 until you get to the main Hope exit.

Hope has the appeal of a small rural community and feels as if it's in the Alps. Quaint churches, murals, Native totems and wood sculpture around the City Park, and Hope Brigade Days (first weekend in September) bring people here again and again. The Hope Museum has a charming local history display next to the Information Centre and across from Rolley's Restaurant & Motel, a locally popular breakfast place. We tried Lee's Cafe on Main Street across from City Park, along with several locals having their regular burgers and Lee's famous fish and chips.

Important: At Hope you part from Highway 1, which turns north. Take Highway 3 heading east through the breathtaking Coquihalla Canyon Provincial Recreation Area in the Skagit Range, after which the road turns right (southeast) and becomes the Crowsnest Highway (3) at Nicolum River Provincial Park. You start the climb over the summit about 3 miles (5 kilometers) southeast of Hope.

In another 4 miles (6.7 kilometers) you enter one of nature's best, Manning Provincial Park, and pass an Esso station, the last gasoline station for 64 kilometers. It is now 133.2 miles (222 kilometers) to Penticton, our goal for today. The popular rest stop and Manning Provincial Park Resort are actually 27 miles (45 kilometers) farther ahead on Highway 3.

In the meantime, Highway 3 narrows to two lanes for a while, the air becomes cooler and crisper, the grasses become more lush and green, the mountains become more sheer, and the woods beside the road become deeper and more beautiful. Obey the speed limits here if you want to survive.

The park and the MANNING PARK RESORT are named for Edward C. Manning, who once served as British Columbia's legendary chief forester. Elegantly simple, the resort has forty-one motel rooms, a few cabins, and triplexes, most in beautiful log-cabin style.

The resort's restaurant and Cascade Cafe are open to the public, although both are closed midafternoon. The gift shop offers souvenirs as well as a few snacks and bottled water. Enjoy the picnic tables, clean rest rooms, historical exhibits, and spacious lawns open to public use.

✿ *Manning Park Resort, Box 1480, Highway 3, Manning Provincial Park; phone (250) 840–8822. American Express, MasterCard, and Visa; checks not accepted. Wheelchair accessible.*

After the past few hours' drive beyond Manning Park, the town of Princeton looks like an enormous small town. Be sure to turn right (southeast) on Highway 3 at Princeton toward Hedley and Keremeos.

Princeton offers some crucial pit stop features: the Bromley Station Pub just before town, a Mohawk station with diesel fuel, the Copper Town Motel, Santo's Pizza and Steak House, the Golden Hills Deli, and that oasis Dairy Queen. Just before you cross the blue bridge back to the highway, there's a helpful Visitors Information Centre.

Bʀɪᴛɪꜱʜ Cᴏʟᴜᴍʙɪᴀ Wɪɴᴇ Iɴꜰᴏʀᴍᴀᴛɪᴏɴ Cᴇɴᴛʀᴇ

Twenty-seven miles (45 kilometers) west of Princeton, you come to Hedley, another small town with an interesting-looking Colonial Inn and Tea Room. The Nickel Plate Restaurant and Western Gift Shop look as if they, too, could get you through the day.

Another 6 miles (9 kilometers) marks the beginning of the Okanagan's fruit stands. For the next 2 miles (3.3 kilometers) they line the road and the air smells like sweet fruit, at least in August and September. April is blossom time, another popular visiting month. You can sample and take home apricots, peaches, apples, cherries, asparagus, and smoked salmon (a local orchard crop, of course). There are abundant U-pick opportunities and bargain prices at these stands. Antiques shops have infiltrated the neighborhood, so beware!

Turn north on Highway 3A to Penticton and notice the historic 1877 gristmill, as well as more fruit stands.

When Highway 3A stops at Highway 97, take extreme care while turning left toward Penticton, another 8.4 miles (14 kilometers). You pass the fabulous Okanagan Game Farm, where you can see 120 species including lions, tigers, zebras, and rhinoceros in a 560-acre quasi-natural environment, and Okanagan Amusements as you follow the western shore of Skaha Lake and into downtown Penticton.

Penticton is a largely underrated city, where there truly is something for everyone. Ideally located between two lakes, Skaha to the south and Okanagan to the north, Penticton offers a wide range of vacation activities. The Skaha Lake end of Penticton is loaded with beach activities, including waterskiing, sailing, windsurfing, and swimming as well as go-carts, amusement centers (games!), miniature golf, and water slides. There are plenty of motels (some right across from the water) and camping and RV parks. The Okanagan Lake end is slightly more subtle, and the lake itself stretches north for 68 miles (113 kilometers).

A great place to get your bearings in Penticton are the exquisite new BRITISH COLUMBIA WINE INFORMATION CENTRE and Penticton Visitor Information Centre at 888 Westminster Avenue West, Penticton V2A 8S2; phone (250) 490–2006; fax (250) 490–2003; Web site www.bcwineinfo.com. The BC Wine Centre is the largest VQA wine center in Canada. Here you can pick up pounds of brochures, answers to your questions, wines, and wine posters.

Penticton's old downtown reaches a couple of blocks wide from Main Street and lengthwise between Eckhardt and Okanagan Lake.

We have found that one of the most relaxing things to do in Penticton is to walk or run on the path along the Okanagan River Channel and along the path and beaches of Skaha Lake. Remember that some paths are in Penticton Indian Band territory and are offered to the public for your enjoyment. Please respect where you walk.

THEO'S is a favorite hangout for us and for many locals. Winemakers and winery staff members come here often to enjoy the ambience and Mom's Greek food. The fried calamari is exceptional, and the quantities of food served here make it a good idea to order a few favorites and share.

You can select the romantic room that suits your mood of the moment. Rooms have tile floors, heavy wood beams, tall ceilings, lots of large plants, and that ever-present feeling that song should break out at any minute—and it often does, along with dancing and an occasional belly dancer.

Theo's, 687 Main Street near Eckhardt; phone (250) 492–4019; Web site www.eatsquid.com. Open for lunch and dinner until 10:00 P.M., light foods after that. Full bar. American Express, MasterCard, Visa, and Interac. Wheelchair accessible.

Now, let's get on to the wineries! We suggest that you first base yourself in Penticton and make a one- or two-day tour southward to Oliver, and perhaps even to Osoyoos near the U.S. border. Come back to Penticton, spend the night, and then tour the wineries in Naramata, Summerland, Peachland, Westbank, Kelowna, and Winfield. Those with time on their hands might even want to go all the way north to Vernon and Salmon Arm.

If you come into the Okanagan through Osoyoos from Washington, you might want to visit all the wineries south of Penticton, stay in Penticton one night, work your way northward to Kelowna, spend a night or two there, and

MEATLESS DOLMATHES
from Mary Theodosakis of Theo's Restaurant

1 cup long-grain rice	*juice of one lemon*
¼ cup dried currants	*1 tsp sugar*
2 cups olive oil, divided	*½ tsp pepper to taste*
2 Tbs onions, finely diced	*¼ cup pine nuts*
1 Tbs salt to taste	*¼ cup white wine*
¼ cup flat-leaf parsley, chopped	*2 tsp ground cinnamon*
¼ cup fresh dill, leaves only, chopped	*1 16 oz jar grape leaves*
3 Tbs fresh mint leaves, chopped	*1 lemon, thickly sliced*
½ tsp allspice	*6 fresh vine leaves (optional)*

Wash rice and let soak for five to ten minutes. Rinse and dry in a tea towel. Soak currants in white wine. Heat 1 cup of the olive oil in a large saucepan, add onions and a pinch of salt until the onions are wilted—do not brown. Let onions cook, then add parsley, dill, mint, allspice, rice, lemon juice, sugar, salt and pepper, pine nuts, white wine, currants, and cinnamon. Mix and let simmer, covered, for about ten minutes, then cool mixture. Add salt and pepper to taste.

Rinse the grape leaves until no brine remains. Pat them dry and cut off tough stems. Line the bottom of a Dutch oven with broken vine leaves. Place an old plate upside down in the bottom of the Dutch oven.

To prepare the dolmathes, place the grape leaves shiny side down on a flat surface. Place about 1 Tbs of mixture near the base of each grape leaf. Fold each side of the leaf diagonally into the center so they overlap the stuffing. Start rolling the leaf from the base to the tip, making a neat package. Do not overfill, as the rice will swell during cooking.

Place the packages seam down and close together, making a spiral formation all around the plate inside the Dutch oven. Place remaining lemon slices between layers. Cover the grape leaves with a heavy old plate. Add one cup of olive oil and enough water to come to the level of the old plate. Cover and bring to a boil, lower the heat, and simmer for one hour.

After the hour try one of the dolmathes. If the leaves are chewy, simmer again until done. Let cool covered so they will absorb all their liquid. Serve with slices of lemon and natural yogurt at room temperature.

then hop over the Coquihalla to Vancouver, and maybe Victoria, and back to Seattle and wherever else you may want to go in Washington.

In the Penticton area, you can visit seven neighboring wineries on the east side of Okanagan Lake on your way to Naramata: Benchland Vineyards,

Hillside Estate, Lang Vineyards, Red Rooster, Nichol Vineyard, Kettle Valley, and Lake Breeze. On the west side of Okanagan Lake, Scherzinger Vineyards, Sumac Ridge, and brand-new Greata Ranch Estate Winery, which was opened in 2003 by the owners of Cedar Creek Winery.

BENCHLAND VINEYARDS is one of British Columbia's newer wineries, starting small and proud, and practically right downtown in Penticton. Take Eckhardt Avenue to Benchland and Upper Bench Road. Klaus Stadler and host Kerry Russell offer tables for you to enjoy your wine and picnic, as well as a very friendly tasting experience. Their first release was BC's first Zweigelt (1999), a cross between Lemberger and St. Laurent. It is so full-bodied you can almost chew it.

Fine points: Featured wines: Chardonnay, Pinot Blanc, Pinot Noir, Merlot, Cabernet Sauvignon, Zweigelt, and Late Harvest Riesling. Owner: Klaus Stadler. Consulting winemaker: Eric von Krosigk. Cases: 1,500. Acres: 18.

❧ *Benchland Vineyards, 170 Upper Bench Road, Penticton V2A 8T1; phone (250) 770-1733, fax (250) 770-1734. Open 11:00 A.M.–6:00 P.M. Tuesday–Sunday, May–October. Visa. Wheelchair accessible.*

HILLSIDE ESTATE WINERY was once a charming, personal little winery that has become an excellent larger winery. To get there from Penticton turn east on Lakeshore Road, which becomes Vancouver Road, and then left on Naramata Road. Hillside comes up very quickly, and the sign is right at the turnout (there is no blue and white provincial winery sign here).

Founders Vera and Bohumir Klokocka were both natives of Prague, Czechoslovakia, and met while they both worked for the Czech national airline, after which they found their way to Canada and marriage. Eventually they purchased an orchard at Naramata, which they replanted in grapes.

They joined neighbors Guenther Lang, the Zellers, Adolf Kruger, and Terry Wells in a campaign to gain recognition of small "farmgate" wineries, resulting in then-BC premier Bill Vander Zalm's announcement of the 1989 farmgate winery policy.

Hillside's first wine, a 1989 Auxerrois, received both the VQA designation and the coveted VQA gold seal. After her husband's death, Vera sold the winery to John Fletcher—who served many years with Vincor and other Canadian and American wineries—and John Hromyk. They built a striking new winery facility and tasting room. In 1997 they hired winemaker Eric von Krosigk, who had been at Hawthorne Mountain.

Recently a group of investors purchased the winery, with Ken Lauzon as managing partner.

Hillside now boasts a much-needed restaurant in these parts—The Barrel Room Bistro, featuring fresh regional cuisine and breathtaking views of the Okanagan Valley.

Fine points: Featured wines: Chardonnay, Pinot Blanc, Riesling, Sémillon-Chardonnay, Muscat Ottonel, Riesling ice wine, Cabernet Franc, Cabernet Sauvignon, Merlot Syrah, and Gamay Blush. Owners: Group of investors. Winemaker: Eric von Krosigk. Cases: 30,000. Acres: 73.

Hillside Estate Winery, 1350 Naramata Road, Penticton V2A 6J6; phone (250) 493–6274; toll free in Canada (888) 923–9463; fax (250) 493–6294; Web site www.hillsideestate.com. Open 10:00 A.M.–5:00 P.M. daily, April–mid-October; noon–4:00 P.M. mid-October–Christmas. Visa and MasterCard. Wheelchair accessible.

From Hillside Estate turn north (right) on Naramata Road. Notice the OSTRICH MEAT FOR SALE sign and Three Mile House on the left.

Naramata is truly the place at the end of the road. The road up the east side of Okanagan Lake simply ends in the charming small town of Naramata, although the community's territory spreads far beyond the burg. Naramata was named for the spirit of an Indian woman who spoke to the town's founder through a medium at a seance.

To get to LANG VINEYARDS from Naramata Road, turn right on Arawana Road straight up the hill, and right again on dirt Gammon Road for 1.2 miles (2 kilometers). A four-wheel-drive vehicle would be nice here. You can also get there from Gawne Road, which is even rougher. Enjoy one of the best views of Okanagan Lake from here.

Guenther Lang was a rising executive at Daimler Benz in his native Stuttgart, Germany, when he and his wife, Kristina, left for Canada and an outdoor life in the Okanagan. In 1981 they bought nine acres of vineyard and converted from hybrid vines to vinifera before the 1988 Canadian government-sponsored pullout. So the Langs were way ahead of their colleagues, who would have to wait longer for their new vines to mature.

Guenther began his unstoppable crusade to get the provincial legislature to recognize small farm wineries and made up to 1,500 gallons of wine in 1989, counting on his powers of persuasion to convince the government to give him a license. The bureaucrats came through, and Lang became BC's first farmgate winery after four years of lobbying.

Guenther believes that his site offers growing conditions "as good as Bordeaux's," with warm days and cool nights. He exports his ice wine and

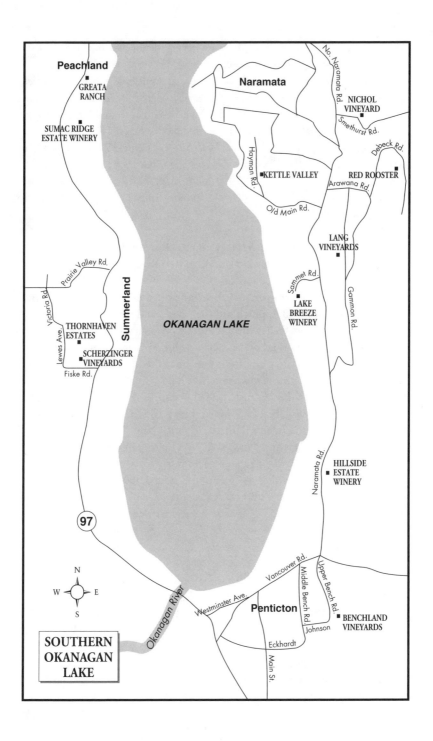

Peachland

GREATA
RANCH

SUMAC RIDGE
ESTATE WINERY

Naramata

No. Naramata Rd.

NICHOL
VINEYARD

Smethurst Rd.

Depeck Rd.

Hayman Rd.

■KETTLE VALLEY

RED ROOSTER

Arawana Rd.

Old Main Rd.

LANG
VINEYARDS

Prairie Valley Rd.

Summerland

OKANAGAN LAKE

Sammet Rd.

Gammon Rd.

Victoria Rd.

LAKE
BREEZE
WINERY

THORNHAVEN
ESTATES

Lewes Ave.

SCHERZINGER
VINEYARDS

Fiske Rd.

Naramata Rd.

HILLSIDE
ESTATE
WINERY

97

N
W   E
S

Okanagan River

Vancouver Rd.

Upper Bench Rd.

Middle Bench Rd.

Westminster Ave.

Penticton

Johnson

BENCHLAND
VINEYARDS

SOUTHERN
OKANAGAN
LAKE

Eckhardt

Main St.

dessert wines to Singapore and Taiwan, having discovered fortuitously that "Lang" means "beautiful" in Chinese.

 Fine points: Featured wines: Five or six Rieslings from dry to ice wine, Gewürztraminer, Auxerrois, Maréchal Foch, Pinot Noir, Pinot Meunier, and Merlot. Owners: Guenther and Kristina Lang. Winemaker: Petra Koeller. Cases: 5,000. Acres: 15.

❧ *Lang Vineyards, 2493 Gammon Road, Site 11, Comp 55, Naramata V0H 1N0; phone (250) 496–5987; fax (250) 496–5706; Web site www.vignoble wines.com. Open 11:00 A.M.–6:00 P.M. daily, May–mid-October; weekdays by appointment and 11:00 A.M.–4:00 P.M. Saturday–Sunday, November–April. No credit cards. Wheelchair accessible.*

From Lang Vineyards, turn left on Gammon Road, right on Arawana Road, and left on Debeck Road, and wind around to **RED ROOSTER WINERY** and some of the best views in British Columbia.

Beat and Prudence Mahrer sold their fitness center in Basel, Switzerland, came to Canada in the '80s, purchased their farm, and planted their vineyard. A carpenter, Beat built their winery and sold off orchards to concentrate on grape vines. Both Mahrers far prefer their new life to their old. You might even leave with some rooster lore and fresh eggs from the henhouse. For a varying price, you can adopt a row of vines and have a flag with your name at the end of your row. Every year Red Rooster hosts a picnic for adoptive families.

 Fine points: Featured wines: Pinot Gris, Chardonnay, Riesling, Gewürztraminer, Bantam, Pinot Noir, Merlot, Meritage, Merlot/Cabernet Sauvignon, Vin Santo, Golden Egg, Brut, Late Harvest Chardonnay, and Chardonnay Ice wine. Owners: Beat and Prudence Mahrer. Winemaker: Greg Larson. Cases: 8,500. Acres: 25.

❧ *Red Rooster Winery, 891 Naramata Road, Penticton V0H 1N0; phone (250) 496–4041; fax (250) 496–5674; e-mail: redroosterwinery@shaw.ca. Open 10:00 A.M.–6:00 P.M. daily, April–December; by chance or appointment January–March. Visa and MasterCard. Wheelchair accessible.*

From Red Rooster you can either drive on to Nichol or visit Lake Breeze on the lake side of Naramata Road. If you make an appointment ahead of time, you can visit **KETTLE VALLEY**, 2988 Hayman Road, RR #1, Site 2, Comp 39 (phone 250–496–5898; fax 250–496–5298), to taste Chardonnay, Pinot Noir, Cabernet Sauvignon, and Merlot, plus rare (and possibly the first) ice wines made from Pinot Noir and Chardonnay.

To get to **NICHOL VINEYARD**, go back down to Naramata Road and turn north (right). Follow it as it twists and turns, pass the turnoff to Naramata proper, and turn right on Smethurst Road. Pass Albrecht and turn with Smethurst Road to the left and into the winery driveway. Nichol is at the end.

Nichol Vineyard is best known as the first vineyard to plant Syrah in Canada and the only winery to make Syrah commercially available in Canada.

Kathleen and Alex Nichol left the worlds of library science, computers, and classical music for their rocky vineyard. Alex later took a wine appreciation course while studying double bass in London in 1979, and upon returning to Vancouver, he wrote *Wine and Vines of British Columbia* (1983). They finally found an alfalfa field and one-time pear orchard on a rocky bench beneath a south-facing granite cliff below the abandoned Kettle Valley Railway. Building unusual wooden trellises to open their vines up to the sun, they maximized exposure and reflections off the cliff's rock, enabling them to grow more warm-climate varietals, such as Cabernet Franc and Syrah, than many of their neighbors.

Kathleen is an organizer of the Association of British Columbia Winegrowers, whose purpose is to promote BC wineries that are dedicated to using only BC grapes in their wines, or only Vancouver Island grapes if they call their wines Vancouver Island, and only Canadian grapes if labeling their wines "Product of Canada." Check out Nichol's Bohemian Wine Festival, the first weekend in August, with local artists, an art auction, jazz and blues bands, and dancing human sculptures.

Fine points: Featured wines: Syrah, Pinot Gris, Cabernet Franc, Pinot Noir, and St. Laurent. Owners: Kathleen and Alex Nichol. Winemaker: Alex Nichol. Cases: 1,000–1,200. Acres: 5.

❧ *Nichol Vineyard, 1285 Smethurst Road, RR# 1, Site 14, Comp 13, Naramata V0H 1N0; phone (250) 496–5962; fax (250) 496–4275; e-mail nicholvineyard@shaw.ca; Web site www.nicholvineyard.com. Open 11:00 A.M.– 5:00 P.M. Tuesday–Sunday, June–mid-October, or by appointment all year. Visa, MasterCard, and American Express. Wheelchair accessible.*

Next we head to LAKE BREEZE WINERY. You will see the sign to Lake Breeze near Hillside and can make a circle visit, or you can hit it on the way back to Penticton from Nichol Vineyard.

Paul and Verena Moser, both Swiss natives, created one of the most pleasant wineries and winery sites. Verena had winemaking in her blood from her mother's Swiss-Italian side and grew up on her parents' vineyard in Switzerland.

After starting several successful companies, in 1993 they took off for France and then British Columbia to find the perfect place to settle. In 1995 they

LAKE BREEZE WINERY

purchased Rock Oven Vineyards, the oldest vineyard in Naramata, from Barry and Sue Irvine.

The vineyards here originally were planted in 1924, and the house and cellar were built in 1929. The Irvines planted Pinot Blanc and Pinot Noir in the mid-1980s, and the Mosers imported and planted a rare Pinotage, known widely as "the noble grape of South Africa," which was the first planting of Pinotage in Canada.

The ultimate view of Okanagan Lake beyond the vineyards provided the setting for the popular Canadian movie *My American Cousin.* The tasting room is on the north side of the gardens, all done in tasteful white stucco and birch to remind the Mosers of their one-time home of South Africa.

In early 2000 the Mosers sold Lake Breeze to Joanne and Wayne Finn, who formerly owned a helicopter firm. The Finns in turn sold to a new group, who serve lunch on the patio with a breathtaking view of the lake in summer and open the guest cottage to visitors year-round ($150–$200 per night).

 Fine points: Featured wines: Pinot Blanc, Pinot Gris, Merlot, Blanc de Noir, Ehrenfelser, Gewürztraminer, Sémillon, Chardonnay, Merlot, Cabernet Franc, Pinot Noir, Merlot, Pinotage (a South African cross between Pinot Noir and Hermitage [Syrah]), Pinot

Blanc Icewine, and Zephyr Brut. Owners: Drew and Barbara MacIntyre, Tracey Ball, and Gary Reynolds. Winemaker: Garron Elmes. Cases: 5,000. Acres: 13.

❧ *Lake Breeze Winery, Sammet Road, Box 9, Naramata V0H 1N0; phone (250) 496–5659; fax (250) 496–5894; e-mail lakebreeze@telus.net; Web site www.lakebreezewinery.ca. Open hours vary, but try 10:00 A.M.–6:00 P.M. daily, mid-May–October; winter by appointment. Visa, MasterCard, and American Express. Wheelchair accessible.*

Naramata is becoming a superb destination with its wineries, Robinson's Road Bistro (serving Naramata wines exclusively), and the newly restored Naramata Heritage Hotel, a ten-room bed-and-breakfast. To see more of what Naramata has to offer, visit www.discovernaramata.com.

Also try the Shimmering Lake Bed & Breakfast, a Swiss-style log house near Lake Breeze Vineyards (Web site www.bbcanada.com/shimmeringlake). The Naramata General Store, 224 Robinson Road, has everything from liquor to postal services, fresh local produce, coffee, baked goods, and general local charm.

Pick organically grown blueberries on a gorgeous half acre overlooking Okanagan Lake at Sutherland Blueberries in July or August by calling Pam or Gary ahead of time at (250) 496–5767.

Visit James Hibbert, a potter, at 3015 Naramata Road 10:00 A.M.–5:00 P.M. or by chance, or call (250) 496–5150. Raccoon Ridge features handmade arts and crafts by local artists (enjoy some warm tea) at 1150 Upper Debeck Road, Naramata, noon–6:00 P.M. Wednesday–Sunday, June–September 1. Visit Naramata Art Gallery, 3064 Debeck Road East, to see Angela C. Roth McIntosh's watercolors and sculptor Brenda Fredrick's Objects of Desire Atelier.

When you return to Penticton, be sure to drop in at Martha's Jams & Jellies, 1250 Naramata Road (250–490–9164), to sample Okanagan fruits and berries fresh and canned with no artificial additives or preservatives. Martha Fehr opens her doors daily year-round.

Scherzinger Vineyards and Sumac Ridge Estate Winery are around the southern tip of Okanagan Lake. From Vancouver Avenue, turn a soft left onto Front Street, and ease right onto Westminster at Main Street past the PLEASE COME AGAIN sign.

Follow Highway 97 north along the western side of the lake for fifteen to twenty minutes to Summerland, passing Kickininee Provincial Park and Summerland Beach. About 2 miles (3.3 kilometers) north of the beach is a sign guiding you up the hill to the left to SCHERZINGER VINEYARDS.

MUSHROOM SOUP
from Scherzinger Vineyards

2 Tbs butter or olive oil

2 cups chopped onion

1 lb mushrooms, sliced

1–2 Tbs fresh dill

1 Tbs paprika

pinch of dried red pepper

2 Tbs Tamari soy sauce

2 cups water or stock

2 Tbs butter

3 Tbs whole wheat flour

1 cup milk

2 tsp fresh lemon juice

4 Tbs sour cream

4 Tbs red wine (Scherzinger Pinot
Noir or Merlot)

Sauté the onion in the oil until golden. Add sliced mushrooms, dill weed, paprika, and pepper, and sauté for five minutes. Add the Tamari and 1 cup of the stock, then cover and simmer for fifteen minutes. Set aside.

Melt 2 Tbs butter in a large pan and add the flour slowly. Cook for two to three minutes, whisking, then add milk, stirring constantly. Simmer on low heat, stirring often until mixture is thick.

Stir in mushrooms and remaining stock. Cover and simmer for fifteen minutes. Just before serving, whisk in the lemon juice, sour cream, and red wine.

Highly recommended on a cold winter night along with good bread, good salad, and a good glass of wine, such as Scherzinger Vineyards Merlot or Pinot Noir.

The son of a master wood-carver, Edgar Scherzinger and his wife, Elizabeth, moved here from the Black Forest via Vancouver for wood carving and grape growing. They bought a cherry orchard, which Edgar converted to grapes while Elizabeth ran a deli downtown. The vineyards are picturesquely located in Trout Creek Canyon next to historic Kettle Valley Railway. Until they started their own winery in 1995, they sold their grapes to nearby Sumac Ridge Estate Winery. In 2001 the Scherzingers retired and sold the winery to good friends Cher and Ron Watkins.

Fine points: Featured wines: Dry Gewürztraminers, Chardonnay, Pinot Noir, Select Late Harvest Gewürztraminer, Late Harvest Chardonnay, Opus 2000 (Trockenbeerenauslese), and Sweet Caroline dessert wine. Owners: Cher and Ron Watkins. Winemaker: Ron Watkins. Cases: Unspecified. Acres: 6.6.

✤ Scherzinger Vineyards, 7311 Fiske Road, RR #2, Site 68, Comp 13, Summerland V0H 1Z0; phone (250) 494–8815; fax (250) 494–8850; e-mail info@ scherzingervineyards.com; Web site www.scherzingervineyards.com. Open 10:00 A.M.– 5:30 P.M. daily, April 1–October 1; call ahead the rest of the year. Visa and MasterCard. Wheelchair accessible.

Just north of the center of Summerland, you will see signs to SUMAC RIDGE ESTATE WINERY. Take the left driveway to avoid the golf course and its clubhouse. Follow the steep driveway (watch the trucks) around the back of the winery to a large parking lot, and then walk between the buildings to the smallest of all, which houses the tasting room and highly awarded Cellar Door Bistro, featuring the best of regional cuisine. The casual cafe's patio tables and dining room look out toward the east and Okanagan Lake. We enjoyed the lasagna and salad. The pizza of the day, quiches, sandwiches, and other specials all looked good as well.

Harry McWatters, cofounder of Sumac Ridge, is founder of several entities important to the Okanagan and BC wines: Okanagan Wine Festival, the Okanagan Estate Wineries Association, and the British Columbia Wine Institute.

McWatters and Lloyd Schmidt originally purchased thirty-eight acres, which included a nine-hole golf course (the old clubhouse is now McWatters's tasting room and cafe). Vines weave along the fairways, an often precarious inconvenience to golfers and dangling grapes.

Eventually Schmidt sold his interest to Bob Wareham, whose business talents allow Harry to sell, sell, sell, and market to the wine industry. The land, however, turned out not to be great vineyard property, so Sumac buys from Lake Breeze and from their own Black Sage Vineyards near Oliver.

Sumac Ridge publishes an extremely informative newsletter about wine and food. The wine shop sells other Okanagan Valley wineries' best wines—one-stop shopping at its best.

Fine points: Featured wines: Chardonnay, Gewürztraminer, Pinot Blanc, Riesling, Sauvignon Blanc, White Meritage, Okanagan Blush, Chancellor, Merlot, Cabernet Franc, Cabernet Sauvignon, Red Meritage, Cabernet Merlot, Pinot Noir, Okanagan Blush, Meritage White, sparkling wines, Steller's Jay Brut, Blanc de Noirs, and dessert wines. Owners: Harry McWatters, Bob Wareham, and partners. Winemakers: Mark Wendenburg and Harold Bates. Cases: 50,000. Acres: 110.

✤ Sumac Ridge Estate Winery, 17403 Highway 97, Box 307, Summerland V0H 1Z0; phone (250) 494–0451; fax (250) 494–3456; e-mail info@

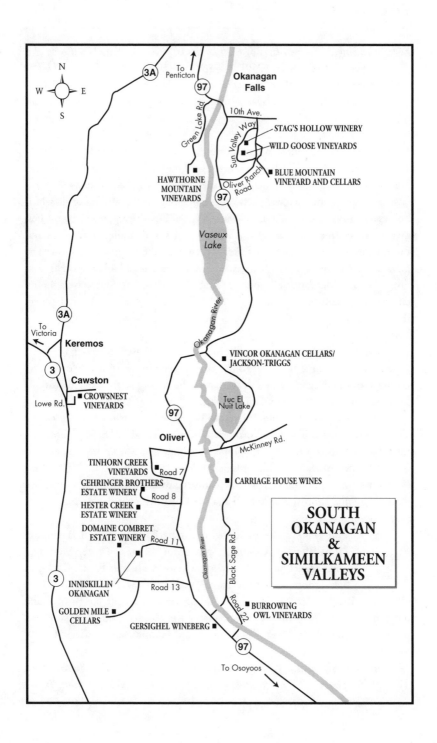

SOUTH OKANAGAN & SIMILKAMEEN VALLEYS

sumacridge.com; Web site www.sumac ridge.com. Cellar Door Bistro serves lunch 11:00 A.M.–2:30 P.M. daily, dinner from 5:00 P.M. Thursday–Sunday. Winery open 9:00 A.M.–6:00 P.M. daily; tours hourly 10:00 A.M.–4:00 P.M. Visa, MasterCard, and American Express. Wheelchair accessible.

Now we will take you on our tour of the wineries south of Penticton, particularly those that are open to visitors: Hawthorne Mountain Vineyards (Le Comte), Tinhorn Creek Vineyards, Gehringer Brothers Estate Winery, Hester Creek Estate Winery, Inniskillin Okanagan Vineyards, Golden Mile Cellars, Domaine Combret Estate Winery, and Gersighel Wineberg on the west side of Highway 97. Then we

CELLAR DOOR BISTRO AT
SUMAC RIDGE ESTATE
WINERY

go to Burrowing Owl, Carriage House, Vincor Okanagan, Blue Mountain, Stag's Hollow, and Wild Goose. Crowsnest Vineyards is a bit out of the way but an excellent wine experience.

We purposely take you down one side of the road and back the other for your safety. This way you avoid crisscrossing the highway.

To visit these wineries, cross the channel at Penticton and turn south on Highway 97 along the west side of Skaha Lake and beaches covered with soft, fine sand. On the way up the hill you again pass, or perhaps stop at, the Okanagan Amusement and Fun Centre and the Okanagan Game Farm.

Be sure to go straight following the sign to Osoyoos via Highway 97, and do not turn to the right toward Vancouver. For a fascinating experience, you might want to detour and follow the signs to the White Lake Dominion Astrophysical Observatory just 0.7 mile from the Vancouver turnoff.

To get to HAWTHORNE MOUNTAIN VINEYARDS, turn right up Green Lake Road just before the bridge across the channel between Skaha Lake and Vaseux Lake and southwest of Okanagan Falls. It's actually 3 miles (5 kilometers) up this old but paved winding road past Okanagan Falls Campground. Sharp cliffs and rock slides, occasionally warranting caution, intermingle with lush green pastures. Watch the hairpin turn and steep climb in the last kilometer.

A curiosity here are the headstones of settler Major Hugh Fraser's twelve dogs, who were his trusted companions after his English bride decided she couldn't handle the place and bolted, leaving nothing but a note saying "SYL"—See You Later.

In 1995 Harry McWatters and his group (also Sumac Ridge) bought Le Comte and renamed it Hawthorne Mountain after the land where it's located. Hawthorne still sells Le Comte wines and established its Hawthorne Mountain label in 1996 for its premium wines.

McWatters turned the house full of antiques into a professional tasting room and wine shop decorated with elegant woods. Enjoy the expansive view, deck, and picnic tables as well as its annual fall pig roast and daily BBQs noon–3:00 P.M. in summer.

In 2000 McWatters sold to giant Canadian wine company Vincor International.

 Fine points: Featured wines: Pinot Gris, Gewürztraminer, Auxerrois, Riesling, Ehrenfelser, Pinot Noir, Meritage, Gamay Noir, Cabernet Franc, Merlot, Brut, and Select Late Harvest Optima VQA. Owner: Vincor. Winemaker: Dave Carson. Cases: 6,500. Acres: 170.

🍇 *Hawthorne Mountain Vineyards, Green Lake Road, P.O. Box 480, Okanagan Falls V0H 1R0; phone (250) 497–8267; fax (250) 497–8073; e-mail info@hmvineyard.com; Web site www.hmvineyard.com. Open 9:00 A.M.–5:00 P.M. weekdays, noon–5:00 P.M. Saturday–Sunday. Visa and MasterCard. Wheelchair accessible.*

Turn right at the bottom of Hawthorne's driveway, cross the bridge, and continue south on Highway 97, which, you may remember, continues all the way into the state of Washington.

Okanagan Falls is a small, old town, whose highlights are the OK Falls Hotel and the Okanagan Falls Restaurant. About 4 miles (6.7 kilometers) south of the turn to Hawthorne Mountain, Oliver Ranch Road takes off up to the left to Wild Goose Vineyards. Wait to visit this winery until you are on your way back to be safe.

The beautiful body of water on your right 0.4 mile (0.7 kilometer) south of Oliver Ranch Road is Vaseux Lake, nestled under the high cliffs on the west. Highway 97 skims along the edge of this calm, mirrorlike, and seemingly unused lake bordered by mowed peach orchards. We found the pine trees, fruit stand, and general landscape to be mindblowingly lovely. The Gallagher Lake KOA Campground is supposed to be excellent and extremely popular in the summer.

About 4.5 miles (7.5 kilometers) south of the campground you reach Oliver, a wonderful midwestern sort of town with a definite main street and

YE OLDE WELCOME INN & PUB

cruisers of all ages checking out the tourist influx at all times of day and night. You might find the Oliver Heritage Museum, 9728 356th Avenue (250–498–4027), an interesting respite.

Our favorite stop (19.8 miles, or 33 kilometers, south of Penticton) and that of many local winemakers is YE OLDE WELCOME INN & PUB, one of the best pubs in BC. Here's where you hear the local gossip; pet the house dog and feed her scraps; gorge on great sandwiches, salads, and fish and chips; and sip local brews.

Lunch is served all afternoon, thank heavens, in comfortable rooms full of heavy, dark wood walls, tables, and benches.

❧ *Ye Olde Welcome Inn & Pub, 39008 Eighty-seventh Street, Gallagher Lake; phone (250) 498–8840. Visa and MasterCard. Wheelchair accessible.*

About 4 miles (6.6 kilometers) south of Oliver, take Road 7 west from Highway 97 to TINHORN CREEK VINEYARDS and TINHORN CREEK ESTATE WINERY. The rough paved road takes you past a flower and fruit stand beside the road and over a busy, narrow bridge. Take the left fork, which is Tinhorn Creek Road, through the stone gateposts up the one-lane paved road to the winery, watching for trucks. Drive around behind the building to the front door on the west side. Tinhorn's wines are made exclusively from grapes grown right here in their vineyard.

To your right as you enter the vestibule are a play table and chairs with drawing materials and toys for little kids, a welcome sight to wine enthusiasts with small children.

Designed by Richard Lindseth of Calgary, Tinhorn Creek offers the best educational winery experience in the Okanagan Valley. Study aerial maps of the winery's plantings and learn tons on the well-outlined self-guided tour. Displays in the North Gallery (to your left) show you harvest, crushing, and winemaking, while the South Gallery (to your right) shows barrel aging and bottling. The Northwest Gallery houses the stainless steel fermentation tanks, all named for Tinhorn Creek mentors, including five professors from the U.C. Davis Department of Viticulture and Enology and several friends. The Southeast Gallery serves as the barrel cellar in which flavor and aging are nurtured.

A century ago gold was mined in the hills above the winery site at the Tinhorn Creek Quartz Mining Company. The archway of the winery is made from stones from the mine and is patterned after the arched entrance to the gold mine stamp mill.

The East Deck gives you a view of Osoyoos Lake and the mountains as well as Tinhorn's manicured Demonstration Vineyard for grape growing and training. Tinhorn encourages day-hiking in the hills.

Tinhorn Creek's ownership is a perfect marriage between Alberta oilman Bob Shaunessy, "mother superior" Barb Shaunessy, General Manager and Viticulturist Kenn Oldfield, and Winemaker Sandra Cashman Oldfield. Don't miss their Spring Lamb Roast during the Spring Wine Festival.

A native of Oakland, California, Sandra got her first degree in business administration and went to work for the fun of it in Rodney Strong's tasting room near Healdsburg. She got hooked on the wine biz, worked there for three vintages, and went to U.C. Davis to earn an M.S. in enology. Kenn was also studying at Davis, and Sandra became Tinhorn Creek's winemaker and Kenn's wife in 1995.

Kenn reminds us that Americans will find it economical to take BC wine south across the Canadian-U.S. border because the duty is so low.

 Fine points: Featured wines: Pinot Gris, Chardonnay, Gewürztraminer, Pinot Meunier, Pinot Noir, Cabernet Franc, Merlot, and Kerner/Riesling ice wine. Owners: Bob and Barb Shaunessy, Kenn Oldfield, and Sandra Cashman Oldfield. Winemaker: Sandra Cashman Oldfield. Cases: 16,000. Acres: 160.

TINHORN CREEK'S EDUCATIONAL VINEYARD

❧ *Tinhorn Creek Vineyards and Tinhorn Creek Estate Winery, Road 7, RR #1, Sit 58 Comp 10, or 32830 Tinhorn Creek Road, Oliver V0H 1T0; phone (250) 498–3743 or (888) 4–TINHORN; fax (250) 498–3228; e-mail winery@ tinhorn.com; Web site www.tinhorn.com. Open 10:00 A.M.–5:00 P.M. daily. Visa and MasterCard. Wheelchair accessible.*

As you leave Tinhorn Creek, go down the driveway in low gear. Stop at the stop sign, cross the little bridge, and go back to Highway 97.

To get to GEHRINGER BROTHERS ESTATE WINERY from Tinhorn Creek, turn right onto Highway 97 and immediately turn right again onto 326th Street, which is Road 8. As you reach the top of the road, it forks to the right to Gehringer's driveway and to the left to Hester Creek.

Both Walter and Gordon Gehringer studied winemaking in Germany, although they were born in Oliver. Walter, the tasting-room front man, was the first Canadian graduate in viticulture and enology at Germany's famed University of Geisenheim, whose director of grapevine breeding, Dr. Helmut Becker, had an enormous influence on vine development throughout the Okanagan. Gordon, who studied in Weinsberg, Germany, serves as vineyard manager and winemaker.

Fine points: Featured wines: Pinot Gris, Dry Riesling, Ehrenfelser, Pinot Noir, Optimum Pinot Noir, Merlot, Pinot Blanc, Blush, Cabernet-Merlot, Schonburger, Riesling Icewine, and Cabernet Franc. Owners: The Gehringer family. Winemasters: Walter and Gordon Gehringer. Cases: 18,000. Acres: 42.

❧ *Gehringer Brothers Estate Winery, RR #1, Road 8, Site 23, Comp 4, Oliver V0H 1T0; phone (250) 498–3597 or toll free in Canada (800) 784–6304; fax (250) 498–3510. Open 10:00 A.M.–5:00 P.M. daily, July–September; 10:00 A.M.–5:00 P.M. Monday–Friday, October–June; also open Victoria Day and Thanksgiving Day weekends. Visa and MasterCard. Wheelchair accessible.*

Just sail back down Gehringer's driveway to HESTER CREEK ESTATE WINERY, with its vineyards growing right up to the lawn's edge. Exquisite heavy oak doors with dark gray metal hinges open into a tasting room with high ceilings and a grape leaf motif. Open beamed ceilings with oak tables and picnic tables under grapevine trellises invite visitors to stay awhile. Pure white Irish golden retrievers J.D. and Cooper greet guests happily.

After leaving his native Austria with his family for Canada in 1982, Hans Lochbichler created and then built up the Uncle Willy's Buffet chain in western Canada. In 1992 he sold the enterprise and "retired" into the wine business in the Okanagan, and in 1996 he purchased and renamed Hester Creek. Partnered with entrepreneur Henry Rathje and former Vincor winemaker Frank Supernak, Hans moved his winery rapidly into the forefront of the Okanagan wine industry, with Corrie Warwick taking over in the early 2000s.

Hester Creek is now a fun place for lunch during the summer with Duffy's Emporium Ice Cream and Gelato next door. There's also an Easter egg hunt and an August salmon BBQ.

Fine points: Featured wines: Pinot Blanc, Kerner, Pinot Gris, Chardonnay, Cabernet Franc, Gamay, Merlot, Blanc de Noir, Pinot Blanc, Late Harvest Trebbiano, and Pinot Blanc Icewine. Owner: Boltons Capital Corporation. Winemaker: Glenn Barry. Cases: 25,000. Acres: 70.

❧ *Hester Creek Estate Winery, 13163 326th Street, P.O. Box 1605, Oliver V0H 1T0; phone (250) 498–4435; fax (250) 498–0651; e-mail info@ hestercreek.com; Web site www.hestercreek.com. Open 10:00 A.M.–5:00 P.M. daily; phone in winter to confirm hours. Visa and MasterCard. Wheelchair accessible.*

About a mile south on Highway 97 from the turn to Gehringer Brothers and Hester is INNISKILLIN OKANAGAN. Turn right (west) up 322nd Avenue

GEHRINGER BROTHERS ESTATE WINERY

(Road 11 W) and go up the soft grade and turn left at 123rd Street to the Inniskillin Wine Boutique and Tasting Bar, previously that of much turned-over Okanagan Vineyards.

This is the adoptive baby of a much-merged enterprise now called Vincor. The original Inniskillin in Ontario merged with the Cartier wine group, which then merged with Brights to yield the now enormous Vincor International.

 Fine points: Featured wines: Pinot Blanc, Chardonnay, Gewürztraminer, Cabernet Franc, Pinot Noir, Merlot, Meritage, and Riesling Icewine. Owner: Vincor. Winemaker: Sandor Mayer.

🌱 *Inniskillin Okanagan Vineyards, Road 11 West, Oliver V0H 1T0; phone (250) 498–6663 or (800) 498–6211; fax (250) 498–4566; e-mail inniskil@inniskillin.com; Web site www.inniskillin.com. Open 9:00 A.M.–5:00 P.M. daily in summer; 9:00 A.M.–3:00 P.M. Monday–Friday the rest of the year. Visa and MasterCard. Wheelchair accessible.*

As you turn off Highway 97 onto Road 13 south of Oliver, you will see Peter and Helga Serwo's GOLDEN MILE CELLARS' Teutonic castle surrounded by vineyard and circular trellises outside the wine shop. What a view and experience! Wings of the castle actually function as winery.

 Fine points: Featured wines: Optima, Riesling, Bacchus, Kerner, Chardonnay, "Al Vinifera" white blend, Blanc de Noir, Pinot Noir, Merlot, and Botrytis Riesling. Owners: Peter and Helga Serwo. Winemaker: Ross Mirko.

🍂

✹✧ Golden Mile Cellars, *13140-316A Avenue, Road 13, Oliver; V0H 1T0; phone (250) 498–8330; fax (250) 498–8331. Open 10:00 A.M.–5:00 P.M. May 1–October 20; winter hours by appointment.*

To get to DOMAINE COMBRET ESTATE WINERY from Golden Mile Cellars, turn left on Road 13 and then follow the sign to the winery. Enjoy the fabulous views!

Olivier Combret, a graduate of Montpellier's wine school, designed the winery for his father, Robert, and family—a group with wine and vines in their French heritage. Robert and Olivier represent the tenth and eleventh generations of Combrets involved in wine, the first ten in Provence beginning in 1638.

Having run into bureaucratic hassles over importing French vines, the Combrets have overcome these adversities and produced some remarkable wines. The Combrets entered their first wines in French judgings and won a silver medal for their 1993 Riesling at the International Wine Challenge at Blaye-Bourg near Bordeaux and a bronze medal at the 1995 Chardonnay du Monde in Burgundy for their first 1993 Chardonnay.

Fine points: Featured wines: Chardonnay, Riesling, Cabernet Franc, Gamay, Pinot Noir, Late Harvest Chardonnay, Riesling Icewine, and Pinot Noir Icewine. Owner: Olivier Combret family. Winemaker: Olivier Combret. Cases: 10,000. Acres: 40.

✹✧ Domaine Combret Estate Winery, 32057 131 Street, P.O. Box 1170, Oliver V0H 1T0; phone (250) 498–8878 or 498–6966; fax (250) 498–8879; e-mail domaine_combret@telus.net. Open 9:00 A.M.–dusk. Ring bell. Visa and MasterCard. Wheelchair accessible.

The most southern winery in the Okanagan Valley is also the first winery north of Osoyoos and has the smallest tasting room, but locals and visitors drop in to buy the ice wine and have a chat.

GERSIGHEL WINEBERG is just 100 feet off the highway on a short gravel driveway. The signs are handmade, old car seats serve as park benches under trees, and the tasting room occupies the family home's former garage.

Flemish-born father and owner Dirk DeGussem made up the winery's name by combining parts of his three children's names: Gerd, Sigrid, and Helgi. Dirk grew up on his family's potato farm near Ghent, Belgium, and worked as a grape picker near Pomerol, France, in the mid-1960s. He and his wife, Gerda, searched throughout Europe and South Africa for the best place to grow grapes and make wine, and finally found it right here. Replacing fruit trees with vines in 1989, Dirk started out by planting Pinot Noir, Pinot Blanc, and Chardonnay grapes.

Fine points: Featured wines: Chardonnay, Pinot Blanc, Riesling, Gewürztraminer, Merlot, Pinot Noir, and ice wine. Owner and winemaker: Dirk DeGussem. Cases: 3,000. Acres: 7.

➳ *Gersighel Wineberg, 29690 Highway 97, RR #1, Site 40, Comp 20, Oliver V0H 1T0; phone (250) 495–3319; fax (250) 495–3319. Open 9:30 A.M.–8:00 P.M. year-round. No credit cards. Wheelchair accessible.*

For a recreational distraction, you might want to try Wolf Creek Trail Rides about a mile south of the winery on Highway 97 (phone 250–498–3269).

If you want to continue the few miles on to Osoyoos or are coming through Osoyoos from Washington, we will give you a few points of interest. Osoyoos decided to make itself an imitation Mexican village in line with several BC cities' efforts to establish an identity and attract visitors. It is a great place to sample rich and succulent fruits in the summer at many roadside fruit stands or enjoy year-round golf and other recreational pleasures.

"Osoyoos" is an Indian word meaning "the narrows of the lake," an appropriate handle for this town. Just north of Osoyoos you pass through the Vest Pocket Desert, Canada's only desert, where you can see rare species of birds, bats, prickly pear cactus, rock rose, antelope bush, and Canada's smallest hummingbirds. All sand dunes and desert around here belong to the Osoyoos Indian Reserve, and you can get permission to enter at the Inkameep Campsite on Highway 3 East and Forty-fifth Street (phone 800–205–6288).

Pioneer Walkway along Lake Osoyoos in the middle of the hotel and motel district is a great place to get in your daily walk and enjoy flowers maintained by local volunteers. Or visit Klikuk (Spotted Lake) 5.5 miles (8.8 kilometers) west on Highway 3 where naturally occurring Epsom salts, calcium, magnesium, and other trace minerals are combined into a healing mud to alleviate aches and pains.

The Osoyoos Museum at the end of Main Street calls itself the "Best Small Town Museum in BC," boasting "one of the finest displays from the archives of the BC Provincial Police," Indian artifacts, an 1891 log building, and the "only liquor distilling apparatus in a BC museum." Check out the Osoyoos Art Gallery in the Cultural Centre on Main Street, or play golf at one of several golf courses.

Mt. Baldy Ski Area is forty-five minutes away for winter pleasures. Just west of Osoyoos off Kobau Road is Mount Kobau, a splendid place to hike. Trails include the Kobau Lookout Trail to the fire lookout (3 miles, or 5 kilometers) and Testalinden Trail (3 miles, or 5 kilometers), which loops around with smashing views of the Similkameen Valley.

A beautifully scenic detour will take you to CROWSNEST VINEYARDS. Take Highway 3 north and turn east on Lowe Drive, then turn north on Surprise Street to Crowsnest.

Andrea and Hugh McDonald converted the twelve-acre orchard owned by Hugh's parents to vineyards in the late 1980s. Swiss native Andrea lived in Spain, Chile, and Peru before moving to Penticton with her family. She graduated from the BC Institute of Technology, working at both Okanagan Vineyards and Vincor labs, leaving for Crowsnest and their own small family.

The McDonalds sold the winery to Olaf and Sabine Heinecke, who have vineyards in Naramata, and Klaus Cavada of Germany. The Heineckes have added a German-style restaurant serving lunch and dinner, filling another culinary void in the region. Check out their music festival the second week in September and a five-course Rabbit Feast the first weekend in October.

 Fine points: Featured wines: Auxerrois, Riesling, Chardonnay, Gewürztraminer, Maréchal Foch, Merlot, and Pinot Noir. Owners: Olaf and Sabine Heinecke. Winemakers: Ann Heinecke and Todd Moore. Cases: 6,200. Acres: 50.

🐾 *Crowsnest Vineyards, Surprise Road, RR #1, Site 18, Comp 18, Cawston V0X 1N0; phone and fax (250) 499–5129; e-mail info@crowsnestvineyards.com; Web site www.crowsnestvineyards.com. Open 10:00 A.M.–6:00 P.M. daily. Visa and MasterCard. Wheelchair accessible.*

To visit more wineries, retrace your route back to Highway 97 at Osoyoos and head north.

The first winery on the east side of Highway 97 going north from Osoyoos (or south from Oliver) is BURROWING OWL VINEYARDS. For years Jim Wyse and his family have grown wine grapes for some of the finest wineries in Canada. A wine made from their Merlot grapes won a gold medal at the 1997 International Wine Competition in London. That same year the Wyse family decided to set aside 50 acres of its 292 for production of their own wine. To get here take Road 22 east from Highway 97, then turn left (north) on Black Sage Road and right on Burrowing Owl Lane. If you are hungry, try their Sonora Room Restaurant for lunch.

The Wyses use environmentally safe fertilizers. Groupings of one hundred or more bluebird boxes and two bat nurseries invite insect-eating guests to stay awhile and dine in the vineyards. Ground nests of meadowlarks are protected by barriers in spring to prevent farm machinery and vineyard workers from accidentally destroying them. Burrowing Owl also uses a gravity-flow system to handle grapes delicately.

 Fine points: Featured wines: Chardonnay, Pinot Gris, Merlot, and Cabernet Sauvignon. Owner: Jim Wyse. Winemaker: Bill Dyer. Cases: 12,000. Acres: 292.

*✤ **Burrowing Owl Vineyards**, *RR#1, Site 52, Comp 20, Oliver V0H 1T0; phone (250) 498–0620 or toll-free (877) 498–0620; fax (604) 984–2753; e-mail info@bovwine.com; Web site www.bovwine.com. Open 11:00 A.M.–5:00 P.M. daily. Visa and MasterCard. Wheelchair accessible.*

From Burrowing Owl, follow Black Sage Road north to **CARRIAGE HOUSE WINES**. David and Karen Wagner bought an old fruit orchard in 1992 and began building a winery in the architectural style of eastern carriage houses. They opened the winery in 1995, putting to use David's training in microbiology and biochemistry at Simon Fraser University, while Karen followed the advice to the beginning vintner, "keep your day job," by continuing her long-time position with BC Hydro. The Wagners produce a unique blend of Okanagan Pinot Blanc, Kerner, and Chardonnay lightly aged in French oak, which they have named Ebonage Blanc, as well as the three component varietals plus Merlot that debuted in 1998.

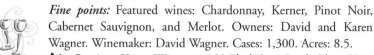

Fine points: Featured wines: Chardonnay, Kerner, Pinot Noir, Cabernet Sauvignon, and Merlot. Owners: David and Karen Wagner. Winemaker: David Wagner. Cases: 1,300. Acres: 8.5.

*✤ **Carriage House Wines**, *32764 Black Sage Road, Oliver V0H 1T0; phone and fax (250) 498–8818; e-mail wineinfo@carriagehousewines.com; Web site www.carriagehousewines.com. Open 10:00 A.M.–6:00 P.M. daily, April–October; by appointment only November–March. Visa only. Not wheelchair accessible.*

Almost 12 miles (20 kilometers) north of Carriage House Wines or 4.5 miles (7.5 kilometers) north of Ye Olde Welcome Inn & Pub, turn right (east) up Oliver Ranch Road to Stag's Hollow Winery & Vineyard, Wild Goose Vineyards, and Blue Mountain Vineyard & Cellars. Stag's Hollow and Wild Goose are next door to each other on Sun Valley Way. You can also get to these wineries from Penticton by taking Tenth Avenue east from Highway 97 and then going right on Maple Street to Sun Valley Way or Allendale Road.

Oliver Ranch Road takes you through this rattlesnake country 2.5 miles to Sun Valley Way, then turn left to **STAG'S HOLLOW WINERY & VINEYARD**. Stag's Hollow fulfills the dream of oil company alumni Larry Gerelus and Linda Pruegger, a husband-and-wife team. They purchased the vineyard in 1992, had the Chasselas vines grafted over to Pinot Noir and Merlot, others to Chardonnay, and kept two acres of Vidal. Their small, tasteful tasting room was built on top of their winery.

Fine points: Featured wines: Chardonnay, Vidal-Ehrenfelser, Vidal, Pinot Noir, Merlot, Clarete, Serenata, and Late Harvest Vidal. Owners and winemakers: Larry Gerelus and Linda Pruegger. Cases: 1,500. Acres: 10.

❧ *Stag's Hollow Winery & Vineyard, Sun Valley Way, RR #1, Site 3, Comp 36, Okanagan Falls V0H 1R0; phone and fax (250) 497–6162; e-mail stagwine@vip.net. Open 10:00 A.M.–5:00 P.M. daily. Visa and MasterCard. Not wheelchair accessible.*

Walk next door to WILD GOOSE VINEYARDS, where Susanna Kruger answers questions and pours wine in the white stucco tasting room. If Adolf Kruger isn't in the tasting room, she will get him from the winery below or from their home next door.

Adolf, Susanna, and their sons Hagen and Roland left Berlin, Germany, in 1949 and came to Canada in 1951. Adolph worked on a Manitoba wheat farm and became an electrical and yacht (yes) designer, moved here in 1983, began planting in 1984, became involved in securing farmgate status for small wineries in 1988, and moved on to an ever-expanding wine business. Adolph is a great storyteller. Bring your lunch to enjoy on their new patio. Enjoy the salmon BBQ during the Okanagan Fall Wine Festival.

STAG'S HOLLOW WINERY & VINEYARD

Fine points: Featured wines: Gewürztraminer, Riesling, Pinot Blanc, Pinot Gris, Autumn Gold Riesling, Dry Riesling, Pinot Noir, Merlot, and Wild Goose Pipe. Owners: The Kruger family. Winemaker: Hagen Kruger. Cases: 6,000. Acres: 15.

⟡ *Wild Goose Vineyards, Sun Valley Way, RR #1, Site 3, Comp 11, Okanagan Falls V0H 1R0; phone (250) 497–8919 or (888) 497–8918; fax (250) 497–6853; e-mail roland@wildgoosewinery.com; Web site www.wildgoosewinery.com. Open 10:00 A.M.–5:00 P.M. daily, April–October; by appointment only, November–March. Visa, MasterCard, and Interac. Wheelchair accessible.*

From Wild Goose or Stag's Hollow, go back down the hill to Oliver Ranch Road and turn left, then right on Allendale Road. If you go right out of Wild Goose, turn right on Maple Street and left on Allendale Road.

BLUE MOUNTAIN VINEYARD AND CELLARS overlooks Okanagan Lake from an intriguing stone building. Since Blue Mountain is open only by appointment, we drove up in the wake of a tour to arrive at one of the world's most exquisite views from the Mavety property.

Ian Mavety equates his particular microclimate to Burgundy's, and he may be correct, considering the fine wines he produces. A Vancouver native, Ian moved here and planted vines in 1971, an early bird in these parts. Ian produces grapes for other wineries, grows vines in his nursery and sells them to other vineyardists, and served for nearly ten years on the Grape Growers Marketing Board. The Mavetys' son and daughter-in-law, Matt and Corrie, have joined the winery.

Blue Mountain's wines enjoy a wide reputation for excellent quality, and the view of the lake and the dramatic cliffs on the lake's west side also make it worthwhile to arrange an appointment.

Fine points: Featured wines: Pinot Blanc, Pinot Gris, Chardonnay, Pinot Noir, Gamay Noir, and sparkling wines. Owners: Ian and Jane Mavety. Winemakers: Ian and Matt Mavety. Cases: 8,000. Acres: 65.

⟡ *Blue Mountain Vineyard and Cellars, Allendale Road, RR #1, Site 3, Comp 4, Okanagan Falls V0H 1R0; phone (250) 497–8244; fax (250) 497–6160; e-mail bluemountain@bluemountainwinery.com; Web site www.bluemountain winery.com. Open by appointment. Visa and MasterCard. Wheelchair accessible.*

Heading northward on Highway 97 past Penticton, the towns on the west side of Okanagan Lake are Summerland (where we already visited Scherzinger and Sumac Ridge in a quick trip from Penticton), Peachland, and Westbank. Hainle is in Peachland, while just beyond Westbank are Mission Hill, Quail's

Gate, and little Slamka. After visiting these we'll turn east, crossing over Okanagan Lake on a floating bridge into the city of Kelowna. In Kelowna you can visit Pinot Reach, Summerhill, St. Hubertus, and CedarCreek south of the city, Calona right downtown, and House of Rose and Gray Monk to the north.

The first in order (and first in many innovations) is HAINLE VINEYARD ESTATE WINERY. Highway 97 begins to climb just north of Peachland. Turn left 0.6 mile (1 kilometer) from town and then immediately turn right on Trepanier Bench Road toward Hainle and go up the hill. The driveway curves rather steeply upward and the parking lot is on a slant.

Walter Hainle left Germany with his wife, Regina, and son Tilman for Vancouver, where he made Riesling wines in his home from 1971. (Tilman returned to Germany to attend wine school at Weinsberg in 1982.) Walter made the first ice wine in Canada, a fad that caught on with Canadians' taste for things sweet. He passed away in his vineyard while walking his dogs on New Year's Day, 1995.

Tilman and Sandra Hainle's totally organic vineyards and winery was the first BC winery to get a "J" license, allowing them to sell food and wine by the glass in addition to bottled wines. In 2002 the Huber family bought Hainle instead of building their own winery, and Tilman Hainle still serves as wine-maker—thank heavens!

HAINLE VINEYARD ESTATE WINERY

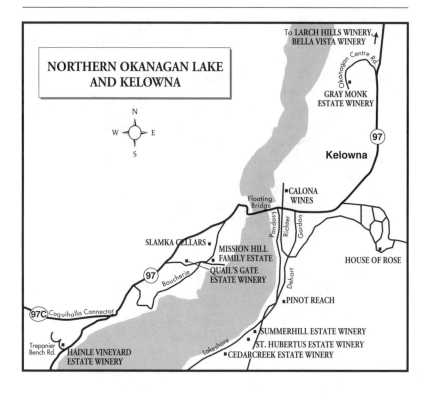

NORTHERN OKANAGAN LAKE
AND KELOWNA

You will enjoy the fabulous seasonal Amphora Bistro and studio kitchen featuring Italian and Mediterranean cuisine and occasional cooking classes.

The wine shop features a wide array of interesting local cookbooks and local food products, including sheep and goat cheeses and salmon as well as souvenirs of your visit.

 Fine points: Featured wines: Riesling, Pinot Blanc, Zweigelt, Gewürztraminer, Pinot Gris, Bibendum, Chardonnay, Cabernet Franc, Syrah, Pinot Noir, Merlot, Bibendum Red, Riesling Cuvée Ice, and Dolce Amore picked on Valentine's Day (February 14). Try the new Deep Creek Wine Estate label as well. Owners: The Huber family. Winemaker: Tilman Hainle. Cases: 15,000. Acres: 43 and buy from others.

❧ *Hainle Vineyard Estate Winery, 5355 Trepanier Bench Road, P.O. Box 650, Peachland V0H 1X0; phone (250) 767–2525 or (800) 767–2525; fax (250) 767–2543; e-mail info@hainle.com; Web site www.hainle.com. Open 10:00 A.M.–7:00 P.M. Tuesday–Sunday, May–October; call or check Web site in winter. Visa and MasterCard. Wheelchair accessible around back.*

Next in your journey northward look for MISSION HILL FAMILY ESTATE. To get there and to Quail's Gate, take Gellatly toward the lake off Highway 97 and turn left on Boucherie, then up the hill to the left on Mission Hill Road.

A highly professional commercial family winery, Mission Hill reminds us of Sebastiani in Sonoma or Mondavi in Napa with its upscale presentation. Wine guides and hostesses speak several languages, including Japanese. The cheerful, bustling tasting room exudes success and offers a 360-degree view of the Okanagan Valley, with loads of landscaping and patios in the new facility.

Known for years as the "rotgut" wine producer (see chapter 5, History of Winemaking in the Pacific Northwest), Mission Hill survived decades of buy-outs, sellouts, and Fuddle Duck, copying Baby Duck, and finally was rescued in 1981 by Anthony von Mandl and Nick Clark.

As an industry triumph, Mission Hill's 1992 Grand Reserve Barrel Select Chardonnay won the 1994 Avery's Trophy at the prestigious International Wine and Spirits Competition in London, the work of New Zealand cum Mission Hill winemaker John Simes. Also try their excellent Okanagan Cider Company ciders.

 Fine points: Featured wines: Private Reserve and Grand Reserve Chardonnays, Pinot Gris, Merlot, Pinot Noir, Cabernet-Merlot, Cabernet Franc, Shiraz, and Vidal Icewine. Owners: Anthony von Mandl and Nick Clark. Winemaker: John Simes. Cases and acres: Unspecified.

✦ℒ *Mission Hill Family Estate, 1730 Mission Hill Road, Westbank V4T 2E4; phone (250) 768–7611; fax 768–2044; e-mail info@missionhillwinery.com; Web site www.missionhillwinery.com. Open 9:00 A.M.–7:00 P.M. in summer, with hourly tours from 10:00 A.M.–5:00 P.M.; 9:00 A.M.–5:00 P.M. in winter, with tours at noon and 2:00 P.M. Visa, MasterCard, and American Express. Wheelchair accessible.*

To get to QUAIL'S GATE ESTATE WINERY from Mission Hill, go back down Mission Hill Road, turn left on Boucherie for about 2 miles (3.3 kilometers), and watch for the Quail's Gate sign. There is no provincial sign because it's on First Peoples' lands.

Originally the 1873 home of pioneers John and Susan Allison, who mapped the route between Hope and Princeton, BC, the attractive, homey log cabin houses Quail's Gate's extremely popular tasting room, supervised by Valerie Burleigh.

Founded by Richard Stewart in 1961, Quail's Gate is now run by his sons, Ben and Tony, who have benefited from an original 1963 planting mistake in which Chasselas was shipped instead of labrusca vines.

Quail's Gate has an excellent alfresco restaurant, Old Vines Patio, overlooking the vineyard and Lake Okanagan.

MISSION HILL FAMILY ESTATE

 Fine points: Featured wines: Chasselas, Gewürztraminer, Harvest White Riesling, Chardonnay, Chenin Blanc, Cabernet Sauvignon, Merlot, Old Vines Foch, Pinot Noir, Riesling ice wine, and Late Harvest Optima Botrytis Affected. Owners: Ben and Tony Stewart. Winemaker: Grant Stanley. Cases: 20,000. Acres: 115.

❧ *Quail's Gate Estate Winery, 3303 Boucherie Road, Kelowna V1Z 2H3; phone (250) 769–4451 or (800) 420–WINE; fax (250) 769-3451; e-mail info@quailsgate.com; Web site www.quailsgate.com. Open 10:00 A.M.–6:00 P.M. daily, June–September; close at 5:00 P.M. the rest of the year; tours 11:00 A.M., 1:00, and 3:00 P.M. in summer. Visa and MasterCard. Wheelchair accessible.*

SLAMKA CELLARS FARM WINERY is much harder to find. To get there, turn right (north) out of Quail's Gate, continue north on Boucherie Road, turn left on Ogden Road, and turn right (north) on Ourtoland Road until the end. Take the little dirt road on the right.

This is one true, small, family operation. Joe Slamka left his native Czechoslovakia in 1948 before the Communist takeover and went to Britain, where he worked as a coal miner. Joe moved on to Canada in 1952, first settling in Edmonton to work in a pipe mill.

Joe felt at home here on Boucherie Mountain, replanting his orchard with grapes in 1970 while working at a truck assembly plant. Son Peter began making wine for the family and realized that they, too, could create a farmgate winery success. The tasting room occupies their former machine shed.

Fine points: Featured wines: Tapestry (Gewürztraminer blend), Rosé, Pinot Noir, Cellar Red blend, Auxerrios Icewine, and Select Harvest Riesling. Owners: Joe, Freya, Pete, Tim, and Rick Slamka. Winemaker: Pete Slamka. Cases: 2,500. Acres: 11 of 24.

Slamka Cellars Farm Winery, 2815 Ourtoland Road, Lakeview Heights, Kelowna V1Z 2H5; phone (250) 769–0404; fax (250) 763–8168; e-mail slamka@silk.net; Web site www.slamka.bc.ca. Open 10:00 A.M.–5:30 P.M. daily, April–November. Call ahead other months. Visa, MasterCard, and American Express. Wheelchair accessible.

After you find your way back down to Highway 97, turn left (north) and proceed 2 miles (3.3 kilometers) and across the floating bridge to downtown Kelowna.

Kelowna has strip malls and feels like the last-chance-to-buy city before heading off to the wilds of the north and east and to Calgary. Every fast-food chain in North America is represented here. Kelowna is also a major Canadian vacation and recreational water sports center, as well as a great place to view and sniff local blossoms and harvest fruits.

The BRITISH COLUMBIA ORCHARD MUSEUM, 1304 Ellis Street (phone 250–763–0433; fax 250–868–9792), tells the story of the Okanagan Valley's transformation from wide open cattle range to beautifully manicured orchards and vineyards, with exhibits on packing, processing, home preserving, picking, marketing, and hands-on artifacts, a 50-foot model railroad set, and a great gift shop. Open 10:00 A.M.–5:00 P.M. Monday–Saturday, July–August; closed Monday, September–June.

The WINE MUSEUM, 1304 Ellis Street (phone 250–868–0441; fax 250–868–9272), in the same Laurel Packing House as the Orchard Museum, is one of the best sources of information about the history of wine in BC and the Northwest. You can also buy award-winning and limited-edition VQA BC wines here. Open 10:00 A.M.–5:00 P.M. Monday–Saturday, noon–5:00 P.M. Sunday.

Check out the KELOWNA MUSEUM, 470 Queensway Avenue (250–763–2417), one of British Columbia's oldest museums, just a block from the Orchard Museum. Based on a Boy Scout collection of natural history specimens, the museum also houses exhibits on the history of Kelowna and on African, Pacific, and American cultures. Open 10:00 A.M.–5:00 P.M. Monday–Saturday, July–August; Tuesday–Saturday, September–June. All three museums are managed by the Kelowna Museum Association.

Kelowna sports fifteen golf courses, some of which have fruit trees growing down the fairways, while others have beautiful, sparkling lakes or rivers running through them. Call the T Times Booking Service at (250) 762–7844 or (800) 689–4653 to book your tee times.

The PANDOSY MISSION, at Benvoulin and Casorso Roads, still reflects the peace and tranquillity of pioneer Father Pandosy's Oblate Mission, which he founded here more than 140 years ago. Three of the original log buildings still stand on the first agricultural land-use settlement in British Columbia. Father Pandosy became a great friend of the Okanagan Indians, and subsequently the mission was known as the Okanagan Mission. Pandosy also is believed to have planted the first fruit trees in the Okanagan. You can even visit Father Pandosy's grave on the Mission grounds. Open dawn to dusk daily.

The wineries here are all slightly different in feeling from those of the southern Okanagan. They seem self-sufficient and enjoy their relative isolation at this tip of the wine country.

First we will take you to CALONA WINES, LTD. Go north on Richter Street from Highway 97 just east of Pandosy. Calona is in an industrial building flush on the sidewalk just before the hills.

Some of the great characters of the Okanagan Valley and Canadian wine

MICROBREWERY ALERT!

Tree Brewing Co. Ltd., *1083 Richter Street (phone 250–860–8836; fax 250–860–8839), is one of the finest microbreweries in British Columbia. While they want you to notice their beer first, check out their unusual and eye-catching graphics.*

Created in 1995, Tree Brewing makes only a few beers but makes them very well. They get their hops from the Yakima Valley (doesn't everybody?), malt from the Gambrinus Maltery in Armstrong, BC, and Cara Munch and Carafa from Europe, and local pure mountain water to yield all-natural, unpasteurized brews.

Featured beers: Fireweed Honey Pilsner, Tree Pale Ale, Hophead IPA, London Spy Porter, and Amber Ale. Store open noon–5:00 P.M. Monday–Friday. E-mail info@treebrewery.com; Web site www.treebrewery.com.

business have been involved in Calona, including Carlo Ghezzi, Pasquale (Cap) Capozzi, and BC premier W. A. C. Bennett, as well as lots of other local and old-country Italians. From the 1940s the Capozzi brothers borrowed ideas from whomever they thought was successful. For example, they copied Gallo with sweet wines, bottle sizes, and prices. At one point they asked Gallo to buy 49 percent of their company; when Gallo asked for 51 percent they said no way, and that's the polite version.

In the early 1960s, Growers', their chief Canadian competitor, bought a majority of the operation and later offered its shares back to Capozzi Enterprises. The Capozzis then sold the works for just under $10 million to Standard Brands of New York. Finally Potter Distilling Corp. of Vancouver bought Calona in 1995 for almost $17 million from Heublein and renamed it Cascadia Brands Inc.

One of the benefits of this enormous company is that you get to taste Calona wines, as well as purchase Granville Island Brewery beers and Potter's spirits. Wander through the rooms where you can watch a wine video and browse through history. The beer and wine plants cover 8.5 acres.

Fine points: Featured wines: Ehrenfelser, Sémillon, Fumé Blanc, Pinot Blanc, Pinot Noir, Chardonnay, Gewürztraminer, Merlot, Pinot Blanc Icewine, Sonata Port, and Sovereign Opal. Owner: Cascadia Brands, Ltd. Winemaker: Howard Soon. Cases: 1,250,000. Acres: 300.

🍇 *Calona Wines, Ltd., 1125 Richter Street, Kelowna V1Y 2K6; phone (250) 762–3332 or (888) 246–4472; fax (250) 762–2999; Web site www.calonavine yard.ca. Open 9:00 A.M.–6:00 P.M. daily. Visa and MasterCard. Wheelchair accessible.*

All the wineries around Kelowna are close by, so you don't really have to make choices. Pinot Reach, Summerhill, St. Hubertus, and CedarCreek are all in the general vicinity of Lakeshore Road just south of town, and House of Rose is east of downtown Kelowna.

To get to PINOT REACH, take Pandosy Road south from Highway 97 in Kelowna, turn east on Dehart Road, and at the fork keep right on Dehart Road. The winery entrance and driveway will be on your left.

Winemaker Susan Dulik, the new generation of a longtime Kelowna wine- and grape-growing family, began working in the tasting room at Ste. Michelle. She later moved on to CedarCreek and Summerhill.

Fine points: Featured wines: Chardonnay, Pinot Blanc, Riesling, Bacchus, Bacchus Dry, Pinot Noir, Pinot Meunier, Cabernet Sauvignon, Riesling Icewine, Late Harvest Optima, Riesling Brut, Blanc de Noir Brut de Brut, and Pinot Meunier Brut. Owners: Den and Pat Dulik. Manager and winemaker: Susan Dulik. Cases: 3,000. Acres: 50.

❧ *Pinot Reach*, *1670 Dehart Road, Kelowna V1W 4N6; phone (250) 764–0078 or toll free in Canada (877) 764–0078; fax (250) 764–0771; e-mail pinot@direct.ca. Open noon–5:00 P.M. Tuesday–Saturday, summer; October–May by appointment only. Visa and MasterCard. Wheelchair accessible.*

Next we will visit SUMMERHILL ESTATE WINERY. To get here, follow Pandosy until it becomes Lakeshore Road. When you reach the flashing traffic light, do not turn to the right as Lakeshore does. Proceed ahead onto Chute Lake Road. The winery sign is a few hundred yards farther, and the winery is on the west side of the road.

You'll know you're there when you see the tour buses and the giant pyramid and wine bottle overlooking the winery and the valley below. This is a tourist destination.

Stephen Cipes is a New Yorker and developer who shows his smarts in every way: Japanese signage, free putting hole, climbing gym for kids, lounge chairs on the 200-foot deck, huge carved doors, dark plank flooring. All of this adds up to a long, huge, bustling tasting room with a small hofbrau-style restaurant, Veranda, at the end of the room, serving lunch 11:00 A.M.–3:00 P.M. daily (less than $10) and dinner at sunset. Stephen believes in the power of pyramids and places his wines in the shape of a Cheops pyramid for aging.

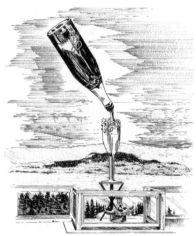

SUMMERHILL ESTATE WINERY "STATUARY" OVERLOOKING OKANAGAN LAKE

Enjoy the organic herb and vegetable garden grown for Veranda. Tasting room staff speak Japanese, Italian, Spanish, French, Mandarin, and Cantonese. You can buy jellies, books, oils, soaps, and breads and occasionally enjoy the sound of the grand piano and take the only "champagne" making tour in Canada.

Fine points: Featured wines: Sparkling *Méthodes Traditionelles*, Ehrenfelser, Blau Fränkisch (Lemberger), Pinot Blanc, Gewürztraminer, Chardonnay, Merlot, Pinot Noir, Cabernet Sauvignon, Cabernet Sauvignon-Merlot, Cipes Aurora, Chardonnay Cuvée, Cipes Gabriel, Pinot Noir Brut, and Riesling ice wine. Owner: Stephen Cipes. Winemaker: Bruce Ewert. Cases: 25,000. Acres: 35 planted of 185.

⤞ *Summerhill Estate Winery, Unit 1, 4870 Chute Lake Road, Kelowna V1W 4M3; phone (250) 764–8000 or (800) 667–3538; fax (250) 764–2598; e-mail summerhill@summerhill.bc.ca; Web site www.summerhill.bc.ca. Open 9:00 A.M.–8:00 P.M. daily in summer; 10:00 A.M.–7:00 P.M. daily in winter. Visa, MasterCard, and American Express. Wheelchair accessible.*

Next we visit ST. HUBERTUS ESTATE WINERY. From Summerhill, go back down the driveway, turn left toward the lake on Chute Lake Road, and left again on Lakeshore Road. From Kelowna, just go out Lakeshore Road until you see St. Hubertus signs. Before the great fire throughout northeastern British Columbia, you felt as if you were entering a small Swiss village. But when BC was swept by massive forest fires in the summer of 2003, the charming Swiss chalet tasting room and the home of co-owners Leo and Barbara Gebert burned down—the only winery in the province to be lost. With courage and determination, as well as community support, the Geberts (including Andy Gebert) were soon back in business.

You can enjoy the wines under both the St. Hubertus and Oak Bay Vineyards labels, both overseen by St. Hubertus, Swiss patron saint of huntsmen.

Fine points: Featured wines: Oak Bay Chardonnay-Pinot Blanc, Riesling, Pinot Noir, Gamay Noir, Maréchal Foch, Merlot, and Pinot Meunier; St. Hubertus, Bacchus, Riesling, Pinot Blanc, Chasselas, Gewürztraminer, Rosé Gamay Noir, Gamay Noir, Summer Symphony, and Riesling ice wine. Owners: Leo, Andy, and Barbara Gebert. Winemaker: Cherie Mirk. Cases: 7,000. Acres: 40 planted of 80.

⤞ *St. Hubertus Estate Winery, 5225 Lakeshore Road, Kelowna V1W 4J1; phone (250) 764–7888 or (800) 989–WINE; fax (250) 764–0499; e-mail wine@st-hubertus.bc.ca; Web site st-hubertus.bc.ca. Open 10:00 A.M.–5:30 P.M. daily, May–October; noon–5:00 P.M. Tuesday–Saturday, November–April. Visa and MasterCard. Wheelchair accessible.*

The heavy pall of smoke that hung over the mainland due to the forest fires in summer 2003 dusted many growing grapes with a smoky flavor. There were several close calls from the roaring flames. One narrrow escape was St. Hubertus's neighbor, CEDARCREEK ESTATE WINERY, considered by many to be one of the best producers of quality wines in BC. The winery was purchased in 1986 by Ross Fitzpatrick, a native of Kelowna who had returned to his roots after a career in business, government, and politics. His early business successes included an oil company, an aircraft parts enterprise in Seattle, and even a

California gold mine. In addition to directing the winery, Fitzpatrick was former Prime Minister Jean Chrétien's personal leader in the province and was appointed a federal senator in 1998.

He pumped a million and a half dollars into upgrading the winery, renamed it CedarCreek for the creek that runs through the vineyards down to Okanagan Lake, shifted from the Germanic to what he called a "northwest" style of wines, and promoted wine tours of the property with its sweeping vistas. In addition to the forty acres on site, CedarCreek acquired the forty-acre Greata Vineyards between Peachland and Summerland.

Fine points: Featured wines: Pinot Blanc, Pinot Noir, Meritage, Gewürztraminer, Chardonnay, Ehrenfelser, Riesling, and Merlot. Owners: Ross and Linda Fitzpatrick. Winemaker: Tom DiBello. Cases: 28,000. Acres: 80.

CedarCreek Estate Winery, 5445 Lakeshore Road, Kelowna V1W 4S5; phone (250) 764–8866 or (800) 730–9463; fax (250) 764–2603; Web site www.cedar creek.bc.ca. Open 10:00 A.M.–6:00 P.M. daily, tours on the hour 11:00 A.M.–3:00 P.M. daily. Closed Sunday November–March. Visa, MasterCard, and American Express. Not wheelchair accessible.

Now we'll take you northward to House of Rose and Gray Monk. HOUSE OF ROSE VINEYARDS is the closer of the two. To get there take Highway 97 through Kelowna and go east out of town. Just north of the Orchard Park Shopping Centre, turn east on Highway 33 for 4 miles (6 kilometers). Turn south (right) on Garner Road and follow signs to House of Rose.

A former teacher from Alberta, Vern Rose grows grapes and makes his wine on the Rutland Bench, a rare cool Okanagan site for grape growing. He opened the winery in 1995. Because of this microclimate, Rose studied cool-climate viticulture in New Zealand.

Fine points: Featured wines: Okanagan Trocken Riesling, Chardonnay, Auxerrois, Verdelet, Perle of Zala, Maréchal Foch, Auxerrois, Sémillon, Vintners' Choice, Rosé, Merlot, de Chaunas, Pinot Noir, late harvest ice wine blend, Sherry, and Port. Owners: Vern, Aura, and Russell Rose. Winemaker: Vern Rose. Cases: 4,000. Acres: 7.

House of Rose Vineyards, 2270 Garner Road, RR #5, Kelowna V1X 4K4; phone (250) 765–0802; fax (250) 765–7762; e-mail arose@showswap.net; Web site www.winterwine.com. Open 10:00 A.M.–5:00 P.M. daily. Visa and MasterCard. Wheelchair accessible.

Make the effort to go a little more out of your way for a special winery: GRAY MONK ESTATE WINERY, one of the first farmgate wineries. Gray Monk is Official Sighting Station #5 for the legendary Okanagan Lake monster, Ogopogo. Created by two former hairdressers, George and Trudy Heiss, Gray Monk is worth the visit just for the beauty of the site. North of 50° north latitude, the international northern limit for viticulture, Gray Monk has named one of its best-known generic white wines Latitude Fifty, of course. Cold snaps have ruined a few vintages, which makes the survivors all the more precious.

Fine points: Featured wines: Chardonnay, Pinot Blanc, Pinot Gris, Pinot Auxerrois, Riesling, Rotberger, Siegerrebe, Gewürztraminer, Latitude Fifty, Cabernet Franc, Gamay Noir, Merlot, and Pinot Noir. Owners: The Heiss family. Winemaker: George Heiss Jr. Cases: 60,000. Acres: 40 and buy grapes locally.

❧ *Gray Monk Estate Winery, 1055 Camp Road, Okanagan Centre V4V 2H4; phone (250) 766–3168 or (800) 663–4205; fax (250) 766–3390; Web site www.graymonk.com. Open 9:00 A.M.–9:00 P.M. Monday–Saturday, July–August; 10:00 A.M.–5:00 P.M. daily, June, September, October, tours every hour on the hour; 11:00 A.M.–5:00 P.M. Monday–Saturday, November–April, tour at 2:00 P.M. Visa and MasterCard. Wheelchair accessible.*

The most northerly wineries, actually, are Bella Vista near Vernon and Larch Hills in Salmon Arm.

To get to BELLA VISTA WINERY, follow Highway 97 north with Kalamalka Lake on your right into Vernon. Turn left on Thirtieth Avenue and then right on Agnew to the winery overlooking this finger of Okanagan Lake about five minutes from downtown Vernon.

The 1994 creation of fifteen investors known to enjoy a good glass of wine, Bella Vista welcomes visitors of somewhat alternative nature to come and share in the work and fun (drinking). Larry Passmore, who used to run an amateur wine- and beermakers store, coordinates the operation.

Fine points: Owners: Group of fifteen investors. Winemaker: Larry Passmore. Cases: 40,000. Acres: 12.

❧ *Bella Vista Winery, 3111 Agnew Road, Vernon V1T 5J8; phone (250) 558–0770; fax (250) 542–1221. Open noon–5:00 P.M. daily. Visa and MasterCard. Wheelchair accessible.*

While Bella Vista claims to be BC's most northerly winery, as does Gray Monk, LARCH HILLS WINERY was until Recline Ridge cropped up 3 miles north. It is just north of Enderby, right off Highway 97 south of the intersection of the TransCanada Highway and Highway 97.

Arriving from Vienna in 1970, Hans and Hazel Nevrkla settled in Calgary and took some winemaking courses. They came to the Okanagan to buy grapes for Han's amateur winemaking habit and got hooked.

Hans and Hazel have four acres of vineyard scratched out of their seventy-three acres of rocky cliffs, most of which are inaccessible for the toughest agricultural equipment. With the vineyards facing south—wise move—the Nevrklas believe profoundly in forcing the vines to work hard to produce rich fruit in the short growing season.

Fine points: Featured wines: Riesling, Gewürztraminer, Pinot Noir, Ortega, and Northern Lights. Owners and winemakers: Hans and Hazel Nevrkla. Cases: 300. Acres: 4.

❧ *Larch Hills Winery, 110 Timms Road, Salmon Arm V1E 4M3; phone (250) 832–0155 or (250) 832–9419; Web site larchhillswinery.bc.ca. Open noon–5:00 P.M. daily May–October; call ahead November–April. Visa and MasterCard. Wheelchair accessible.*

For your return to Vancouver, we recommend that you take the route west over the mountains from Westbank, called the Coquihalla Connector (Highway 97C), until you reach Highway 5A, turning briefly north to the town of Merritt, and then head south on the Coquihalla (Highway 5), which is a multilane highway with a $10 toll. The Coquihalla provides some of the most

---

NEW WINERIES TO WATCH IN THE OKANAGAN VALLEY

The western bluffs above Lake Okanagan are the new frontier for new wineries in the Okanagan Valley.

GREATA RANCH ESTATE WINERY, the newest enterprise of Ross and Linda Fitzpatrick of CedarCreek, with magnificent views of Okanagan Lake north and south, opened its doors in spring 2003; 697 Highway 97 South, Peachland, BC V0H 1X9; phone (250) 767–2605.

THORNHAVEN ESTATES WINERY, built in 1999, emphasizes Pinots and has other varieties; 6816 Andrew Avenue (off Highway 97 at Arkell), Summerland, BC V0H 1Z0; phone (250) 494–7778; e-mail info@thornhaven.com; Web site www.thornhaven.com.

NEW FAR-OUT WINERIES IN
BRITISH COLUMBIA

For the adventurous wine aficionado willing to drive a distance, several small new wineries in beautiful British Columbia have been established since 1999. These include: **ARROWLEAF CELLARS,** 1574 Camp Road, Lake Country, BC V4V 1K1 (phone 250–766–5033); **BONAPARTE BEND WINERY,** Highway 97, Cache Creek, BC V0K 1H0 (phone 250–457–6667); **COLUMBIA GARDENS VINEYARD & WINERY,** 9340 Station Road, Trail, BC V1R 4W6 (phone 250–367–7493); **HUNTING HAWK VINEYARDS,** 4758 Gulch Road, Spullumcheen, BC V0E 1B4 (phone 250–546–2164); **PEMBERTON VALLEY VINEYARD & INN,** 1427 Collins Road, Pemberton, BC V0N 2L0 (phone 604–894–5857); **RECLINE RIDGE VINEYARDS & WINERY,** 2640 Skimikin Road, Tappen, BC V0E 2X0 (phone 250–835–2212), which, despite other claims, is apparently the most northerly winery in the western hemisphere, if not the world.

remarkable scenery as you drive downhill on perfectly engineered, banked curves through forests, past 1,000-foot-high cliffs, and beside sparkling creeks. The views and nature experiences on this route are exquisite.

We recommend you leave the Okanagan early in the morning, with the sun at your back to avoid the five hours of sun in your face. Be sure your car is full of gas, as chances to get gas are few and far between.

CHAPTER 4

IDAHO

f you are curious about Idaho wines and are a devoted wine fan, you really should visit Idaho for a new wine-tasting and visual experience. The drive to Idaho is refreshingly beautiful. Eastern Washington vintners and vineyardists encourage exploration of the growing Idaho wine industry as well as the area's outdoor beauty. Some want to give a boost to their brothers and sisters in the business, while others want to see their neighbors succeed because they sell them grapes.

The best way to get to the southern part of Idaho wine country is via Interstate 84 eastward from Portland, Oregon, along the Columbia River to Pendleton. You can also head south from Walla Walla, Washington, to I–84, and then southeast from Pendleton on 84 to Caldwell and Boise, Idaho. (You can always fly to Boise, but then you will need to rent a car.)

Ste. Chapelle, Idaho's largest winery, is located in Caldwell, just west of Boise, and is open to the public. Hells Canyon Winery and Koenig Vineyards are also in Caldwell, but open by appointment only and on weekends, respectively. To complete your Boise-area tour, visit Sawtooth Winery in Nampa and Indian Creek Winery in Kuna.

There are several ways to tour Idaho's small wineries, which are strung out along State Highway 55 and then 95. This tour covers a total of 500 miles, from Boise northward until one reaches beautiful Sandpoint not far from the Canadian border. Take a couple of days to drive all the way. There is a long pull to Moscow, where Camas Winery is located. Finally there is Pend d'Oreille Winery in the resort town of Sandpoint.

Another plan: Make the tour of Moscow and Sandpoint a one- or two-day side-trip from a tour of the Spokane, Washington, winery area, just across the border. Head east from Spokane to Coeur d'Alene on I–90, then turn north to Sandpoint on Highway 95 to arrive at Pend d'Oreille about noon, then have lunch by the lake, and head back to Moscow, arriving just before dark. Or come to Moscow from Pullman.

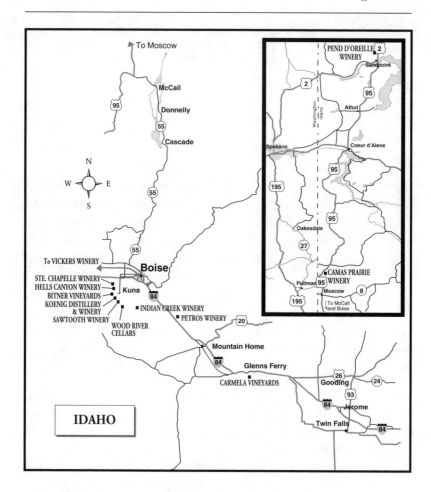

As you enter Idaho from Portland or Walla Walla, you first come to STE. CHAPELLE WINERY. To get there from I–84, take exit 35 to Highway 55 South and head south for about 13 miles to Caldwell. Turn left onto Lowell Road and follow signs to the winery.

Ste. Chapelle is the largest and oldest (since 1976) winery in Idaho, and one of the biggest in the Northwest. It receives accolades from wine experts around the world.

Slightly incongruous with the location and terrain, Ste. Chapelle's winery is modeled after the style of a Parisian cathedral and feels like an oasis amid surrounding orchards and vineyards. Ste. Chapelle makes a big point of keeping prices low while producing large quantities of excellent still and sparkling wine to gain both exposure and fans.

You might want to plan your visit for a July Sunday afternoon, when you can enjoy great jazz concerts, splendid food, and wine outdoors. They suggest you bring a blanket, a picnic, and a visor.

 Fine points: Featured wines: Chardonnay, Fumé Blanc, Riesling, Chenin Blanc, Cabernet Sauvignon, Merlot, Syrah, and bulk sparkling wines. Owner: Constellation Brands of New York. Winemaker: Chuck Devlin. Cases: 150,000. Acres: Lease 1,000.

Ste. Chapelle Winery, 19348 Lowell Road, Caldwell 83605; phone (208) 459–7222; fax (208) 459–9783; Web site stechapelle.com. Open 10:00 A.M.–5:00 P.M. Monday–Saturday; noon–5:00 P.M. Sunday. Tours on the hour. Visa, MasterCard, and American Express. Wheelchair accessible.

Also in Caldwell, HELLS CANYON WINERY offers a fun interlude. From Ste. Chappelle, continue east on Lowell Road, turn right on Chicken Dinner Road, and left on Symms Road. Steve and Leslie Robertson founded the winery in 1980 and named it for the famous canyon created by Idaho's Snake River. Hells Canyon Winery includes some humorously named blends worth trying. Steve studied at the Culinary Institute of America and loves to create foods to pair with his wines. Their 1998 Idaho Reserve Merlot won Best Idaho Wine.

 Fine points: Featured wines: Premium Idaho Chardonnay, Cabernet Sauvignon, Cabernet Franc, Syrah, Merlot, Bird Dog White, Retriever Red, Seven Devils Red, Deerslayer Syrah, and Crooked Chardonnay. Owners: Steve and Leslie Robertson. Winemaker: Steve Robertson. Cases: 3,000. Acres: 40.

Hells Canyon Winery, 18835 Symms Road, Caldwell 83605; phone (208) 454–3300; Web site www.hellscanyonwinery.com. Open noon–5:00 P.M. Saturday–Sunday, or by appointment. Visa and MasterCard. Wheelchair accessible.

To get to KOENIG DISTILLERY & WINERY from Hells Canyon, go back to Lowell Road and head west. Turn right on Plum Road and right on Grape Lane.

Brothers Andy and Greg Koenig studied for several years with their father's family in Austria and learned to make fine brandies in the European tradition. From their mother's family in the Nampa area, they learned about Idaho fruit. They planted Merlot and Cabernet Sauvignon grapes, pears, Italian prunes, apricots, and peaches, and they buy fruit from their Sunny Slope neighbors.

The Koenig brothers built an Italian-style hillside villa, the first building of several to surround a central courtyard to make wine and distill fruit, much as they did at their own Knob Hill Inn in Ketchum.

Fine points: Featured wines: Merlot, Cabernet Sauvignon, and brandies. Owners, winemakers, and distillers: Andy and Greg Koenig. Cases: 1,000 wine; 1,000 brandy. Acres: 70.

❧ *Koenig Distillery & Winery, 20928 Grape Lane, Caldwell 83605; phone (208) 455–8386; fax (208) 455–8038; Web site www.idahowine. com/Koenig.htm. Open noon–5:00 P.M. Saturday–Sunday, by appointment during the week. Visa and MasterCard. Wheelchair accessible.*

SAWTOOTH WINERY is in the neighboring town of Nampa. It is open only on weekends, so plan accordingly. Take exit 36 off I–84 and go south on Franklin Avenue, turn right on Eleventh Avenue, then left on Third Street South on a minor jog right over to Twelfth Avenue South, and follow it south. Turn right on Missouri Road, left on Sky Ranch, and follow signs to Sawtooth Winery.

The founding Pintler family has grown various kinds of fruit for generations. They planted grapes in the early 1980s after they saw Ste. Chapelle's success, and now they enjoy their own. You will too. Recently the Pintlers sold their winery to Corus Brands of Woodinville, Washington. Sawtooth is located on the rim of Hidden Valley and has a panoramic view of the Owyhee Mountains and the Boise Valley. Enjoy its beautiful, landscaped grounds.

You might want to plan your trip around the winery's Mother's Day Wine and Food Festival or its Thanksgiving Weekend Open House.

Fine points: Featured wines: Reserve Chardonnay, Riesling, Cabernet Sauvignon, Merlot, Syrah, Pinot Gris, and Viognier. Owner: Corus Brands. Winemaker: Brad Pintler. Cases: 10,000. Acres: 600.

❧ *Sawtooth Winery, 13750 Surrey Lane, Nampa 83651; phone (208) 467–1200. Open noon–5:00 P.M. Friday–Sunday. Visa, MasterCard, and American Express. Wheelchair accessible.*

A short distance closer to Boise, INDIAN CREEK WINERY—often referred to as the STOWE WINERY—has the in-house expertise of highly respected winemaker Bill Stowe. (Stowe also consults with Wood River Cellars.) Bill, Mui, Will, Greg, and Tammy Stowe and John and Mary Ann Ocker grow all the winery's grapes. Indian Creek is located 2 miles west of Kuna on North McDermott Road midway between Deer Flat and Kuna Roads, both of which run east and west. Enjoy the picnic grounds. Visitors usually get to talk to Bill while tasting his wines.

Fine points: Featured wines: Red and white Pinot Noirs, Chardonnay, Riesling, Cabernet Sauvignon, Merlot, and occasional Gewürztraminers and ice wines. Owners: The Stowe family. Winemaker: Bill Stowe. Cases: 2,500. Acres: 27.

SAWTOOTH WINERY LABEL

❧ *Indian Creek (Stowe) Winery, 1000 North McDermott Road, Kuna 83634; phone (208) 922–4791; fax (208) 922–9463; e-mail icwinery@micron.net; Web site www.indiancreekwinery.com. Open noon–5:00 P.M. Friday–Sunday or by appointment. Visa and MasterCard. Wheelchair accessible.*

In the greater Boise area several wineries are not open to the public but are worth mentioning here. In Caldwell: Bitner Vineyards is headed by respected winemaker Ron Bitner; Vickers Winery is owned by Kirby and Cheryl Vickers and sells at the Boise Consumer Co-op. In Nampa: Wood River Cellars is quite new. And in Boise: Petros Winery.

Another winery-tour route takes you southeast from Boise on I–84. First stop is Glenns Ferry less than 100 miles down the road.

CARMELA VINEYARDS is one of the most convenient wineries in Idaho and one with the most conveniences in the entire Northwest. Situated next to Three Island State Park, it overlooks the Snake River. Carmela is one of the few Northwest wineries that appreciate the need of wine fans to eat and eat well. Its deli-restaurant is a godsend for many travelers and has become an attraction itself, to say nothing of the popular, low-key golf course. This is also a great place to end your touring day because the whole facility is open until 9:00 P.M.

Fine points: Featured wines: Chardonnay, Riesling, Sémillon, Lemberger, Cabernet France, Cabernet Sauvignon, Merlot, Pinot Noir, and Old Vine Sweet (red). Owner: Roger Jones. Winemaker: Neil Glancey. Cases: 20,000. Acres: 48.

⊱ Carmela Vineyards, 1289 West Madison, Glenns Ferry 83623; phone (208) 366–2313; e-mail carmelawinery@aol.com. Open 9:00 A.M.–9:00 P.M. daily in summer. Restaurant open 11:00 A.M.–9:00 P.M. Monday–Saturday, 10:00 A.M.–8:00 P.M. Sunday, with brunch served 10:00 A.M.–3:00 P.M. Visa, MasterCard, and American Express. Wheelchair accessible.

The wineries along the westward line of Idaho between Moscow and Sandpoint that are regularly open to the public are Camas Prairie Winery and Pend d'Oreille Winery.

CAMAS PRAIRIE WINERY is conveniently located in downtown Moscow. Named for the camas lily whose roots sustained Nez Perce Indians, and which appears on the winery's labels, Camas also honors early settlers' pigs that dug for the camas bulbs. The Palouse—the region on both sides of the Washington-Idaho line—acquired the name "hog heaven," which Camas recognizes with its Hog Heaven White and Hog Heaven Red blend wines.

Obviously deeply rooted in the community, owners Stuart and Susan Scott started their winery in their "basement and two garages," eventually moving downtown to a century-old building that had housed an old tire shop. Now the wine bar is on the mezzanine in the beautifully restored old brick building, displaying local artists' work.

 Fine points: Featured wines: Chardonnay, Riesling, Lemberger, Cabernet Sauvignon, five meads, sparkling wines, and Star Garnet Red dessert wine. Owners: Stuart and Susan Scott. Winemaker: Stuart Scott. Cases: 4,000. Acres: None, buy from Columbia Valley in Washington.

⊱ Camas Prairie Winery, 110 South Main Street, Moscow 83843; phone (208) 882–0214; e-mail scottcamas@turbonet.com; Web site www.camasprairie.com. Open noon–6:30 P.M. Tuesday–Saturday. Visa, MasterCard, American Express, and Discover. Wheelchair accessible.

There are several attractions in the Moscow area besides wine. These include the work of at least eighty-five professional quality craftsmen and -women, specialty foods grown in the region, and the University of Idaho, which has many programs that attract hundreds each year. Also just 6 miles across the state line is Washington State University in Pullman.

Finally, but far from least, we reach the most northerly winery in the American Northwest, PEND D'OREILLE WINERY. It is well worth the trip here for the magnificent countryside, lake, the wines of this winery, and the enthusiasm

Grilled Ahi
from Pend d'Oreille Winery

4 6-oz ahi tuna steaks, skinless, boneless	1 Tbs olive oil
2 limes, juiced	salt and pepper to taste
	fresh lime wedges

Marinate ahi steaks in lime juice and olive oil for ½ to 1½ hours (no longer!).

When ready to cook, remove steaks from marinade and sprinkle both sides with salt and pepper. Position grill 4 to 6 inches above hot coals; when grill is very hot, place ahi on it. Cook for three to five minutes, turn; cook other side two to three minutes. (It should be light pink.) Serve with Pend d'Oreille Chardonnay.

---

of its owners, Stephen and Julie Meyer. Pend d'Oreille (pronounced *pond der ray*) took its name from a nearby popular lake. French for earring (ear pendant), the lake was named for Native Americans who wore pendants hanging from their earlobes.

Stephen, who has a degree in accounting, spent a summer working for a winery in Burgundy, caught the winemaking bug, and took courses at University of California Davis in enology. He and Julie decided to establish the winery in Sandpoint, which was her hometown. Their first release was in 1995. Pend d'Oreille was named Idaho Winery of the Year for the third time in 2003. The winery recently moved into new facilities, including a large tasting room and gift shop stocked with items for the home.

Fine points: Featured wines: Chardonnay, Pinot Gris, Syrah, Cabernet Sauvignon, Cabernet Franc, Merlot, Pinot Noir, Riesling, and Huckleberry. Owners: Stephen and Julie Meyer. Winemaker: Stephen Meyer. Cases: 7,000. Acres: None, buy from Washington and Idaho vineyards.

➳ *Pend d'Oreille Winery, 220 Cedar Street (mailing address: P.O. Box 1821, Sandpoint 83864); phone (208) 265–8545; e-mail steve@powine.com. Open in summer 10:00 A.M. Monday–Saturday, 11:00 A.M. Sunday; close 6:00 P.M., later Wednesday–Saturday; in winter close an hour earlier; also by appointment. Visa, MasterCard, and American Express. Wheelchair accessible.*

Until 1988 Idaho's few wineries were barred by law from selling directly to the public—this included a prohibition on selling to retail stores and taverns. Tasting rooms did not exist, and wineries could only sell their wines through distributors. These legal shackles had a chilling effect on the potential development of the state's wine industry.

Thanks in great measure to the lobbying efforts of a group of small winery owners, including Bill Stowe, Steve Robinson, Brad Pintler, and Idaho wine pioneer Cheyne Weston, the Idaho legislature removed these restrictions. The result was a rebirth of Idaho winemaking.

CHAPTER 5

HISTORY OF WINEMAKING IN THE PACIFIC NORTHWEST

he War of 1812 ended in a negotiated settlement between the United States and Britain. The two nations agreed in 1818 to table the issue of authority over what the Americans called Oregon (Shoshone for "place of plenty") Country and what the British called the Columbia Department, which included modern British Columbia, Washington, Oregon, Idaho, and a corner of western Montana. In the meantime citizens of both countries were allowed to settle there. No one asked the native residents what they thought.

THE FIRST GRAPE VINES

The infancy of the Northwest wine industry can be traced to 1825, when the Hudson's Bay Company (HBC), a British fur-trading monopoly, established Fort Vancouver as its western headquarters on the north shore of the Columbia River. At the fort (now Vancouver, Washington), Dr. John McLoughlin, HBC's western chief, planted Black Hamburg and Black Prince grape seeds brought from Britain. When the grapes matured, McLoughlin sent cuttings to HBC outposts.

American minister/physician Marcus Whitman and his bride, Narcissa, led a covered wagon train in 1836 to a site just west of Walla Walla ("Little Running Water") to found a mission from which to Christianize the local Indians. Narcissa recorded that grape vines had already been planted by French Canadian settlers, who were making wine.

The joint authority over the Oregon Country was extended for another ten years in 1827, and again in 1837. Concerned that the territory would be divided between the United States and Britain at a line north of Fort Vancouver, the HBC established Fort Victoria at the southern tip of Vancouver Island in 1843.

In December 1845 President James K. Polk claimed that all of Oregon Country should belong to the United States. The British countered with a proposal that the Columbia River be the dividing line, attaching most of modern-day Washington to Canada. While the negotiators sparred, American wagon trains full of settlers were trundling into the Columbia and Willamette basins.

OREGON COUNTRY DIVIDED

On May 13, 1846, the United States declared war on Mexico. Needing to address only one war at a time, the U.S. Senate quickly approved a resolution accepting a new British proposal: The Forty-ninth Parallel would be the new border. Vancouver Island, including Victoria, would remain British. Once American authority below the border was established, the invasion of settlers from the United States—over the Oregon Trail and by ships from California—grew from a trickle to a tidal wave.

In eastern Washington, however, a tragic incident stifled migration. During a measles epidemic more than 200 Cayuse Indians, who lacked natural immunity to the disease, died while the white settlers did not. As a result the natives suspected Marcus Whitman was poisoning them. They attacked his mission in November 1847 and killed Whitman, his wife, and eleven other settlers. In retaliation roving bands of settlers began to massacre Indians on sight.

During a ten-year "Indian War," U.S. Army troops that were sent west to protect the immigrants attacked Indian villages on the slightest provocation. To add to this injustice, the indigenous people also lost great numbers to epidemics (smallpox was the worst) and much of their land due to broken treaties and bad deals.

The underlying issue was land. The settlers wanted a place to farm, build, and live, without regard to Indian rights, treaties, or any other obstructions. Claims of ex-trappers in Washington who thought they had title to land through the HBC were also ignored by aggressive American squatters. Under an 1843 U.S. statute, a white male could get title to a square mile by marking its boundaries and building a cabin.

Around Fort Victoria the HBC tried to limit sales and settlement to its own employees, which deterred immigration until 1858. Then a gold strike in the Fraser Valley attracted thousands of former forty-niners who poured into British Columbia and overran both HBC and native land claims.

During the 1840s Oregon's population more than doubled each year. The Willamette Valley was fully claimed by 1855.

Dr. John McLoughlin, who retired from the Hudson's Bay Company in 1846, opted to stay south of the newly drawn American–Canadian border. He founded Oregon City (his home can be visited) and became a leader of the push for Oregon statehood.

Due to the Indian Wars, however, much of Washington Territory (split off from Oregon in 1853) was closed to set-

DR. JOHN MCLOUGHLIN

tlement until 1859, the same year Oregon was admitted to the Union as a non-slave state.

NURSERYMEN DISTRIBUTE VINES

Among the earliest settlers into Willamette Valley were nurserymen with wagons of cuttings, plants, and seeds—Henderson Luelling and William Meek, who arrived in 1847, being the first. They brought cuttings of Isabella, an American hybrid grape popular in the east, where Cincinnati, Ohio, was the heart of grape-growing in the United States. Various entrepreneurs soon carried Luelling and Meek cuttings and plants to other areas, such as Olympia. The name was changed to Lewelling and Meek in 1848 when Henderson sold out to his brother Seth, who spelled the family name differently.

Other sources of wine, cuttings, and grapes included the Hudson's Bay Company station at Fort Vancouver, which continued operation until 1868, and shipments from San Francisco in the late 1850s. Among the early cuttings from California were Mission grapes from the vineyards planted by California mission fathers between the 1760s and 1834.

Since 1837 wine had been produced on a small scale around the Catholic missions near Centralia and the Cowlitz River. Using varieties shipped from France, French Canadians were making wine in the Willamette Valley near modern-day Newburg.

When the Indian War cooled down, Walla Walla became a nursery head-quarters for the inland valleys. The leading nurserymen were A. B. Roberts, starting in 1859, and Philip Ritz, founder of the Columbia Valley Nursery, who both sold a wide variety of grapevine cuttings.

In eastern Washington, U.S. soldiers accused the Catholic priests of helping the Indians (protecting them from being massacred) and burned down one of the Oblate missions. Thus, in 1859 Father Charles Pandosy, a husky Slovakian priest with an imposing black beard, led his priests north in search of a more friendly neighborhood.

FATHER PANDOSY PLANTS A VINEYARD

When Pandosy came to Lake Okanagan (local native dialect for "meeting place" and spelled Okanogan in Washington) in British Columbia, he judged it perfect for agriculture—particularly fruit trees and grapes. Forty miles up the lake he founded a mission, which you can visit today, just east of the present-day city of Kelowna. With grape cuttings sent from a mission in the Willamette Valley, Pandosy laid out a vineyard overlooking the lake at the site where St. Hubertus Winery is today. The Kelowna Mission wines were used for celebrating masses and personal use, but they were not sold.

FATHER PANDOSY

Competition from California wineries was a major deterrent to expansion of the wine business in the Pacific Northwest. In 1858 Hungarian émigré promoter Agoston Haraszthy planted Zinfandel cuttings on the former mission vineyard land in Sonoma, California. He then imported 100,000 seedlings from Europe to launch California's commercial wine business big-time.

With the best of European and California wines arriving regularly from San Francisco, it was difficult for Northwestern vineyardists and winemakers to compete. Ironically, California vine cuttings were also providing the basis for the few vineyards being planted in the Northwest.

THE EARLY WINEMAKERS

The first commercial winemaker in Oregon was Peter Britt, a Swiss photographer, who planted a vineyard at Jacksonville in Oregon's Rogue Valley during the 1850s, using California vine cuttings. His winery, which he named Valley View Vineyards, yielded its first vintage in 1858. Britt soon sold his Claret, Muscatel, and Zinfandel to saloons and stagecoach stations for 50 cents a gallon. When the Oregon taxing authority sued him for unpaid taxes on the profit from his fifteen acres, he claimed it was "just an overgrown hobby," but was ordered to pay up. Nowadays he is honored by the Peter Britt Music Festival at Jacksonville.

Britt's success was followed by vineyard and winery expansion by others in the Umpqua Valley in the 1860s and 1870s. Willamette Valley, which got a headstart with the Luelling and Meek vines in the late 1840s, continued apace with an influx of cuttings from California and Europe. By the mid-1870s the Oregon State Fair began awarding prizes in separate categories for the best wines produced by state wineries and for imported wines.

Quite a few vintners preferred hybrids of varying strains of vines native to the western hemisphere (labrusca), which were thought to be hardier but not as tasty as the vinifera. Toughness was considered necessary to survive freezing weather, the rigors of shipping, and the infestation of voracious insects. The debate continues to this day.

Although it became a backwater far from the coastal market, Walla Walla continued to be the major grape-growing and wine-producing area in Washington until many vines died in the great freeze of 1883, with temperatures of minus 20 degrees Fahrenheit.

The first vines in the Yakima Valley were planted by Charles Schanno, a French brewer, who came from The Dalles in 1869 with cuttings from Fort Vancouver wrapped in wet straw. Following the example of the HBC at Fort Vancouver and Yakima chief Yamiakin, Schanno and Sebastian Lauber had an irrigation ditch dug from the Yakima River into Yakima to bring irrigated agriculture to the valley. Schanno's mercantile and agricultural career ended rather abruptly when he was convicted of the murder of one of his brewery employees.

Next came a German homesteader, Anthony Herke. He was a baker and butcher, who planted a one-acre vineyard next to his house (which is still owned by his descendants) west of Yakima in 1871, for wine drunk at home and donated to the Catholic mission in the valley. He also gave grape cuttings to settlers headed for Wenatchee to the north.

The first vineyard in the Wenatchee region was planted by "Dutch John" Galler, an ex-trapper, who settled on the Columbia River with his second wife, Mary. Theirs was a romantic story: Accompanied by a group of Indians, John fell into a river. When the others left him, a young Indian woman stayed and kept the half-drowned, hypothermic John warm by cuddling him close to her body. Not long after, they were married. They planted one of the first irrigated orchards in the area. In 1873 he added grapes, eventually reaching twenty acres, and he used them to make a German wine, which he sold.

Meanwhile, in the late 1870s the California wine boom burst spectacularly. The dreaded *phylloxera vestratix,* an insect that attacked vine roots, crippled Sonoma Valley wineries within three years and later infested vineyards in Napa County. Pierce's Disease wiped out the vineyards planted by Germans in Anaheim (now the site of Disneyland) in southern California.

The good news in the Northwest was that California competition was sharply curtailed. The bad news was that there were fewer cuttings of first-class vines available. California grape growers would make a comeback, however, assisted by the research program on viticulture and enology at the University of California, founded in 1880.

VINE PLANTING SPREADS

In the 1870s Lambert Evans, a Confederate Army veteran from Florida, planted grapes on little 350-acre Stretch Island in the lower reaches of Washington's Puget Sound and delivered them by rowing his skiff to Olympia.

A former liquor store owner from New York, Adam Eckert bought forty acres from Evans in 1889. Becoming an ardent nurseryman, he used a hybrid grape, Campbell Early, to produce what he called Island Belle (thought by most experts to be identical to select Campbell Early), which he promoted as a West Coast original. Within a decade Island Belle became the most common new grape planted in Washington.

Eckert emerged as the spokesman on grape growing for the Puget Sound region, was elected president of the West Coast Growers (which included California, Washington, and Oregon), and in 1910 published a booklet titled *Grape Growing in the Pacific Northwest.*

In the Yakima Valley and east of Kennewick, grape growing roller-coasted between boom and bust in the 1890s. A major irrigation project built in 1892 suffered a disastrous break the next year, followed by a national economic panic. Most of the grape farmers gave up, leaving the vines to fend for themselves, or sold the land to hop growers.

Anxious to ship farm products, beginning in 1903 the Northern Pacific Railroad sold some of its excess land to finance large irrigation projects at Kennewick. In the Tri-City region this triggered a revival of grape growing and wine production as well as development of agriculture in general. More than a dozen grape varieties were being pressed.

In 1910 Elbert F. Blaine, a water and irrigation attorney, built the Stone House Winery in Grandview. Blaine was one of the first to hire a professional winemaker, French Canadian Paul Charvet, who ran a small winery at his own home. Several Italian families in the Grandview area were also bottling wine.

That same year Kennewick held its first Grape Festival with entries of European varieties and several American standards of that period: Catawba, Campbell Early, and Concord. Concord rapidly became the most popular wine grape in eastern Washington, in part because it had a tough surface, which made it easy to ship. Parallel to wine production was that of grape juice, invented by Charles Welch of New York in 1890. The Church Grape Juice company of Kennewick began squeezing tons of Concords in 1913.

Rogue Valley growers expanded what Britt had begun. By the first decade of the 1900s the A. H. Carson vineyard was one of the largest in Oregon. A second wave of *phylloxera*, however, soon made its way north from California and virtually wiped out the Rogue Valley vines.

The Klondike/Alaska Gold Rush between 1897 and 1900 swelled the populations of British Columbia and Seattle. In the face of the bad example of the hard-drinking Klondike miners, table wine was touted as the drink of moderation, a family beverage. Seattle was now linked directly to the east by James J. Hill's Great Northern Railroad, and Tacoma was the terminus of the rival Northern Pacific. The prospects of growth and prosperity for the Pacific Northwest grape and wine industries were most favorable.

PROHIBITION CRUSHES THE WINERIES

The one cloud on the horizon was the growing prohibition movement in both the United States and Canada. The original targets of the prohibitionists were saloons where men hung out, spent the rent money, got drunk, met ladies of the evening, and neglected their families. But as "dry" political power grew, prohibition of all liquor manufacture and sales became a real possibility.

The British Columbia parliament enacted a prohibition against the manu-facture and sale of all alcoholic beverages as a "war time measure" effective October 1, 1917. Within a few weeks, dozens of pubs in British Columbia closed their doors. BC physicians issued so many prescriptions for "medicinal" liquor that the provincial parliament clamped a limitation on the number a doc-tor could write each year. In the same year, Washington State's legislature passed a bill that outlawed even the consumption of alcohol.

American vintners expected that if Congress adopted national prohibition, wine would be exempted or at least could be voted legal by local option. No such luck.

The Eighteenth Amendment to the Constitution passed on December 18, 1917, and was sent to the states for ratification. The amendment prohibited "the manufacture, sale or transportation of intoxicating liquors . . ." Three-quarters of the states ratified it by January 16, 1919, to take effect a year later. There were some exceptions: Wine for sacramental and medicinal purposes could be made and sold (on the technical basis that it was not used for "beverage purposes"), and limited production of 200 gallons of wine a year for personal use was permitted.

Prohibition was an obvious disaster for the American wine industry. It did not kill the grape-growing business, however, since grapes could still be used for homemade wines as well as eating. Washington became a prime source for grapes sent to the East Coast, and its vineyard production actually increased after the start of Prohibition. Grape juice and dehydrated grape mash were shipped with a label warning not to add yeast since it might cause "illegal fermentation." Many tons of California grapes, particularly Zinfandel, were shipped into Oregon and Washington for home production by hundreds of amateurs.

William B. Bridgman, a Canadian-born lawyer and former mayor of Sunnyside in Yakima Valley, became the chief advocate of expansion of vine-yards in Washington and planted more acreage each year during Prohibition. Other Washington growers followed his advice. In Oregon, however, discour-aged grape growers more often gave up, uprooting and burning their vines to replace them with pear trees fertilized with the ashes.

Meanwhile, in 1921 British Columbia repealed its provincial prohibition act, leaving municipalities with the local option to ban sales of "liquor by the glass"—a restriction adopted by Victoria—putting a considerable crimp in the saloon and pub business. It was a shot in the arm for liquor smuggling from BC to the United States as speedy motorboats and false-bottomed little freighters sailed from Canadian coves (or openly from the ports) to Washington inlets or waiting American boats. Trucks with dimmed lights rumbled through the night over back roads, eluding American revenuers.

Prohibition also stimulated thousands of home winemakers who learned how to make wine, often of barely passable quality but less toxic than the bath-tub gin, white lightning, and other intoxicants being distilled or mixed through-out the United States. It also created a taste for wine among those who shied away from bootleg booze. But the established American wineries were dead, except for the handful that were producing sacramental wines in amounts that were a shadow of their pre-dry output.

LIQUOR CONTROL IN BRITISH COLUMBIA

With the end of outright prohibition in British Columbia, the so-called Moderation Act in 1921 established the Liquor Control Board to regulate dis-tribution of alcoholic beverages and license retail outlets to sell alcoholic bever-ages. The three-man board set up provincial liquor stores—more than fifty the first year—which were nicknamed "John Oliver's Drug Stores" in honor of ide-alistic BC premier "Honest John" Oliver.

Some members of the board were not so squeaky clean. Financial irregular-ities, payoffs for licenses, and conflicts of interest were common, resulting in investigations followed by efforts at reform. But the British Columbia wine industry in the 1920s was scarcely a blip on the alcoholic beverage radar. There was only one established winery, there were no trained winemakers, and the grape output had only reached 135 tons by 1930.

Growers Wines, Ltd. opened the first commercial winery in Victoria in 1921, producing loganberry wine from berries grown on Vancouver Island in the Saanich area. In 1925 pioneering American horticulturist J. W. Hughes began planting grapes for wine just south of Kelowna above Okanagan Lake. It remained the only winery in the province until 1932, when Domestic Fruits & By-Products was established in Kelowna to make apple wine. Hughes sold his vineyards to his foremen in 1944, including Danie Dulik, whose descendants own Pinot Reach.

Domestic Fruits was the brainchild of Italian immigrant winemaker Giuseppi Ghezzi, who was joined by Pasquale "Cap" Capozzi, a grocer and lead-er of the Italian community, and teetotaler W. A. C. "Wacky" Bennett, a local hardware store owner. Together they raised about $5,000 and set up shop in a beat-up warehouse, with Bennett as nominal company president. In the mid-1930s the company switched from apple to grape wines and became Calona Wines, Ltd., a name sent in by the winner of a publicity-gimmick name-picking contest for a grand prize of $20 and a case of wine.

When Bennett was elected to the provincial legislature in 1940, he resigned and sold his stock. He became premier of British Columbia in 1952, serving twenty years. In 1960 the dapper Ghezzi departed for the winery business in the United States, leaving Calona Wines to Cap Capozzi and his sons.

The reformed Liquor Board became a cash cow for the province, pulling in millions of dollars in revenue from the liquor stores and licenses. The Board had little regulatory impact on BC wineries until 1960, since there were only Calona and Growers Wines.

REPEAL OF PROHIBITION

On February 20, 1933, Congress passed the Twenty-first Amendment, which repealed Prohibition, and submitted it to the states. Three-quarters of the legislatures ratified repeal by December 7, 1933.

The next day Ron Honeyman and John Wood of Salem, Oregon, hustled over to the capitol building to apply for a license for a bonded winery, which they called Columbia Distilleries. In Olympia, Washington, Charles Somers, a professional real estate man who owned the historic Evans Vineyard on little Stretch Island, could not find any state official with authority to issue a bonded winery permit. So he applied to the Federal Department of the Treasury for a license for what he "modestly" named St. Charles Winery. The confused Treasury Department bureaucracy issued the permit for medicinal wines, so for the first few months St. Charles could only sell its wine in drug stores.

Columbia Distilleries (shortly renamed Honeywood Winery) opened its doors in downtown Salem with production of brandies and liqueurs but soon shifted its emphasis to fruit wines. Honeywood remains the oldest continuously operating winery in Oregon and Washington.

Washington's St. Charles was soon joined as a licensed winery by Pommerelle, a Seattle apple juice company located in a warehouse at the site of the latter-day Kingdome, and William B. Bridgman's new Upland Winery at Sunnyside in the Yakima Valley.

It was only natural that former illicit operators from Prohibition days would get into the wine business. Frank Alvau, a builder of liquor stills for bootleg liquor, and Dominic Depoulis, a smuggler of hooch across the border (whose wife ran a whorehouse on Vancouver Island), headed a group of their friends who founded the National Wine Company in 1935.

At the time of repeal there was only one professionally trained enologist in the Northwest: a young German immigrant, Erich Steenborg, who had studied at the Geisenheim Wine Institute. Steenborg's talent was promptly put to work by Somers at St. Charles in developing a sweet sipping wine, and as a consultant to Washington University professors in developing a technique for "high fermentation" to balance grape, sugar, and yeast to yield wines at an alcohol content as high as 17 percent.

But Steenborg's big chance came in late 1934 when the prophetic Bridgman hired Steenborg to create table wines for Upland Winery, a task he relished and for which he was trained. At the time the taste of both Americans and Canadians was for sugary wines, so promoting varietals like dry Sémillon or Pinot Noir was an evangelistic effort.

LIQUOR LEGISLATION IN WASHINGTON AND OREGON

With repeal Washington's legislature passed the Washington Liquor Act (also called the Steele Act) aimed at moderation in drinking of alcoholic beverages. The act (1) prohibited sales of hard liquor by the glass—thus banning bars and saloons, (2) permitted "taverns" to sell beer (and in 1935 wine) by the glass, (3) established the Washington State Liquor Control Board, (4) set up a network of state liquor stores, (5) authorized the Liquor Control Board to purchase liquor and wines for the state stores, (6) allowed retail stores to sell bottled wine, and (7) gave a tax break to Washington wineries that grew their own grapes or fruit.

Oregon set up a similar system of state stores, which had little effect on that state's winery business because in the 1930s it was infinitesimal.

A vital side effect of these systems was protection of the local wine industries from the overwhelming production capacity and quality of California wineries. Only Washington wines were poured in that state's taverns, and the lower tax rate for small wineries was pro–home state because Washington wineries were little family affairs.

Lobbying for the state's growing wine industry was the Washington Wine Producers Association, formed in 1935, which became the Washington Wine Council three years later, with forty-two winery members. Between 1938 and 1942 Washington wineries' share of the state market jumped from 38 to 65 percent.

Some of the Washington wine business tactics during the late 1930s were cutthroat. In 1938 when National Wine Company (Nawico) refused to sell an interest to a potential investor, the investor went to the Feds and reported the pre-repeal bootlegging activity of three of its principals. Although their crimes were more than five years in the past, they were charged with illegal liquor trafficking. One of the accused agreed to tell all in return for not losing his license, but the others resigned and went into grape growing.

Despite its somewhat shady origins, Nawico was successful from the beginning, holding more than 12 percent of the Washington market in the late 1930s. At that time the company established its principal wine-production facility in Grandview, the Yakima Valley location of its vineyards, while maintaining the business and sales operations near Seattle.

THE FORTIFIED FAD

World War II had a profound effect on wine production. In the United States and Canada hard liquor "went to war" because distilleries were producing alcohol for military purposes (for explosives), resulting in a liquor shortage. Wine filled the gap and gained in popularity with the public. But former whiskey drinkers wanted something stronger. Natural fermentation to produce a higher alcohol content required lots of sugar, and sugar was rationed because the Japanese had overrun the sugar-producing Philippines.

To meet the demand, Washington wineries began producing "fortified" wines, beefed up in alcohol by blending in brandies distilled from fruits like apricots and peaches. Calona Wines in Kelowna, BC, fermented raisins in the wine mash as a substitute for the missing sugar. The vast majority of British Columbia's production was in fortified wines starting in 1930 and remained so until the end of the 1950s. By the end of the war, most of the twenty surviving Washington wineries produced primarily fortified wines.

In 1948 the previously clairvoyant Bill Bridgman dropped his crystal ball. Caught up in the flood tide of fortified wine, Bridgman abandoned his promotion of varietal table wine as the wave of the future and by 1948 was concentrating his Upland Winery on the fortifieds. His timing could not have been worse. That year the state legislature approved sale of hard liquor by the glass in restaurants. Given the choice of a real drink, many drinkers shifted away from fortified wine. Two years of record freezes were followed by winemaker Steenborg's resignation in 1951. In 1960, at age eighty-two, Bridgman sold the winery, which staggered to a close twelve years later.

Nawico was absorbed by Pommerelle Winery, another post-repeal pioneer, and in 1954 the two wineries were restructured as American Wine Growers. In came new management, which began looking to vinifera for table wines to challenge California in the Washington market. In 1956 AWG purchased one of Bridgman's vineyards in Grandview, the start of an acquisition program in Yakima Valley.

THE END AND THE BEGINNING

Oregon's fledgling wine industry suffered a near deathblow in 1957 when the state legislature repealed tax breaks for Oregon wines. These laws had been adopted to get around the U.S. constitutional prohibition against duties on commerce between states, and to protect Oregon wineries from California competition. Shortly after their repeal, California wines accounted for more than 92 percent of wine sales in Oregon. Only Honeywood Winery—Oregon's oldest—survived.

Richard Sommer, however, one of the first of the wave of University of California at Davis graduates to head for the Northwest, figured the Oregon soil and weather would produce competitive quality wine. So in 1961 he planted a vineyard of Riesling in the Umpqua Valley to provide grapes for HillCrest Winery, which he would open in 1963. Another U.C. Davis grad, David Lett, planted Pinot Noir in McMinnville in 1966 for his Eyrie Vineyards, which would produce its first wine in 1970, despite warnings by his famous professor Maynard Amerine against attempting to grow vinifera in the cold climate.

A handful of professors at the University of Washington in the mid-1950s put together an informal wine club, led by Lloyd Woodbourne, professor of psychology. They bought California grapes, which they pressed in a hand crusher, and then divided the juice among the members, who fermented the wines in their homes. They gradually brought in new members, with the goal of producing top-quality table wines.

Woodbourne's organization was incorporated as Associated Vintners in 1962. Then they bought a vineyard from Bridgman located on a hill in Woodinville, called Harrison Hill. The next year the shareholders personally planted new vines ordered from U.C. Davis. While waiting for their first crop, they bought grapes from American Wine Growers (the future Chateau Ste. Michelle) and Upland Winery, until those wineries began to suspect they were nurturing a rival.

Calona and Growers Wine Company of Victoria were the only wineries in British Columbia at the close of 1959. Within a year the number doubled. First came the incorporation of West Coast Wines, a subsidiary of Jordan Wines of Ontario, based in New Westminster outside Vancouver. Then brewer Andrew Peller founded Andres Wines Ltd. in Port Moody. Peller soon established wineries in other provinces, and for a time Andres was the largest wine company in Canada.

Calona Wines was swimming in profits by the 1950s, helped by its monopoly on selling sacramental wines to the Catholic churches in western Canada. Cap Capozzi became the CEO in 1951 and bought out the nonfamily investors. Calona was making an applejack called Doublejack and other fortified berry beverages called Berryjack, Blackjack, and Cherryjack. In 1965 Calona planted grapes near Osoyoos, at the south end of the Okanagan, pioneering vines in that region.

Jacks, Ducks, and Rotgut

Andres and Growers were both pandering to the popularity of American-born Cold Duck, a sparkling pink pseudo-Champagne. Andres went it one better with Baby Duck, a lower-alcohol version of the fizzy Cold Duck. It became an overnight favorite of Canadians who liked sweeter light drinks.

Mission Hill Vineyards, built by a group of local investors above Okanagan Lake in Westbank, entered the BC wine business in 1966. Mission Hill's grapes were barely ripe when it went broke in 1970. It was purchased at a distress price by flamboyant Ben Gintner, millionaire roadbuilder and brewer, who changed the name to Uncle Ben's Gourmet Wines, Ltd. Salesmanship was Gintner's game, and he tried to match the Berryjacks and Baby Ducks with a series of duck wines that Gintner said met the public's taste for "rotgut." They had splashy names like Hot Goose and Yellow Bird.

Gintner's most famous brand was Fuddle Duck, a name that came from a well-known Canadian political slip of the tongue. Prime Minister Pierre Trudeau, usually the model of propriety, while listening to his administration being roasted in parliament, blurted into an open microphone a two-word epithet, which included a well-known four-letter word beginning with the letter F. When criticized for his bad language, Trudeau claimed he had said "fuddle duck." The people of Canada laughed at this lame excuse. Gintner knew a popular joke when he heard one and put it on his bottles.

The old Growers Wine Company was purchased in 1965 by Imperial Tobacco Company, which changed the name to Ste. Michelle (by a remarkable coincidence it would not be the last tobacco company to diversify by acquiring a winery named Ste. Michelle). In two years Imperial sold Ste. Michelle to Jordan of Ontario. Eventually Jordan would be acquired by T. G. Bright's, then Canada's oldest and largest wine corporation, now Vincor International.

Capozzi's sons Tom (by then head of the company) and Herb wanted to either sell or expand with the help of a major investor. The Capozzi brothers visited the Gallo brothers, offering 49 percent of Calona in exchange for expansion capital. The Gallos' counteroffer was zero money but the benefit of the Gallo name in payment for 51 percent and control of Calona. This was an offer the Capozzis could refuse. Tom responded: "If I wanted a job as a salesman for Gallo Wines, I would have filled out an application."

In 1971 they sold Calona to Standard Brands, Inc., the American-Canadian food company, for $9.6 million. Newcomer wineries were discouraged by British Columbia's rules against liquor advertising and sales to the public from the winery, thus barring tasting rooms.

Enter the Experts

Two wine experts made a major impact on the struggling Washington wine industry. One of these was Walter J. Clore, a friendly Oklahoman, who in 1934 became a scholarship graduate student in horticulture at Washington State College (now University) at Pullman. Beginning in 1937 as a horticulturist at the state's agricultural experimental station near Prosser, he established a reputation as an expert in Washington's vegetables (in 1967 he was named "Mr. Asparagus") and fruits, especially grapes.

Clore became more than an expert on grapes, wines, soil, water, and weather. He got to know people, encouraged would-be growers and vintners, advised a generation of qualified winemakers, and put them together to develop and improve wineries and vineyards. Dr. Clore became a champion of the future of Washington wines, particularly those made from vinifera grapes. He capped off his technical career by directing the Wine Project, a long-term, in-depth study of vines and wines beginning in 1964.

While the Washington wine leaders (including Bridgman) continued to fight to shield Washington's wine industry from California competition, Clore believed that the underlying issue was making Washington's wine live up to its potential so the state would be competitive with other wine-producing regions of the world.

He did not limit his optimism to Washington. "The states of Washington and Oregon, and the province of British Columbia, are in the latitudes of the fine wine regions of Europe—France and Germany," he testified in 1969. He felt the problem of subzero temperatures some nights was matched by the insect and disease depredations in California and Europe. After all, he argued, a bad freeze might cost you one year's crop, but not a vineyard.

European-born André Tchelistcheff, winemaster at Napa Valley's Beaulieu Vineyard, was recognized as California's leading wine expert. In 1967 he visited American Wine Growers (the future Ste. Michelle) to advise them how they could improve their wines. The outspoken André was unimpressed and said he thought AWG had to adopt new methods. Before he caught his plane back to California, he dropped by little Associated Vintners and, along with a salmon dinner, tasted a glass of Gewürztraminer made at home by AV's treasurer. Tchelistcheff was ecstatic, calling it the "best in the world." He repeated this opinion in the days ahead, which gave Associated Vintners credibility.

The ubiquitous Dr. Clore induced Tchelistcheff to visit his project headquarters in Prosser the next year, where he served wines developed by his associates, Dr. Charles Nagel and George Carter. André liked what he tasted and became an apostle of the future of Washington wines. Howard Somer, American Wine Growers' winemaster and son of the founder of St. Charles Winery, which he had sold in 1965, retained Tchelistcheff as a consultant to AWG to tone up its table wines.

André's positive comments about the potential of Washington wines were echoed within the next decade by Leon Adams in the 1978 edition of *Wines of America* (particularly praising Ste. Michelle's Cabernet Sauvignon) and Terry Robards in *The New York Times Book of Wine*, which appeared in 1977. Robards enthused: "The astonishing wines that have come out of Washington's Yakima Valley have inspired some experts to proclaim that this region one day will be America's greatest." In regard to Oregon he reported that its "fledgling wine industry is tiny but has a promising outlook." He praised Eyrie, HillCrest, and Tualatin Vineyards for their "worthy efforts."

1969: A Turning Point

In his *Vineyard Tales,* wine writer Gerald Asher calls 1969 "a turning point for wine in Washington." Under pressure from California wine interests (which threw legislative campaign money around) and the Washington Liquor Board, which wanted to buy more out-of-state wines, the legislature repealed the tax on "foreign" wines. This forced the Washington wineries and vineyardists to become competitive by producing better table wines from vinifera as urged and predicted by Clore and his fellow experts. The state's vinifera acreage in the next three years jumped from 400 acres to 1,200.

Associated Vineyards purchased the entire crop of one Yakima Valley vineyard's grapes for Cabernet Sauvignon. With its Ste. Michelle brand, Nawico increased its planting of vinifera grapes for table wines. They were the only two Washington wineries that would last intact from that era. Winery owners Charles Henderson in Bingen, Lincoln and Joan Wolverton (the state's first female vintner) with Salishan Vineyards, Gary Figgins in Walla Walla, and Mike Wallace at Hinzerling would all start up a half dozen years in the future.

The year 1969 was a turning point for Washington wines in a strange way, too. The *Seattle Post-Intelligencer* ran a series on Associated Vintners (writer Stan Reed called AV "revolutionary" and some of its varietals the equal of California's best) that crossed the desk of Wally Opdycke, a young investment manager for Safeco Insurance Company in San Francisco. Opdycke liked to take tasting tours of Napa Valley and had placed investments in Washington. So he wrote to Dr. Clore, who took him on a tour of his Prosser research center and urged him to consider investing in a Washington winery. In cold business terms Opdycke felt that only American Wine Growers was a viable option in Washington.

Opdycke's offer was a leveraged buyout, which was mostly bluff and guts with very little cash. He did have a commitment for a large bank loan to be secured by the winery, which he intended to acquire. The aging partners who owned American Wine Growers eagerly sold their winery and its brands (Nawico, Pommerelle, and Ste. Michelle) to Opdycke's newly incorporated Ste. Michelle Vintners.

He kept the technical management (general manager Vic Allison, vineyard manager Les Fleming, and consultant Tchelistcheff) and pushed a pair of young distributors to unload the inventory of second-rate Nawico and Pommerelle outside the Northwest, while building up sales of the vinifera Ste. Michelle brand. With the remainder of his borrowed funds he bought some vineyards, since Nawico had owned only 400 acres at the time of sale, and used the first year's profit to upgrade with new steel tanks, oak barrels, and equipment.

A record freeze swept across the Pacific Northwest in 1971, destroying some vineyards and discouraging many growers, but the high percentage of survival of vinifera vines gave hope to vintners who believed in making quality table wines.

Opdycke's money was running out. He threw out feelers for investors and got a serious response from Canada's Labatt's Beer, followed by a competing bid from U.S. Tobacco, the chewing tobacco company based in Connecticut. He chose U.S. Tobacco, which gave him and his coinvestors equivalent stock in the parent company and was happy to pony up $150 million for expansion. The infusion of so much capital was a sea change in the Washington wine industry.

U.S. Tobacco acted swiftly. It built a $6 million Versailles-like headquarters in Woodinville, northeast of Seattle, on the eighty-seven-acre estate designed for lumber magnate Frederick Stimson in 1912, while keeping the principal vine-

yards and wine processing in Yakima Valley. In 1976 the name was changed
from Ste. Michelle Vintners to Chateau Ste. Michelle, and in 1982 the company (still a subsidiary of U.S. Tobacco) would be renamed Stimson Lane
Vineyards and Estates. Chateau Ste. Michelle, however, remained the popular
name for both the principal label and the company.

MATURING THE WINE INDUSTRY

David Lake, a thirty-four-year-old Canadian from Vancouver Island with a
rare master's degree in enology from University of California at Davis, was hired
as Associated Vineyards' winemaster in 1979 after an apprenticeship with David
Lett at Eyrie Vineyards in Oregon. Putting a highly trained young professional
in charge of wine production symbolized Associated Vineyards' transition from
a winery operated by dedicated amateurs into a business.

Within two years AV installed attorney Willard Wright as president,
hired a business manager, sold Harrison Hill in Woodinville and the Church
vineyard near Sunnyside to raise money, and brought in cash from new
investors. By 1983 it had nearly quadrupled its annual production from
25,000 gallons to 96,000 gallons. That year AV took a new public name,
Columbia Winery, although the holding corporation is still officially
Associated Vineyards. Shortly the new management purchased a large mansion across the road from Chateau Ste. Michelle in Woodinville as its headquarters, winery, and tasting room.

Lake's arrival was also evidence of the importance of U.C. Davis to the
development of Washington and Oregon wineries in the 1970s. Winemakers
and owners from the west's principal enological training ground included
Richard Sommer (HillCrest Vineyards), David Lett (Eyrie), Mike Wallace
(Hinzerling), Chuck Henderson (Bingen, later Mount Elise Vineyards), Mike
Moore (Blackwood Canyon), Tom Campbell (Horizon's Edge), David Forsythe
(Hogue), David Crippen (Covey Run), Dr. Dan Jeps (Alpine), Mike Januik and
Erick Olsen (both of Ste. Michelle), and several others. Jerry and Jean
Bookwalter (Bookwalter Winery) met at Davis in the late 1950s.

Dr. Clore was a regular visitor at Davis and looked to it for both talent and
vines. The university's enology influence is also felt across the border, as evi-
denced by Davis alumni Kenn Oldfield as vineyard manager and Sandra
Cashman Oldfield as winemaker for the modern Tinhorn Creek Vineyards in
Oliver, British Columbia, founded in 1995. Dr. Clore died in 2003, sixty-nine
years after his first taste of northwest wines.

Farm owner Bill Preston planted fifty acres of vinifera grapes on a parcel of his property north of Pasco and opened Preston Wine Cellars (which became Preston Premium Wines) in 1976. He soon hired young Rob Griffin from historic Buena Vista Winery in Sonoma, California. In 1979 Preston's Chardonnay won Best of Show at the first Northwest Wine Festival. Preston and his family rapidly increased vineyard acreage and case production.

Griffin moved on to Hogue Cellars in Prosser, which had just been founded by Wayne Hogue, and worked his magic there while Hogue grew to become one of the largest wine producers in Washington. Griffin left in 1990 to start his own winery, Barnard Griffin, in Richland, and was succeeded by U.C. Davis alumnus David Forsythe.

OREGON'S NEW WAVE

In Oregon Richard Sommer and David Lett were joined in serious wine development by Dick Erath and Scott Henry. Erath was a natural and innovative vineyardist and vintner who began his career in an unheated log cabin with a vineyard he planted on the land of wealthy lumberman Cal Knudsen, forming Erath Knudsen Winery (now just Erath) in 1970.

Henry was an aeronautical engineer whose family owned a ranch in the Umpqua Valley. After planting thirty-five acres of viniferas in 1972, he and his wife, Sylvia, opened Henry Estate Winery in 1978. Scott gained international renown in viticulture by inventing the "Scott Henry Trellis System," which spreads the vine canes and leaves to allow the sun to ripen the grape clusters in regions without as many sunny days as California.

He was one of the first of a wave of winery owners who came from other professions and disciplines: engineers, physicians, airline pilots, chemists, professors, business executives, lawyers, teachers, a newspaper reporter, an economist, a retired army officer, a Silicon Valley pioneer, a housewife, and a banker. Dick Ponzi was an amalgam of all types: a California engineer who took courses at U.C. Davis, planted in 1970 outside Beaverton, and then involved the entire family in Ponzi Vineyards.

In addition there were Oregon families with a history of farming or grapegrowing, like Dave and Margy Buchanan at Tyee Winery on land homesteaded by Dave's grandfather. Several children of those who made all that homemade wine during Prohibition or of European immigrants who grew up with a wine tradition decided to plant grapes and make quality wine. In recent years they have been joined by larger corporate entities, exemplified by Willamette Valley Vineyards.

THE WINE BARREL THAT SHOOK THE WORLD

One barrel of Pinot Noir put Oregon on the world wine map. In 1979 Dave Lett daringly sent his 1975 Eyrie Vineyards Pinot Noir to the Gault-Millau blind tasting in Paris. To the astonishment and chagrin of the Europeans, Lett's wine upset the grape cart by finishing a close third, ahead of dozens of Burgundies from leading French wineries.

The French had a beret-full of excuses. Robert Drouhin of the distinguished French wine family demanded a rematch and set up a special competition at the Hall of Justice of ancient Burgundy with a panel of European wine experts. So in January 1980, Lett returned with another bottle drawn from his barrel of Pinot Noir to compete against carefully selected French entries. This time the Eyrie entry finished second by two-tenths of a point behind a 1959 Chambolle-Musigny (a Burgundian village that produces the richest and smoothest of reds), with the next wine some three full points back.

Lett had proved that Oregon's Pinot Noir could stand up to European standards. His triumph drew worldwide attention and proved an economic boon to McMinnville, which now draws thousands of wine tourists each year. Significantly, it accelerated the shift in Oregon emphasis from berry-based wines and liqueurs to the varietals.

Oregon wineries specializing in Pinot Noir sprang up all over the Willamette and Rogue Valleys like dandelions after a rain. New wineries included Rex Hill, Chateau Benoit, Adelsheim, Yamhill Valley, Cooper Mountain, Sokol Blosser, Amity, St. Innocent, Girardet, Callahan Ridge, Bridgeview, and France's Domaine Drouhin, suitably impressed by Lett's barrel. In recent years they have been joined in Pinot Noir upper rankings by Torii Mor, Duck Pond, Lange, Willakenzie, Champoeg, Oak Knoll, Brick House, David Hill, Stag's Hollow, and Domaine Serene, among others.

CHATEAU STE. MICHELLE GROWS AND GROWS

Allen Shoup was selected as president of Stimson Lane (a.k.a. Chateau Ste. Michelle) by founder Wally Opdycke in 1980. Shoup was a businessman (Amway, Chrysler, Boise Cascade) who thought big and could persuade U.S. Tobacco top brass to spend their money on marketing.

Under Shoup's direction Stimson Lane began an ambitious acquisition program. A Ste. Michelle vineyard and wine plant named Columbia Ridge, at a dot on the map called Paterson overlooking the Columbia River, was expanded in acreage and provided with state-of-the-art equipment, huge tanks, and a drip irrigation system. In 1987 it was renamed Columbia Crest as a separate label. With 2,000 acres of vinifera grapes as well as an extensive farming operation, Columbia Crest is now the number one producer of Merlot in the world.

Stimson Lane bought Saddle Mountain Winery in 1982, Snoqualmie Winery (founded by former Ste. Michelle winemaker Joel Klein) in 1987, and Indian Wells, Cold Creek, Weinbau, Black Rock, and other vineyards. For variety they acquired Whidbey's on Whidbey Island (1987), which produces loganberry liqueur. Next door to Columbia Crest, Stimson Lane purchased what became Canoe Ridge Estates (not the same as Walla Walla's Canoe Ridge Winery, which has vineyards along the same ridge) in 1993. They also launched Domaine Ste. Michelle at the Woodinville headquarters in 1988 to produce sparkling wines.

Chateau Ste. Michelle/Columbia Crest also brought on board the latest U.C. Davis wunderkind, Mike Januik, and assigned him Snoqualmie in 1990. In short order he was chief winemaker overseeing all Chateau Ste. Michelle winemaking, working with winemasters given authority over each of the company's winemaking operations. There is also one person responsible for all vineyards, viticulturalist Charlie Hassom. By 1997 a stunning three-quarters of all Washington wine was produced by Stimson Lane's wineries.

Associated Vintners/Columbia Winery initiated an acquisition program of its own, although considerably more modest than Stimson Lane's. Coming under their umbrella were Paul Thomas Winery and Quail Run Winery (which became Covey Run Vineyards) in the Yakima Valley. For Paul Thomas (founded in 1979) AV built a modern winery in Sunnyside, which soon produced 150,000 cases annually, and founded Zillah Oakes at Zillah.

When dominant Stimson Lane began a program of buying and planting its own vineyards, it let the contracts with their vineyardist suppliers expire. As a result, many of the grape growers went into the winery business, greatly increasing the number of wine producers. In the last two decades, the number of Washington State wineries jumped from 19 to 145 by 2000. In the same period the acreage planted in grapes grew from 5,000 to 25,000.

David Lake at Columbia holds the longevity record as a professional winemaker at the same Washington winery (1979 to the present). When in 1987 the company acquired what became Covey Run, Associated Vintners hired David Crippen, who like Lake had a master's in enology from U.C. Davis. Crippen was also given the position of general manager. The day of the highly trained wine professional as a management official had arrived.

ESTATE WINERIES APPROVED IN BRITISH COLUMBIA

Since the commercial production of British Columbia wines for sale to the public was confined to a handful of large wineries (Calona, Andres, Mission Hill, and Casobello owned by Labatt Brewery), the government had not set any regulations for licensing of medium-size wineries. The Liquor Administration Branch of the Liquor Control Board had not been concerned with modest sales to friends, but there were now seven applicants with proposed midsize wineries anxious to sell to the public.

They pressed the Consumer Affairs Ministry for the right to be licensed, arguing that they could produce carefully crafted wines. At last in 1980 guidelines were announced by the board for obtaining a license for a "Cottage" winery, which had to own twenty acres of vineyard but was limited to production of 30,000 gallons, which had to be from BC-grown grapes. Later the maximum was raised to 40,000 gallons for sale in the province, and the title was changed to "Estate" wineries.

First in the field were George and Trudy Heiss, who had been growing grapes at the north end of Okanagan Valley since 1972. The Heisses amassed an inventory of wine for their Gray Monk Winery even before they got their license. Their first year proved that the smaller wineries had much to offer, receiving two golds and a silver in the 1981 initial Okanagan Wine Festival.

When a freeze in the mid-1980s cut their production, they were denied a waiver to be allowed to purchase wine from Washington to fulfill orders. To their rescue came giant Brights, which sold them some BC wine. George Heiss Jr., with a degree from Weinsberg, joined his parents as winemaker, and the winery continued to collect medals.

Sumac Ridge, founded by Harry McWatters (formerly with Casobello) and Lloyd Schmidt, was also in business by 1980 overlooking Lake Okanagan. Gehringer Brothers Estate Winery was founded by Helmut and Karl Gehringer who bought property near Oliver in Okanagan Valley in 1981 and began planting vineyards. They were soon joined by Helmut's sons, a pair of serious enologists, Walter (the first Canadian to graduate from the Geisenheim Institute) and Gordon (who learned winemaking at Weinsberg).

Hainle Estate Winery, which opened in 1988 at Peachland on Lake Okanagan, has a history of firsts. The family patriarch, Walter Hainle, who planted a vineyard in the early 1970s on doctor's orders to get exercise, was the first Canadian to intentionally make ice wine (a few had saved a crop frozen by unseasonable weather), created the first organic winery in the province, and was first in BC to get a "J" license to serve food in its tasting room. Son Tilman graduated from Weinsberg in 1982 to join his father in developing the winery.

Within a few years the ranks of estate wineries grew: LeComte (now Hawthorne), CedarCreek, St. Hubertus (on land where Father Pandosy once planted vines), Summerhill, Quail's Gate, and Blue Mountain all bottled competitive wines and were financially viable.

If 1969 was a turning point for Washington's wineries, and 1980 for Oregon with Lett's Pinot Noir, 1989 was the crucial year for British Columbia and very nearly spelled fatal disaster.

THE GREAT PULLOUT

Through the Liquor Distribution Branch of the Liquor Board, the government had protected British Columbia wineries in a method analogous to the tax breaks that had once been in place for Washington and Oregon. Each commercial winery was guaranteed listings with provincial liquor stores, and since the board controlled prices, it marked up the price of imported wines to almost double the margin for BC wines. Thus, the local product was cheaper and more attractive to Canadian consumers.

Then came the American-Canadian free trade agreement of 1988. The price differential that protected British Columbia wines was abrogated by the agreement. Many growers and vintners panicked. To compensate for anticipated loss of business, the national and provincial governments created a $28 million fund to pay growers to pull up "inferior" vines. More than half of BC grape growers accepted the deal. Worse yet, the Liquor Board marketing branch recommended that the viniferas should be the ones to go.

In the ensuing chaos, half the vines of British Columbia were victims of "The Great Pullout." Vineyard workers—mature, tough-handed men—cried unashamedly as the bulldozers tore out the vines. The danger to the wine industry became so desperate that BC premier Bill Vander Zalm ordered a halt to the suicidal program. In 1988 BC's vineyards had produced 18,397 tons. In 1989 tonnage fell through the floor down to 3,830. Those who had refused to take the money (like Joe Busnardo of Divino) were considered the lucky ones.

Free trade and the Great Pullout had also made some vintners realize that British Columbia had to compete on terms of quality in the long term, although the mechanics of the provincial acquisition system still favored local wineries. Bulk wines had made up 90 percent of BC wine production. New plantings would be heavily in favor of vinifera.

GUENTHER GETS HIS FARMGATE

Guenther Lang, a young executive with Daimler Benz in Germany, and his wife emigrated to Naramata above Lake Okanagan and planted nine acres in grapes in 1971. He was soon making wine that won medals in amateur wine contests. When the Estate Winery regulations were adopted, his was too small an operation to qualify. In 1985 he applied for a license anyway and was turned down. He became the leader of a number of small growers/winemakers who wanted to make good wine from their grapes for sale under a new category for those with fewer than twenty acres. Some of their number threatened to make wine and sell it, challenging the authorities to stop them.

In the wake of the 1989 disaster, these small producers were seen as one means to revive the level of BC wine production. Lang and his supporters pushed harder and began storing wine in anticipation of victory. Before the end of the year, a license category for Farmgate Wineries was approved. The wine had to be made from the licensee's own grapes, and production could not exceed approximately 10,000 gallons (45,000 liters), which was a fourth of the amount allowed Estate Wineries. The smaller wineries were on their way.

With the door open to new vintners from the ranks of growers, there was concern about quality controls to prove to the world that British Columbia wines were top drawer. Harry McWatters and the British Columbia Wine Institute (formed in 1990) thought they had part of the answer: empower the Wine Institute to enforce standards. The result was the BC Wine Act of 1990.

VINTNERS' QUALITY COMES TO BRITISH COLUMBIA

The Wine Act's Vintners Quality Alliance (generally called VQA) standards became effective in May 1991 and were based on a similar system developed in Ontario. To obtain VQA approval all grapes must be grown in British Columbia and the wine must have been made in BC, with 85 percent of the grapes from the variety stated on the label and 95 percent grown in the year on the label. In addition the wine must pass muster with a wine-tasting panel. While the requirements are not mandatory, the VQA-approved label is considered a test of quality the buyer would expect.

Most BC wineries agreed to the VQA system and were eager to get the approved labels. There were a few rebels, most notably Joe Busnardo of Divino Winery, who argued that the standards were too narrow and that the real test was the wine itself.

Farmgate (today usually just called Estate Wineries) licenses encouraged small growers to start wineries. Added to the mix were two Frenchmen with family histories in wine dating back to the seventeenth century: Claude Violet with Domaine de Chaberton at Langley in the Fraser Valley and Olivier Combret of Domaine Combret near Oliver in the Okanagan. Vancouver Island became a new growing region, with several new wineries opening by 1998.

Calona's ownership took several turns before it was purchased in 1989 by International Potter Distilling Corporation, which became Cascadia Brands, Inc. in 1995. Brights, the more than one-hundred-year-old Canadian winery in Ontario, merged with Carter & Inniskillin (which had bought Casabello) and eventually wound up with the name Vincor (featuring the brand Jackson-Triggs). With two wineries in the southern Okanagan Valley, Vincor is Canada's largest wine company.

In 1981 new investors bought out Ben Gintner, of Fuddle Duck fame, reinstated the name Mission Hill, and chucked the Ducks in favor of quality varietals. They launched an advertising campaign, acquired new equipment, and improved its wines and reputation. But Mission Hill's most important acquisition would be winemaker John Simes from New Zealand in 1992. Simes changed the harvesting times, delayed picking for greater ripeness, and brought in American oak barrels.

British Columbia's wines gained world acclaim in 1994 when Mission Hill's 1992 Grand Reserve Barrel Select Chardonnay won the International Wine and Spirits Competition in London and was awarded Avery's Trophy. It was a defining moment.

The wines of the Pacific Northwest have come a long way since Dr. McLoughlin planted those first seeds. Despite erratic weather, fewer sunny days than their southern neighbors, inconsistent government regulation, and fickle public tastes, the growers and vintners are now prospering. In addition to some excellent soil, there is one constant: the people who have cared. They have braved the rains, freezes, financial difficulties, good and bad advice, and disappointment, but persevered. When Richard Sommer set out to plant his HillCrest Vineyards in 1961, he was told "he would be frosted out in the spring, rained out every autumn, and would get athlete's foot up to his knees." Like a good Northwester he went ahead anyway. This pioneer spirit is still alive and well among the vines and vats of the Northwest.

CHAPTER 6

THE NORTHWEST WINE COUNTRY LIST OF LISTS

hese are lists of all Northwest wineries, the best wine and food events, farmers' and farm markets, as well as suggested restaurants and lodgings near the wineries listed in the book. Detailed descriptions of the wineries that are open to the public are in the main text.

OREGON WINERIES
NOT DISCUSSED IN TEXT

The Academy, 18200 Highway 238 (Applegate), Grants Pass 97527; phone (541) 846–6817; e-mail academy@internetcds.com. Open 2:00–5:00 P.M. by appointment.

Adelsheim Vineyard, 16800 Northeast Calkins Lane, Newberg 97132; phone (503) 538–3652. Not open to visitors, except Memorial Day weekend and Thanksgiving.

Ankeny Vineyards, 2565 Riverside Drive South, Salem 97306; phone (503) 378–1498. Open noon–5:00 P.M. Wednesday–Sunday.

Beaux Freres, 15155 Northeast North Valley Road, Newberg 97132; phone (503) 537–1137. Appointments only.

Beran Vineyards, 30088 Southwest Egger Road, Hillsboro 97123; phone (503) 628–1298. Open by appointment.

Bergstrom, 18405 Northeast Calkins Lane, Newberg 97132; phone (503) 554–0468. Open Memorial and Thanksgiving Days.

Brick House Vineyards, 18200 Lewis Rogers Lane, Newberg 97132; phone (503) 538–5136. Not open to visitors.

Cameron Winery, 8200 Worden Hill Road, Dundee 97115; phone (503) 232–6652. Appointments only.

Chehalem, 31190 Northeast Veritas Lane (off Highway 99W), Newberg 97132; phone (503) 538–4700. Not open to visitors except on Thanksgiving and Memorial Day weekends.

Domaine Meriwether, 801 North Scott Street, Carlton 97111; phone (503) 852–6100. Open noon–5:00 P.M. Saturday except January; also Memorial Day and Thanksgiving weekends.

Domaine Serene, 338 West Main Street, Carlton 97111; phone (612) 473–9825 (not to premises). Not open to visitors.

Evesham Wood Vineyard and Winery, 4035 Wallace Road NW, Salem 97304; phone (503) 371–8478. Appointments only.

Flying Dutchman Winery, 301 Otter Crest Loop, Otter Rock 97369; phone (541) 765–2060. Open noon–6:00 P.M. daily.

Helvetia Winery and Vineyard, 22485 Northwest Tungen Road, Hillsboro 97124; phone (503) 647–5169; e-mail helvwine@aol.com; Web site www.helvetia winery.com. Open Memorial Day, July 4, Labor Day, Thanksgiving, or by appointment.

High Pass Winery, 24757 Lavell Road, Junction City 97448; phone (541) 998–1447. Appointments only except Memorial Day and Thanksgiving weekends.

Houston Vineyards, 86187 Hoya Lane, Eugene 97405; phone (503) 747–4681. Appointments only.

James Scott Winery, 27675 Southwest Ladd Hill Road, Sherwood 97140; phone (206) 896–9869. Appointments only.

La Meurlasine, 9100 Holland Loop, Cave Junction 97523; phone (503) 537–0730. Not open to visitors.

Laurel Ridge Winery, 13301 Northeast Kuehne Road, Carton 97111; phone (503) 852–7050, (888) 311–9463; fax (503) 852–7404; e-mail info@laurel ridgewines.com; Web site www.laurelridgewines.com. Recently moved into new building; contact to find out if new tasting room is open yet.

LaVelle Vineyards, 89697 Sheffler Road, Elmira 97437; phone (541) 935–9406. Open noon–6:00 P.M. daily, Memorial Day through October; noon–5:00 P.M. Saturday and Sunday rest of the year.

Lawton Winery, 20990 Northeast Kings Grade, Newberg 97132; phone (503) 538–6509. Open Memorial Day and Thanksgiving weekends.

Madrona Hill Winery, 2412 North Mississippi, Portland 97227; phone (503) 284–5153. Open noon–5:00 P.M. Friday–Sunday.

Marquam Hill Vineyards, 35803 South Highway 213, Molalla 97038; phone (503) 829–6877. Open 11:00 A.M.–6:00 P.M. daily, May 15–November; 11:00 A.M.–5:00 P.M. Saturday and Sunday, February–May 15 and Thanksgiving and Christmas week.

McKinlay Vineyards, 7120 Earlwood Road, Newberg 97132; phone (503) 625–2534. Appointments only. Events on Memorial Day and Thanksgiving weekend.

Morgan Lake Cellars, 119975 Smithfield Road, Dallas 97338; phone (503) 623–6420. Open 11:00 A.M.–5:00 P.M. Saturday and Sunday.

Mystic Wines, 3995 Deepwood Lane NW, Salem 97304; phone (503) 581–2769. Open 11:00 A.M.–5:00 P.M. Saturday–Sunday, April–October.

Nehalem Bay Winery, 34965 Highway 53, Nehalem 97131; phone (503) 368–5300. Open 9:00 A.M.–6:00 P.M. daily.

Oak Grove Orchards Winery, 6090 Crowley Road, Rickreall 97371; phone (503) 364–7052. Open noon–6:00 P.M. Tuesday–Sunday.

Orchard Heights Winery, 6057 Orchards Heights Road Northwest, Salem 97304; phone (503) 363–0375. Open 11:00 A.M.–5:00 P.M. Tuesday–Sunday.

Panther Creek Cellars, 455 North Irvine Street, McMinnville 97128; phone (503) 472–8080. Open Memorial Day and Thanksgiving weekends.

Rainsong Vineyards Winery, 92989 Templeton Road, Cheshire 97419; phone (503) 998–1786. Appointments only.

Raptor Ridge Winery, 29090 Southwest Wildhaven Lane, Scholls 97123; phone (503) 887–5595. Appointments only, including tours.

RoxyAnn, 3285 Hillcrest Road, Medford 97504; phone (541) 776–2315; Web site www.roxyann.com. Open times not determined.

Schwarzenberg Vineyards, 11975 Southfield Road, Dallas 97338; phone (503) 623–6420. Open 9:00 A.M.–5:00 P.M. Monday–Friday, 10:00 A.M.–5:00 P.M. Saturday, 1:00–5:00 P.M. Sunday.

Seven Hills Winery, 235 East Broadway, Milton Freewater 97862; phone (503) 938–7710. Appointments only. Some open houses (call). Note: Seven Hills is in the Walla Walla, Washington, wine area.

Shallon Winery, 1598 Duane Street, Astoria 97103; phone (503) 325–5978. Open noon–6:00 P.M. daily.

Silver Falls Winery, 4972 Cascade Highway SE, Sublimity 97385; phone (503) 769–9463. Open noon–5:00 P.M. Saturday and Sunday.

St. Innocent Winery, 1360 Tandem Street NE, Salem 97303; phone (503) 378–1526. Appointments only. Open Memorial Day weekend and Thanksgiving weekend.

St. Josef's Wine Cellar, 28836 South Barlow Road, Canby 97013; phone (503) 651–3190. Open 11:00 A.M.–5:00 P.M. Thursday–Monday, May–September; 11:00 A.M.–5:00 P.M. Saturday and Sunday, October–April.

Starr & Brown, 10610 Northwest St. Helens Road (Highway 30), Portland 97231; phone (503) 289–5974. Open 11:00 A.M.–5:00 P.M. Saturday and Sunday.

Tempest Vineyard, 6000 Karlas Lane, Amity 97101; phone (503) 252–1383. Open Saturday and Sunday during summer; call for times. Also open Memorial Day and Thanksgiving weekends. Otherwise appointments only.

Territorial Vineyards, 907 West Third Avenue, Eugene 97402; phone (541) 684–WINE. By appointment.

Walnut City Wineworks, 475 Northeast Seventeenth Street, McMinnville 97128; phone (503) 472–3215. Open Memorial Day and Thanksgiving weekends; taste Iris Hill Winery here.

Wasson Brothers Winery, 41901 Highway 26, Sandy 97055; phone (503) 668–3124. Open 9:00 A.M.–5:00 P.M. daily.

Westrey Wine Company, 705 Northwest Winchester Terrace, Portland 97210; phone (503) 224–7360. Appointments only.

Wine Country Farm Cellars, 6855 Breyman Farm Cellars, Dayton 97114; phone (503) 864–3446. Open 11:00 A.M.–5:00 P.M. Saturday and Sunday (tasting room only).

_W_ASHINGTON WINERIES
NOT DISCUSSED IN TEXT

Alexia Sparkling Wines. 18658 142nd Avenue NE, Woodinville 98072; phone (206) 985–2816; e-mail gordyrawson@msn.com. Open noon–4:00 P.M. Saturday.

Ambrosia by Kristy, 4921 Eighty-fifth Avenue W, University Place 98467; phone (253) 307–5156; e-mail hampton@wa.net; Web site www.wa.net/ ambrosia/.

Andrew Will Winery, 12526 Southwest Bank Road, Vashon 98070; phone (206) 463–3290. Not open to visitors.

Balcom & Moe Winery, 2520 Commercial Avenue, Pasco 99301; phone (509) 547–7307; Web site www.balcomandamoewines.com. Not open to visitors, except group tours by appointment.

Birchfield Winery, 921–B Middle Fork Road, Onalaska 98570; phone (360) 978–5224. Open daily 10:00 A.M.–2:00 P.M., August–October; by appointment the rest of the year.

Bunchgrass Winery, P.O. Box 1503, Walla Walla 99362; e-mail rocher@bmi.net. Open only on local release weekends.

Cadence, 432 Yale Avenue N, Seattle 98109; phone (206) 381–9507; Web site www.cadencewinery.com. Call for appointment.

Cavatappi Winery, 9702 Northeast 120th Place, Kirkland 98034; phone (425) 823–6533. Appointments only.

Cayuse Vineyards, 17 East Main Street, Wall Walla 99362; phone (509) 526–0686. Open by appointment only.

Chateau Gallant, South 1355 Gallant Road, Pasco 99301; phone (509) 545–9570 Not open to visitors.

Coventry Vale Winery, Wilgus and Evans Roads (P.O. Box 249), Grandview 98930; phone (509) 882–4100. Appointments only.

DeLille Cellars/Chaleur Estate, P.O. Box 2233, Woodinville 98072; phone (425) 489–0544. Open to wine club members.

Dunham Cellars, 150 East Boeing, Walla Walla Regional Airport, Walla Walla 99362; phone (509) 529–4685; e-mail dunham@wwics.com; Web site www.dunhamcellars.com. Open by appointment.

E. B. Foote Winery, 127-B Southwest 153rd Street, Burien 98166; phone (206) 242–3852. Open 10:00 A.M.–4:00 P.M. Saturday or by appointment.

FairWinds Winery, 1924 Hastings Avenue West, Port Townsend 98368; phone (360) 385–6899. Open 1:00–5:00 P.M. Saturday and Sunday.

Glen Fiona, Mill Creek Road (P.O. Box 2024), Walla Walla 99362; phone (509) 522–2566. Open by appointment. Open houses second weekend of May, September, and December.

Greenbank Cellars Ltd., 3112 South Day Road, Greenbank 98253; phone (360) 678–3964; e-mail wine@whidbey.com; Web site www.whidbey.com/wine. Open 11:00 A.M. to 5:00 P.M. Saturday and Sunday, April–October.

Johnson Creek Winery, 19248 Johnson Creek Road SE, Tenino 98589; phone (360) 264–2100. Open daily evenings.

Leonetti Cellar, 1321 School Avenue, Walla Walla 99362; phone (509) 525–1428. Not open to public.

Lopez Island Vineyards, 724 Fisherman Bay Road, Lopez Island 98261; phone (360) 468–3644; e-mail lopezvineyards@yahoo.com. Open noon–5:00 P.M. Friday–Saturday, March 15–May 31 and September 9–December 20; noon–5:00 P.M. Wednesday, Friday, and Saturday, June 1–September 7 or by appointment.

Manfred Vierthaler Winery, 17136 Highway 410 East, Sumner 98390; phone (253) 863–1633. Open daily 11:00 A.M.–10:00 P.M. (at restaurant).

McCrea Cellars, 13443 118th Avenue SE, Rainier 98576; phone (360) 458–9463. Appointments only.

Mont Elise Vineyards, 315 West Steuben, Bingen 98605; phone (509) 493–3001. Open daily 11:30 A.M.–5:00 P.M.

Mount Baker Vineyards, 4298 Mount Baker Highway, Deming 98244; phone (360) 592–2300; fax (360) 592–2526; Web site www.mountbakervine yards.com. Open 11:00 A.M.–5:00 P.M. daily year-round.

Mountain Dome Winery, 16315 East Temple Road, Spokane 99207; phone (509) 928–2788. Open by appointment only.

Pasek Cellars Winery, 511 South First, Mt. Vernon 98273; phone (360) 336–6877. Open 11:00 A.M.–6:00 P.M., Monday–Saturday, Sunday by chance.

Patrick M. Paul Vineyards, 1554 School Avenue, Walla Walla 99362; phone (509) 526–0676; e-mail paulte@wwwics.com. Open 1:00–4:00 P.M. Saturday–Sunday on Balleer Stampede Weekend (May) and Christmas Barrel Tasting (December). Call for appointment the rest of the time.

Paul Thomas Estate and Winery, 2310 Golmanson Road, Sunnyside 98944; phone (509) 837–5605. Not open to visitors. Tasting at Zillah Oakes Winery.

Quilceda Creek Vineyards, 5226 Old Machias Road, Snohomish 98290; phone (360) 568–2389. Appointments only.

Rich Passage Winery, 7869 Northeast Day Road W, Building A, Bainbridge Island 98110; phone (206) 842–8199. Appointments only

San Juan Vineyards, 2000 Roche Harbor Road, P.O. Box 1127, Friday Harbor 98250; phone (360) 378–9463; fax (360) 378–3411; e-mail sjvineyards@rockisland.com; Web site www.sanjuanvineyards.com. Open 11:00 A.M.–6:00 P.M. daily, less in winter.

Soos Creek Wine Cellars, 20404 140th Avenue SE, Kent 98042; phone (253) 631–8775. Not open to visitors.

Widgeon Hill Winery, 121 Widgeon Hill Road, Chehalis 98532; phone (360) 748–0407. By appointment only.

Wilridge Winery, 1416 Thirty-fourth Avenue, Seattle 98122; phone (206) 447–0849. Appointments only.

*B*RITISH COLUMBIA WINERIES
NOT DISCUSSED IN TEXT

Andres Wines and Big Horn Vineyards, 2120 Vintner Street, Port Moody V3H
1W8; phone (604) 937–3411.

Chateau Wolff, 2534 Maxey Road, Nanaimo V95 5V6; phone (250)
753–4613. Open 10:00 A.M.–5:00 P.M. Saturday, or call for an appointment.

Divino Estate Winery, 1500 Freeman Road (off Highway 1), Cobble Hill V0R
1L0; phone (250) 743–2311. Call for hours.

Okanagan Vineyards, Road 11, RR #1, S24, C5, Oliver V0H 1T0; phone
(250) 498–6663. Open 10:00 A.M.–4:00 P.M. daily, Victoria Day to Labour
Day; Monday–Friday rest of year.

Vincor Okanagan Cellars/Jackson-Triggs, 38691 Highway 97, Oliver V0H
1T0; phone (250) 498–4981. No longer open to the public.

*I*DAHO WINERIES
NOT DISCUSSED IN TEXT

Bitner Vineyards, 16645 Plum Road, Caldwell 83605; phone (208) 454–0086.
Not open to visitors.

Petros Winery, 2303 Table Rock Road, Boise 83712; phone (208) 345–6283;
fax (208) 345–5723. Not open to visitors.

Vickers Winery, 15646 Sunny Slope Road, Caldwell 83605. Not open to visitors, but can purchase wines at Boise Consumer Co-op.

Wood River Cellars, 2606 San Marco Way, Nampa 83686; phone (208)
888–9358. Not open to visitors.

*Here we list in chronological order events
not presented by individual wineries.*

*O*REGON WINE AND FOOD EVENTS

Friday Afternoon Escapes, bus tours (smart idea) led by Grape Escape Winery Tours, leaving from downtown Portland, 1:30–4:30 P.M. Reservations required, $45. Phone (503) 282–4262.

Old Ashland Story Tours. One-hour walks meet at Plaza in downtown Ashland by information booth, Monday–Saturday, 10:00 A.M. Admission $5.00. Phone (541) 488–1993.

Third Thursday Educationals at the Portland Wine and Culinary Center, Atwater's Restaurant, 111 SW Fifth Avenue near West Burnside, Portland. Usually $26 per person. Phone (503) 275–3600.

Oregon Shakespeare Festival, last weekend of February to first weekend of October, 15 South Pioneer Street, P.O. Box 158, Ashland 97520. Phone (541) 482–4331; fax (541) 482–8045; Web site www.mind.net/osf.

McMinnville Wine & Food Classic, third weekend in March, featuring thirty-five choice Oregon wineries, thirty restaurants and culinary experts, thirty Northwest artists, and live music all weekend long. Phone (503) 472–4033.

Blossom Festival, third weekend in April, stages loads of celebratory events marking the beauty of thousands of acres of pink and white pear and apple blossoms in the Hood River Valley, with pancake breakfasts, BBQ, arts, crafts, and antique shows. Phone (800) 366–3530.

Spring Beer & Wine Fest, third Saturday and Sunday in April, Oregon Convention Center, noon–10:00 P.M. Beer and wine sampling (charge); food, seminars, entertainment (free). Phone (503) 238–3770.

Memorial Weekend in the Wine Country, last weekend in May. Forty tasting rooms in Yamhill County participate. Phone (503) 646–2985; Web site www.yamhillwine.com.

Heritage Wine & Art Festival, last weekend in May–first in June, Clackamas County Fairgrounds, Canby. Oregon winery booths, food, art, entertainment. Admission $5.00 adults, $4.00 seniors and teens, kids free. Phone (503) 266–1136.

At the Songbird Celebration, first weekend in June at the Hutson Museum in Parkdale. Kid and adult activities welcome migratory songbirds home to Hood River. Bird numbers are down, but humans enjoy plays, puppet shows, storytelling, live music, crafts, food, birdhouse or feeder building. Phone (541) 352–6002.

Portland Rose Festival is celebrated throughout the Rose City for twenty-four days in June. Don't miss the Grand Floral Parade, first Saturday following the opening of the Rose Festival, and the Festival of Flowers in Pioneer Courthouse Square, first week of the Rose Festival. (Don't forget to stop in at Powell's Travel Store beneath the square while you're there.) Phone (503) 228–9411 or call festival association at (503) 227–2681.

Vintage Food and Wine Festival, mid-June, Jacksonville. Phone (541) 899–8118.

Peter Britt Musical Festival, June–September, Jacksonville. Music and dance outdoors under the trees, honoring pioneer Oregon winemaker. Phone (800) 88–BRITT or (541) 773–6077.

Oregon Bach Festival, late June or early July, Eugene. Phone (860) 457–1486.

At a Berry Good Cherry Time, first week in July, Hood River. You can sample ten kinds of cherries including Bing, Ranier, and Black Republican (What?!) in every humanly crafted form imaginable.

Ashland Vineyards Art & Wine Festival, July 4th weekend, 11:00 A.M.–6:00 P.M., 1775 East Main Street, Ashland. Phone (541) 488–0088.

Bend Summer Festival, second weekend in July, downtown Bend. Winery booths, food booths, fine arts and crafts, live music. Free, with charges for food and wine. Phone (541) 389–0995.

Salem Arts Festival, third weekend in July, Bush Park, Salem. The state's biggest juried arts festival. Phone (503) 581–2228.

Bite of Salem, last weekend in July, Waterfront Park, Salem. Salem's premier food and wine event. Don't miss it! Phone (503) 581–4325.

International Pinot Noir Celebration, last weekend in July, Linfield College campus, McMinnville. Sixty of the finest Pinot Noir producers from around the world are invited to participate on a rotating basis in this three-day orgy of seminars, tastings, tours, and extraordinary meals celebrating and featuring Pinot Noir. Winemakers present their wines and even act as tour guides to the select 550 guests who are lucky enough to get much sought-after tickets. The Northwest's top chefs create lunches, dinners, and a traditional Northwest salmon bake. Seminars may include how to make a wine barrel in one easy lesson, pinot and everything pairing, making wine and terroir, tasting, tasting, and tasting. Expensive. P.O. Box 1310, McMinnville 97128. Phone (503) 472–8964 or (800) 775–4762; Web site www.yamhillwine.com.

Chief Joseph Days, last full weekend in July, Joseph. Native American demonstrations rodeo, exhibits. Phone (541) 432–1015.

Mount Hood Festival of Jazz, first full weekend in August, Mount Hood Community College, Gresham. Phone (503) 232–3000.

The Bite—A Taste of Portland, second or third weekend in August, Waterfront Park, Portland. Benefit for Oregon Special Olympics with twenty winery booths, nineteen local restaurant booths, continuous live entertainment on five stages, children's activities. Admission $2.00, additional $1.00 for Oregon Wine Pavilion, charge for food and wine. Phone (503) 248–0600.

Gravenstein Apple Days, third weekend in August, Hood River. Guarantees country fun for the whole family with "the best" judgments and prices for pies, sauces, tarts; friendly farm animals; BBQ; trout fishing; rides on the Mt. Hood Railroad; 10K Volkswalk. Phone (800) 366–3530.

Wine, Arts & Crafts, last weekend in August/first in September, Wy'East Day Lodge, Timberline Lodge, Government Camp. Wine tasting by eight local wineries, crafts, live music. Free admission, charge for wine. Phone (503) 231–7979.

Umpqua Valley Wine, Art & Music Festival, first weekend in September, historic Oakland. Sixteen wineries, regional artists, food, live music. Carnivores: Don't miss the lamb barbecue. Admission $6.00, or $13.00 "weekend passport" for both days and wineglass, extra for barbecue. Phone (800) 444–9584.

Newberg Vintage Celebration, first weekend in September, Sportsman Airpark, Highway 219, Newberg. Yamhill County wineries' booths, Vintage Aircraft Fly-in, classic autos, boats and motorcycles, art, food, live entertainment. Phone (503) 538–2014.

Indian Summer at Champoeg State Heritage Area, third weekend in September. Phone (503) 678–1251, ext. 222.

Oregon Grape Stomp Championship and Harvest Festival, mid-September, Willamette Valley Vineyards, Turner (just off Highway 5). Food, music. Phone (503) 588–9463.

The Pumpkin Funland, October 1–November 12 at fruit stands and Rasmussen Farms, Hood River. A must for generations of kids, with all sorts of wild characters created from pumpkins, squash, and other garden produce, and an optional mysterious trip through the Rasmussen Corn Maze.

Harvest Fest, first weekend in October, Hood River Expo Center. A truly local celebration of the harvest and crafts with more than one hundred vendors and all the food and crafts you can stand, plus tour of "fruit loop." Phone (800) 366–3530.

Gorge Fruit & Craft Fair, third weekend in October, Hood River. The best of the region's harvest season produce and crafts by Gorge artisans; local firemen's breakfast. Phone (541) 354–2865.

Yamhill County Wine Country Thanksgiving, Thanksgiving weekend, Yamhill County. Thirty-five tasting rooms open, including many usually by appointment only. Phone (503) 646–2985; Web site www.yamhillwine.com.

*W*ASHINGTON WINE AND FOOD EVENTS

Red Wine & Chocolate, Valentine's Day, Zillah and Granger in Yakima Valley. Phone (800) 258–7270.

Passport to Woodinville, first Saturday and Sunday in April, is winery tour in Woodinville. Phone (425) 424–9002.

Tasting Washington, second Saturday and Sunday in April, Stadium Exhibition Center, Seattle.

Spring Barrel Tasting, last full weekend in April, Yakima Valley wineries. Phone (800) 258–7270.

Washington Cheese Festival, last weekend in April, Tucker Cellars, 70 Ray Road, Sunnyside. Phone (509) 837–8701.

Hot Air Balloon Stampede & Winery Open House, first weekend in May, most wineries. Tri-Cities.

Cherry Festival & Parade, first weekend in May, Granger.

Yakama Nation Treaty Day Commemoration of 1855, first week in June, Toppenish. Includes Mural in a Day. Phone (800) 369–3982.

Tri-Cities Air Show, late June or early July, Tri-Cities area. Features loud noise, military planes, and vehicles.

Toppenish Pow Wow & Rodeo and July 4th Parade, July 4 weekend, Toppenish. A spectacular tribal gathering and rodeo with parades, dancing, crafts, and Native foods.

Bluegrass & Micro-Brew Hop Festival, July, Toppenish.

Seafair, July to early August, Seattle. Parades, festivals, hydroplane races, large attendance. Phone (206) 728–0123.

Columbia Cup Hydroplane Race, late July or early August, Tri-Cities. A wild time; dubbed "Thunder-on-the-Columbia." Families turn this into a noisy fair atmosphere full of local fun.

Chili Pepper Festival, first weekend in August, Washington Hills Cellars, 111 East Lincoln Avenue, Sunnyside. Phone (509) 839–WINE.

Pacific Northwest Wine Festival, first Saturday in August, Seattle. Sample wines from Washington, Oregon, and Idaho. Sponsored by the Enological Society of the Pacific Northwest, Seattle Chapter. Phone (206) 667–9463 for details.

Walla Walla Fair & Frontier Days, last week and weekend in August, Walla Walla. This is a week of rodeo, country singers, horse racing, huge Western parade downtown on Saturday, and general Western dress-up and cavorting. Be ready to ride, Sally. Phone (509) 527–3250 or 527–3247.

Wheelin' Walla Walla Weekend, second weekend in September, Main Street, Walla Walla. This is a hilarious reliving of fifties and sixties popular culture with the Twilight Valley Cruise at 6:00 P.M. Friday and a Cost-U-Less Cruise from 9:00 to 11:00 P.M., an all-day "Show 'n Shine" of your favorite wheels, an Evening Streetdance with the Bouncin' Baby Boomer Band, and a Sunday Pancake Breakfast from 7:00 to 11:00 A.M. Can't get more down-home.

Tri-Cities Northwest Wine Festival, mid-November. Phone (509) 588–6716.

Thanksgiving in the Wine Country, last weekend in November, Yakima Valley wineries. Phone (800) 258–7270.

ℬritish Columbia Wine and Food Events

Wine & Oyster Festival, late January, at the Westin Bayshore in Vancouver. Sponsored by the Liberty Wine Merchants. Thirty-four BC wineries pour tastes to allow guests to match wines with oysters, oysters, oysters.

Pacific Northwest Wine Festival, February or March; at sites throughout Victoria; tastings and banquet featuring wineries of BC, Washington, Oregon, Idaho; call any local Victoria wineshop.

Vancouver Playhouse International Wine Festival, last full weekend in April, Vancouver. Features 153 wineries from BC, Washington, Oregon, California, Japan, and Austria. Enjoy a full range of wine and food tasting events at a full range of ticket prices. Phone (604) 280–4444; Web site www.winefest.mybc.com.

Spring Festival, usually May 1–4, Kelowna. Residents and visiting wine fans celebrate the new growing season. Cosponsored by twenty-five wineries and the Ramada Lodge Hotel. Spring Tasting takes place at the Boardwalk, 1030 McCurdy Street, 6:30–9:30 P.M. Tickets $30 through TicketMaster. Phone (250) 860–1470.

South Okanagan Horse Trials, Victoria Day weekend (often the next-to-last Monday in May), at Desert Park, Osoyoos.

Cowichan Bay Boat Festival, first or second weekend in June, Duncan. Contact: Cowichan Wooden Boat Society, P.O. Box 787, Duncan V9L 3Y1; phone (250) 746–4955.

Cherry Fiesta Day, July 1, Osoyoos. Parade and cherry foods.

Salt Spring Island Wine Festival, Saturday closest to July 4. BC, Washington, and Oregon wineries pour tastes on Salt Spring Island, sponsored by the Tuned Air Choral Society.

Symphony Splash, first Sunday in August, Inner Harbor, Victoria. Afternoon pop concert by Victoria Symphony from barge, draws 50,000 to Parliament lawn. Phone (250) 385–9771.

British Columbia Square Dance Jamboree, first week in August, Penticton (the "Square Dancing Capital of Canada"). Phone (250) 493–5922.

Penticton Peach Festival, second week in August, Penticton. Family entertainment, music, community theater, fireworks, boat show, tea and peach shortcake, sandcastle competition, carnival and rides, volleyball tournament, pancake and sausage breakfast, parade down Main Street, picnic, land luge competition, country music, kids' parade, wine tasting, and much more. Phone (604) 975–9642; e-mail peachfest@img.net.

First Peoples' Festival, Victoria, second full weekend in August. Three-day free event in Heritage Court and Thunderbird Park of cultural activities of island's first people. Phone (250) 384–3211 and (250) 387–2134.

Cardboard Boat Race, second weekend in August, Penticton. Phone (250) 492–3011.

Artathon, most of August, at Leir House Cultural Centre, Manor Park Avenue, Penticton. Displays and exhibits and craft fair from artists of the South Okanagan. Phone (250) 492–7997.

Ironman Canada Triathlon, last weekend in August, Penticton. Draws athletes and spectator/athletes from around the world. Phone (250) 490–8787; fax (250) 490–8788.

Dixieland Jazz Festival, Labor Day weekend, Penticton. Usually ten top Dixieland bands at four venues, plus big band swing, New Orleans funk, boogie and blues piano, western swing, and gospel. Dancing is encouraged! Phone (250) 770–DIXI.

Fall Festival, a weeklong celebration starting on the first Friday in October, Kelowna and Penticton. Wine tastings and food pairings for commercial buyers of wine and hospitality industry personnel, the Kelowna Consumer Tasting featuring VQA wines from twenty-five wineries at the Coast Capri Hotel in Kelowna ($35), Winemasters' Luncheon & Awards luncheon with fabulous wines and foods at the Clarion Lakeside Resort in Penticton ($35). At Grand Finale Fall Consumer Tasting, the Fall Festival's largest event, sample VQA wines from all member wineries at the Penticton Trade & Convention Centre, 6:00–9:00 P.M. Tickets $30 or two-night package $50. All tickets available through TicketMaster, (250) 860–1470. Information: (800) 972–5151 (from Canada only).

Fraser Valley Wine Festival, first Saturday in November, Willowbrook Shopping Centre, Langley. Local restaurants and merchants provide hors d'oeuvres to accompany BC wines.

Sonoma-British Columbia Wine Festival, first weekend in November at the Empress Hotel, Victoria. More than 150 wines from twenty-six Sonoma County wineries and eighteen BC wineries are poured at an afternoon trade show and an evening public tasting.

Great Canadian Beer Festival, second weekend in November, Victoria Conference Centre, 4:00–9:00 P.M. All-natural beers. Phone (250) 595–7729.

*F*ARMERS' MARKETS

Oregon

Ashland

Rogue Valley Growers & Crafters Market, Water and Main Streets. Open on Tuesday.
U-Pick at Valley View Orchards, 1800 North Valley View Road; (541) 488–2840.

Eugene

Eugene's Saturday Market, High Street and Broadway.

Hood River

Farmers in the Park, Thirteenth and May Streets. Open 9:00 A.M.–2:00 P.M. Saturday, May–October.
Saturday Market, Trout Lake; (509) 395–2679. Open July–Labor Day.

Portland

Portland Farmers' Market, Alber's Mill under the Broadway Bridge. Open Saturday morning April–October.
Saturday Market, 108 West Burnside near the Skidmore Fountain at SW First Avenue and SW Ankeny Street.

Washington

Grandview

The Melon Man, corner of Wine Country and County Line Roads; (509) 786–3600. Open 9:00 A.M. to dusk beginning in mid-March.

Granger

Granger Berry Patch, 1731 Beam Road; (509) 854–1413. Open 8:00 A.M.–5:00 P.M. daily June–October.

Jones Farms, 2020 Thacker Road; (509) 829–6024. Open 7:00 A.M.–5:00 P.M. daily, Sunday in August–September only.

R. A. Rasmussen & Sons, Inc., 1183 Indian Church Road; (509) 854–1365. Open 8:00 A.M.–5:00 P.M. Monday–Friday, 8:00 A.M.–3:00 P.M. Saturday, in season.

Prosser

Bushel's and Peck's, 611 Wine Country Road; (509) 786–1600. Open 9:00 A.M.–6:00 P.M. Monday–Friday, 9:00 A.M.–4:00 P.M. Saturday, 10:00 A.M.–3:00 P.M. Sunday, May–October 31.

Chukar Cherry Store, 320 Wine Country Road; (509) 786–2055.

Prosser Farmers' Market, 1230 Bennett Avenue; (509) 786–3600. Open 8:00 A.M.–1:00 P.M. Saturday, June–October.

Sunnyside

Darigold Dairy Fair, 400 Alexander Road; (509) 837–4321. Open all day daily.

Guerra's Produce, 4800 Maple Grove Road; (509) 837–8897. Open 9:00 A.M.–6:00 P.M. Monday–Saturday, 10:00 A.M.–6:00 P.M. Sunday.

Tucker Cellars and Farmers' Market, 70 Ray Road; (509) 837–8701. Open 8:00 A.M.–6:00 P.M. summer, 9:00 A.M.–4:30 P.M. winter.

Toppenish

Schell Farms Bean & Produce, 10 Harris Road; (509) 865–4511. Open 9:00 A.M.–6:00 P.M. Monday–Saturday, 9:00 A.M.–4:00 P.M. Sunday, mid-June–October 30.

Walla Walla

Farmers' Market, Fourth and Main Streets. Open Saturday 8:00 A.M.–noon, May 24–November 1.

Wapato

Caribou Ranches, Inc., 7281 Progressive Road; (509) 848–2277; fax (509) 848–2523.

Donald Fruit & Mercantile, 2560 Donald-Wapato Road; (509) 877–3115. Open 9:00 A.M.–6:00 P.M. daily June 13–October 31.

Imperial's Garden, 2701 Corner Lateral A and Lateral I; (509) 877–2766. Open 7:00 A.M.–7:00 P.M. daily June–October.

Krueger Family Peppers & Produce, Inc., 462 Knights Lane; (509) 877–3677. Open daylight hours Sunday–Thursday, Friday until 3:00 P.M., closed Saturday.

Turcott Orchard & Benson Ranches, 801 Clark Road; (509) 877–2688. Open 8:00 A.M.–6:00 P.M. Wednesday–Monday.

Yakima

Johnson Orchards, 4906 Summitview Avenue; (509) 966–7479. Open 9:00 A.M.–6:00 P.M. daily.

Residential Fruit Stands, South Second and Third Avenues, Nob Hill, South 58th and Summitview Avenue (next to Smooty's); (509) 575–5358. Open 9:00 A.M.–dusk daily, July–November.

British Columbia

Cobble Hill

Arbutus Ridge Farms, 3295 Telegraph Road; (250) 743–7599. Open sunup to sundown daily.

Cobble Hill Orchard, 1310 Fairfield Road; (250) 743–9361. Open Friday–Sunday 10:00 A.M.–5:00 P.M. in season.

Kilrenny Farm, 1470 Cowichan Bay Road; (250) 743–9019. Open 11:00 A.M.–4:00 P.M. Saturday–Monday and Wednesday from mid-July through October.

Old Farm Market and *Moby Chix*, on the east side of Highway 1. Open 11:00 A.M.–sundown, summer.

Silverside Farms, 3810 Cobble Hill Road; (250) 743–9149.

Penticton

Fruit and vegetable stands line all roads in and around Penticton and the Okanagan Valley. July, August, and September are the best months to enjoy the bounty.

*R*ESTAURANTS

Oregon

Ashland

Ashland Bakery Cafe, 38 East Main Street; (541) 482–2117
Brothers' Restaurant, 95 North Main Street; (541) 482–9671
Chateaulin, 50 East Main Street; (541) 482–2264
Gen Kai, 180 Lithia Way, just off Plaza; (541) 482–9632
Geppetto's, 345 East Main Street; (541) 482–1138
Monet, 36 South Second Street, just off Main; (541) 482–1339
Plaza Cafe, 47 North Main Street; (541) 488–2233
Primavera, First and Hargadine; (541) 488–1994
Thai Pepper: Some Like It Hot, 84 North Main Street; (541) 482–8058

Corvallis

The Gables, 1121 Northwest Ninth Street; (541) 752–3364

Dayton

Joel Palmer House, 600 Ferry Street; (503) 864–2995

Dundee

Dundee Bistro, 100A Southwest Seventh Street (corner of Highway 99W); (503) 554–1650
Red Hill Provincial Dining, 276 Highway 99W; (503) 538–8224
Tina's, 760 Highway 99W; (503) 538–8880

Eugene

Excelsior Cafe, 754 East Thirteenth Avenue; (541) 342–6963
Zenon Cafe, 898 Pearl Street; (541) 343–3005

Hood River

Big City Chicks, 1302 Thirteenth Street at B Street; (503) 387–3811
Purple Rocks Art Bar and Cafe, 606 Oak Street west of town; (503) 386–6061
Stonehedge Inn, 3405 Cascade Drive, exit 62 off Highway 84; (503) 386–3940

Jacksonville

Bella Union Restaurant, 170 West California Street; (503) 899–1710

McMinnville

Nick's Italian Cafe, 521 East Third Street; (503) 434–4471

Oakland

Tolly's, 115 Locust Street; (541) 459–3796

Portland

Cafe des Amis, 1987 Northwest Kearny Street at Twentieth; (503) 223–3302
Genoa, 2832 Southeast Belmont Street; (503) 238–1464
The Heathman Restaurant and Bar, 1001 Southwest Broadway at Salmon, just off Pioneer Square; (503) 790–7752
Pazzo Ristorante, 627 SW Washington at Southwest Broadway; (503) 228–1515

Roseburg

Los Dos Amigos, 53 Southeast Jackson; (541) 673–1351

Salem

Alessandro's Park Plaza, Trade and High Streets; (503) 370–9951
The Inn at Orchard Heights, 695 Orchard Heights Road NW; (541) 378–1780
Kim Huong, 2950 Silverton Road; (503) 581–0884
McGrath's Publick Fish House, Chemeketa and Liberty Streets; (503) 362–0736
Morton's Bistro Northwest, 1128 Edgewater, West Salem; (503) 585–1113

Troutdale

Black Rabbit Restaurant & Bar, 2126 Southwest Halsey Street; (503) 665–2992
Tad's Chicken 'n' Dumplings, 943 Southeast Crown Point, (503) 666–5337

Washington

Bainbridge Island

Cafe Nola, 101 Winslow Way; (206) 842–3822
Ruby's on Bainbridge, 4569 Lynwood Center; (206) 780–9303

Kennewick

The Blue Moon, 21 West Canal Drive; (509) 582–6598
Casa Chapala, 107 East Columbia Drive; (509) 586–4224
Chez Chaz, 5001 Clearwater Avenue; (509) 735–2138

Othello

Brunswich Bar & Grill, 28 East Main; (509) 488–9861
Casa Mexicana, 1224 East Main; (509) 488–6163
El Caporal, 1244 East Main; (509) 488–0487

Paterson

Paterson Store & Restaurant, Highway 221 near Highway 14; (509) 875–2741

Prosser

The Blue Goose, 306 Seventh Street; (509) 786–1774

Richland

Emerald of Siam, 1314 Jadwin; (509) 946–9328
Giacci's, 94 Lee Boulevard; (509) 946–4855

Seattle

Brie & Bordeaux, 2227 North Fifty-sixth Street; (206) 633–3538
Cafe Campagne, 1600 Post Alley at Pine; (206) 728–2233
Campagne, 86 Pine Street near Post Alley; (206) 728–2800
El Puerco Lloron, 1501 Western Avenue; (206) 624–0541
Elliott's Oyster House, Pier 56; (206) 623–4340
Kaspar's, 2701 First Avenue; (206) 441–4805
The Metropolitan Grill, 820 Second Avenue; (206) 624–3287

Spokane

The Downtown Onion, 302 West Riverside at Bernard; (509) 747–3852
Luna, 5620 South Perry; (509) 448–2383
Milford's Fish House and Oyster Bar, North 719 Monroe; (509) 326–7251
Patsy Clark's, West 2208 Second Avenue; (509) 838–8300

Sunnyside

Taqueria La Fogata, 1204 Yakima Valley Highway; (509) 839–9019
Vannini's Italian Restaurant, 111 North Sixth; (509) 837–2225

Touchet

Alkali Flats Cafe, Highway 12; (509) 394–2310

Vashon Island

Express Cuisine, 17629 Vashon Highway SW; (206) 463–6626
Turtle Island Cuisine, 9924 Southwest Bank Road (near its intersection with
   Vashon Highway); (206) 463–2125

Walla Walla

Jacobi's, 416 North Second Street; (509) 525–2677
Merchant's Ltd. & French Bakery, 21 East Main Street; (509) 525–0900
Pastime Cafe, 215 West Main Street; (509) 525–0873
Whitehouse-Crawford, 55 West Cherry Street; (509) 525–2222

Whidbey Island

Lucy's Mi Casita, 1380 West Pioneer Way, Oak Harbor; (360) 675–4800

Yakima

Gasperetti's Restaurant, 1013 North Front Street; (509) 248–0628
The Greystone Restaurant, 5 North Front Street (and East Yakima); (509)
   248–9801
Santiago's, 111 East Yakima at First; (509) 453–1644

Zillah

The Squeeze Inn, downtown on First Avenue; (509) 829–6226

British Columbia

Cowichan Bay

The Blue Nose, two doors up the road from the Rock Cod; (250) 748–2841
Rock Cod Cafe, 1759 Cowichan Bay; (250) 746–1550

Kelowna

De Montreuil, 368 Bernard Avenue at Pandosy; (250) 860–5508
Kitchen Cowboy, 353 Bernard near Pandosy; (250) 868–8288
Schroth Wood Fire Bakery, 2041 Harvey on Highway 97 north; (250) 762–2626

Malahat

The Aerie, 600 Ebedora Lane; (250) 743–7115

Naramata

The Country Squire, 3950 First Street; (250) 496–5416

Oak Bay

Oak Bay Beach Hotel, 1175 Beach Drive; (250) 598–4556

Oliver

Jacques Neighborhood Grill, 34646 Highway 97 across from Oliver Place Mall; (250) 498–4418

Osoyoos

Diamond Steak & Seafood House, Main Street near Eighty-ninth Street; (250) 495–6223

Penticton

Front Street Pasta Factory, 75 Front Street; (250) 493–5666
Granny Bogner's, 302 Eckhardt Avenue W (2 blocks off Main Street); (250) 493–2711
Theo's, 687 Main Street; (250) 492–4019
Villa Rosa Restaurante, 795 Westminster Avenue W; (250) 490–9595

Sooke

Sooke Harbour House, 1528 Whiffen Spit Road; (250) 642–3421

Vancouver

Bishop's, 2183 West Fourth Avenue between Arbutus and Yew; (604) 738–2025
Carpaccio's, 1809 West First; (604) 732–1632

The Fish House at Stanley Park, 2099 Beach Avenue near the entrance to Stanley Park; (604) 681–7275
Le Grec, 1447 Commercial; (604) 253–1253
Topanga Cafe, 2904 West Fourth; (604) 733–3713

Victoria

Blue Fox Cafe, 919 Fort Street; (250) 380–1683
Camille's Fine West Coast Dining, below 45 Bastion Square; (250) 381–3433
Dilettantes, 787 Fort Street; (250) 381–3327
Foster's Eatery, 753 Yates Street (across from Odeon Theatre); (250) 382–1131
Herald Street Caffe, 546 Herald Street; (250) 381–1441
J & J Wonton Noodle House, 1012 Fort Street; (250) 383–0680
John's Place, 723 Pandora; (250) 389–0711
Pagliacci's, 1011 Broad Street; (250) 386–1662
San Remo Restaurant, 2709 Quadra Street; (250) 384–5255

Idaho

Boise

B. B. Strand's, 310 North Fourth Street; (208) 342–7777
Gamekeeper Restaurant & Lounge, 1109 Main Street; (208) 343–4611
Tablerock, 705 Fulton; (208) 342–4900
Trolley House, 1821 Warm Springs Avenue; (208) 345–9255

Caldwell

Dos Amigos Restaurant, 420 North Fifth Avenue; (208) 459–2190
Sunrise Family Restaurant, 2601 Cleveland Boulevard; (208) 459–8557

Hagerman

Snake River Grill, corner of Hagerman Avenue and State Street; (208) 837–6227

Kuna

Peregrine Steaks & Spirits, 414 West Third Street; (208) 922–9797

McCall

Mill Steaks & Spirits, 324 North Third Street; (208) 634–7683
Romano's Italian Restaurant, 203 East Lake; (208) 634–2128

Moscow

Gambino's Italian Restaurant, 308 West Sixth Street; (208) 882–4545
Nobby Inn Restaurant, 501 South Main Drive; (208) 882–2032

Nampa

Country Inn Family Restaurant, 803 Twelfth Avenue; (208) 466–2181
Dutch Inn Restaurant, 1120 Twelfth Avenue; (208) 467–2737
Lakeside Inn, Lake Shore Drive; (208) 466–1551

Sandpoint

Beach House Restaurant, 56 Bridge Street; (208) 263–8612
Eichard's Pub, Grill & Coffee House, 212 West Cedar Street; (208) 263–1613
Ivano's, 124 South Second Avenue; (208) 263–0211
Swan's Landing, Lakeshore Drive at Highway 95; (208) 265–2000

*L*ODGINGS

Oregon

Ashland

Ashland's Bed and Breakfast Network; phone (541) 482–BEDS or (800) 944–0329
Ashland's Main Street Inn, 142 North Main Street; phone (541) 488–0969
Best Western Bard's Inn Motel, 132 North Main Street; phone (541) 482–0049; fax (541) 488–3259
Country Willows, 1313 Clay Street; phone (541) 488–1590 or (800) 945–5697; Web site www.willowsinn.com
McCall House, 153 Oak Street; phone (541) 482–9296; Web site www.McCallhouse.com; historic landmark
Mount Ashland Inn, 550 Mount Ashland Road; phone (541) 482–8707
Peerless Hotel, 243 Fourth Street; phone (541) 488–1082; Web site www.peerlesshotel.com
Romeo Inn, 295 Idaho Street at Holly; phone (541) 488–0884 or (800) 915–8899; Web site www.romeoinn.com
Stratford Inn, 555 Siskiyou Boulevard; phone (541) 488–2151 or (800) 547–4741; fax (541) 482–4474

Windmill's Ashland Hills Inn, 2525 Ashland Street, just east of I–5; phone (541) 482–8310 or (800) 547–4747; fax (541) 488–1783

Beaverton

Courtyard by Marriott, 8500 Southwest Nimbus Avenue; phone (503) 641–3200; fax (503) 641–1287

Greenwood Inn, 10700 Southwest Allen Boulevard; phone (503) 643–7444 or (800) 289–1300; fax (503) 626–4553; Web site www.greenwoodinn.com

Peppertree Motel, 10720 Southwest Allen Boulevard; phone (503) 641–7477 or (800) 453–6219

Phoenix Inn, 15402 Northwest Cornell Road; phone (503) 614–8100 or (888) 944–8100; e-mail phoen707@pine.net

Corvallis

Best Western Grant Manor Inn, 925 Northwest Garfield; phone (541) 758–8571 or (800) 626–1900; fax (541) 758–0834

Patricia Covey's Hanson Country Inn, 795 Southwest Hanson Street; phone (541) 752–2919

The Dalles

Best Western River City Inn, Second and Liberty; phone (541) 296–9107; fax (541) 296–3002

Williams House Inn, 608 West Sixth Street at Trevett; phone (541) 296–2889

Dayton

Wine Country Farm B&B and Cellars, 6855 Breyman Orchards Road; phone (503) 864–3446 or (800) 261–3446; e-mail innkeeper@winecountryfarm.com; Web site www.winecountryfarm.com

Eugene

Best Western Greentree Inn, 1759 Franklin Boulevard; phone (541) 485–2727 or (800) 528–1234; fax (541) 686–2094

Best Western New Oregon Inn, 1655 Franklin Boulevard; phone (541) 683–3669 or (800) 528–1234; fax (541) 484–5556

Campbell House, 252 Pearl Street; phone (541) 343–1119 or (800) 264–2519; fax (541) 343–2258; e-mail campbellhouse@campbellhouse.com; Web site www.campbellhouse.com

Eugene Hilton, 66 East Sixth Avenue; phone (541) 342–2000

Valley River Inn, 1000 Valley River Way; phone (541) 687–0123; e-mail reserve@valleyriverinn.com; Web site www.valleyriverinn.com

Forest Grove

Forest Grove Inn, 4433 Pacific Avenue; phone (503) 357–9700 or (800) 240–6504

Hood River

Best Western Hood River Inn, 1108 East Marina Way; phone (541) 386–2200; fax (541) 386–8905

Columbia Gorge Hotel, 4000 Westcliff Drive; phone (541) 386–5566 or (800) 345–1921; e-mail cghotel@gorge.net; Web site www.gorge.net/lodging/cghotel/

Hood River Hotel, 102 Oak Street; phone (541) 386–1900

King City (near Newberg)

Best Western Northwind Inn and Suites, 16105 Southwest Pacific Highway 99W; phone (503) 431–2100; fax (503) 431–2115

McMinnville

Best Western Vineyard Inn, 2035 South Highway 99W; phone (503) 472–4900 or (800) 285–6242; fax (503) 434–9157

Safari Motor Inn, 345 North Highway 99W; phone (503) 472–5187 or (800) 321–5543; fax (503) 434–6380

Youngberg Hill Vineyard and Inn, 10660 Southwest Youngberg Hill Road; phone (503) 472–2727 or (888) 657–8668; Web site www.youngberghill.com

Newberg

Partridge Farm B&B, 4300 East Portland Road just off Highway 99W north of Newberg; phone (503) 538–2050

Shilo Inn, 501 Sitka Avenue; phone (503) 537–0303 or (800) 222–2244; fax (503) 537–0442

Springbrook Hazelnut Farm, 30295 North Highway 99W north of Newberg; phone (503) 538–4606 or (800) 793–8528

Portland

The Benson, 309 Southwest Broadway, corner of Oak; phone (503) 228–2000; fax (503) 226–4603

Governor Hotel, 611 Southwest Tenth Avenue; phone (503) 224–3400 or (800) 554–3456; fax (503) 241–2122

Heathman Hotel, 1001 Southwest Broadway at SW Salmon; phone (503) 241–4100 or (800) 551–0011; fax (503) 790–7110

Mallory Hotel, 729 Southwest Fifteenth Avenue, corner SW Yamhill; phone (503) 223–6311 or (800) 228–8657; fax (503) 223–0522

Portland Hilton, 921 Southwest Sixth Avenue; phone (503) 226–1611; fax (503) 220–2565

Portland Marriott Hotel, 1401 Southwest Front Avenue; phone (503) 226–7600 or (800) 228–9290; fax (503) 221–1789

Salem

Best Western New Kings Inn, 3658 Market Street, from I–5, exit 256 east onto Market; phone (503) 581–1559; fax (503) 364–4272

Marquee House Bed & Breakfast, 333 Wyatt Court, NE near corner of Seventeenth and Center; phone (503) 391–0837

Shilo Inn, 3304 Market Street, from I–5, exit 256 west onto Market; phone (503) 581–4001 or (800) 222–2244; fax (503) 399–9385

Washington

Bainbridge Island

The Bombay House, 8490 Beck Road; phone (206) 842–3926 or (800) 598–3926; Web site www.bombayhouse.com

Island Country Inn, 920 Hildebrand Way Northeast; phone (206) 842–6861 or (800) 842–8429

Bothell

Residence Inn by Marriott—Seattle Northeast/Bothell, 11920 Northeast 195th Street, east at exit 24 on Highway 405; phone (206) 485–3030 or (800) 223–9290; fax (206) 485–2247

Wyndham Garden Hotel, 19333 North Creek Parkway; phone (206) 485–5557; fax (206) 486–7314

Coupeville (Whidbey Island)

Anchorage Inn, 807 North Main Street; phone (360) 678–5581; e-mail anchorag@whidbey.net; Web site www.anchorage-inn.com

The Captain Whidbey Inn, 2072 West Captain Whidbey Inn Road; phone (360) 678–4097 or (800) 366–4097; fax (360) 678–4110

The Coupeville Inn, 200 Coveland Street; phone (360) 678–6668; fax (360) 678–3059

Kennewick

Cavanaugh's at Columbia Center, 1101 North Columbia Center Boulevard; phone (509) 786–0611; fax (509) 735–3087

Comfort Inn, 7801 West Quinault Avenue; phone (509) 783–8396; fax (509) 783–8396

Fairfield Inn by Marriott, 7809 West Quinault Avenue; phone (509) 783–2164; fax (509) 783–2164

Silver Cloud Inn, 7901 West Quinault Avenue; phone (509) 735–6100 or (800) 205–6938; fax (509) 735–3084

Kirkland

Silver Cloud Inn at Kirkland, 12202 Northeast 124th Street, reach from Highway 405, exit 20B (northbound), exit 20 (southbound); (206) 821–8300 or (800) 551–7207

The Woodmark Hotel on Lake Washington, 1200 Carillon Point; phone (425) 822–3700; fax (425) 822–3699

Oak Harbor (Whidbey Island)

Acorn Motor Inn, 8066 Highway 20; phone (360) 675–6646

Auld Holland Inn, 33575 Highway 20; phone (360) 675–2288 or (800) 228–0148; fax (360) 675–2817

Coachman Inn, 32959 Highway 20; phone (360) 675–0727 or (800) 635–0043; fax (360) 675–1419

Othello

Aladdin Motor Inn, 1020 East Cedar Street; phone (509) 488–5671

Cimmaron Motel, 1450 Main Street; phone (509) 488–6612

Pasco

Red Lion Inn-Pasco, 2525 North Twentieth Avenue; phone (509) 547–0701; fax (509) 547–4278

Prosser

Best Western Prosser Inn, 225 Merlot Drive; phone (509) 786–7977 or (800) 688–2192

Wine Country Inn Bed & Breakfast, 1106 Wine Country Road; phone (509) 786–2855

Richland

Best Western Tower Inn, 1515 George Washington Way; phone (509) 946–4121 or (800) 635–3980

Hampton Inn, 486 Bradley Boulevard; phone (509) 943–4400 or (800) HAMPTON

Shilo Inn–Richland Rivershore, 50 Comstock Street; phone (509) 946–4661 or (800) 222–2244

Seattle

Best Western—Continental Plaza, 2500 Aurora Avenue North; phone (206) 284–1900

Best Western Executive Inn of Seattle, 200 Taylor Avenue North; phone (206) 448–9444

Best Western Loyal Inn, 2301 Eighth Avenue; phone (206) 682–0200

Claremont Hotel, 2000 Fourth Avenue; phone (206) 448–8600

Crowne Plaza Hotel, 1113 Sixth Avenue (corner of Seneca); phone (206) 464–1980

Four Seasons Olympic Hotel, 411 University Street; phone (206) 621–1700; fax (206) 682–9633

Hampton Inn Downtown Seattle Center, 700 Fifth Avenue North; phone (206) 282–7700

Hotel Vintage Park, 1100 Fifth Avenue at Spring Street; phone (206) 624–8000; fax (206) 623–0568

Inn at the Market, 86 Pine Street; phone (206) 443–3600 or (800) 446–4484; fax (206) 448–0631

The Madison Renaissance Hotel, 515 Madison Street at Sixth Avenue; phone (206) 583–0300 or (800) 278–4159; fax (206) 624–6125

Pioneer Square Hotel, 77 Yesler Way; phone (206) 340–1234

Seattle Inn, 225 Aurora Avenue North; phone (206) 624–0500

Sorrento Hotel, 900 Madison Street; phone (206) 622–6400 or (800) 426–1265

The Warwick Hotel, 401 Lenora Street; phone (206) 443–4300; fax (206) 448–1662

Spokane

Cavanaugh's Inn at the Park, 303 North River Drive; phone (509) 326–8000 or (800) THE INNS; fax (509) 325–7329

Doubletree, 322 North Spokane Falls Court; phone (509) 455–9600 or (800) 848–9600; fax (509) 455–6285

Fairfield Inn, 311 North Riverpoint Boulevard; phone (509) 747–9131 or (800) 228–2800; fax (509) 747–9131

Fotheringham House, 2128 West Second Avenue; phone (509) 838–1891

Spokane Bed and Breakfast Reservation Service; (509) 328–1856

Waverly Place, 709 West Waverly Place; phone (509) 326–8000 or (800) 843–4667

Sunnyside

Sun Valley Inn, 724 Yakima Valley Highway; phone (509) 837–4721

Sunnyside Inn B&B, 800 East Edison Avenue; phone (509) 839–5557 or (800) 221–4195; fax (509) 839–3520

Walla Walla

Comfort Inn, 520 North Second Street; phone (509) 525–2522; fax (509) 522–2565

The Marcus Whitman, 107 North Second; phone (509) 525–2200

Pony Soldier Motor Inn—Howard Johnson, 325 East Main Street; phone (509) 529–4360; fax (509) 529–7463

Yakima

Best Western Rio Mirada Motor Inn, 1603 Terrace Heights Drive; phone (509) 457–4444; fax (509) 453–7593

Cavanaugh's at Yakima Center, 607 East Yakima Avenue; phone (509) 248–5900 or (800) THE INNS; Web site www.cavanaughs.com

Holiday Inn of Yakima, 9 North Ninth Street, exit 33 or 33B; phone (509) 452–6511; fax (509) 457–4931

British Columbia

Kelowna

Best Western Kelowna, 2402 Highway 97 North (continuation of Harvey); phone (250) 890–1212 or (800) 667–9210; fax (250) 860–0675
Capri Hotel, 1171 Harvey Avenue at Gordon; phone (250) 860–6060
Grand Okanagan Lakefront Resort, 1310 Water Street; phone (250) 763–4500 or (800) 465–4651; fax (250) 763–4565
Holiday Inn Express—Kelowna, 2429 Highway 97 North at Banks Road; phone (250) 763–0500 or (800) 465–0200; fax (250) 763–7555
Hotel Eldorado, 500 Cook Road; phone (250) 763–7500

Langley

Best Western Langley Motor Inn, 8 Glover Road; phone (604) 530–9311
Westward Inn, 9650 Fraser Highway; phone (604) 534–9238 or (800) 667–4557

Malahat

Aerie Resort, 600 Ebedora Lane; phone (250) 743–7115; fax (250) 743–4776

Oak Bay

Oak Bay Beach Inn, 1175 Beach Drive; phone (250) 598–4556 or (800) 668–7758; fax (250) 598–6180

Oliver

Anne Marie's B&B, 34427 Ninety-seventh Street (Highway 97); phone (250) 498–0131; fax (250) 498–0131
Lakeside Resort, 37005 Eighty-first Street; phone (250) 498–2177; fax (250) 498–0011
Southwind Inn, 34017 Highway 37 South; phone (250) 498–3442 or (800) 661–9922; fax (250) 498–3938

Osoyoos

Falcon Motel, 7106 Sixty-second Avenue (Highway 3 East); phone (250) 495–7544
Plaza Royale Motor Inn, Highway 3 at junction with Highway 97; phone (250) 495–2633

Poplars Motel, 6404 Sixty-seventh Avenue; phone (250) 495–6035; fax (250) 495–2736

Richter Pass Motor Inn, 7304 Sixty-second Avenue (Highway 3 East); phone (250) 495–7229

Starlite Motor Inn, 7906 Main Street (Highway 3); phone (250) 495–7223; fax (250) 495–6899

Penticton

Beachside Motel, 3624 Parkview Street; phone (250) 492–8318

Best Western at Penticton, 3180 Skaha Lake Road; phone (250) 493–0311 or (800) 668–6746

The Brough House B&B, 185 Middle Bench Road South; phone (250) 490–9958 or (800) 774–4866

Castle Rock Bed & Breakfast, 2050 Sutherland Road; phone (250) 492–4429

Clarion Lakeside Resort, 21 Lakeshore Drive West; phone (250) 493–8221 or (800) 663–9400

Empire Motel, 3495 Skaha Lake Road; phone (250) 492–4255 or (800) 681–2323; fax (250) 493–4270

Hansel and Gretel Motel, 2872 Skaha Lake Road; phone (250) 493–1528; fax (250) 490–8863

The Lakeside B&B, 4537 Lakeside Road; phone (250) 493–6404; fax (250) 493–0170; e-mail lcorrao@cln.etc.bc.ca

Log Cabin Motel, 3287 Skaha Lake Road; phone (250) 492–3155 or (800) 342–5678; fax (250) 492–8468

Penticton Inn—Howard Johnson, 333 Martin Street; phone (250) 492–3600 or (800) 665–2221

Sooke

Sooke Harbour House, 1528 Whiffen Spit Road; phone (250) 642–3421; fax (250) 642–6988

Vancouver

English Bay Inn, 1968 Comox Street; phone (604) 683–8002

The Four Seasons, 791 West Georgia Street; phone (604) 689–9333 or (800) 332–3442; Web site www.fshr.com

Sutton Place Hotel, 845 Burrard Street; phone (604) 682–5511; e-mail info@fcr.suttonplace.com; Web site www.travelweb.com/sutton.html

Sylvia Hotel, 1154 Gilford Street; phone (604) 681–9321

Victoria

Bedford Regency Hotel, 1140 Government Street; phone (250) 384–6835 or (800) 665–6500

Days Inn on the Harbour, 427 Belleville Street; phone (250) 386–3451 or (800) 325–2525

The Empress Hotel, 721 Government Street; phone (250) 384–8111 or (800) 441–1414; fax (250) 381–4334

Laurel Point Inn, 680 Montreal Street; phone (250) 386–8721

Ocean Pointe Resort, 45 Songhees Road; phone (250) 360–2999 or (800) 667–4677; fax (250) 360–1041

Royal Scott Inn, 425 Quebec Street; phone (250) 388–5463

Idaho

Boise

Best Western Safari, 1070 Grove Street; phone (208) 344–6556

University Inn, 2360 University; phone (208) 345–7170

Caldwell

Holiday Motel & Cafe, 512 Huckleberry; phone (208) 453–1056

Hagerman

Rock Lodge Motel, Route 30; phone (208) 837–4822

Moscow

Cavanaugh's Motor Inn, 645 Pullman Road; phone (208) 882–1661 or (800) THE–INNS

Sandpoint

Connie's Motor Inn–Best Western, 323 Cedar Street; phone (208) 263–9581

The Edgewater, 56 Bridge Street (on lake); phone (208) 263–3194

INDEX

G

H

𝓜

ABOUT THE AUTHORS

*K*athleen and Gerald Hill are native Californians who now live in Sonoma in the northern California wine country after selling their home in Vancouver Island, British Columbia. As a team the Hills have written all six books in the Hill Guides series in addition to *The People's Dictionary of the Law, The Real Life Dictionary of American Politics, Facts on File Dictionary of American Politics, Encyclopedia of Federal Agencies and Commissions,* and an international exposé, *Aquino Assassination,* as well as articles for *National Geographic Traveler* magazine and *Wine Spectator.* Kathleen is the author of *Festivals USA* and *Festivals USA— Western States,* and she has written articles for *The Chicago Tribune, San Francisco Magazine, Cook's Illustrated, San Francisco Examiner Magazine, James Beard Newsletter,* and other periodicals. Gerald was editor and co-author of *Housing in California* and practices law to support their writing habit. The Hills occasionally teach U.S. government and politics at the University of British Columbia, University of Victoria, and Sonoma State University.